RWANDA

MINING LAWS AND REGULATIONS HANDBOOK

VOLUME 1
STRATEGIC INFORMATION AND REGULATIONS

International Business Publications, USA
Washington DC, USA - Rwanda

RWANDA
MINING LAWS AND REGULATIONS HANDBOOK
VOLUME 1 STRATEGIC INFORMATION AND REGULATIONS

UPDATED ANNUALLY

We express our sincere appreciation to all government agencies and international organizations which provided information and other materials for this handbook

Cover Design: **International Business Publications, USA**

2016 Edition Updated Reprint International Business Publications, USA
ISBN 1-4330-7812-0

For customer service and information, please contact:

in the USA: **International Business Publications, USA**
P.O.Box 15343, Washington, DC 20003
Phone: (202) 546-2103, Fax: (202) 546-3275.
E-mail: ibpusa3@gmail.com
Global Investment and Business Info Databank - www.ibpus.com

Printed in the USA

RWANDA

MINING LAWS AND REGULATIONS HANDBOOK

VOLUME 1

STRATEGIC INFORMATION AND REGULATIONS

TABLE OF CONTENTS

STRATEGIC & DEVELOPMENT PROFILES

Capital (and largest city)	Kigali 1°56.633′S 30°3.567′E1.943883°S 30.05945°E
Official language(s)	Kinyarwanda, French, English
Demonym	Rwandan, Rwandese
Government	Unitary parliamentary democracy and Presidential republic
- President	Paul Kagame
- Prime Minister	Pierre Habumuremyi
	Independence
- from Belgium	1 July 1962
	Area
- Total	26,338 km^2 (148th) 10,169 sq mi
- Water (%)	5.3
	Population
- 2011 estimate	11,370,425[1] (73rd)
- 2002 census	8,162,715[2]
- Density	419.8/km^2 (29th) 1,087.2/sq mi
GDP (PPP)	2011 estimate
- Total	$13.109 billion[3]
- Per capita	$1,284[3]
GDP (nominal)	2011 estimate
- Total	$6.055 billion[3]
- Per capita	$593[3]
Gini (2003)	41.1 (medium)
HDI (2010)	▲0.385[4] (low) (152nd)
Currency	Rwandan franc (RWF)
Time zone	CAT (UTC+2)
- Summer (DST)	not observed (UTC+2)
Drives on the	right
ISO 3166 code	RW
Internet TLD	.rw
Calling code	250

[1] Estimates for this country explicitly take into account the effects of excess mortality due to AIDS; this can result in lower life expectancy, higher infant mortality and death rates, lower population and growth rates, and changes in the distribution of population by age and sex than would otherwise be expected.

Rwanda is a sovereign state in central and east Africa and one of the smallest countries on the African mainland. Located a few degrees south of the Equator, Rwanda is bordered by Uganda, Tanzania, Burundi and the Democratic Republic of the Congo. Rwanda is in the African Great Lakes region and is highly elevated; its geography dominated by mountains in the west and savanna to the east, with numerous lakes throughout the country. The climate is temperate to subtropical, with two rainy seasons and two dry seasons each year.

The population is young and predominantly rural, with a density among the highest in Africa. Rwandans are drawn from just one cultural and linguistic group, the Banyarwanda, although within this group there are three subgroups: the Hutu, Tutsi and Twa. The Twa are a forest-dwelling pygmy people descended from Rwanda's earliest inhabitants. Scholars disagree on the origins of and differences between the Hutu and Tutsi; some believe differences are derived from former social castes within a single people, while others believe the Hutu and Tutsi arrived in the country separately, and from different locations. Christianity is the largest religion in the country; the principal language is Kinyarwanda, spoken by most Rwandans, with French and English serving as official languages. Rwanda has a presidential system of government. The president is Paul Kagame of the Rwandan Patriotic Front (RPF), who took office in 2000. Rwanda today has low corruption compared with neighbouring countries, although human rights organisations report suppression of opposition groups, intimidation and restrictions on freedom of speech. The country has been governed by a strict administrative hierarchy since precolonial times; there are five provinces delineated by borders drawn in 2006. Rwanda is one of only two countries with a female majority in the national parliament.

Hunter gatherers settled the territory in the stone and iron ages, followed later by Bantu peoples. The population coalesced first into clans and then into kingdoms. The Kingdom of Rwanda dominated from the mid-eighteenth century, with the Tutsi kings conquering others militarily, centralising power, and later enacting anti-Hutu policies. Germany colonised Rwanda in 1884 as part of German East Africa, followed by Belgium, which invaded in 1916 during World War I. Both European nations ruled through the kings and perpetuated a pro-Tutsi policy. The Hutu population revolted in 1959. They massacred numerous Tutsi and ultimately established an independent, Hutu-dominated state in 1962. The Tutsi-led Rwandan Patriotic Front launched a civil war in 1990. Social tensions erupted in the 1994 genocide, in which Hutu extremists killed an estimated 500,000 to 1 million Tutsi and moderate Hutu. The RPF ended the genocide with a military victory.

Rwanda's economy suffered heavily during the 1994 Rwandan Genocide, but has since strengthened. The economy is based mostly on subsistence agriculture. Coffee and tea are the major cash crops for export. Tourism is a fast-growing sector and is now the country's leading foreign exchange earner. Rwanda is one of only two countries in which mountain gorillas can be visited safely, and visitors are prepared to pay high prices for gorilla tracking permits. Music and dance are an integral part of Rwandan culture, particularly drums and the highly choreographed *intore* dance. Traditional arts and crafts are produced throughout the country.

STRATEGIC PROFILE

Background: Throughout their colonial rule, first Germany and then Belgium favored Rwanda's minority Tutsi ethnic group in education and employment. In 1959, the majority ethnic group, the Hutus, overthrew the ruling Tutsi monarch. The Hutus killed hundreds of Tutsis and drove tens of thousands into exile in neighboring countries. The children of these exiles later formed a rebel group, the Rwandan Patriotic Front (RPF), and began a civil war in October 1990. The war, along with several political and economic upheavals, exasperated ethnic tensions culminating in April 1994 in a genocide in which roughly 800,000 Tutsis and moderate Hutus were killed.

The Tutsi rebels defeated the Hutu regime and ended the genocide in July 1994, but approximately 2 million Hutu refugees -many fearing Tutsi retribution - fled to neighboring Burundi, Tanzania, Uganda, and Zaire, now called the Democratic Republic of the Congo (DROC). According to the UN Office of the High Commissioner for Refugees, in 1996 and early 1997 nearly 1.3 million Hutus returned to Rwanda. Even with substantial international aid, these civil dislocations have hindered efforts to foster reconciliation and to boost investment and agricultural output. Although much of the country is now at peace, members of the former regime continue to destabilize the northwest area of the country through a low-intensity insurgency. Rwandan troops are currently involved in a crisis engulfing neighboring DROC.

RWANDA, A COUNTRY OF A THOUSAND HILLS

Rwanda is etended over an exiguous territory of 26,338 square kilometers. It is a small country in the heart of Africa with almost 7,223,255 inhabitants. Rwanda possesses natural ressources of exceptional beauty and variety: its countless lakes and rivers, fauna and flora as well as its magnificient volcanoes and mountains, natural ressources, its expressive folklore and traditional handcraft ...constitute a considerable source of attraction and assets for the country.

Rwanda is located in the Great Lakes region between the Central and Eastern parts of Africa and shares common borders with:

- Uganda in the North
- Burundi in the South
- The Democratic Republic of Congo in the West
- Tanzania in the East

Rwanda is a land-locked country, with no access to the Ocean: The Indian ocean is 1200 km and the Atlantic ocean is 2200 km away from Rwanda. The country is between the 7 400km distance from the Cape to Cairo.

Because of its countless elevations, Rwanda is known as a country of a thousand hills. It is also called "country of perpetual spring". Throughout the year, country has favourable climate: soft, sunny, stable and temperate. The average annual temperature is 18°C. It results from the effect of the trade wind and the coolness from its mountains.

The climate of Rwanda is caracterized by:

- A short rainy season from September to December
- A short dry season from end of January to February
- A long rainy season from March to end of May
- A long dry season from June to August

BASIC INFORMATION

Location: Central Africa, east of Democratic Republic of the Congo
Geographic coordinates: 2 00 S, 30 00 E
Map references: Africa

Area:
total: 26,340 sq km
land: 24,950 sq km
water: 1,390 sq km

Area—comparative: slightly smaller than Maryland
Land boundaries:
total: 893 km

Rwanda and Burundi

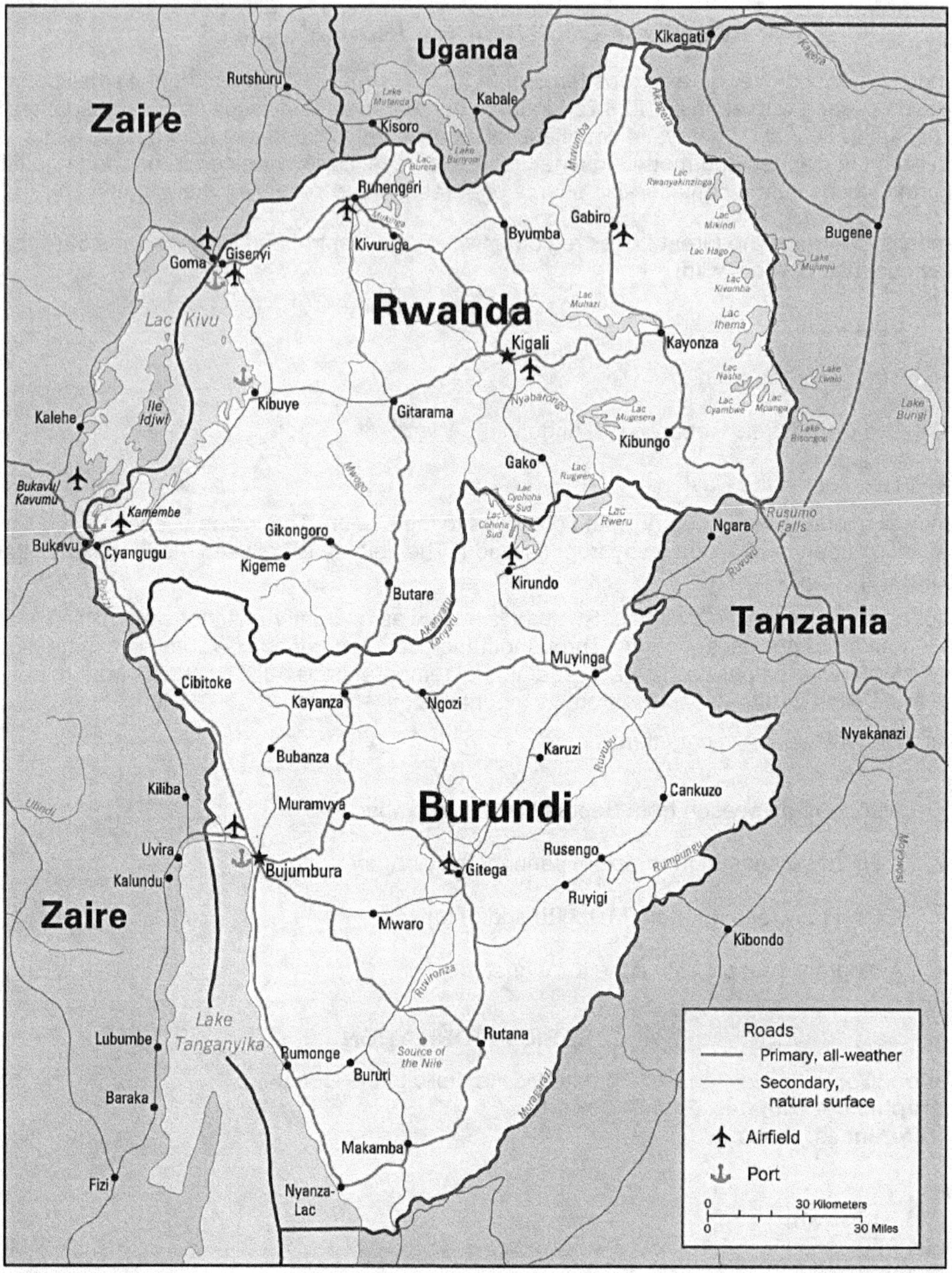

740959 (R01374) 11-96

border countries: Burundi 290 km, Democratic Republic of the Congo 217 km, Tanzania 217 km, Uganda 169 km

Coastline: 0 km (landlocked)
Maritime claims: none (landlocked)

Climate: temperate; two rainy seasons (February to April, November to January); mild in mountains with frost and snow possible
Terrain: mostly grassy uplands and hills; relief is mountainous with altitude declining from west to east
Elevation extremes:
lowest point: Rusizi River 950 m
highest point: Volcan Karisimbi 4,519 m

Natural resources: gold, cassiterite (tin ore), wolframite (tungsten ore), methane, hydropower

Land use:
arable land: 35%
permanent crops: 13%
permanent pastures: 18% forests and woodland: 22%
other: 12%
Irrigated land: 40 sq km
Natural hazards: periodic droughts; the volcanic Birunga mountains are in the northwest along the border with Democratic Republic of the Congo

Environment—current issues: deforestation results from uncontrolled cutting of trees for fuel; overgrazing; soil exhaustion; soil erosion; widespread poaching
Environment—international agreements: party to: Biodiversity, Climate Change, Desertification, Endangered Species, Nuclear Test Ban signed, but not ratified: Law of the Sea
Geography—note: landlocked; predominantly rural population

PEOPLE

Population: 8,154,933

Age structure:
0-14 years: 44% (male 1,807,695; female 1,793,590)
15-64 years: 53% (male 2,148,477; female 2,179,119)
65 years and over: 3% (male 92,490; female 133,562)

Population growth rate: 2.43%
Birth rate: 38.97 births/1,000 population **Death rate**: 19.53 deaths/1,000 population

Net migration rate: 4.91 migrant(s)/1,000 population
note: following the outbreak of genocidal strife in Rwanda in April 1994 between Tutsi and Hutu factions, more than 2 million refugees fled to neighboring Burundi, Tanzania, Uganda, and Democratic Republic of the Congo (formerly Zaire); according to the UN High Commission on Refugees, in 1996 and early 1997 nearly 1.3 million Hutus returned to Rwanda - of these 720,000 returned from Democratic Republic of the Congo, 480,000 from Tanzania, 88,000 from Burundi, and 10,000 from Uganda; probably fewer than 100,000 Rwandans remained outside of Rwanda by the end of 1997
Sex ratio:
at birth: 1.03 male(s)/female
under 15 years: 1.01 male(s)/female
15-64 years: 0.99 male(s)/female

65 years and over: 0.69 male(s)/female
total population: 0.99 male(s)/female

Infant mortality rate: 112.86 deaths/1,000 live births

Life expectancy at birth:
total population: 41.31 years
male: 40.84 years
female: 41.8 years

Total fertility rate: 5.8 children born/woman

NATIONALITY

noun: Rwandan(s)
adjective: Rwandan
Ethnic groups: Hutu 80%, Tutsi 19%, Twa (Pygmoid) 1%
Religions: Roman Catholic 65%, Protestant 9%, Muslim 1%, indigenous beliefs and other 25%
Languages: Kinyarwanda (official) universal Bantu vernacular, French (official), English (official), Kiswahili (Swahili) used in commercial centers
Literacy:
definition: age 15 and over can read and write
total population: 60.5%
male: 69.8%
female: 51.6%

GOVERNMENT

Country name:
conventional long form: Rwandese Republic
conventional short form: Rwanda
local long form: Republika y'u Rwanda
local short form: Rwanda

Data code: RW
Government type: republic; presidential, multiparty system
Capital: Kigali
Administrative divisions: 12 prefectures (in French—prefectures, singular—prefecture; in Kinyarwanda—plural—NA, singular—prefegitura); Butare, Byumba, Cyangugu, Gikongoro, Gisenyi, Gitarama, Kibungo, Kibuye, Kigali, Kigaliville, Umutara, Ruhengeri

Independence: 1 July 1962 (from Belgium-administered UN trusteeship)
National holiday: Independence Day, 1 July (1962)

Constitution: on 5 May 1995, the Transitional National Assembly adopted a new constitution which included elements of the constitution of 18 June 1991 as well as provisions of the 1993 Arusha peace accord and the November 1994 multi-party protocol of understanding

Legal system: based on German and Belgian civil law systems and customary law; judicial review of legislative acts in the Supreme Court; has not accepted compulsory ICJ jurisdiction

Suffrage: NA years of age; universal adult

Executive branch:

chief of state: President Paul KAGAME (since 22 April 2000)

head of government: Prime Minister Pierre Damien HABUMUREMYI (since 7 October 2011)

cabinet: Council of Ministers appointed by the president
elections: President elected by popular vote for a seven-year term (eligible for a second term); elections last held on 9 August 2010 (next to be held in 2017)

election results: Paul KAGAME elected to a second term as president; Paul KAGAME 93.1%, Jean NTAWUKURIRYAYO 5.1%, Prosper HIGIRO 1.4%, Alvera MUKABAR 0.4%

Legislative branch:
description: bicameral Parliament consists of the Senate or Senat (26 seats; 12 members indirectly elected by local councils, 8 appointed by the president, 4 appointed by the Political Organizations Forum - a body of registered political parties, and 2 selected by institutions of higher learning; members serve 8-year terms) and the Chamber of Deputies or Chambre des Deputes (80 seats; 53 members directly elected by proportional representation vote, 24 women elected by special interest groups, and 3 selected by youth and disability organizations; members serve 5-year terms)
elections: Senate - NA; Chamber of Deputies - last held on 16-18 September 2013 (next to be held in 2018)
election results: Chamber of Deputies percent of vote by party - RPF 76.2%, PSD 13%, PL 9.3%, other 1.5%; seats by party - RPF 41, PSD 7, PL 5, 27 members indirectly elected

Judicial branch: Constitutional Court, consists of the Court of Cassation and the Council of State in joint session

Political parties and leaders: significant parties include: Rwandan Patriotic Front or RPF [Charles MULIGANDE, secretary general]; Democratic Republican Movement or MDR [leader NA]; Liberal Party or PL [leader NA]; Democratic and Socialist Party or PSD [leader NA]; Christian Democratic Party or PDC [leader NA]; Islamic Democratic Party or PDI [leader NA]; Rwandan Socialist Party or PSR [leader NA]; National Movement for Democracy and Development or MRND (former ruling party) [leader NA]

Political pressure groups and leaders: Rwanda Patriotic Army or RPA [Maj. Gen. Paul KAGAME, commander]; Rally for the Democracy and Return (RDR)

International organization participation: ACCT, ACP, AfDB, CCC, CEEAC, CEPGL, ECA, FAO, G-77, IBRD, ICAO, ICFTU, ICRM, IDA, IFAD, IFC, IFRCS, ILO, IMF, Intelsat, Interpol, IOC, IOM (observer), ITU, NAM, OAU, OPCW, UN, UNCTAD, UNESCO, UNIDO, UPU, WCL, WHO, WIPO, WMO, WToO, WTrO

DIPLOMATIC REPRESENTATION IN THE US:

chief of mission: Ambassador Theogene N. RUDASINGWA
chancery: 1714 New Hampshire Ave. NW, Washington, DC 20009
telephone: [1] (202) 232-2882
FAX: [1] (202) 232-4544

Diplomatic representation from the US:
chief of mission: Ambassador George M. STAPLES
embassy: Boulevard de la Revolution, Kigali
mailing address: B. P. 28, Kigali
telephone: [250] 756 01 through 03, 721 26, 771 47
FAX: [250] 721 28

Flag description: three equal vertical bands of red (hoist side), yellow, and green with a large black letter R centered in the yellow band; uses the popular pan-African colors of Ethiopia; similar to the flag of Guinea, which has a plain yellow band

ECONOMY

Economy - overview:	Rwanda is a poor rural country with about 90% of the population engaged in (mainly subsistence) agriculture. It is the most densely populated country in Africa and is landlocked with few natural resources and minimal industry. Primary foreign exchange earners are coffee and tea. The 1994 genocide decimated Rwanda's fragile economic base, severely impoverished the population, particularly women, and eroded the country's ability to attract private and external investment. However, Rwanda has made substantial progress in stabilizing and rehabilitating its economy to pre-1994 levels, although poverty levels are higher now. GDP has rebounded and inflation has been curbed. Despite Rwanda's fertile ecosystem, food production often does not keep pace with population growth, requiring food imports. Rwanda continues to receive substantial aid money and obtained IMF-World Bank Heavily Indebted Poor Country (HIPC) initiative debt relief in 2005-06. Rwanda also received Millennium Challenge Account Threshold status in 2006. Kigali's high defense expenditures have caused tension between the government and international donors and lending agencies. Energy shortages, instability in neighboring states, and lack of adequate transportation linkages to other countries continue to handicap growth.
GDP (purchasing power parity):	$13.7 billion
GDP (official exchange rate):	$1.968 billion
GDP - real growth rate:	5.8%
GDP - per capita (PPP):	$1,600
GDP - composition by sector:	*agriculture:* 39.9% *industry:* 20.3% *services:* 39.7%
Labor force:	4.6 million
Labor force - by occupation:	*agriculture:* 90% *industry and services:* 10%
Unemployment rate:	NA%
Population below	60%

poverty line:	
Household income or consumption by percentage share:	*lowest 10%:* 2.1% *highest 10%:* 38.2%
Distribution of family income - Gini index:	46.8
Inflation rate (consumer prices):	8.8%
Investment (gross fixed):	22.5% of GDP
Budget:	*revenues:* $682.4 million *expenditures:* $714.6 million; including capital expenditures of $NA
Agriculture - products:	coffee, tea, pyrethrum (insecticide made from chrysanthemums), bananas, beans, sorghum, potatoes; livestock
Industries:	cement, agricultural products, small-scale beverages, soap, furniture, shoes, plastic goods, textiles, cigarettes
Industrial production growth rate:	7%
Electricity - production:	95 million kWh
Electricity - consumption:	198.4 million kWh
Electricity - exports:	10 million kWh
Electricity - imports:	120 million kWh
Oil - production:	0 bbl/day
Oil - consumption:	5,400 bbl/day
Oil - exports:	NA bbl/day
Oil - imports:	NA bbl/day
Oil - proved reserves:	0 bbl
Natural gas - production:	0 cu m
Natural gas - consumption:	0 cu m

Natural gas - proved reserves:	54.32 billion cu m
Current account balance:	$-174 million
Exports:	$146 million f.o.b.
Exports - commodities:	coffee, tea, hides, tin ore
Exports - partners:	China 10.3%, Germany 9.7%, US 4.3% (2006)
Imports:	$436 million f.o.b.
Imports - commodities:	foodstuffs, machinery and equipment, steel, petroleum products, cement and construction material
Imports - partners:	Kenya 19.6%, Germany 7.8%, Uganda 6.8%, Belgium 5.1%
Economic aid - recipient:	$576 million
Reserves of foreign exchange and gold:	$439.7 million
Debt - external:	$1.4 billion
Market value of publicly traded shares:	$NA
Currency (code):	Rwandan franc (RWF)
Exchange rates:	Rwandan francs per US dollar - 560 (2006), 610 (2005), 574.62 (2004), 537.66 (2003), 476.33 (2002)
Fiscal year:	calendar year

COMMUNICATIONS

Telephones - main lines in use:	22,000
Telephones - mobile cellular:	290,000
Telephone system:	*general assessment:* telephone system primarily serves business and government *domestic:* the capital, Kigali, is connected to the centers of the provinces by microwave radio relay and, recently, by cellular telephone service; much of the network depends on wire and HF radiotelephone *international:* country code - 250; international connections employ microwave radio relay to neighboring countries and satellite communications to more distant countries; satellite earth stations - 1 Intelsat (Indian Ocean) in Kigali (includes telex and telefax service)

Radio broadcast stations:	AM 0, FM 8 (two main FM programs are broadcast through a system of repeaters, three international FM programs include the BBC, VOA, and Deutchewelle), shortwave 1 (2005)
Television broadcast stations:	2
Internet country code:	.rw
Internet hosts:	1,592
Internet users:	65,000

TRANSPORTATION

Railways: 0 km
Highways:
total: 12,000 km
paved: 1,000 km
unpaved: 11,000 km

Waterways: Lac Kivu navigable by shallow-draft barges and native craft
Ports and harbors: Cyangugu, Gisenyi, Kibuye
Airports: 7
Airports - with paved runways:
total: 4
over 3,047 m: 1
914 to 1,523 m: 2
under 914 m: 1
Airports - with unpaved runways:
total: 3
914 to 1,523 m: 1
under 914 m: 2

MILITARY

Military branches: Army, Gendarmerie
Military manpower - availability:
males age 15-49: 1,964,118
Military manpower - fit for military service:
males age 15-49: 1,000,204
Military expenditures - dollar figure: $92 million
Military expenditures - percent of GDP: 3.8%

TRANSNATIONAL ISSUES

Burundi and Rwanda dispute two sq km (0.8 sq mi) of Sabanerwa, a farmed area in the Rukurazi Valley where the Akanyaru/Kanyaru River shifted its course southward after heavy rains in 1965; fighting among ethnic groups - loosely associated political rebels, armed gangs, and various government forces in Great Lakes region transcending the boundaries of Burundi, Democratic Republic of the Congo (DROC), Rwanda, and Uganda - abated substantially from a decade ago due largely to UN peacekeeping, international mediation, and efforts by local governments to create civil societies; nonetheless, 57,000 Rwandan refugees still reside in 21 African states, including Zambia, Gabon, and 20,000 who fled to Burundi in 2005 and 2006 to escape drought and recriminations from traditional courts investigating the 1994 massacres; the 2005 DROC and Rwanda border verification mechanism to stem rebel actions on both sides of the border remains in place

Refugees and internally displaced persons:

refugees (country of origin): 77,610 (Burundi); 73,992 (Democratic Republic of the Congo) (2016)

IDPs: undetermined (fighting between government and insurgency in 1998-99; returning refugees) (2012)

IMPORTANT INFORMATION FOR UNDERSTANDING RWANDA[1]

PROFILE

Geography
Area: 26,338 sq. km. (10,169 sq. km.); about the size of Maryland.
Cities: *Capital*--Kigali (est. pop. 800,000). *Other cities*--Muhanga (formerly Gitarama), Huye (formerly Butare), Musanze (formerly Ruhengeri), Rubavu (formerly Gisenyi).
Terrain: Uplands and hills.
Climate: Mild and temperate, with two rainy seasons.

People
Nationality: *Noun and adjective*--Rwandan(s); Rwandese.
Population (est.): approximately 9,997,614.
Annual population growth rate (2008 est.): 2.8%.
Religions (2002 est.): Christian 93.5%, traditional African 0.1%, Muslim 4.6%, 1.7% claim no religious beliefs.
Languages: Kinyarwanda, French, English.
Education: *Years compulsory*--9. *Attendance* (prewar)--75%. *Literacy* (2008)--70%.
Health: *Infant mortality rate* (2008 est., Rwandan Government)--62 deaths/1,000. *Life expectancy* (2008 est.)--49.8 years.
Work force (2000): *Agriculture*--90%; *industry and commerce, services, and government*--10%.

Government
Type: Republic.
Independence: July 1, 1962.
Constitution: May 26, 2003.
Branches: *Executive*--president (chief of state), prime minister (head of government). Broad-based government of national unity formed after the 1994 genocide. *Legislative*--80-seat Chamber of Deputies; 26-member Senate. *Judicial*--Supreme Court; High Courts of the Republic; Provincial Courts; District Courts; mediation committees.
Administrative subdivisions: 4 provinces plus Kigali; 30 districts; 416 sectors; 2,148 cells.
Political parties: There are 10 political parties, including the ruling Rwandan Patriotic Front (RPF), which leads a coalition that includes the Centrist Democratic Party (PDC), the Rwandan Socialist Party (PSR), the Ideal [formerly Islamic] Democratic Party (PDI), the Prosperity and Solidarity Party (PSP), and the Democratic Popular Union (UPDR). Other parties include the Social Democratic Party (PSD), the Liberal Party (PL), the Concord Progressive Party (PPC), and the Social Party Imberakuri (PS-Imberakuri).
Suffrage: Universal for citizens over 18--except refugees, prisoners, and certain categories of convicts.
Central government budget (2009-2010 est.): 900 billion Rwandan francs ($1.5 billion).

Economy
Agriculture: 36% of GDP. *Products*--coffee, tea, pyrethrum (insecticide made from chrysanthemums), bananas, beans, sorghum, potatoes, livestock.
Industry: 14.2% of GDP. *Types*--cement, agricultural products, beer production, soft drinks, soap, furniture, shoes, plastic goods, textiles, cigarettes, pharmaceuticals.
Services: 43.7%.
Trade (est.): *Exports*--$193 million: tea, coffee, coltan, cassiterite, hides, iron ore, and tin. *Major*

[1] US State Department Profile

markets--China, Belgium, and Germany. *Imports*--$963 million f.o.b.: foodstuffs, machinery and equipment, steel, petroleum products, cement, and construction material. *Major suppliers*--Kenya, Germany, Belgium, France, Uganda, and Israel.

GEOGRAPHY

Rwanda's countryside is covered by grasslands and small farms extending over rolling hills, with areas of rugged mountains that extend southeast from a chain of volcanoes in the northwest. The divide between the Congo and Nile drainage systems extends from north to south through western Rwanda at an average elevation of almost 9,000 feet. On the western slopes of this ridgeline, the land slopes abruptly toward Lake Kivu and the Ruzizi River valley, which form the western boundary with the Democratic Republic of the Congo (formerly Zaire) and constitute part of the Great Rift valley. The eastern slopes are more moderate, with rolling hills extending across central uplands at gradually reducing altitudes, to the plains, swamps, and lakes of the eastern border region.

Although located only two degrees south of the Equator, Rwanda's high elevation makes the climate temperate. The average daily temperature near Lake Kivu, at an altitude of 4,800 feet (1,463 meters) is 73° F (23° C). During the two rainy seasons (February-May and September-December), heavy downpours occur almost daily, alternating with sunny weather. Annual rainfall averages 80 centimeters (31 in.) but is generally heavier in the western and northwestern mountains than in the eastern savannas.

PEOPLE

Rwanda's population density is currently the highest in continental sub-Saharan Africa. It is still a very rural society, and many families live in a self-contained compound on a hillside. The urban concentrations are grouped around administrative centers. The indigenous population consists of three groups, or *ubwoko*--Bahutu, Batutsi, and Batwa. Traditionally, the population also is affiliated with one of 18 clans--all with more than one *ubwoko* or group.

Accounts of the respective arrivals of each *ubwoko* centuries ago in the area of modern Rwanda were highly politicized throughout much of the 20th century, and the Belgian colonialists' "racialization" of differences among *ubwoko* was used by the Rwandan Government to fuel the 1994 state-orchestrated genocide. As part of political efforts to overcome divisions that led to the genocide, the Rwandan Government does not collect data on *ubwoko* and banned its inclusion on identity cards. Rwandans share the same language and culture, so *ubwoko* today reflects a family identity that has been passed patrilineally and often a historical narrative. The Rwandan Government does not permit politicization of this identity, any form of discrimination, or "genocide ideology" (hate speech) based on *ubwoko*.

Education

Until 1994, educational opportunities for Rwandans were extremely limited. After the genocide, most primary schools and more than half of prewar secondary schools reopened, though no more than 5% of the adult population received secondary education through 1996. Although educational quality remains an issue, access to education expanded dramatically in recent years and the Government of Rwanda's Nine-Year Basic Education policy, implemented in 2010, contributed to an increase of the primary school completion rate from 52.4% in 2008 to 75.6% in 2010.

The National University (NUR) in Huye (formerly Butare), Rwanda's sole university prior to 1994, reopened in April 1995; enrollment is over 7,000 students. Today, there are about 20 institutions of higher learning in Rwanda. Between 1963-1993, Rwandan university graduates numbered roughly 1,900; today, Rwandan university graduates exceed 44,000. Seventy percent of the adult population is literate (2008). Rebuilding the educational system continues to be a high priority of the Rwandan Government. Rwanda has three official languages--Kinyarwanda, French, and English. The recent transition to English as the language of instruction in schools presents pedagogical challenges even as if offers prospects for increased opportunity within the East African Community and internationally.

HISTORY

Beginning in the 15th century, Rwandans established a monarchy headed by a Tutsi *mwami* (king) with a hierarchy of Tutsi nobles and gentry. In some areas of the country, independent Hutu principalities continued to exist, and in other areas, Tutsi and Hutu lineages lived in interdependent cooperation under the nominal control of the king. Within the monarchy, through a contract known as *ubuhake*, the Hutu farmers pledged their services and those of their descendants to a Tutsi lord in return for the loan of cattle and use of pastures and arable land, creating a relationship somewhat similar to serfdom. However, membership in a *ubwoko* and class were fluid. Affiliation was determined by paternal ancestors. Intermarriage and multiple marriage was common. Some Hutus took Tutsi status and some Tutsis lost their status as Tutsis. Most rural Tutsis enjoyed few advantages over rural Hutus). The first European known to have visited Rwanda was German Count Von Goetzen in 1894. He was followed by missionaries called the "White Fathers." In 1899, the mwami submitted to a German protectorate without resistance. Belgian troops from Zaire chased the small number of Germans out of Rwanda in 1915 and took control of the country.

After World War I, the League of Nations mandated Rwanda and its southern neighbor, Burundi, to Belgium as the territory of Ruanda-Urundi. Following World War II, Ruanda-Urundi became a UN Trust Territory with Belgium as the administrative authority. Reforms instituted by the Belgians in the 1950s encouraged the growth of democratic political institutions but were resisted by the Tutsi traditionalists who saw in them a threat to Tutsi rule. Hutu leaders, encouraged by the Belgian military, sparked a popular revolt in November 1959, resulting in the overthrow of the Tutsi monarchy. Two years later, the Party of the Hutu Emancipation Movement (PARMEHUTU) won an overwhelming victory in a UN-supervised referendum.

During the 1959 revolt and its aftermath, more than 160,000 Tutsis fled to neighboring countries. The PARMEHUTU government, formed as a result of the September 1961 election, was granted internal autonomy by Belgium on January 1, 1962. A June 1962 UN General Assembly resolution terminated the Belgian trusteeship and granted full independence to Rwanda (and Burundi) effective July 1, 1962.

Gregoire Kayibanda, leader of the PARMEHUTU Party, became Rwanda's first elected president, leading a one-party government chosen from the membership of the directly elected unicameral National Assembly. The Kayibanda government promoted a Hutu-supremacist ideology, and a series of anti-Tutsi “pogroms” and other violence gravely affected internal security and provoked the flight of Rwandan Tutsis.

Rwanda established relations with 43 countries, including the United States, during the first 10 years. Despite some progress made, inefficiency and corruption festered in government ministries in the mid-1960s. On July 5, 1973, the military took power by force under the leadership of Maj. Gen. Juvenal Habyarimana, who dissolved the National Assembly and the PARMEHUTU Party and abolished all political activity.

In 1975, President Habyarimana formed the National Revolutionary Movement for Development

(MRND) as Rwanda's only legal party. The movement was organized from the "hillside" to the national level and included elected and appointed officials. During his tenure, violence against Tutsis continued without effective prosecution of wrongdoers, prompting more exoduses.

Under MRND aegis, Rwandans went to the polls in December 1978, overwhelmingly endorsed a new constitution, and confirmed President Habyarimana as president. President Habyarimana was re-elected in 1983 and again in 1988, when he was the sole candidate. Responding to international as well as public pressure for political reform, President Habyarimana announced in July 1990 his intention to transform Rwanda's one-party state into a multi-party democracy. He also indicated that Rwanda "had no room" for its largely Tutsi population living in exile, so they were not welcome to return to Rwanda.

On October 1, 1990, Rwandan exiles banded together as the Rwandan Patriotic Front (RPF) and invaded Rwanda from their base in Uganda. The rebel force, composed primarily of ethnic Tutsis who had not been allowed to return to Rwanda under the Kayibanda or Habyarimana regimes, blamed the government for failing to democratize and resolve the problems of some 500,000 Tutsi refugees living in the diaspora around the world. The war dragged on for almost 2 years until a cease-fire accord was signed July 12, 1992, in Arusha, Tanzania, fixing a timetable for an end to the fighting and political talks, leading to a peace accord and power sharing, and authorizing a neutral military observer group under the auspices of the Organization for African Unity. A cease-fire took effect July 31, 1992, and political talks began August 10, 1992. The talks concluded in a peace accord that was not implemented.

On April 6, 1994, the airplane carrying President Habyarimana and the President of Burundi was shot down as it prepared to land at Kigali. Both presidents were killed. As though the shooting down was a signal, military and militia groups began rounding up and killing all Tutsis and political moderates, regardless of their *ubwoko*.
The Rwandan prime minister and her 10 Belgian bodyguards were among the first victims. The killing swiftly spread from Kigali to all corners of the country; between April 6 and the beginning of July, a genocide of unprecedented swiftness left an estimated 800,000 Tutsis and moderate Hutus dead at the hands of organized bands of militia--*Interahamwe.* Even ordinary citizens were called on to kill their neighbors, friends, and even family members by local officials and government-sponsored radio; many complied. The president's MRND Party was implicated in organizing many aspects of the genocide.

The RPF battalion stationed in Kigali under the Arusha accords came under attack immediately after the shooting down of the president's plane. The battalion fought its way out of Kigali and joined up with RPF units in the north. The RPF then resumed its invasion, and civil war raged concurrently with the genocide for 2 months. French forces landed in Goma, Zaire, in June 1994 on a humanitarian mission. They deployed throughout southwest Rwanda in an area they called "Zone Turquoise," ostensibly to quell the genocide and stop the fighting there, though some Rwandans asserted that they were complicit; many members of the genocidal rump regime established after the genocide began escaped through the French zone to eastern Congo. The RPF defeated the Rwandan Army, which crossed the border to Zaire followed by some 2 million Rwandans who fled to Zaire, Tanzania, and Burundi as refugees. The RPF took Kigali on July 4, 1994, and the war ended on July 16, 1994. The country was decimated, having been ravaged by war and a brutal genocide. Up to 1 million had been murdered, another 2 million or so had fled, and another million or so were displaced internally.

The international community responded to the humanitarian disaster that developed among the refugees in Zaire with one of the largest humanitarian relief efforts ever mounted. The United States was one of the largest contributors. The UN peacekeeping operation, UNAMIR, was drawn down during the fighting but brought back up to strength after the RPF victory. UNAMIR remained in Rwanda until March 8, 1996.

Following the establishment of armed groups and a local rebellion in the camps in eastern Zaire, Rwandan and Ugandan troops invaded in late 1996. This triggered the return of more than 800,000 back to Rwanda in the last 2 weeks of November, followed at the end of December 1996 by the return of another 500,000 from Tanzania, both of which occurred in huge waves. Fewer than 50,000 Rwandans are estimated to remain outside of Rwanda, and they include remnants of the defeated army of the former genocidal government, its allies in the civilian militias known as *Interahamwe*, soldiers recruited in the refugee camps before 1996, as well as children of those groups and opponents of today's government.

In 2001, with over 120,000 Rwandans in prison and virtually no judicial system in existence (most lawyers and judges had been killed or fled during the genocide), the government began implementing a grassroots village-level justice system, known as *gacaca* to address the enormous backlog of genocide cases. Although many convicted were sentenced to public service rather than prison, because of the continuing high numbers of prisoners, the Government of Rwanda periodically arranged prison releases, including the January 2006 release of approximately 7,000 prisoners. By December 2010, *gacaca* officials reported having concluded more than 1.2 million cases. These courts planned to complete their caseload in 2010.

GOVERNMENT AND POLITICAL CONDITIONS

After its military victory in July 1994, the RPF organized a coalition government called "The Broad Based Government of National Unity." Its fundamental law was based on a combination of the June 1991 constitution, the Arusha accords, and political declarations by the parties. The government outlawed the MRND Party. In April 2003, the transitional National Assembly recommended the dissolution of the Democratic Republican Party (MDR), one of eight political parties participating in the Government of National Unity since 1994. Human rights groups noted the subsequent disappearances of political figures associated with the MDR, including at least one parliamentarian serving in the National Assembly. On May 26, 2003, Rwanda adopted a new constitution that eliminated reference to *ubwoko* and set the stage for presidential and legislative elections in August and September 2003. The seven remaining political parties endorsed incumbent Paul Kagame for president, who was elected to a 7-year term on August 25, 2003. Rwanda held its first-ever legislative elections September 29 to October 2, 2003. A ninth political party formed after these 2003 elections.

In the spring of 2006, the government conducted local non-partisan elections for district mayors and for sector and cell executive committees. Elections for the Chamber of Deputies occurred in September 2008; the RPF won an easy victory in coalition with six small parties, taking 42 of 53 directly-elected seats. As provided in the constitution, 24 seats were also accorded to women candidates in indirect elections. Women now hold 45 of the 80 seats in the Chamber. The elections were peaceful and orderly, despite irregularities. A tenth political party formed in 2010.

Presidential elections were held in August 2010; the National Electoral Commission reported that President Kagame won re-election with roughly 93% of the vote. The presidential election was peaceful and orderly, with heavy turnout. However, the pre-election period was marked by events of concern, including waves of terrorist attacks using grenades in populous areas, the murder of a journalist, the unexplained murder of the vice president of the Democratic Green Party, an assassination attempt on a former high-ranking government official accused of fomenting attacks, and the suspension of two local-language newspapers. In addition, two political opposition figures were arrested on criminal charges, and a party that had been seeking to register for many months was unable to do so.

Challenges facing the government include maintaining internal and regional security, promoting further democratization and judicial reform; completion of prosecution of remaining individuals for crimes relating to the 1994 genocide, either by the regular court system or the *gacaca* system; integrating former combatants and prisoners; preventing the recurrence of any insurgency directed by ex-military and *Interahamwe* militia who remain in eastern Congo; and the continuing work on medium- and long-term development.

PRINCIPAL GOVERNMENT OFFICIALS

Cabinet

PRIME MINISTER'S OFFICE

Rt. Hon. Anastase Murekezi Prime Minister

The Prime Minister's Office, PMO in short, under the authority of the Prime Minister, is entrusted with assisting the Prime Minister in the implementation of national policies, leading Government activities along the major guidelines given by the President of the Republic and ensuring law enforcement.

The PMO is also entrusted with the function of formulating the Government programme of action in consultation with Ministerial Departments. In addition to that, PMO provides advice to ministries and supporting agencies in order to speed service delivery.

For more information: www.primature.gov.rw

MINISTRY OF NATURAL RESOURCES

Hon. Dr. Vincent Biruta- Minister of Natural Resources (Land, Forests, Environment and Mining)Hon. Dr. Vincent Biruta - Minister of Natural Resources (Land, Forests, Environment and Mining)

About MINIRENA

The Ministry of Natural Resources (MINIRENA) was established to ensure sustainable management and rational use of natural resources. The imbalance between population and natural resources is the biggest challenge that Rwanda has with regard to the management and protection of the environment and natural resources (land, water resources, forests, minerals, etc.). Degradation has occurred over the decades causing serious ecological and socio-economic problems that, if no adequate recovery measures are undertaken, would lead to an irreversible damage.

For more information: www.minirena.gov.rw

Hon. Evode Imena - Minister of State in the Ministry

For more information: www.minirena.gov.rw

MINISTRY OF FINANCE AND ECONOMIC PLANNING

Hon. Claver Gatete - Minister of Finance and Economic Planning

About MINECOFIN

The Ministry of Finance and Economic planning is responsible for sustainable growth, economic opportunities and living standards of all Rwandans. The ministry is also responsible for establishing and monitoring the highest standards of accountability and transparency in public finance management.

The Ministry of Finance and Economic Planning mobilises internal and external resources and works with public institutions to improve the delivery of public services and accountability through effective financial and fiscal decentralisation.

For more information: www.minecofin.gov.rw

Hon. Uzziel Ndagijimana - Minister of State in the Ministry of Finance and Economic Planning in charge of Economic Planning

For more information: www.minecofin.gov.rw

MINISTRY OF AGRICULTURE AND ANIMAL RESOURCES

Hon. Geraldine Mukeshimana

About MINAGRI

The Ministry of Agriculture's mission is to develop and manage suitable programmes of transformation and modernisation of agriculture and livestock to ensure food security and to contribute to the national economy.

The Ministry's vision is to modernize Agriculture and Livestock to achieve food security. The key pillars of this vision is the transformation of Agriculture from subsistence to a productive high value, market oriented farming that is environmentally friendly and has an impact on other sectors of the economy.

The Ministry also oversees the development and implementation of policy of to increase animal and crop production, modernize farming, reduce poverty, ensure food security and have surplus for the market. This will ultimately result in the increase of the standard of living of the population.

For more information: www.minagri.gov.rw

Hon. Tony Nsanganira - Minister of State in the Ministry of Agriculture and Animal Resources in charge of Agriculture

For more information: www.minagri.gov.rw

MINISTRY OF EDUCATION

Dr. Musafiri Papias Malimba Minister of Education

About MINEDUC

The mission of the Ministry of Education is to transform the Rwandan citizen into skilled human capital for socio-economic development of the country by ensuring equitable access to quality education focusing on combating illiteracy, promotion of science and technology, critical thinking and positive values.

For more information: www.mineduc.gov.rw

Hon. Olivier Rwamukwaya Minister of state in charge of Primary and Secondary Education.

MINISTRY OF HEALTH

Hon. Agnes Binagwaho - Minister of Health

About MOH

The main goal of the Ministry of Health is to provide and continually improve the health services of the Rwandan population through the provision of preventive, curative and rehabilitative health care thereby contributing to the reduction of poverty and enhancing the general well-being of the population.

For more information: www.moh.gov.rw

Hon. Patrick Ndimubanzi - Minister of State in the Ministry of Health in charge of Public Health and Primary Health Care

For more information: www.moh.gov.rw

MINISTRY OF DEFENCE

Hon. James Kabarebe - Minister of Defence

About MINADEF

The Ministry of Defence is responsible for ensuring the sovereignty and defence of the country by protecting Rwanda's interests, territorial integrity, vital resources of the population and of the national values under the ambit of the Constitution and International Law.

The overall goal of the Ministry of Defence is to generate, employ and sustain combat-ready, integrated and rapidly deployable Defence Force, capable of quick assemblage to meet varying contingencies both at home and abroad.

For more information: www.mod.gov.rw

MINISTRY OF JUSTICE

Hon. Johnston Busingye - Minister of Justice / Attorney General

About MINIJUST

The vision of Ministry of Justice is to promote and facilitate the Rule of law in the country by emphasizing equality of all persons before the law and ensuring that judicial institutions are effective and efficient in the provision of legal services to the public.

The Minister of Justice also serves as the Republic of Rwanda's Attorney General.

For more information: www.minijust.gov.rw

MINISTRY OF FOREIGN AFFAIRS AND COOPERATION

Hon. Louise Mushikiwabo - Minister of Foreign Affairs and Cooperation

About MINAFFET

The Ministry of Foreign Affairs is responsible for establishing and maintaining quality relationships with other countries for peace, security and stability of Rwanda, the region and the world while participating in wealth creation through more efficient cooperation for development, promotion of investments and tourism, the transfer of know-how and technologies, and more equitable worldwide trade regional integration.

The Ministry of Foreign Affairs is also responsible for elaborating strategies and programmes, whose objectives are to implement, monitor and evaluate Rwanda's foreign policy as well as to clearly articulate this policy both inside and outside the country.

For more information: www.minaffet.gov.rw

Hon. Amb. Eugène-Richard Gasana - Minister of State at the Ministry of Foreign Affairs and Cooperation

For more information: www.minnaffet.gov.rw

MINISTRY OF GENDER AND FAMILY PROMOTION IN THE PRIME MINISTER'S OFFICE

Dr. Diane Gashumba - Minister of Gender and Family Promotion in the Prime Minister's Office

About MIGEPROF

The Ministry in the Prime Minister's office in charge of Gender and Family Promotion aims at promoting equality and equity for both men and women and ensure empowerment of women through the national development processes of Rwanda. The Ministry further aims at promoting the family, as a natural and cultural basis of the Rwandan society and provide a conducive environment for the overall development of the nation's children according to internationally agreed standards and principles.

For more information: www.migeprof.gov.rw

MINISTRY OF INFRASTRUCTURE

Hon. Musoni James - Minister of Infrastructure

About MININFRA

The mission of the Ministry of infrastructure is to ensure the sustainable development of infrastructure and contribute to economic growth with a view to enhancing the quality of life of the population. To develop institutional and legal frameworks, national policies, strategies and master plans relating to transport, energy, habitat and urbanism, meteorology, and water and sanitation subsectors; To initiate programs to develop, rehabilitate and maintain an efficient and integrated national transport infrastructure network, including roads, bridges, airports, railways, and water transportation which will contribute towards economic development and regional integration.

For more information: www.mininfra.gov.rw

Hon. Germaine Kamayirese - Minister of State in charge of Energy and Water

Hon. Dr Alexis Nzahabwanimana - Minister of State in charge of Transport

For more information: www.mininfra.gov.rw

MINISTRY OF INTERNAL SECURITY

Hon. Sheikh Mussa Harerimana - Minister of Internal Security

About MININTER

The Ministry of Internal Security was formed grouping together, the National Police and Prisons with a perspective of efficiently giving appropriate solutions to requirements of the Rwandan Society in perpetual mutations. The formation of this Ministry is a clear indication that the High Authorities of this country put in issues of security and peace at the centre of governmental priority programmes.

The Ministry of Internal Security's mission is to guarantee the safety and security of Rwandans and their property respecting all relevant international conventions. The Police and Correctional Services work throughout the country, in collaboration where necessary.

For more information: www.mininter.gov.rw

MINISTRY OF EAST AFRICAN COMMUNITY

Hon. Valentine Rugwabiza - Minister of East African Community

About MINEAC

The Ministry of East African Community was established by the Government of Rwanda in 2008 in line with EAC member states' joint commitment to establish national coordinating ministries with primary responsibility for EAC matters. MINEAC serves as an operational link between the Government of Rwanda and other national stakeholders, and the EAC organs and Institutions.

MINEAC's main mission is to lead the widening and deepening of the EAC integration process in order to promote the development goals of Rwanda and the region.

For more information: www.mineac.gov.rw

MINISTRY OF DISASTER MANAGEMENT AND REFUGEE AFFAIRS

Hon Serafine Mukantabana - Minister of Disaster Management and Refugee Affairs

About MIDIMAR

The Ministry of Disaster Management and Refugee Affairs was established to attain a highly proficient mechanism for preventing, mitigating, responding, recovering, securing, monitoring and timely acting positively in order to promote disaster awareness culture within a sector policy framework oriented to management of natural and manmade disasters. The Ministry is tasked with developing a pro- active refugee policy and good mechanism for handling of Rwandan and Foreign Refugees affairs in respect of Rwandan law and international treaties signed for protection of refugees which permit to develop a comprehensive advance response strategy.

For more information: www.midimar.gov.rw

MINISTRY OF CABINET AFFAIRS

Stella Ford MugaboStella Ford Mugabo

Ministry of Cabinet Affairs (MINICAAF)

About MINICAAF

The Ministry of Cabinet Affairs (MINICAAF) is headed by the Minister for Cabinet Affairs, Stella Ford Mugabo, and comprises the Cabinet Secretariat and the Official Gazette of Rwanda.

MINICAAF was established by the Cabinet decision of 28 January 2008 and its mandate is set out in Presidential Order No 03/01 of 02/04/2008 determining the functioning of Cabinet, its membership and procedures for decision making.

The mission of MINICAAF is to ensure that the Cabinet process is run effectively and efficiently and that proper consultations take place before policy decisions are taken. MINICAAF also works to achieve coordination of policy across State institutions in collaboration with the Strategy and Policy Unit in the Office of the President.

For more information: www.minicaaf.gov.rw

MINISTRY OF LOCAL GOVERNMENT

Hon. Francis Kaboneka - Minister of Local Government

About MINALOC

The Ministry of Local Government was established with the main mission of "Promoting the well-being of the population by good governance, community development and social affairs." Among its objectives, the Ministry is tasked with Putting in place democratic, decentralized administrative structures, which are able to mobilize the population in order to implement Government programs and resolve problems.

For more information: www.minaloc.gov.rw

Hon. Dr. Alvera Mukabaramba - Minister of State in the Ministry of Local Government in Charge of Social Affairs.

For more information:www.minaloc.gov.rw

Hon. Judith Uwizeye - Minister of Public Service and Labor

About MIFOTRA

The Ministry of Public Service and Labour was established to Strengthen Institutional and Legal framework to improve conditions of employment in Public and Private sector. The Ministry's mission is to reinforce the national labour standards, promote job creation and institutionalize an efficient and modern public service management framework that will enable private and public sector organizations to perform at their best and effectively contribute to improving the lives of the Rwandan population.

For more information: www.mifotra.gov.rw

MINISTRY OF TRADE AND INDUSTRY

Hon François Kanimba - Minister of Trade and Industry

About MINICOM

The Ministry of Trade and Industry has a vision to achieve accelerated and sustained economic growth led by a dynamic and competitive private sector. The Ministries mission is to facilitate

Rwanda's economic transformation through enabling a competitive private sector integrated into regional and global markets, while ensuring a level playing field and the protection of consumers.

For more information: www.minicom.gov.rw

MINISTRY OF SPORTS AND CULTURE

Hon. Julienne Uwacu - Minister of Sports and Culture

About MINISPOC

The Ministry of Sports and Culture was established with a mission to develop, coordinate, monitor, evaluate and support implementation of policies and strategies that promote Sports and Cultural development initiatives that lead to the economic and social transformation as well as to a productive and patriotic generation.

The Ministry's mission is to develop and support implementation of policies and strategies that lead to a winning culture in sports and to make culture foundational to our development agenda.

For more information: www.minispoc.gov.rw

For more information: www.minispoc.gov.rw

MINISTRY OF YOUTH AND ICT

Hon. Jean Philbert Nsengimana - Minister of Youth and ICT

About Ministry of Youth and ICT

The Ministry of Youth and ICT develops, coordinates, monitors, evaluates and supports implementation of policies and strategies that promote youth development aimed at economic and social transformation and a productive and patriotic generation. The ministry is also charged with integrating and disseminating ICT through policy, strategy and action to empower both public and private sectors, in order to accelerate the transformation of Rwanda into a middle-income economy and information society by 2020.

For more information: www.myict.gov.rw

MINISTER IN THE OFFICE OF THE PRESIDENT

Hon. Venantia Tugireyezu - Minister in the Office of the President

About MINIPRESIREP

The Minister in the Office of the President reviews all legislation before promulgation by the President of the Republic. The Minister works closely with the National Unity and Reconciliation Commission, Office of the Ombudsman and National Intelligence Security Service and ensures the establishment and implementation of policies and legislation related to those institutions attached to the Office of the President. The Minister is also charged with resolving the citizen complaints addressed to the President and supervises implementation of Presidential pledges; and serves as liaison between Cabinet and Parliament by briefing both bureaus of the Senate and Chamber of Deputies on Cabinet resolutions or any other issues from the two Chambers concerning government.

RWANDA DEVELOPMENT BOARD

Hon. Francis Gatare - RDB's Chief Executive Officer

About RDB

The Rwanda Development Board was set up by bringing together all the government agencies responsible for the entire investor experience under one roof. This includes key agencies responsible for business registration, investment promotion, environmental clearances, privatization and specialist agencies which support the priority sectors of ICT and tourism as well as SMEs and human capacity development in the private sector.

The RDB is independent and influential. It reports directly to the President and is guided by a Board that includes all the key Ministers (e.g., finance, commerce, infrastructure, agriculture).

For more information: www.rdb.gov.rw

Rwanda maintains an **embassy** in the United States at 1714 New Hampshire Avenue NW, Washington, DC 20009 (tel. 202-232-2882).

ECONOMY

Currency	Rwandan franc (RWF)
Fiscal year	calendar year
Trade organisations	WTO, ECCAS, EAC, COMESA
Statistics	
GDP	$7 billion
GDP rank	144th (nominal) / 136th (PPP)
GDP growth	8.3%
GDP per capita	$644
GDP by sector	agriculture: 33%, industry: 16%, services: 45%
Inflation (CPI)	6.7% (
Population below poverty line	55%
Gini coefficient	24.9
Labour force	5.0 million
Labour force by occupation	agriculture: 90%, industry and services: 10%
Unemployment	no data
Main industries	cement, agricultural products, small-scale beverages, soap, furniture, shoes, plastic goods, textiles, cigarettes
Ease-of-doing-business rank	32nd
External	
Exports	$152.8 million
Export goods	coffee, tea, hides, tin ore
Main export partners	Kenya 32.6% DR Congo 13.1% China 11.7% Malaysia 10.4% United States 5.6% Swaziland 5.2% Pakistan 4.1%
Imports	$365.7 million (
Import goods	foodstuffs, machinery and equipment, steel, petroleum products, cement and construction material
Main import partners	Kenya 18.4% Uganda 16.6%

	United Arab Emirates 8.3% China 6.9% India 5.4% Tanzania 5.4% Belgium 4.3%
	Public finances
Public debt	$0.7 billion (2010) (external)
Revenues	$560.9 million
Expenses	$654 million
Economic aid	recipient: $285 Million

Rwanda is a rural country with about 90% of the population engaged in (mainly subsistence) agriculture. It is the most densely populated country in Africa; is landlocked; and has few natural resources and minimal industry. Primary exports are coffee and tea. By 1994, farm size, on average, was smaller than one hectare, while population density was more than 450 persons per square kilometer of arable land.

The Rwandan economy is based on the largely rain-fed agricultural production of small, semi-subsistence, and increasingly fragmented farms. It has few natural resources to exploit and a small, noncompetitive industrial sector. While the production of coffee and tea is well-suited to the small farms, steep slopes, and cool climates of Rwanda and has ensured access to foreign exchange over the years, farm size continues to decrease.Prewar population was growing at the high rate of 3% a year.

During the 5 years of civil war that culminated in the 1994 genocide, GDP declined in 3 out of 5 years, posting a dramatic decline at more than 40% in 1994, the year of the genocide. The 9% increase in real GDP for 1995, the first postwar year, signaled the resurgence of economic activity and massive foreign aid inflows.

In the immediate postwar period--mid-1994 through 1995--emergency humanitarian assistance of more than $307.4 million was largely directed to relief efforts in Rwanda and in the refugee camps in neighboring countries where Rwandans fled during the war. In 1996, humanitarian relief aid began to shift to reconstruction and development assistance.

Since 1996, Rwanda has experienced steady economic recovery, thanks to government reforms and foreign aid (now over $500 million per year). Since 2002, the GDP growth rate ranged from 3%-11% per annum, and inflation ranged between 2%-9%. Rwanda depends on significant foreign imports (over $900 million per year). Exports have increased, up to $193 million in 2009. Private investment remains below expectations despite an open trade policy, a favorable investment climate, cheap and abundant labor, tax incentives to businesses, stable internal security, and crime rates that are comparatively low. Investment insurance also is available through the Africa Trade Insurance Agency, the Overseas Private Investment Corporation, and the World Bank's Multilateral Investment Guarantee Agency (MIGA). The weakness of exports and low domestic savings rates are threats to future growth. The global economic crisis has impacted Rwanda. However, while there was a decline in overall exports (28% between 2008 and 2009), remittances, and nongovernmental organization (NGO) transfers in 2009, the agricultural sector performed strongly, propelling Rwanda to a 4% growth in GDP, well above the sub-Saharan average growth for the year. Amidst obstacles, Rwanda appears committed to economic reform and private sector investment. In the World Bank's "Ease of Doing Business" report released in September 2009, Rwanda catapulted from number 143 to number 67; in the 2010 report, Rwanda improved its ranking to number 58.

The Government of Rwanda remains dedicated to a strong and enduring economic climate for the country, focusing on poverty reduction, infrastructure development, privatization of government-owned assets, expansion of the export base, and trade liberalization. The implementation of a value added tax of 18% and improved tax collections are having a positive impact on government revenues and thereby on government services rendered. Banking reform and low corruption also are favorable current trends. Agricultural reforms, improved farming methods, and increased use of fertilizers are improving crop yields and national food supply. Moreover, the government is pursing educational and healthcare programs that bode well for the long-term quality of Rwanda's human resource skills base.

Many challenges remain for Rwanda. The country is dependent on significant foreign aid. Exports continue to lag far behind imports and will continue to affect the health of the economy. The persistent lack of economic diversification beyond the production of tea, coffee, and minerals keeps the country vulnerable to market fluctuations. Perhaps the largest constraint on private sector development is the cost of electricity, which is currently among the highest in the world at about 24.6 cents per kilowatt hour. Given Rwanda's landlocked geography, strong highway infrastructure maintenance and good transport linkages to neighboring countries, especially Uganda and Tanzania, are critical. Transportation costs remain high and, therefore, burden import and export costs. Rwanda has no railway system for port access to Tanzania or Kenya. The limited availability and high cost of power also continues to impede the growth of manufacturing enterprises. The tourism industry has undeveloped potential for growth given the current political stability, travel infrastructure, and extensive national parks as well as other potential tourist sites. In 2006, Rwanda completed the Multilateral Debt Relief Initiative and the Heavily Indebted Poor Countries (HIPC) debt initiative, significantly lowering its foreign debt load.

American business interests in Rwanda are modest, and the African Growth and Opportunity Act (AGOA) has yet to make a significant impact in Rwanda. In addition to long-standing tea production by an American firm, in 2008 a U.S. corporation concluded an agreement with Rwandan authorities to produce 100 megawatts of electrical power from methane extraction operations in Lake Kivu. In 2009 a U.S.-British consortium signed an agreement with the government to develop a biofuel project based on jatropha, and a U.S. mining company expanded its investment in local mineral production. In 2010, RwandAir signed a contract with Boeing for the purchase of two Boeing 737-800 aircraft, for an estimated $80 million. American exports of aviation, telecommunications, and construction equipment have increased in recent years. Energy needs will stress natural resources in wood and gas, but hydroelectric power development is underway, albeit primarily in the planning stages, as is methane development. Rwanda does not have nuclear power or coal resources. Finally, Rwanda's fertility rate--averaging 5.5 births (2008 est.) per woman--will continue to stress services, and diseases such as HIV/AIDS transmission, malaria, and tuberculosis will have a major impact on human resources.

Rwanda's government-run radio broadcasts 15 hours a day in Kinyarwanda, English, and French, the national languages. News programs include regular re-broadcasts from international radio such as Voice of America, BBC, and Deutsche Welle. There is one government-operated television station. In addition to government-operated Radio Rwanda, there are a number of independent FM radio stations. There are few independent newspapers; most newspapers publish in Kinyarwanda on a weekly, biweekly, or monthly basis. Several Western nations, including the United States, are working to encourage freedom of the press, the free exchange of ideas, and responsible journalism.

The country entered a high period of economic growth in 2006, and the following year managed to register 8% economic growth, a record it has sustained since, turning it into one of the fastest-growing economies in Africa. This sustained economic growth has succeeded in reducing poverty, with growth between 2006 and 2011 reducing the percentage of the country's population living in poverty from 57% to 45%.The country's infrastructure has also grown rapidly, with connections to electricity going from 91,000 in 2006 to 215,000 in 2011.[6]

Existing foreign investment is concentrated in commercial establishments, mining, tea, coffee, and tourism. Minimum wage and social security regulations are in force, and the four prewar independent trade unions are back in operation. The largest union, CESTRAR, was created as an organ of the government but became fully independent with the political reforms introduced by the 1991 constitution. As security in Rwanda improves, the country's nascent tourism sector shows great potential to expand as a source of foreign exchange.

MINING IN RWANDA

Mining in Rwanda consists of extracting such minerals as tin, tantalum, and tungsten. In 2010, Rwanda earned about US$67.8m from mineral exports which constitute 14.9% of total exports, making mining the biggest source of export revenues.

MINERALS EXTRACTED

- Cassiterite (tin ore) had the largest production and export volume at about 3,874 tons valued at US$42.2m in 2010 (down from 4,269 tons in 2009);
- It was followed by coltan with 749 tons in 2010 valued at $18.48m (949 tons in 2009), and wolfram (tungsten ore) with 843 tons in 2010 valued at $7.1m, down from 874 tons in 2009.
- Rwanda produces about 9% of the world's tantalum, used in electronics manufacturing, and about 4% of global tungsten.[1]

In October 2012, Rwanda's Ministry of Natural Resources suspended mining activities in the country's western province on the basis that they were endangering the River Sebeya. The decision was met with negativity due to the affected mining companies' loss of production and the loss of thousands of jobs for workers at the mines

DEFENSE

The military establishment is comprised of a well-trained army and a small, rotary-wing air force. The Rwandan Defense Forces (RDF) is on an aggressive plan to professionalize its military. Following withdrawal of Rwandan Armed Forces from the Democratic Republic of the Congo in October 2009, the government completely restructured the military and launched an ambitious plan to demobilize thousands of soldiers. At end state, Rwanda will have a small, well-equipped army of 20,000 soldiers and a reserve force of more than 100,000. Rwanda has deployed 3,326 peacekeepers to Darfur and Liberia, as well as 21 police officers to Haiti.

FOREIGN RELATIONS

Rwanda is an active member of the international community and has remained in the international spotlight since the genocide. Rwanda is an active member of the UN, having presided over the Security Council during part of 1995. The UN assistance mission in Rwanda (UNAMIR), a UN Chapter Six peacekeeping operation, involved personnel from more than a dozen countries. Most of the UN development and humanitarian agencies have had a large presence in Rwanda. At the height of the humanitarian emergency, more than 200 nongovernmental organizations were carrying out humanitarian operations. In addition to receiving assistance from the international community, Rwanda has also contributed to international peacekeeping missions. Currently, the RDF has four 800-strong battalions deployed in support of the UNAMID Mission in Darfur and one company in UNMIS (Khartoum). As of June 2009, Rwanda was training its 22nd peacekeeping battalion since 2006.

Several nations--including Belgium, Canada, China, Egypt, France, Germany, Japan, the United Kingdom, Libya, the Netherlands, Russia, Sweden, the Holy See, and all members of the EAC (Kenya, Tanzania, Uganda, Burundi) as well as the Democratic Republic of the Congo (D.R.C.)--maintain diplomatic missions in Kigali, as does the European Union.

In December 2008, after months of bilateral discussions, Rwanda and the D.R.C. announced a joint military operation against a root cause of instability in the Great Lakes Region--the FDLR (Democratic Forces for the Liberation of Rwanda), which took place in January and February 2009. In January 2009 the governments of the D.R.C. and Rwanda accelerated efforts to achieve the rapprochement that they had initiated in late 2008. The two nations' forces also cooperated in reintegrating renegade general Laurent Nkunda's CNDP rebel force into the Congolese armed forces (FARDC); Nkunda was detained by Rwandan authorities.

In the fall of 2006, Rwanda broke diplomatic relations with France, following a French judge's indictment of senior Rwandan officials on charges of having participated in the shooting down of the presidential jet in 1994. Rwanda rejects these charges. In January 2010, Rwanda and France renewed their diplomatic relations after France indicated it had reopened its investigation of the 2006 charges. Rwanda, along with Burundi, joined the EAC in 2007, and it acceded to the Commonwealth in 2009.

U.S.-RWANDAN RELATIONS

U.S. Government interests have shifted significantly since the 1994 genocide from a strictly humanitarian concern focused on stability and security to a strong partnership with the Government of Rwanda focused on sustainable development. The largest U.S. Government programs are the President's Emergency Plan for AIDS Relief (PEPFAR) and the President's Malaria Initiative, which aim to reduce the impact of these debilitating diseases in Rwanda. In partnership with the Government of Rwanda, U.S. Government agencies--Centers for Disease Control and Prevention, Department of Defense, Peace Corps, State Department, and U.S. Agency for International Development (USAID)--work to strengthen the Rwandan health system and build local capacity.

The **USAID** program plays a strong role in helping Rwanda to improve the health and livelihoods of its people and increase economic and political development. To achieve this, USAID activities focus on:

- Prevention, treatment, and care of HIV/AIDS;
- Reducing mortality and morbidity due to malaria;
- Increasing access to, and use of, voluntary family planning methods;
- Improving maternal and child health;
- Promoting rural economic growth through staple crops, specialty coffee, dairy, and eco-tourism;

- Reducing post-harvest losses of agriculture produce;
- Expanding the use of information technology in primary education;
- Encouraging participatory governance and decentralization; and
- Promoting a democratic Rwanda, where the government respects human rights, civil liberties, and the rule of law.

In September 2008, Rwanda signed a Threshold Country Plan (TCP) agreement with the Millennium Challenge Corporation (MCC). USAID implements these programs, which focus on strengthening civil society, the judiciary, police, and media sectors and promoting civic participation and civil society.

The State Department's Public Affairs section (PAS) maintains an Information Resource Center (IRC) in Kigali, which offers public access to English-language publications, an English language lab for those preparing for English language exams, information on the United States, and information on studying in the U.S. PAS also maintains an American Corner at the National University of Rwanda (NUR) in Huye (formerly Butare) and supports an English Language Resource Center at the Catholic Institute of Kabgayi (ICK) in Gitarama.

American business interests have been small; currently, private U.S. investment is limited to the tea industry, franchising (FedEx, Coca-Cola, Western Union, and Moneygram) and small holdings in service and manufacturing concerns. Annual U.S. exports to Rwanda, under $10 million annually from 1990-93, exceeded $40 million in 1994 and 1995. Although exports decreased in the years immediately after the genocide, in 2007 they were estimated at approximately $17 million, a 20% increase over 2006.

Principal U.S. Officials
Ambassador--**W. Stuart Symington**
Deputy Chief of Mission--Anne Casper
USAID Mission Director--Dennis Weller

The **U.S. Embassy** is located on 2657 Avenue de la Gendarmerie, Kigali (tel. 250-596-400, fax 250-596-591).

TRAVEL AND BUSINESS INFORMATION

Travel Alerts, Travel Warnings, Trip Registration
The U.S. Department of State's Consular Information Program advises Americans traveling and residing abroad through Country Specific Information, Travel Alerts, and Travel Warnings. **Country Specific Information** exists for all countries and includes information on entry and exit requirements, currency regulations, health conditions, safety and security, crime, political disturbances, and the addresses of the U.S. embassies and consulates abroad. **Travel Alerts** are issued to disseminate information quickly about terrorist threats and other relatively short-term conditions overseas that pose significant risks to the security of American travelers. **Travel Warnings** are issued when the State Department recommends that Americans avoid travel to a certain country because the situation is dangerous or unstable.

For the latest security information, Americans living and traveling abroad should regularly monitor the Department's Bureau of Consular Affairs Internet web site at http://travel.state.gov, where current Worldwide Caution, Travel Alerts, and Travel Warnings can be found. The travel.state.gov website also includes information about passports, tips for planning a safe trip abroad and more.

More travel-related information also is available at http://www.usa.gov/Citizen/Topics/Travel/International.shtml.

The Department's Smart Traveler app for U.S. travelers going abroad provides easy access to the frequently updated official country information, travel alerts, travel warnings, maps, U.S. embassy locations, and more that appear on the travel.state.gov site. Travelers can also set up e-tineraries to keep track of arrival and departure dates and make notes about upcoming trips. The app is compatible with iPhone, iPod touch, and iPad (requires iOS 4.0 or later).

The Department of State encourages all U.S. citizens traveling or residing abroad to register via the State Department's travel registration website or at the nearest U.S. embassy or consulate abroad (a link to the registration page is also available through the Smart Traveler app). Registration will make your presence and whereabouts known in case it is necessary to contact you in an emergency and will enable you to receive up-to-date information on security conditions.

Emergency information concerning Americans traveling abroad may be obtained by calling 1-888-407-4747 toll free in the U.S. and Canada or the regular toll line 1-202-501-4444 for callers outside the U.S. and Canada.

Passports
The National Passport Information Center (NPIC) is the U.S. Department of State's single, centralized public contact center for U.S. passport information. Telephone: 1-877-4-USA-PPT (1-877-487-2778); TDD/TTY: 1-888-874-7793. Passport information is available 24 hours, 7 days a week. You may speak with a representative Monday-Friday, 8 a.m. to 10 p.m., Eastern Time, excluding federal holidays.

MINERAL AND MINING SECTOR

RWANDA

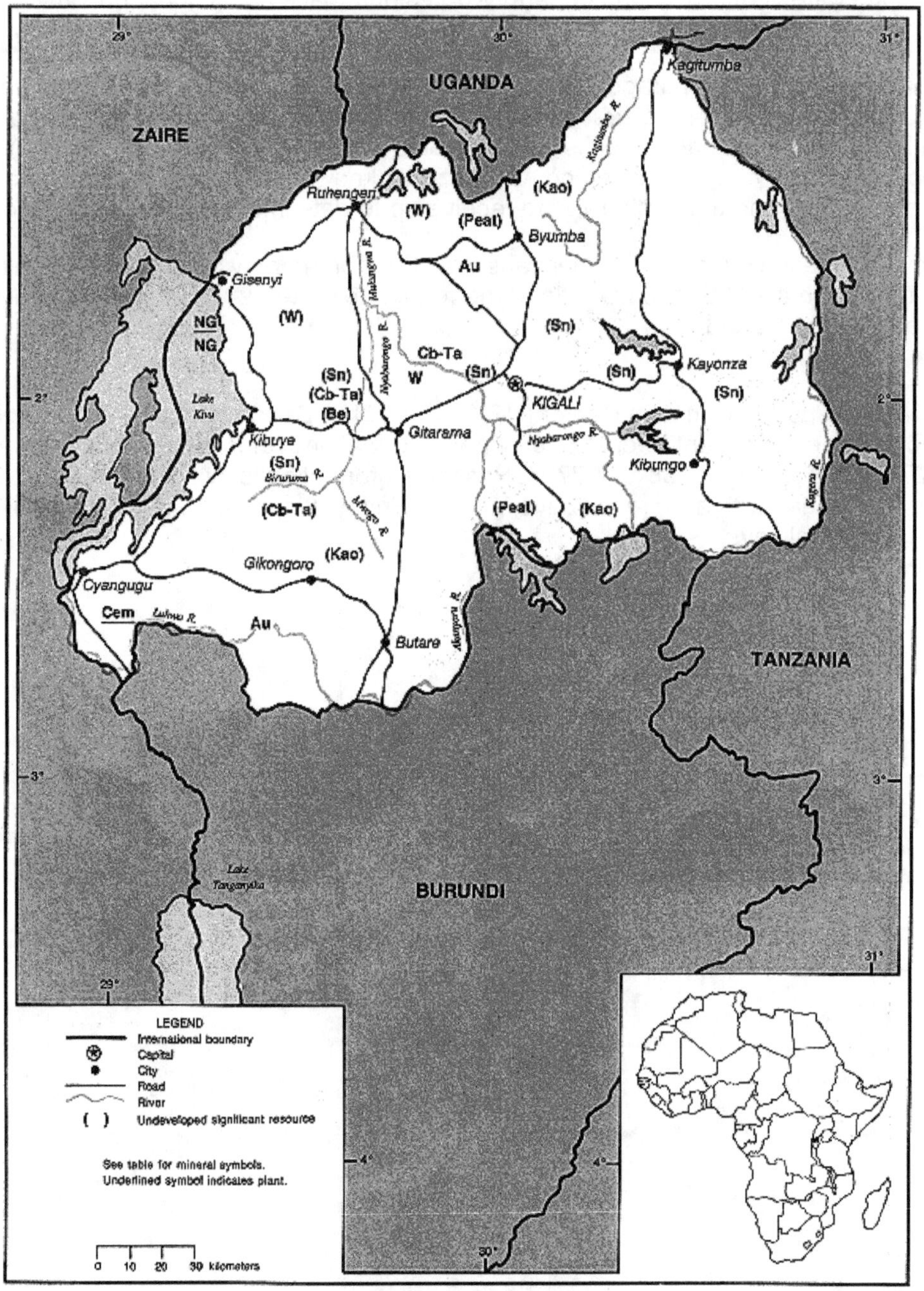

THE MINERAL INDUSTRY OF RWANDA

Rwanda was not a globally significant consumer of minerals. In 2009, however, Rwanda's share of the world's tantalum mine production amounted to about 9%, and tungsten, 1%. In 2008 (the latest year for which data were available), the mining and quarrying sector accounted for about 1% of the gross domestic product. About 50,000 Rwandans were employed in the mining sector in 2007. Rwanda's exports of columbite-tantalite, cassiterite (tin ore), and wolframite (tungsten ore) were from domestic mining operations and reexports from mining operations in the Democratic Republic of the Congo [Congo (Kinshasa)] (Banque Nationale du Rwanda, 2009, p. 128; Garrett and Mitchell, 2009, p. 39-41; Papp, 2010; Shedd, 2010).

PRODUCTION

In 2009, peat production increased by an estimated 300%, and natural gas, by about 100%. Production of tungsten decreased by an estimated 14% in 2009, and niobium (columbium), tantalum, and tin, by an estimated 13% each.

STRUCTURE OF THE MINERAL INDUSTRY

The state-owned Régie d'Exploitation et de Développement des Mines (REDEMI) produced columbite-tantalite, cassiterite (tin ore), and wolframite (tungsten ore); privately owned companies, cooperatives, and artisanal miners also produced these mineral commodities. In 2006, the Government privatized 20 of REDEMI's concessions. The privately owned Cimenterie du Rwanda (Cimerwa) was the country's only cement producer.

METALS

Gold.—TransAfrika Resources Ltd. of Mauritius engaged in a drilling program at its Byumba concession in the Gicumbi District from October 2008 to September 2009. In October 2009, Transafrika started work on a resource estimate at Byumba. Kivu Gold Corp. of Canada also engaged in gold exploration. Rogi Mining Ltd. of Russia held the Miyove concession.

Niobium (Columbium) and Tantalum.—Columbite-tantalite was mined in the Gatsibo and the Kamonyi Districts by companies that included Centrale Multi-Services SARL (CMS), Eurotrade International S.A., Gatumba Mining Concessions Ltd. (GMC), Munsad Minerals, and Natural Resources Development Rwanda Ltd. (NRD) of Germany. CMS produced at the rate of 180 metric tons per year (t/yr) of columbite-tantalite in 2009. GMC planned to spend $2.5 million on building 10 new small processing plants by late 2014 (Holland, 2009b; Centrale Multi-Services SARL, 2010).

Tin.—Cassiterite was mined in 26 of Rwanda's 30 districts. CMS produced cassiterite at the rate of 300 t/yr in 2009 compared with 174 t/yr in 2007. In 2009, NRD produced cassiterite at Ntemba at the rate of nearly 220 t/yr compared with 56 t/yr in 2007. NRD planned to increase production to about 430 t/yr. GMC produced cassiterite at Gatumba at the rate of 60 t/yr in 2009 compared with 10 t/yr in 2007. The company was considering the development of medium-scale cassiterite and columbite-tantalite mines at Gatumba that would increase output to between 1,200 and 2,400 t/yr of cassiterite. Columbite-tantalite prices were $38 per pound in late November 2009; GMC's expansion depended on prices increasing to $60 per pound (Garrett and Mitchell, 2009, p. 38; Holland, 2009a, b; New Times, 2009; Centrale Multi-Services SARL, 2010).

Umlhaba Mining of South Africa was engaged in a joint venture with the Government to revamp the Rutongo Mines in Rulindo District. The cost of the project was estimated to be about $5 million (Karuhanga, 2009).

Tungsten.—Privately owned companies, such as Africa Primary Tungsten SARL, CMS, Eurotrade International S.A., Pyramid International, Rwanda Allied Partners, and Wolfram Bergbau- und Hütten GmbH Nfg of Austria, accounted for about 50% of Rwanda's wolframite production in 2007; cooperatives, nearly 40%; and artisanal miners, about 10%. In 2009, CMS produced about 300 t/yr of wolframite (Centrale Multi-Services SARL, 2010; Transafrika Resources Ltd., 2010).

INDUSTRIAL MINERALS

Cement.—Rwanda imported 116,000 t of cement in 2008; Ciments du Rwanda Ltd. (Cimerwa) [Rwanda Investment Group S.A. (RIG), 90%] was unable to meet domestic demand in spite of producing at about its full capacity of 100,000 t/yr. Cimerwa planned to build a new plant with a capacity of 600,000 t/yr at a cost of $70 million. In June 2009, Cimerwa was trying to secure financing for the project (Majyambere, 2009).

MINERAL FUELS

Natural Gas.—State-owned company Kibuye Power 1 Ltd. extracted natural gas from Lake Kivu; the company's 2-megawatt (MW)-capacity gas-fired power station produced electricity for the local power grid. Starting in December 2009, RIG planned to supply a new gas-fired power station with an initial capacity of 3.6 MW using natural gas from beneath Lake Kivu (Africa Energy Intelligence, 2009).

In March 2009, CountourGlobal LLC of the United States signed an agreement with the Government to extract natural gas from Lake Kivu and to build a new gas-fired power station. In the first phase of the project, the plant was expected to have a capacity of 25 MW starting in 2010; full capacity of 100 MW would be reached by 2012. The estimated cost of the project was $325 million (African Power Mining & Oil Review, 2009).

Peat.—In 2008, Peat Energy Co. (a subsidiary of RIG) started peat production at Gishoma in Rusizi District. By October 2009, production amounted to 20,000 t. Cimerwa planned to use peat as a source of energy; the company planned to replace about 70% of its fuel oil consumption with peat. RIG also planned to develop the Gihitasi and the Masya peat deposits (Gahigi, 2009).

Petroleum.—At the end of 2009, Vangold Resources Ltd. of Canada spun off its concession in Lake Kivu and southwest Rwanda to a new company called Vanoil Energy Ltd. of Canada Vanoil planned to complete a seismic survey at Lake Kivu in the third quarter of 2010.

TABLE 1
RWANDA: PRODUCTION OF MINERAL COMMODITIES[1]

(Metric tons unless otherwise specified)

Commodity[2]		2005	2006	2007	2008[e]	2009[e]
Cement		101,128	102,589	103,034	103,244[3]	100,000
Columbite-tantalite, ore and concentrate:						
Gross weight	kilograms	276,000	188,000	490,000	490,000	430,000
Nb content[e]	do.	87,000[r]	59,000[r]	150,000[r]	150,000[r]	130,000
Ta content[e]	do.	68,000[r]	46,000[r]	120,000[r]	120,000[r]	104,000

Gold, mine output, Au content[e]	do.	10	15	17[3]	20	20
Natural gas:						
Gross	million cubic meters	(4)	--	--	NA	NA
Dry	do.	(4)	--	--	2	4
Peat		--	--	--	5,000	20,000
Tin:						
Mine output:[e]						
Gross weight		215[3]	600	1,141[3]	1,500[r]	1,300
Sn content		140[r]	390[r]	740[r]	980[r]	850
Refined[e]		200	50	--[3]	--[3]	--[3]
Tungsten, mine output:						
Gross weight		557	1,436	2,988	1,708[r, 3]	1,500
W content		270[r]	680[r]	1,400[r]	810[r]	700

[e]Estimated; estimated data are rounded to no more than three significant digits. [r]Revised. do. Ditto. NA Not available. -- Zero.
[1]Table includes data available through May 27, 2010.
[2]In addition to the commodities listed, sapphire and pozzolanic materials are also known to be produced, but information is inadequate to make
reliable estimates of output.
[3]Reported data.
[4]Less than one-half unit.

IMPORTANT LAWS AND REGULATIONS

LAW NO. 37 / 2008 FOR THE MINING AND CAREERS

CHAPTER 1. GENERAL PROVISIONS

Article 1:

Purpose of the Act

This Act regulates mining and quarrying in Rwanda.

Article 2:

Definition of Terms

For the purposes of this Act, the terms listed below have the following meanings:

1 **Administration:** Department, Office of Geology and Mines in Rwanda or any other competent body;

2 **Minerals useful** minerals or fossil concessible in terms of the statutory scheme;

3 Career: mineral or fossil concessible not in terms of the statutory scheme. From the technical point of view, this is "an open-pit mining;

4 **Mine:** place of extraction of useful minerals and career;

5 ° **tile mine:** instead of mining operations, and career;

6 **Environmental Impact Assessment:** report assessing the impact of a proposed activity on the environment;

7 **Operation:** extraction of minerals or fossils to dispose of them for utilitarian purposes, and all operations preparatory to the preceding, accompanying or subsequent to it;

8 Deposit: any natural concentration of minerals and fossils of their career;

9 ° **hydrocarbon:** natural substance in solid, liquid or gas composed of hydrogen and carbon only, and having formed by geological processes. It can be mixed with other substances in the reservoir;

10 ° **Authority:** a person authorized to make decisions in relation to this Act;

11 ° **Ore:** economic output after valuable minerals or their fossil

12 ° **Minister:** Minister in mines and quarries in its jurisdiction;

13 ° **Land use:** land owned or used under the land laws;

14 ° **Scope:** land area subject to a license;

15 ° **Small Mine:** mine whose size is considered small in relation to reserves, the level of investment, production and the degree of mechanization;

16 ° **permits:** prospecting permits, research and mining;

17 ° **policy mining and quarrying:** applicable standards for mining and quarrying;

18 ° **Judicial Police:** all officers of research and bring to justice all persons who violate laws relating to mining and quarrying;

19 ° **state-owned property:** property in which the State has an original title;

20 ° **Exploration:** exploration operations which, based on the general features of geology, are to conduct investigations of superficial or deep to discover and provide information on the unusual nature of the soil, indices or concentrations of substances mineral or fossil;

21 ° **Search:** any set of superficial or deep work and study scientific, technical and applied to:

a. establish continuity indices or concentrations discovered by prospecting, and finding deposits or extensions of deposits of minerals or fossils;

b. determine the interest deposits or deposits and extensions of localized evaluate the reserves and demonstrate operability;

c.estimer investments necessary for their operations, the cost of extraction, recovery and conditioning of minerals or fossil extract and the marketability of the latter;

22 ° **Rules:** Prime Minister's Order, Ministerial Order;

23 ° **Reserve:** quantity of minerals or fossils contained in a exploitable deposit and useful;

24 ° **residues:** residues from sieving or foundry products of mining and quarrying;

25 ° **minerals:** all natural, solid other than oil found in the earth's crust on the surface or at depth, in or under water, and having formed by geological processes;

26 ° **Substances useful for Atomic Energy:** radium, thorium and uranium;

27 ° **Title mining:** prospecting permits, research, mining and concession;

28 ° **Enhancement of revenue from mines and quarries:** provide value-added products of mining and quarrying by any means of treatment or processing by the physical, chemical or industrial value added.

Article 3:

Scope of this Act

This Act shall apply to activities related to prospecting, exploration, exploitation, acquisition, possession, processing, transportation and marketing of concessible substances other than oil and products careers throughout the territory of the Republic of Rwanda.

Article 4:

General Principles

Research and exploitation of mines and quarries must meet the following general principles:

1 ° the useful minerals are the property of all Rwandans;

2 ° The State is empowered to manage these resources for economic development and welfare of the population;

3 ° The State may conduct the business of mining, quarrying and use the resulting products or issuing the related permits to private individuals;

4 mining, quarrying and exploitation of the resulting products must take place in accordance with professional standards and those relating to environmental protection;

5 ° the bodies responsible for mining, quarrying and exploitation of the resulting products must work towards a common goal in the development of this sector;

6 Mining, quarrying and resulting products must comply with laws and regulations on land, environment, trade, labor, security, culture and public health;

7 women and youth should be involved in the management and exploitation of minerals.

CHAPTER 2. CLASSIFICATION OF MINES AND CAREERS

Article 5:

Mining and quarrying

All masses of natural minerals contained in the womb of the earth or existing on the surface are classified under the classification of mines or quarries.

Careers are considered deposits of construction materials, fertilizer, agricultural land and other similar substances, salts and peat.

Mines are considered the masses of natural minerals or fossils that are not classified in the quarries. Oil and gas are also classified in the mineral commodities. An order of the Minister shall determine the classification of minerals.

Article 6:

Careers and location

The quarries are inseparable from the soil that they follow the ownership and are leased, acquired or subject to the operating license pursuant to this Act.

CHAPTER 3. BANNED SITES AND AREAS RESERVED

Article 7:

Matters governed by a Prime Minister's Order

Without prejudice to other specific laws, an order of the Prime Minister determines the prohibited areas and restricted areas.

When areas are prohibited, human exploration and exploitation are suspended.

In special areas, human exploration and exploitation of mines or quarries are reserved to the state or agencies established or approved by the State for this purpose.

Article 8:

Content of technical specifications

The techniques of prospecting, exploration, exploitation and utilization of minerals should be included in the specifications of the project established by the Minister.

Article 9:

Use of dynamite

The import, manufacture, transport, trade and use of dynamite in mining and quarrying require prior approval of the Minister responsible for security in its powers on a proposal of the

Minister. An Ordinance of the Minister determines the requirements for obtaining this authorization.

Article 10:

Bodies authorized to carry out mining operations

Public bodies or bodies approved by the State for that purpose may carry on the prospecting, exploration and exploitation of mines and quarries in accordance with this Act.

Article 11:

Exploration licenses, research and exploitation

Subject to the provisions of Article 7 of this Act, the operations of exploration and research for the discovery of mineral deposits or quarries can be carried out pursuant to a prior permit.

The mines can be operated only under a license.

Improving the quality of the minerals can not be acquired except by permission of the Minister. This improvement in the quality of the minerals back into the responsibilities of the holder of a permit and is in compliance.

Article 12:

Acquired rights under the license for exploration and research

The exploration license and research is a personal right furniture, indivisible, separate from land ownership, which is assigned or transferred. This permit exploration and research is not likely to mortgage.

Article 13:

Rights acquired under the mining license

The mining license is a personal right furniture, of limited duration, indivisible, distinct from the real estate and not subject to mortgage. It is transferable, leased or transferred.

The mining concession is a real estate law, limited in time, separate from land ownership is not subject to the mortgage dealer. Dealer may sell, transfer or mortgage its interest in the concession.

Article 14:

Licensing Authority

Operations provided for 11, 12 and 13 are made in accordance with a ministerial order.

Article 15:

Operation of a mineral deposit and career

The exploitation of a deposit of substance as a career can be made for a profit if it is commercial or non-commercial.

The permit is issued to the person who can request.

The operating license is issued for places that have been approved by the research state.

When the landowner shall submit an application for research permits before the others and it is deemed appropriate, the permit is issued first.

Article 16:

Obligation of an operator discovering the substances not covered by the permit

If, during the mining or quarrying, the operator discovers the substances on which is not his title, he shall immediately notify the authority that issued the current permit, with possible request for extension of its license to this new substance.

If permits for exploration, exploitation or mining concessions granted for different substances, cover the same land, the licensee who are not, under the permit, the substances extracted by him, must return to licensee to whom they rightfully belong, against payment, if any, of just compensation.

Article 17:

Right to use waste

The holder of a mining permit or lease may provide that substances extracted from quarries considered at work to service the mine and outbuildings.

The landowner can claim substances extracted and not used by the licensee on payment of just compensation.

The holder of a prospecting permit, operating or concession may dispose of such of those substances that come from the mechanical preparation of ores.

Article 18:

Incompatibility with the operating activities

No person may obtain a license to operate mines and quarries, when his personal status is incompatible with the exercise of commercial activities.

Article 19:

Authorization of a society for the achievement of operating activities

A company wishing to conduct search operations and mining must be incorporated under the company law and have its head office in Rwanda.

Article 20:

Operating as an act of commerce

Research and exploitation of mines and quarries are considered commercial acts.

Article 21:

Body responsible for determining the boundaries of a mining perimeter

The body responsible for issuing license is the sole authority to determine, at the expense of the applicants, the limits and consistency of such licenses. It also keeps the mining and gives, in case of dispute, the interpretation of the contents of such documents.

Article 22:

Exploitation rights

The licensing dexploitation mines and quarries is accompanied by the fee determined by ministerial order.

CHAPTER 4. MINING LICENCES

Article 23:

Types of Permits

Permits for mining and quarrying under this Act are:

1 ° the exploration license;

2 ° the exploration license;

3 ° the permit to operate mines and quarries;

4 ° concession licenses.

Article 24:

Exploration license

The applicant for a prospecting license must obtain a special certificate when the place of prospection is not prohibited under other laws.

The licensee has the right to, within the boundaries assigned, facilities and work it deems necessary to discover evidence of deposits.

The validity of the exploration license shall not exceed two (2) years.

Article 25:

Conversion of exploration licenses in exploration permit

The holder of a prospecting license may, at least two (2) months prior to expiration of the permit, require its transformation into a research permit.

Article 26:

Scope of survey

The exploration license covers an area which is the maximum range of a thousand square miles (1,000 km2).

Article 27:

Rejection of the application for a prospecting license and waiver of prospecting permits

The request for assignment of a prospecting permit may be rejected. The rejection of the application must be substantiated and notified in writing to the applicant within a period not exceeding thirty (30) days.

The licensee may waive its prospecting permits, provided such waiver to notify the authority that issued it within a period not exceeding sixty (60) days after the waiver decision.

Section 2. From the research permit

Article 28:

Rights over the exploration permit

The exploration license gives its holder the exclusive right of mining research. The permit determines the scope of research and gives its holder an unlimited depth until the right to search for minerals for which it was awarded.

Article 29:

Person who may be issued a permit

The permit can be obtained either by a holder of a prospecting permit still valid, or any other person or entity that requests it.

Article 30:

Terms of acquisition of exploration permit

The applicant's research permits must satisfy the following conditions:

1 ° holds a prospecting permit;

2 present the report of investigations;

3 justify the technical and financial capabilities;

4 present a document of complete environmental impact study and a plan for environmental protection.

Article 31:

Term of an exploration permit

The permit is valid for a period of four (4) years from the date of issue.

It may be renewed once for a further period of four (4) years, when the holder is able to prove that he carried out the work specified in the work program.

The permit holder presents both (2) years a report on its findings.

Article 32:

Scope of Research

The exploration permit covers an area of a square whose sides have a maximum length of two kilometers and are oriented in directions north-south and east-west.

The limits of the search area can be reduced.

Article 33:

Limits the scope of research

The area to which the research permit application is bounded by the surface topography.

Article 34:

Exceeded the scope of research allowed

If the research permit infringes on the surface of a mining previously in force, the rights of the licensee do not wear on the lands included in the mining title as it is in force. The rights are restored on the surface of encroachment on the expiration of the prior.

If the exploration permit area overlaps prohibited or restricted the rights of the licensee shall be reduced accordingly. They are restored automatically when the ban is lifted.

Article 35:

Rejection of application for research permits and waiver of exploration permit

The request for allocation of exploration permits may be rejected. The reasons for rejection of the application must be notified in writing to the applicant within a period not exceeding thirty (30) days.

The licensee may waive his research permit, provided such waiver to notify the authority which issued the license within a period not exceeding sixty (60) days after the waiver decision.

Article 36:

Application for renewal of an exploration permit

The application for renewal of an exploration permit must be in writing and filed at least two (2) months before the expiry of the validity of it.

After this period without any further action will be given to the applicant, the permit is deemed granted.

Article 37:

Obligations associated with the release of a research permit

For the waiver is accepted motion, the request must be accompanied by:

1 ° a certificate of non debt issued by the Treasury;

2 ° a state of environmental rehabilitation satisfactory to the Administration; Otherwise, the permit is canceled. However, the licensee remains responsible for all obligations resulting from its title in relation to the payment of amounts owed to the state and the rehabilitation of the environment. It is recovered them as in direct contributions.

The waiver of the permit void for all purposes.

Article 38:

Exploration permit has not been a renewal application or processing

When a research permit to expire without having been a renewal application or application processing, it is automatically canceled. However, the provisions of Article 37 of this Act continue to apply.

Article 39:

Sale and transfer of exploration permits and mining

The exploration license and mining is assigned or transferred under the conditions laid down in Article 29 of this Act.

The sale and transfer of exploration permits are subject to the payment of fees provided by law.

Article 40:

Research infrastructure perimeter

The licensee has the right to, within the area assigned and in accordance with the provisions of this Act, facilities and the work it considers necessary for the discovery and study of deposits that research . They may, against, engage in any work operating a commercial nature.

Article 41:

Provision of research product

The licensee may dispose of the product of his research on payment of a fee set by law.

Article 42:

Early research

The research must be started within a maximum of three (3) months after the award of licenses and regularly pursued. After this period, the exploration license shall be considered terminated.

Article 43:

Research Report

At the end of the research, the licensee shall prepare a report for the organ that issued the permit.

The body that issued the license shall review the report within a period not exceeding thirty (30) days. Where it is established that a sufficient pool of exploitable mineral was discovered, the licensee is issued a certificate stating the results.

When the permittee requests a permit to operate, it is a priority. If the application is rejected, the rejection is notified in writing to the licensee which conducted the research work within a period not exceeding one month.

CHAPTER 5. LICENCE TO OPERATE SMALL MINES

Article 44:

Person eligible for a license to operate small mines

A ministerial order awarding the license to operate small mines operating license issued to any person or entity holds an exploration license valid and have the technical capacity to suffice.

Article 45:

Term of the operating license for small mine

The operating license for small mine is valid for a period of five (5) years excluding the date of issue. It may be renewed as many times as necessary, for a period of five (5) years, each time a new application of the licensee and when it can demonstrate a business well done.

The application for renewal of a mining license must be filed at least three (3) months before its expiration date.

When a mining license is normally expire before it ruled on an application for renewal regularly introduced, it is automatically extended until the date of the decision on that request.

Article 46:

Scope of small mine

The operating license is for a small mine perimeter of a square whose sides have a maximum length of two (2) km and are oriented in directions North-South and East West.

Article 47:

Rejection of permit application small-scale mining

The application for grant or renewal of operating licenses for small mine may be rejected. The rejection is given by order of the Minister. The reasoned refusal shall be notified in writing to the licensee rejected.

Article 48:

Application for transfer and transmission of the operating license for small mine

The operating license for small mine is assignable and transmissible. It may be to merge with other permits contiguous same substances belonging to the same licensee. It may be waived.

The transfer of the mining license for any reason whatsoever, shall be only on the entire perimeter. The sharing of the permit is prohibited.

The mining license may be farmed out. In this case, the licensee remains responsible for all obligations resulting from its title.

Article 49:

Request to assign, transfer or farm-out of the operating license for small mines

The sale, transfer and permit the leasing of small-scale mining and smelting permits small-scale mining are subject to prior payment of fees provided by law. They take effect only if authorized by order of the Minister.

The application for the assignment, transmission or farmout of a mining license may be rejected. The rejection is given by order of the Minister and notified the licensee in a period not exceeding thirty (30) days.

Article 50:

Discovery of a larger

Upon discovery of a bigger field, the holder of a permit for small-scale mining is required to make a written statement to the Authority within thirty (30) days after discovery. After confirming the existence of this deposit within the scope of the Administration, it requires the licensee to fulfill the requirements for being granted a concession.

Article 51:

Fusion permits

Requests for merging two or more permits on land adjacent on the same substances, are made and investigated under the same conditions that permit applications.

It is ruled by decree of the Minister.

Article 52:

Waiver of permit

The holder of a license to operate small mines may be abandoned. For the waiver is accepted motion, the request must be accompanied by:

1 ° a state of environmental rehabilitation satisfactory to the Administration;

2 ° a certificate of non debt issued by the Rwanda Revenue Authority;

The waiver by the owner of the soil causes the cancellation of the license over its entire extent.

Article 53:

Maximum depth in the small-scale mining

The operating license for small mine opens the right to exploit the deposits of all concessible substances to which it relates, in shallow excavations up to a maximum depth of forty (40) feet from the surface topography.

Beyond forty (40) feet deep, if all requirements are met, the permittee must apply for a driver's license.

Article 54:

Facilities for small-scale mining

The licensee has the right to the perimeter of the mining license and in accordance with the provisions of this Act, facilities and the work it considers necessary for the use of substances licensed. It may freely dispose of the said substances after extraction. However, the State reserves the right to requisition revenues for the general interest. Requisition opens in favor of the licensee the right to compensation and interest equivalent to the value of revenue.

Article 55:

Farm-farm-license license

The operating license for small mine can be farmed out. In this case, the licensee remains responsible for all obligations resulting from its title.

Article 56:

Start of work and protection of areas of small-scale mining

Every licensee is obliged to regularly monitor operational activities in areas which are subject of this permit.It also has the obligation to protect the area covered by the permit. The mining operations shall be commenced within a maximum period of six (6) months after the award of the permit. After this period, the mining license shall be considered terminated.

CHAPTER 6. LARGEST MINING CONCESSION

Article 57:

Rights under a mining lease large

The largest mining concession entitles its holder the exclusive right to explore and exploit concessible substances for which it is granted in the extent of its scope and depth indefinitely.

Article 58:

In the largest mining concession

The dealer has the right to the perimeter of the concession and in accordance with the provisions of this Act, facilities and the work it considers necessary for the use of substances granted. It may freely dispose of such substances after extraction. However, the State reserves the right to requisition revenue recognized in special cases of general interest. Requisition opens in favor of the grantee, the right to compensation and interest equivalent to the value of revenue.

Article 59:

Terms of exploitation of the mining concession largest and licensure

The extensive mining concession is granted solely for mining industry. The largest mining concession can be obtained either by a holder of an exploration permit still valid and so requests, either by tender when the former holder of the exploration permit has not made the request or when it has sufficient capacity. This issue is under the conditions defined by ministerial decree.

Article 60:

Transformation of the exploration permit and small-scale mining in larger mining concession

For a holder of an exploration permit, the license application must be submitted in writing to the Minister at least six (6) months prior to expiration of the permit applicant's research. These conditions also apply to the holder of a license to operate small mines wishing to obtain the largest concession.

Article 61:

Content of a ministerial decree granting the concession largest mining

A ministerial order granting the mining broader defines its size, serial number and its name. One of three copies of the plan duly certified is attached to the order of the Minister and shall be retained by the Minister.Another copy is sent to the office responsible for registering land titles.

The curator of Deeds is to transcribe the concession dealer charges, without further action on the records of land titles. An extract is issued to the Minister.

Article 62:

Effect of the larger mining concession on other permits

Order of the Minister granting a mining concession broader automatically cancels the exploration license or operating license for small mine which it derives and give final allocation, limits and consistency of the concession.

Article 63:

Period of validity of the mining concession

The operating permit larger mine is valid for a period of thirty (30) years and may be renewed several times, if the dealer has maintained an activity deemed compliant with the work program submitted with the application. The concession is an obligation to continue regular activities on pain of forfeiture.

At its expiry, the lease back to the state.

Article 64:

Terminals of the concession

The mining concession covers all or part of the perimeter of the exploration permit.

The area of a concession can not be less than one hundred (100) hectares or greater than four hundred (400) hectares unless a concession resulting from a merger of contiguous concessions. The boundary conditions are determined by order of the Minister.

Article 65:

Slip of the dealer required

The concession is granted only on presentation of proof of payment by the applicant of taxes and charges imposed and subject to the rights of third parties on the same land.

Article 66:

Application for or renewal of a larger concession

The application for grant or renewal of a larger concession may be rejected. Reasons for the rejection is notified in writing to the dealer dismissed within thirty (30) days.

Article 67:

Terms of the application for renewal of the concession

The application for renewal of the concession must be made larger at least one year before the expiry of the concession. If the term of a concession normally comes to an end before it ruled on the request for renewal, the license is deemed granted.

The concession which the dealer has not made an application for renewal shall terminate automatically.

Article 68:

Operator's rights

The dealer may make the mortgage, sale, assignment or farmout of its concession. All these operations are confirmed by order of the Minister.

The transfer of the license for any reason whatsoever, should cover the entire perimeter of the concession.The fragmentation of the license is prohibited.

Article 69:

Required fees

The dealer pays the fees prescribed by tax legislation. The payment of fees applies to the entire area of the concession.

Article 70:

Waiver of the concession

For the dealer waives the concession he must show the following:

1 copy of the concession;

2 ° a certificate of non debt to local financial institutions or the Board of Revenue;

3 ° a state of environmental rehabilitation.

If the concession is burdened with no real right, he is tendering.

If the dealer is accountable to the public treasury, the concession back to the state or is eventually put out to tender. This is where the state of environmental rehabilitation was not considered satisfactory by the Administration.

In the latter case, the proceeds from the auction will be used to rehabilitate the environment.

Article 71:

Consequently whose application for license is not renewed

When a concession expires without having been a renewal application, the grant back to the State on the date of expiry. The forfeiture is imposed by order of the Minister.

Article 72:

Maintenance of a large concession in operation

All grants must be kept active. If for some reason the operation is suspended or restricted, the situation is notified and the Minister in charge of mining within its remit and is approved by the latter.

Article 73:

Rights to the land included in the concession

Rights to occupy land for the farm, buildings and other civil works within the concession, are dependencies of the real estate license and are regulated by the Mining Code.

Article 74:

Public auction of the concession.

When the forfeiture of the concession is granted, there shall be at the public auction of the concession.

The dealer may not participate fallen directly or indirectly to the auction.

The auction takes place at the offices of the Administration, after advertising as is done for public sale by the authority of justice.

Is awarded the contract and the new dealership competitors who will have the most advantageous offer.

However, except in cases of competition from several mortgagees shall be awarded by preference, the creditor who can prove a mortgage on the lease, if he proves to have fulfilled the obligations of the concessionaire fallen as provided by this Act and s undertakes to pay all charges arising out of such subrogation.

Proceeds from the auction of the concession, net of amounts necessary for the rehabilitation of the environment, the back taxes plus the fine, costs of administration and those of the award belongs to the dealer fallen or its assigns. This product, if necessary, legally and distributed in order of "mortgages.

When the award becomes final, there shall be a transfer of the license by order of the Minister.

Article 75:

Concession for which no bidder has been selected

If no bidder has been selected, the grant can be transferred to the State or canceled.

If canceled, the concession and dependencies in real estate follow the fate that are considered under the same conditions.

Article 76:

Reserves estimated by the research

The estimated reserves after the research is directly subject to a researcher prohibited transmitted in a report to the Minister.

Article 77:

Important provisions subject to the publication

Important provisions of the order of the Minister on the establishment, confiscation and cancellation of the concession and the list of expired concessions are published in the Official Gazette of the Republic of Rwanda

CHAPTER 7. LICENCES TO CAREERS

Section 1. General Provisions

Article 78:

Definition

The deposits of mineral substances are called and chosen careers when they are classified by career plan Order of the Minister.

Article 79:

Rights of the owner of the land containing the quarry

The owner of the land containing the quarry which manifests the will to seek a license to operate a priority if they have the required capabilities.

Article 80:

Assignment and transmission

The quarry is transferable or can be given as an inheritance, transferable free, leased or offered for sale.

Article 81:

Conditions required for the operation of the quarry

The procedures for granting permission to quarrying and the requirements of the applicants are determined by order of the Minister.

Article 82:

Authorization for quarrying

The operating permit gives its holder the right to seek, use and dispose of all products for which authorization was granted.

Article 83:

Rejection of the application for leave to quarry

The application for leave to quarries may be rejected. The rejection is pronounced and motivated by the competent authority.

Article 84:

Report quarrying

Permission to quarrying covers an area of any single form.

The holder of a permit to operate quarries must submit a monthly report of operations.

The format of this report is determined by order of the Minister.

Article 85:

Taxes

Revenues careers are subject to taxes provided by law.

Article 86:

Waiver of authorization

The holder of an operating permit may be waived by sending the request to surrender to the authority which issued the authorization.

For the waiver is accepted motion, the request must be accompanied by a statement of environmental rehabilitation. Otherwise, the applicant is charged under the law.

Section 2. The holder of a permit to operate non-commercial mines

Article 87:

Person eligible for an operating license for non-commercial careers

The operating license for non-commercial career is granted to those wishing to make their own work in an area necessary to accomplish the work.

Article 88:

Duration of the license

The duration of the permit for quarrying can not exceed the work for which he was awarded and the products extracted are used solely for this work.

Section 3. From the operating licenses for commercial careers

Article 89:

Person eligible for a license to operate a commercial nature careers

The operating license for careers in commercial is granted for a career with an area does not exceed one hectare.

The operating license for careers in commercial area of more than a hectare is granted for industrial careers.

Article 90:

Duration of the license

The operating license for careers in commercial is awarded for a period of five (5) renewable as many times as necessary.

CHAPTER 8. OPERATING AGREEMENT

Article 91:

Operating Agreement attached to the permit

Permit molding, screening, sales, prospecting, exploration, mining, quarrying come with an agreement determining the various guarantees and commitments assumed by the State and the licensee.

Article 92:

Contents of the Operating Agreement

The operating agreement should at least clarify some of the following:

1 ° the clauses relating to the minimum work of prospecting, exploration, exploitation and marketing of products extracted and planned investments;

2 in terms of the operator as part of the development of products or screening for metal foundry;

3 commitments on safeguarding the security of persons and property;

4 ° commitments to the promotion of employment and vocational training;

5 commitments on environmental protection;

6 commitments in social development;

7 payment and calculation of royalties on products extracted.

CHAPTER 9. FEES AND CHARGES FOR EXPLOITATION

Article 93:

Taxes and Charges

Without prejudice to the laws, work exploitation are acts of commerce subject to the payment of royalties, income tax and tax on the area.

These taxes and fees are determined by law.

CHAPTER 10. PROVISIONS ON SUBSTANCES USEFUL ENERGY AGENCY

Article 94: Exploitation of useful substances for Atomic Energy

Exploration and the search for useful substances to atomic energy are subject to the provisions of this Act. However, the licensee can not dispose freely of its products for exploration and research.

He can not sell to the state that determines the terms of use for the benefit of both parties.

Substances useful for atomic energy can be exploited under the guise of a concession.

Article 95: Rights of the State of substances useful for Atomic Energy

If, subsequent to the awarding of a mining license or concession on a given substance, it is useful substances found in the atomic energy field, the dealer shall immediately notify the State determines what action to take.

CHAPTER 11. TRADE

Article 96:

Trade in minerals

Trade in minerals can be provided by the following:

1 ° the holder of an exploration license, exploitation or concession;

2 ° the holder of an authorization to buy and sell;

3 ° the owner of a screening plant or foundry.

Permission to buy, sell and trade is issued by the Minister having commerce in his attributions.

Article 97:

Standards

Standards of minerals are determined by the competent authority.

Article 98:

Samples of minerals

Export and Import of samples of minerals subject to approval of the Minister. This authorization must specify their, quantity and value as well as their destination.

CHAPTER 12. ENVIRONMENTAL IMPACT STUDY

Article 99:

Certificate of Environmental Impact

The certificate of environmental impact assessment should be appended to the application package for research permits, operating, sifting and smelting of mineral substances and residues thereof in accordance with environmental laws.

CHAPTER 13. RELATIONS BETWEEN THE OWNERS AND LAND ON LEAVE

Article 100:

Mining land

No research or exploitation of mines and quarries can be opened to inhabited land or housing facilities of public utility. However, the authority responsible for issuing permits may authorize the carrying of such works at these places against prior payment of "just compensation.

Article 101:

Rights of co-owners of the land mining

He who performs the research and exploitation of mines and quarries on a hill takes farmout a portion of land necessary to carry out its work and compensate the landowner for the work built on this soil.

Leasehold charges are determined based on the volume, nature and location of the ground and based on current price on the market.

At the end of the work, the perimeter was covered by the research and exploitation rightful occupant of the old ground.

At the end of the exploration permit and exploitation, the holder may retain ownership of the facilities after consultation with the owner of the land and payment of just compensation. Otherwise, the licensee is required to relocate its facilities.

CHAPTER 14. OFFENCES, PENALTIES AND PROSECUTION OF OFFENCES

Article 102:

Category of offenses

Notwithstanding the provisions of other laws, offenses may be committed are:

1 ° prospecting, research, operations, buying and selling without authorization relating thereto;

2 ° non-compliance with technical and operational research;

3 receipt or export of substances in mines and quarries without authorization relating thereto;

4 ° the presentation of false reports of research and operations and irregularities in bids;

5 ° displacement and destruction of the perimeter of the terminals;

6 ° the importation, manufacture, use, transport, purchase and sale of dynamite without a permit;

7 denial of access to all places administration of mining and quarrying.

Article 103:

Prospecting, exploration operations, buying and selling without authorization relating thereto

Whoever carries out exploration work and research without permission is punishable by imprisonment for one (1) year to five (5) years and "a fine of one hundred thousand (100,000 Rwf) and five million (Frw 5,000,000) Rwandan francs or one of these penalties.

Lamende for operation, buying and selling without authorization is three million (3,000,000 Rwf) to twenty million (20,000,000 RWF) Rwandan francs.

Article 104:

Non-compliance with appropriate techniques

Failure to follow proper techniques for exploration and exploitation is punishable by a fine of three hundred thousand (300,000 Rwf) and one million (1,000,000 RWF) Rwandan francs.

Article 105:

Receipt or export of substances from mines and quarries without permission

Receipt or export of substances in mines and quarries thereon without authorization is punishable by a fine of double the amount of materials received or exported and to imprisonment for one to five (5) years or one of these penalties.

Article 106:

Submitting false reports and irregularity in their submission

The submission of false statements in research reports and operating lirrégularité in submitting these reports is punishable by a fine of one hundred thousand (100,000 Rwf) and one million (1000,000 Rwf) Rwandan francs.

Article 107:

Displacement and destruction of terminals

Displacement and destruction of terminals in the scope of research or exploitation is punishable by a fine of one hundred thousand (100,000 Rwf) and one million (1,000,000 RWF) Rwandan francs.

Article 108:

Import, manufacture, use, transport, sale and purchase of dynamite without authorization

The import, manufacture, use, transport, purchase and sale of dynamite for mining operations without authorization related thereto shall be punished by a fine of five hundred thousand (500,000 Rwf) and five million (5,000,000 RWF) Rwandan francs and an imprisonment of one to five (5) years, or one of these penalties.

Article 109:

Refusal to administration to visit the work site

Denial of access to any competent authority places the research and exploitation of mines or quarries shall be punished by a fine of five hundred thousand (500,000 Rwf) and five million (5,000,000 RWF) Rwandan francs .

Article 110:

Confiscation of objects, instruments and proceeds of crime

Instruments and products of offenses under this Act shall be confiscated and auctioned or destroyed.

Article 111:

Recidivism

In case of recidivism, the penalty is maximized for that offense.

The culprit could even be stripped of the permit or "authorization.

Article 112:

Police officers

Some agents ladministration mines and geology shall have the powers of police officers in relation to offenses under this Act.

CHAPTER 15. MISCELLANEOUS, FINAL AND TRANSITIONAL

Article 113:

File admissible

File an application is received until it meets the requirements.

The decision on the request for authorization from exploitation is taken within three (3) months after its introduction. After this period, the application is deemed accepted.

Article 114:

File inadmissible

In case of rejection of a permit application, the rejection must be justified and communicated to the applicant by the competent authority within fifteen (15) days from the date of the decision.

Article 115:

Conditions of admissibility

The competent authority shall list the conditions of admissibility of an application file for business license.

Article 116:

Records Management

Records permit mining are received, managed and maintained by the competent body.

Article 117:

Transitional period

Permits issued for prospecting, exploration and mining are still valid.

Holders of these permits are required to respect the new law. They have a period of one (1) year to bring their work to this Act.

Article 118:

Repealing provision

Decree-Law No. 34/76 of 13/10/1976 relating to the quarrying and the Law of 04.27.1971 amending and supplementing the Law of 30/01/1967 on the Mining Code, and all previous legal provisions contrary to this Act are repealed.

Article 119:

Entry into force of the law

This Act comes into force on the day of its publication in the Official Gazette of the Republic of Rwanda.

MINISTERIAL ORDER NO. 003/MINIFOM/2010 OF 14/09/2010 ESTABLISHING CONDITIONS FOR THE APPROVAL FOR THE PURCHASE AND SALE OF MINERALS IN RWANDA

Chapter I. GENERAL PROVISIONS

Article 1:

Subject to this Order

This Order determines the conditions of approval for the purchase and sale of minerals in Rwanda.

Article 2:

License to operate a sales ore

Except for holders of mining titles which authorized the Minister having commerce in his attributions is adequately informed, any person or entity wishing to operate as a purchase and sale of minerals or precious stones shall send the Minister having trade in its powers, an application for leave to open a counter purchase and sale of minerals, specifying the types of minerals or gems of interest.

Article 3:

Condition for obtaining a permit to purchase and sale of minerals

No person may obtain a license to buy and sell minerals, if not registered in trade register.

Article 4:

Content of the application

The application for opening a sales ore must include the following documents:

1 ° for individuals:

a) a letter of request to the Minister having commerce in his attributions transmitting the appropriate form containing the following:

i. the date of application;
ii. the names of the applicant;
iii. mailing address,
iv. telephone number;
v. his e-mail,
vi. its headquarters;
vii. his signature and seal.

b) a copy of the identity card for nationals or passport for foreigners;

c) a certificate of no tax debt;

d) an initial capital of at least ten million Rwandan Francs (Frw 10 million) certified by a bank statement;

e) a copy of the Register of Commerce for foreigners. This copy is accompanied by a visa.

2 ° for legal persons:

A letter of request to the Minister having commerce in his attributions transmitting the form containing the following:

a) the date of application;

b) the name of the company;

c) mailing address;

d) telephone number;

e) the e-mail;

f) its registered office;

g) the signature of legal representative and the seal of the corporation;

h) of the statutes of the company notarized;

i) for cooperatives, a certificate of registration issued by the Agency Rwanda Cooperatives;

j) an initial capital of at least twenty million Rwandan francs (Rwf 20 million) certified by a bank statement.

Article 5:
Response time

An applicant who fulfills the requirements to receive the permit within thirty (30) days after the filing of the application. Beyond this period unanswered, the license shall be deemed granted.

Chapter II. OPERATION OF A COUNTER SALES OF MINERALS

Article 6:

Conditions of purchase and sale of minerals

Counter purchase and sale of minerals must meet the following requirements:

1 have the local sustainable materials, sufficient for storage;

2 ° have the facilities and equipment that meet the standards of weights and chemical and physical processing of minerals accepted by the institution of standardization in its jurisdiction;

3 Display prices in force at any position to purchase and / or sale;

4 ° provide monthly reports to the Minister having commerce in his attributions and the Minister in mines and quarries in its jurisdiction;

5 ° to allow the duly authorized personnel to access documents and facilities;

6 import and export through legal channels.

Counters in sale and purchase of minerals should not be constructed within mines or mining claims of others.

The Minister having commerce in his attributions granted a certificate stating that the counter purchase and sale of minerals fulfills the requirements.

Article 7:

Activity Report

Any mining operator and owner of a counter purchase and sale of minerals approved are required to file monthly reports containing the following:

1 ° the weight, quality and value of ore processed, bought and sold;

2 addresses of suppliers and recipients of purchases and sales of its ores;

3 ° the difficulties and provide suggested solutions.

Article 8:

Right to purchase and sale of minerals

Have the right to buy and sell minerals, any natural or legal person who has a mining license, the counter purchase and sale, approved an importer or exporter who has an ad hoc authorization, he attributed by the Minister having commerce in his attributions and anyone who has a processing unit and processing of minerals recognized by the Minister in the industry in its functions.

Article 9:

Certificate of origin and packing list

All mining product must be accompanied by a certificate of origin and a deposit slip.

Article 10:

The license to operate a sales counter of minerals

The license to operate a counter purchase and sale of minerals is valid for three (3) years renewable. The installation of the counter must be completed six (6) months after obtaining the permission, otherwise it can be removed.

Article 11:

Renewal of license to operate a sales ore

The application for renewal of license to operate a sales ore occurs in the same conditions and forms that the applicant's license to operate a sales and what minerals within thirty (30) days prior its expiry.

Article 12:

License fees to operate a counter purchase and sale of minerals

The granting of the permit to open a counter purchase and sale is subject to prior payment of three hundred thousand Rwandan Francs (300,000 Rwf) non-refundable.

Article 13:

Obligations of the exploiters of minerals

Exporters of minerals are bound by customs officials and comply with privacy laws.

Article 14:

Content of record export of minerals

Any exporter of minerals must be a complete file containing the following documents:

1 ° a pro forma invoice with the full address of the recipient;

2 ° the weight of exported products;

3 ° quality certification of the exported product;

4 Certificate of Origin documents are shown the circuit of transactions under laws and international conventions ratified by the Republic of Rwanda,

5 ° value of exported products.

Article 15:

Refusal of the application or license renewal

In case of non-compliance specified in this Order, the Minister having commerce in his attributions reserves the right to refuse the permit application, or refuse to renew.

In any event, the Minister having commerce in his attributions sent a letter to the applicant justifying the decision.

Article 16:

Sanctions

Any person contravening the provisions of this Order is punishable under the laws governing trade and industry.

Article 17:

Transitional period

The holder of a counter purchase and sale of minerals has a period of six (6) months from the date of publication of this decree in the Official Gazette of the Republic of Rwanda to comply with the provisions of the said off.

Article 18:

Repealing provision

All previous provisions contrary to this Order are hereby repealed.

Article 19:

Entry into force

This Order comes into force on the day of its publication in the Official Gazette of the Republic of Rwanda.

Kigali, on 14/09/2010

MINISTERIAL ORDER NO. 006/MINIFOM OF 14/09/2010 DETERMINING THE APPLICABLE TAXES ON MINES AND CAREERS

1. Subject to this Order

Article 1:
Subject to this Order
This Order sets the fees paid for mining activities, as follows:

1 ° Prospecting Licence;

2 Research Permit;

3 Licence to operate small mines;

4 ° concession permits;

5 ° quarrying permit commercial

6 Renewal of license;

7 Transfer of permit;

8 rental permit

9 Waiver of permit.

This Order also determines the cost of renting space on which the activities of prospecting, exploration and exploitation of mines and quarries are conducted.

Article 2:
Taxes licenses careers
Taxes licenses careers are:

1 ° permit quarrying business:

a) eligibility for the license, fifteen thousand Rwandan francs (15,000 Rwf)

b) renewal of a license: twenty five thousand Rwandan francs (25,000 Rwf)

c) transfer of a license: twenty five thousand Rwandan francs (25,000 Rwf)

d) transfer of a license: twenty five thousand Rwandan francs (25,000 Rwf)

e) location of a permit: twenty five thousand Rwandan francs (25,000 Rwf)

f) waiver of the permit: twenty five thousand Rwandan francs (25,000 Rwf).

2 ° permits non-commercial quarrying:

a) eligibility for the permit: ten thousand Rwanda francs (10,000 Rwf)

b) renewal of a license: fifteen thousand Rwandan francs (15,000 Rwf)

c) waiver of the license, fifteen thousand Rwandan francs (15,000 Rwf).

Article 3:
Taxes on mining permits
1 ° Prospecting Licence:

a) eligibility for the permit: fifty thousand Rwandan francs (50,000 Rwf)

b) location of a permit: twenty five thousand Rwandan francs (25,000 Rwf)

c) waiver of the permit: twenty five thousand Rwandan francs (25,000 Rwf).

2 Permits for:

a) eligibility for the permit: one hundred thousand Rwandan Francs (100,000 Rwf)

b) renewal of a license hundred and seventy five thousand francs Rwanda (175,000 Rwf)

c) transfer of a license: one hundred and fifty thousand Rwandan Francs (150,000 Rwf)

d) location of a permit: one hundred and fifty thousand Rwandan Francs (150,000 Rwf)

e) waiver of the permit: one hundred thousand Rwandan Francs (100,000 Rwf)

3 Licence to operate small mines:

a) eligibility for the permit: one hundred and fifty thousand Rwandan Francs (150,000 Rwf)

b) renewal of a license: two hundred thousand Rwandan Francs (200,000 Rwf)

c) transfer of a license: two hundred fifty thousand Rwandan Francs (250,000 Rwf)

d) location of a license: two hundred fifty thousand Rwandan Francs (250,000 Rwf)

e) waiver of the permit: one hundred and fifty thousand Rwandan Francs (150,000 Rwf).

4 ° concession permits:

a) eligibility for the license: two hundred fifty thousand Rwandan Francs (250,000 Rwf)

b) renewal of a license, three hundred thousand Rwandan Francs (300,000 Rwf)

c) transfer of a license, three hundred and fifty thousand Rwandan Francs (350,000 Rwf)

d) location of a license, three hundred and fifty thousand Rwandan Francs (350,000 Rwf)

e) sale of a license, one million Rwandan francs (1,000,000 Rwf)

f) mortgage of a concession: one million Rwandan francs (1,000,000 Rwf)

g) a waiver of concession: two hundred fifty thousand Rwandan Francs (250,000 Rwf).

Article 4:
Surface mineable
The cost of renting an exploitable surface mines and quarries are paid out of the area scheduled for mining and quarrying as part of a concession covered by a permit.

This area does not include the non-exploitable such as protected natural resources and infrastructure located within a concession.

Article 5:
Fees paid to the surface used
The fee for the exploitable area is calculated using the area harvested determined in the annual action plan submitted to the Administration Area, to the District, the Office of Geology and Mines Ministry in Rwanda and the mines and quarries within its remit.

Article 6:
Fees payable for a mining area
The fee payable for a mining site shall be as follows:

1 ° prospecting area: twenty five Rwandan franc per hectare (25 Rwf / ha) per year;

2 ° area of research: one hundred Rwandan franc per hectare (100 Rwf / ha) per year;

3 mining area: two hundred Rwandan francs per hectare (200 Rwf) per year.

Article 7:

Fees paid for an area of quarrying
The fee for a quarrying area is calculated using the production reported in the annual report sent to the Administration Area, to the District, the Office of Geology and Mines Ministry in Rwanda and the mines and quarries within its remit.

The fee payable for an area of quarrying amounted to five Rwanda francs (Rwf 5) per year per square meter (1m ^{2}) exploited.

Article 8:
Payment period of one area of operation
For an area of operation, the fee is paid annually within ninety (90) days from the date of calculation by the District that performs mining activities.

After this period, these costs are increased by ten percent (10%) of the amount due. After two (2) months notice without reaction, it follows the withdrawal of operating licenses for the mining and quarrying with the possibility of legal action for recovery of unpaid interest.

All these taxes are paid into the treasury.

Copies of deposit slips are handed to the Administration of Industry and that of the District, the Office of Geology and Mines Ministry in Rwanda and the mines and quarries within its remit.

Article 9:
Repealing provision
All previous provisions contrary to this Order are hereby repealed.

Article 10:
Entry into force
This Order comes into force on the day of sapublication the Official Journal of the Republic of Rwanda.

Kigali, on 14/09/2010

LAND MANAGEMENT LAW

CHAPTER 1 - GENERAL PROVISIONS

Art.1.-This Act shall determine the terms of use and management of land in Rwanda. It also sets out the principles applicable to the rights of all lands within the national territory, and everything in it unites and incorporates it, either naturally or artificially.

Art.2.-In this Act, the following terms are defined as follows:

· 1 · aedificandi Zones are residential areas, areas of commerce and industry, recreational areas and areas reserved for other core activities of public utility.

· 2 · no-building zones are areas reserved for agriculture, forestry, grazing, reservoir zones

Vees, tourism and community green space.

· 3 · Unforeseeable circumstances is a sudden and unpredictable as hail, locust invasion, prolonged drought, the ravages of war, floods, landslides, volcanic eruptions, earthquakes, and other such events .

· 4 ° Title property is an act that contains the recognition of property rights in writing, made and issued under the legislation by the competent authority.

° 5 ° Swamp is a flat surface between the hills and mountains characterized by an accumulation of water, biological diversity, the papyrus, sedges and vegetation of the same family.

° 6 ° Land consolidation is a land development which is to gather

portions of land to better use and rational use, to make it more productive.

° 7 ° Emprise is an area occupied by a road and its annexes up to a certain length from the center line of the roadway. It includes pavement, sidewalks, shoulders on both sides, ditches and other gar-de structures built on the road.

° 8 ° Transfer is a transfer to another person, and definitively, an interest in the property which is the owner or holder.

· 9 · vacant land is land on which person exercises exclusive land rights, either because they have never been employed or they have been abandoned and are therefore fallen into disuse or they are not capable of appropriation by individuals.

· 10 · Land dormant: land which no one claims the estate which is vested in the state.

· 11 · Tenure of "ubugererwa" are rights available to the people who occupied the land as tenants, as defined in the decree No. 530 / 1 of May 26, 1961 on concessions in the territories of Gisenyi and Ruhengeri.

° 12 ° Farm is any activity related to the ground and comes to crops and livestock of all kinds, to forests and nurseries.

· 13 · Lease is a contract between the landowner and another person whereby that person receives from the owner the right to land use and enjoyment of its operations, payment of an agreed rent.

· 14 · Grant is an agreement by which the state authorizes a person,

a fee, to hold or operate as a private, the private land of the State in which there is public infrastructure.

· 15 · Tenure of Ubukonde: As was expected by the edict No. 530 / 1 of May 26, 1961 relating to land "the ubukonde" in the territories of Gisenyi and Ruhengeri, what are the rights enjoyed by a head of household on forest land without an owner he is the first operator, or has received consent of the owners. These rights could be inherited.

· 16 ° Right of alienation is a right to sell his property to give it for free, exchange or transmit by succession.

° 17 ° easements are rights enjoyed by a person on the property of others in certain circumstances, such as right of way through the land of others in an enclave, the servitude of drawing water located in the land of others or from the bondage of the natural water flow of funds to fund higher lower. Legal easements resulting from the location of the property are required by law or from the agreement between the concerned.

· 18 · Land is a surface covering biodiversity as animate beings like human beings, animals and various plants and inanimate objects such as rocks, buildings, various basic infrastructure, rivers, lakes and its subsoil and airspace.

· 19 ° Category environmental and cultural of the Nation are to be specially protected lands, swamps and other wet areas, land for the maintenance and protection of animal and vegetation

such as the parks and forest reserves, as well as regional sites for conservation of cultural heritage, the genocide memorials and cemeteries.

· 20 · Competent is one or more institutions that have the jurisdiction provided by law.

· 21 · Prescription is a situation where a person has permanently of property rights or lose them situation after the expiration of time provided by law.

° 22 ° Expropriation for a public purpose is an expropriation of land for the purpose of general interest, with the formalities prescribed by law and just and prior compensation.

· 23 · Grazing is a surface covered with grass growing confused and intended to graze livestock.

° 24 ° possessor in good faith is one that has a property which he considers his own, under a title beyond doubt.

° 25 ° possessor in bad faith is one that has a precarious or knowingly that he has held a property of another without title, is he availed himself of fraud for this title.

Art.3.-Land is part of the common heritage of all Rwandans; ancestors, present and future generations.

Notwithstanding the rights of people, only the State has a right of eminent management of all lands within the national territory, he exercises in the general interest of all to ensure the rational development economic and social development as defined by law.

As such, the State is the sole authority to grant rights of occupation and land use. It also has the right to order the expropriation for public utility, housing and planning national as defined by law, subject to fair and prior compensation.

Art.4.-Any natural or legal person having a legal personality has the rights as provided by Articles 5 and 6 of this organic law, and exercised freely.

Any form of discrimination, including discrimination based on sex or origin, in terms of access to land ownership and land tenure is prohibited. The man and woman have equal rights to land ownership.

Art.5.-Any natural or legal person who owns the land, acquired under either custom or under a duly granted by competent authorities or by the purchase, ownership is recognized, bound by a long lease contract in accordance with the provisions of this Organic Law.

Art.6.-Any natural or legal person having a legal personality, a Rwandan national or foreign, which has invested in Rwanda may have the right to property, land housing the works for residential, industrial, economic and commercial, social, cultural and scientific.

Terms of availability of authentic documents of this property are covered by the Order of the Minister having Land in its attributions.

Art.7.-This organic law protects equally the rights over land, whether derived from custom or written law.

In the context of this Organic Law, is recognized owner of the land resulting from the usual person who has inherited from his parents received from the competent authority or through other ways known in the custom of the country whether by purchase, gift, exchange and sharing.

It is created Art.8.-land commissions at national level, at the Province and the City of Kigali and the level of Districts and Towns.

The organization, functions, operation and members of land commissions are determined by Presidential order. At each level, the Land Commission should include both men and women.

CHAPTER 2 - CATEGORIES OF LAND

Section 1 - The urban land and rural land

Art.9.-urban land are those that are within the urban boundaries as defined by law. The Presidential Order determines the other land considered urban land included in the outskirts of urban centers and towns. All other land is rural.

Art.10.-Without prejudice to the provisions in Act No. 05/2001 of 18 January 2001 on the organization and functioning of cities in Rwanda as modified and supplemented to date, and Law No. 07/2001 of 19 January 2001 on the organization and operation of the City of Kigali as modified and complemented to date, all the lands in the state, whether urban or rural, are managed by the Ministry having Land in its attributions or other administrative bodies competent.

Section 2 - From the private land area of special

The field-Art.11. individual private land consists of land acquired by the common law and statutory law which are not included in the public domain or in the state or the District of the City and the City of Kigali land granted by the competent authorities and the lands acquired by purchase, donation, exchange and sharing.

Section 3 - From the land area of the State

Subsection 1 - Public Domain of the State

The field-Art.12. public land of the State consists of all lands that are assigned to one use or a public service and public lands that are reserved for environmental protection of the nation. They are:

· 1 ° of beds of lakes, rivers and streams and ranked by order of the Minister having water in its jurisdiction;

· 2 ° of the edges of lakes and rivers up to a length determined by order of the Minister having Environment in his duties, from the furthest point reached by water during floods successive ex-

exception made of the exceptional floods;

· 3 ° of the land housing the sources and points of natural water, determined according to the order of the Minister having water in its jurisdiction;

· 4 ° of national lands for the protection of the environment and consist of natural forests, parks, protected wetlands, gardens and tourist sites;

· 5 ° of the roads and their rights of way as determined by order of the Minister having infrastructure in his duties;

· 6 ° of the land and built buildings affected by the Administration to use or a public service, or those that house the various departments of Public Administration.

Art.13.-waters of rivers and lakes and groundwater is a collective heritage. Without prejudice to legal provisions that determine the use of these waters, as well as special agreements may be concluded between the state and private users, the ability to use it is common to all.

In any case, no one is allowed to sully the water and no one is allowed to deviate the course without the permission of the competent authority.

Subsection 2 - The private domain of the State

Art.14.-The private domain of the state includes all lands that are not tie-in of the public domain and the domain of Land Districts, the City of Kigali and Cities as well as private individuals.

Are part of the private domain of the State:

· 1 ° Vacant land which includes land and unclaimed lands taken over by the state following the confiscation defined by the provisions of Article 75 of this Organic Law;

· 2 ° the public lands of the state but abandoned in accordance with law;

· 3 ° the land purchased by the State, acquired by gift or land being expropriated for public purposes;

· 4 ° swamps usable for agricultural purposes;

· 5 ° the forest areas of the state.

The allocation of public land to the private domain of the state defined by Article 12 of this organic law since its first point to point 4 is by law while from point 5 to point 6, the assignment is made by Prime Minister's Order.

Art.15.-Vacant land and the land on which person exercises exclusive land rights are part of the private domain of the State. They are used for development activities and other activities related to the general development of the national territory and in the distribution to the needy as specified in Article 87 of this organic law.

The Land Commission at the national level regularly inform the Minister having Land in its attributions of land mentioned in the first paragraph of this article.

The Minister having Land in its attributions may transfer the powers to manage these lands to the authorities of the District, the City or the City of Kigali.

Section 4 - From the land area of the District and the City

The domain land-Art.16. District and the City includes the public domain in the District and the City as well as their private domain.

The State may grant a donation of land to the District or the City whether of public or their private domain.

The lands granted to the District or the City from the public lands of the state fall into the public domain in the District or the City, while the land from the private domain of the state are within the private domain District or the City.

The District or the City may also acquire land by purchase or by gift from individuals or legal entities, these lands are within the public or private District or the City.

Subsection 1 - From the public domain land in the District, the City and the City of Kigali

The field-Art.17. public land in the District, the City and the City of Kigali comprises:

· 1 · Land District or the City dedicated to public use or activities of administrative bodies of the District or the City;

· 2 · Roads District and the City as well as their rights of way as determined by order of the Minister having Infrastructure in its attributions;

• 3 ° land for housing in cities.

Decommissioning of public lands in the District or the City in their private domain is done by order of the Minister having Land in its attributions, upon request of the District Land Commission or the City.

Subsection 2 - The private domain of the District, the City and the City of Kigali

Art.18.-land District, the City and the City of Kigali unrestricted public use or activities of the administrative departments of the District, the City or the City of Kigali are part of the private District, the City or the City of Kigali.

CHAPTER 3 - MANAGEMENT, PLANNING AND LAND USE

Section 1 - General Provisions

Art.19.-As part of the development of the country, a pattern of rational use of land is established, whether for housing, agriculture, forestry, livestock, the sites containing the industrial and public activities of the state parks, lakes and rivers, mines etc.., marshes and other natural reserves.

Management, development and use of land as mentioned in the first paragraph of this section are governed by specific laws different.

Art.20.-As part of the public interest and to ensure an economically viable use of rural land, the Minister having Agriculture in its attributions in collaboration with the authorities and the population concerned, may order consolidation of operations landholdings for their operation. Each owner is still entitled to the party is its ownership.

Procedures for consolidation of land holdings comply with the order of the Minister of Agriculture in its attributions, which sets the terms rational for consolidation and exploitation.

Notwithstanding the first paragraph of this article, it is forbidden to divide up the land for agriculture and livestock with an area exceeding one hectare. Similarly, land with an area exceeding five hectares can not be fragmented by the owner as authorized by the Land Commission of the place.

Art.21.-Notwithstanding the provisions governing the sale or lease of land, the conclusion of any contract of sale or lease may be suspended to facilitate unhindered development or execution of the master plan of use of areas with the land.

All contracts for the sale or lease of land must comply with the master plan of the area housing the land under the contract.

Art.22.-land commissions set up under Article 8 of this organic law contribute to the development and implementation of master plan and land use and to transactions consolidation under section 20 of this organic law.

Section 2 - Assignment and lease land

Art.23.-In case of transfer of land, the lessee shall comply with the program management, use and land management as defined by the competent authorities.

Art.24.-Notwithstanding the provisions set out in Article 6 of this Organic Law, the right to property is granted by the State in the form of lease.

The period of the lease of the land can not go below three years or above ninety nine. This period may be extended.

The exact number of years of land lease is determined by Presidential Decree according to the purpose of exploitation of these lands.

Art.25.-The competent authorities to grant the sale or lease of land are assisted at every level, from a land commission.

The procedures for the sale or lease of the land is governed by decree of the Minister having Land in its attributions.

Art.26.-Confirmation of the sale or lease land for a long period is attested by a certificate of registration of land issued by the Registrar of Deeds.

The structure, jurisdiction and functioning of the conservation service land titles are determined by Presidential order.

Section 3 - Transfer and lease of state land

Art.27.-The requirements for the sale or lease of land in the District, the City and the City of Kigali, as well as public institutions with legal personality, the sites of mines and quarries, are determined by order of the Minister having Land in its attributions.

Art.28.-assignment and lease of state land under section 12 of this organic law are defined by the laws.

Art.29.-marsh lands owned by the state. They can not be definitively assigned to individuals or acquired under the pretext of having occupied for a long time.

For their management and rational exploitation, the order of the Minister having environment in his attributions lists and limits of the marshes.

This list determines how real nature and purpose as well as the type of development to promote sustainable development of the people of Rwanda.

The order of the Minister having Environment in his attributions determines the modalities of management, development and operation of marshland.

Section 4 - Registration of land

Art.30.-The Land Registry is required by their owners. The order of the Minister having Land in its attributions govern how the land registration.

Art.31.-Without prejudice to specific legal terms of use and land management of urban districts, it is created an office responsible for land registration of land in each district and each city.

This Office is headed by an officer called Land Officer.

The Land Officer shall keep land records and issues certificates stating that the land law.

With regard to land, it has the jurisdiction of the notary and administrative matters, it is under the orders of the administration of the City or the District housing land it is required to be recorded.

The nature of the documents referred to in paragraph 3 of this Article and other powers and operation of the Land Office are determined by order of the Minister having Land in its attributions.

Art.32.-The request for obtaining a certificate from the landowner must be accompanied by the following:

· 1 · A certificate of complete identity of the applicant and her spouse, if married under community of property;

· 2 ° A brief description of the land, indicating particularly its size, its location relative to

main known landmarks such as roads, rivers, names of occupants of neighboring properties;

• 3 ° Any document necessary to prove the applicant's right on the land which registration is sought, including an affidavit, a certificate of grant of the land by the competent authority or a copy of the ruling cast in force res judicata.

Section 5 - Transfer of land rights

Art.33.-Notwithstanding the provisions of Article 20 of this organic law on the area indivisible, land ownership is real estate, classified as assets successors. Its transfer by succession is acceptable and is the modes of succession established by law on inheritance.

Art.34.-The right to land ownership can be transmitted between people or from the estate and can be transmitted by gift, lease or sale and may be given by mortgage, according to the conditions and manner prescribed by the Code ordinary civilian, without prejudice to specific provisions of this Organic Law.

The definitive transfer-Art.35. land rights, for example by sale, gift or exchange, made by the representative of the family, requires the consent of all members of the family, with whom he shares those rights.

Art.36.-Notwithstanding the provisions of the Civil Code relating to the family, the family members referred to in Article 35 of this organic law are spouses, adult children, minor children in the person their legal representatives and others unable represented by their guardians.

Art.37.-consent referred to in Article 35 of this organic law is found in a document signed by the persons concerned or on which they affixed their fingerprints, before the registrar of civil status or before the Land Officer who records in his documents.

Art.38.-consent referred to in Article 35 of this organic law is also required in case of mortgage of land, leases, long-term leasehold or to the case of easements conventional land, depending on their situation.

The transfer of land rights, mortgage, lease, long lease long-term conventional and easements are binding on third parties only when owners of record.

Section 6 - Lease of land for agricultural purposes

Art.39.-Without prejudice to the provisions of the Civil Code on obligations in general, this section governs the lease of land and other buildings used primarily for farming and livestock, excluding forestry, which is governed by the laws.

Only Art.40.-written lease is recognized and protected by law, regardless of the amount of rent.

Art.41.-Notwithstanding the provisions under Chapter III of this Organic Act, in section 2, the lease of land for agricultural purposes shall be freely determined by the parties to the contract.

However, any lease entered into by a guardian can not go beyond three years.

Art.42.-The lease automatically ceases upon the expiry of fixed term, without the need to give notice. If at the expiration of the lease for a fixed term, the tenant remains on the premises without opposition and without leave of the lessor served, the lease is automatically renewed, without need of further proceedings between the parties.

Leave when there was served, the tenant, though he continued his enjoyment, can not invoke the automatic renewal of the contract if the duration of the expiration date.

However, under paragraph 2 of this article, the deposit for the lease does not extend to obligations under the extension is not subject to special procedures.

Art.43.-Even if the contract was concluded for a fixed term, the landlord may terminate it at any time after giving notice stipulated in the contract.

However, if after notice, the tenant has not yet harvested, the landlord will grant a time to harvest.

Otherwise, it will grant an indemnity equal under the law.

Art.44.-If a lease of land for agricultural purposes, we gave the land an area less than or greater than its actual area, the rent will be on mutual agreement of the parties, increased or decreased in proportion to the area effective the first date following the request, except that the tenant is entitled to request the termination of the contract. The application is admissible for the duration of the lease.

Art.45.-tenant has no right to sublet or assign his lease to another without written permission of the lessor.

Art.46.-lessor is not affected by the disputes created by third parties on the tenant, when they have no rights to the leased land, it is incumbent upon the person of the tenant to refer disputes relevant bodies empowered.

However, the tenant must give the landlord all acts of usurpation or displacement of the ground terminals, within a time limit for the assignment with the court, otherwise he is liable to pay compensation as well as damages.

Art.47.-When the lessor sells the leased land, the purchaser can not evict the tenant before the expiry of the term provided, unless this right has been expressly reserved to the new owner in the lease.

In this case, the purchaser is required to give advance notice to the tenant who was under the contract. When the notice is not provided, it shall allow a period of at least three months.

The buyer is also required to comply with the provisions of Articles 59 to 69.

Art.48.-If it was agreed at the conclusion of the lease, in case of sale the purchaser may evict the tenant, and that no provision had been made on compensation, the lessor is liable to compensate the tenant as provided by Article 43 of this organic law.

Art.49.-In case of death of the tenant, the lease automatically continues with his heirs or assigns.

However, the heirs or assigns of the deceased tenant may terminate the contract within a period of one year counted from the death notice and at least three months.

The landlord can give notice to the heirs or assigns of the deceased tenant before the expiry of the lease term if this power expressly reserved in the contract.

Art.50.-The heirs or assigns of the deceased tenant may agree that they will jointly hire or that it will be entrusted to one or more of them.

Otherwise, everyone has the right to ask the court to be designated as one that continues the lease, but must pay the actual compensation set by the court to the other heirs or assigns of the deceased tenant.

When many of them wish to continue the lease and that there was no compromise, it is the degrees of succession to be followed.

Art.51.-The heirs or assigns of the deceased tenant must notify the landlord that the lease continues.

As long as the decision was not given, the heirs or assigns, jointly and severally liable to pay.

Obligations that arise after the notification of the decision shall be borne by the continuing lease.

Art.52.-The tenant is required to maintain various facilities for the conservation of soil found in the perimeter of the field it operates.

Otherwise, when the report of the Land Commission was empowered fact, the lessor may perform the maintenance and soil conservation in place of the tenant. However, the lessee shall reimburse the actual costs incurred in these facilities.

Art.53.-All disputes relating to land are recognized in courts and tribunals and the procedures prescribed by law.

Before the complaint is brought before the court, both parties trials are required to pass the Mediation Committee in terms of sectors to find a solution to their dispute. This case concerns land holdings without land titles.

CHAPTER 4 - RIGHTS AND OBLIGATIONS OF HOLDERS OF LAND RIGHTS

Section 1 - Rights

Art.54.-Notwithstanding the legal provisions relating to housing and the general arrangement and the use of land, the owner fundamental cial has the right to use its land in accordance with the laws and regulations.

Art.55.-The landowner has no rights to the minerals and other natural resources buried in the basement, they belong to the state. However, the right of removal is granted priority upon request and is able to do so.

Art.56.-Subject to legal provisions on expropriation for public purposes, the State guarantees the landowner the peaceful possession and protects against eviction, partial or total, of which he may suffer.

Art.57.-All buildings, plantations and structures located on the ground are considered to be made by either the landowner's expense or otherwise and that they belong, unless proved otherwise. However, this provision does not prevent a third party to have ownership of buildings, planting or other works of others in the field according to law.

When Art.58.-structures or plantations have been made by a third party in bad faith and with its materials, the landowner has the right to request that such person removes, without prejudice to damages that may result from injury .

If the property owner prefers to keep these buildings or the plantations, he must refund the value-cons.

Section 2 - Obligations

Art.59.-Concession contracts provide for specific conditions

the conservation and development related to land use.

Art.60.-Unless it is necessary, the landowner must not obstruct the rights of others. It can include:

° 1 ° refuse passage to its neighbors if they are landlocked;

· 2 · prevent the natural flow of water in its property funds that come higher;

· 3 · object to the third draw water from wells located on his property unless he proves that they were drilled or developed by its means.

Art.61.-The landowner, as well as any other property operator, must respect the laws and regulations relating to the protection, conservation and wise use of land.

Art.62.-Any private person, holds an interest in land, is required to make use of development land in relation to its nature and destination.

The use of development land is its protection against erosion, conservation of its fertility and its operation continuously.

Any person who occupies the land of another, either through an agreement with the owner or by a loan according to the laws and regulations, is required to ensure its conservation and rational exploitation.

Art.63.-conservation or rational use of land continuously assessed on the basis of its use in accordance with the master plan of allocation, development and land use and particular cultures adopted by the relevant authorized.

Art.64.-maintained and operated shall be deemed rationally managed lands bearing crops or buildings, those relating to the forests so as not to pollute the environment, they prepared for their culture, those cultures are to be collected and set aside for a period that does not go beyond three years, those with newly harvested crops and pastures on which individuals are allowed to graze animals, either individually or in association or organization with legal personality.

Art.65.-Can not be considered to be preserved and used wisely:

· 1 ° the land is not protected against erosion;

· 2 ° the land for agricultural use that is not covered with plantations or crops on at least half (½) of its area;

· 3 ° the land to pastoral use is not effectively or regularly occupied by cattle grazing or not covered forage on at least half (½) of its area;

· 4 ° the land intended for construction of all kinds, but construction has not been achieved for the periods provided by law;

· 5 ° the land intended for use by non-profit organization whose activities have not commenced within three years.

The mere fact of limited, wall or fence a field is not keeping adequate and rational meaning of sections 61A to 64 of this organic law.

Art.66.-Bonds-specific land contract must be specified at its conclusion, either in the contract itself or in a document annexed to these obligations.

The terms imposed by the development plan and national land use must always be respected, whether enacted before the contract or during the execution of it.

Art.67.-The landowner can not object to what is happening in the ground or air of his land to the public interest. If he is that these acts are causing it material injury, it receives appropriate compensation.

All-Art.68. landowner has the obligation to pay a property tax set by a special law.

CHAPTER 5 - PRESCRIPTION

Art.69.-Unless special provisions provided for in this Organic Act, the rules of the law of the Civil Code relating to limitation shall also apply in land matters.

Art.70.-With regard to land, the length of adverse possession and that the time limitation is set at thirty years.

Art.71.-Those who, by force or in bad faith, occupy vacant land and unclaimed property or property of others can never claim the benefit of extinctive prescription is acquisitive or to advance the right of ownership no longer exists or they have acquired the land permanently, even if they have this right for a time beyond the prescription.

Art.72.-Those who have land holdings of others, ie the beneficiaries of rights of use of land and housing on these properties, can not finally dispose off due to what much time elapsed. These properties fall within the private domain of the State.

There is no prescription between members of one family. When a missing person is found, even if his death date for a long time, it may claim its rights under the provisions of the Civil Code relating to the family.

CHAPTER 6 - CRIMINAL PROVISIONS

Section 1 - Administrative sanctions

Subsection 1 - requisitioning of land being degraded and unexploited land

Art.73.-La Land Commission at the District and the City conducts periodic monitoring of the effective conservation and use of land belonging to private individuals and those rental located on the territorial scope of the District and the City. The Commission shall submit an annual report of this control to the Administrative Authority and the District Authorities empowered to grant the transfer or assignment of the private domain of the state.

These authorities may be taken against the owner or lessee fails to conservation and land use specified in this chapter of this organic law.

Art.74.-The Minister having Land in its attributions or any other competent authority to grant the transfer or lease of private land by the State, after consultation with the Land Commission concerned may, if it is clear that the land has passed three successive years without being used, without good cause, order the requisition of the land for a period of three years, extendable up to another three years.

While it is clear that the land is being degraded, the Minister having Land in its attributions or other competent authority, after consultation with the relevant Land Commission, requisition orders without waiting for the period specified in paragraph one of this section.

The requisition shall be only on the undeveloped part or on the current degradation but after a formal notice or acknowledgment of receipt sent to the owner or operator at least six months prior to requisition itself and remained unanswered.

And requisitioned land may be entrusted to another person who so requests and who intends to operate in a profitable manner. If no person is present, the District or the City is responsible for its maintenance and operation.

Subdivision 2 - Confiscation of land degradation being untapped

All land-Art.75. falling within the following categories may be forfeited in the public interest, without good reason recognized:

· 1 ° land requisitioned under Section 74 of the Organic Law and returned to the owner, but he could not fulfill the commitments stipulated in the first paragraph of Article 78 of this Organic Law ;

· 2 ° requisitioned land, which in six years after the requisition has not been a request for surrender;

· 3 ° undeveloped urban land for three consecutive years.

Art.76.-forfeiture is pronounced by the Minister having Land in its attributions, after consultation with the Land Commission at the national level.

Art.77.-The confiscation could only occur after a formal notice and charged with receipt to be sent to the owner at least six months in advance.

When the owner can not be found, the notice shall be served on the occupier of the land during this time and displayed in the office of the District, the City or the City of Kigali and the office sector of the place of the land within six months under paragraph I of this article.

The notice states unequivocally the facts justifying the proposed action and the date from which the abandonment of land was found.

Subsection 3 - The return of the lands requisitioned

Art.78.-The owner of the requisitioned land may request delivery to it. This is granted if it is a written commitment to operate within its operations does not go beyond one year after delivery or when the operation is already underway, and if committed to continue to operate continuously.

The decision to surrender requisitioned land is taken into the same form as the request and authorized by the authority having jurisdiction to authorize their requisitions.

Art.79.-The claim for restitution of land requisitioned or liability resulting from a better notice before the forfeiture must be made in writing and shall state the new operating strategies and the means available to the concerned to immediately resume operations and the pursuit of a development on an ongoing basis. This request must be received by the person making the requisition or notice before the expiry of the period provided for in Articles 74 and 75 in case of requisition. It is the same before the six months of the notice does not flow in case of confiscation.

Art.80.-The administration will evaluate the proposals according to the location of land that can be requisitioned or confiscated, and the reasons for each proposal. The administration accepts the proposal if it appears to him serious or otherwise refuse.

In the latter case, the decision shall specify the reasons of fact justifying the measure and noted the contents of the care and advice and inform the person of what he can contest the decision before the competent court within six months.

Art.81.-The return of requisitioned land shall not be entitled to any compensation.

Art.82.-The transfer of land use to a third party is the subject of a reference to land records only to third parties and unenforceability of the owner.

The return of the right to use land to its rightful owner is by the administrative authority, author of the application after a period of not less than three years from the date of the requisition. In this case, operations conducted by the occupant of the land back to the owner without payment of compensation. However, the occupant of the land receives prior notice of six months before being returned to the owner.

Section 2 - criminal sanctions

Art.83.-Notwithstanding the more serious penalties under the Penal Code, is hereby imposed a prison sentence of five to ten years and a fine of 100,000 to FRW 1,000,000 or to both:

Conservative · 1 ° the land titles that did not follow the rules on conservation and land titling;

· 2 ° any person who has used voluntarily stolen land titles, changed in bad faith or securities containing bad terms;

· 3 ° any person who made the alterations or changes in land titles;

· 4 ° any witness who gives false testimony on the facts committed or uttered

· 5 ° any person who, in bad faith, has given the Conservative Land Titles a false identity and false

ability of the parties concerned, to establish a land title.

Art.84.-A prison sentence of six months to two years and a fine of 100,000 to 5,000,000 FRW or one of these penalties will be imposed on any person who has countered with the provisions of Article 13 of this organic law.

Art.85.-A prison sentence of seven days to six months and a fine of

20,000 to 100,000 FRW or one of its sentences is imposed on any person who has countered with the provisions of Articles 60 and 67 of this organic law. It is further required to do what she did not comply.

Chapter 7 - Transitional and Final Provisions

Art.86.-The traditional institution of "Ubukonde" as governed by the decree No. 530 / 1 of May 26, 1961 relating to tenure of "Ubukonde" in the territories of Gisenyi and Ruhengeri is hereby abolished.

The "Abagererwa" installed by "Umukonde" on the land they farm are treated the same way as other holders of customary land rights.

Art.87.-The State has the duty to find land to those who have been denied their right to land ownership.

These lands are generally comprised of:

· 1 · vacant land;

· 2 · escheated lands;

· 3 · land belonging to the public or private domain of the State;

· 4 · land belonging to the public or private District, the City and the City of Kigali;

° 5 ° sharing of land.

Without prejudice to Article 20 of this organic law on the minimum area that can not be divided, the division of land ownership practiced since the year 1994 is recognized by this organic law. The beneficiaries of this division are considered in law as other landowners who acquired their property according to custom.

The sharing of land referred to in this Article shall not be entitled to any compensation under this Organic Law.

The order of the Minister having Land in its attributions determines the modalities for sharing of land.

Art.88.-All previous provisions contrary to this Organic Law are repealed.

Art.89.-This Act comes into force on the day of its publication in the Official Gazette of the Republic of Rwanda.

MINISTERIAL ORDER OF 14/09/2010 NO. 004/MINIFOM/2010 DETERMINE HOW TO BACKUP FOR THE ENVIRONMENT IN THE MINING AND CAREERS

CHAPTER I. GENERAL PROVISIONS

Article 1:

Subject to this Order

This Order lays down rules for environmental protection applicable to the activities of mining and quarrying.

Article 2:

Respect for the environment

Anyone involved in the activities of prospecting, exploration and exploitation activities in mining and quarrying has a duty to conduct its activities so as not to harm the environment.

CHAPTER II. ENVIRONMENTAL IMPACT STUDY

Article 3:

Form of an Environmental Impact

Every applicant for a mining permit or quarry is required to submit an environmental impact study.

Article 4:

Contents of the Environmental Impact

The EIS must include a description and inventory of the ecosystem, fauna and flora, air quality, groundwater and surface water, soil and topography before mining operations and detailing the aspects that are qualitatively and quantitatively affected by mining.

The impact study shall include at least the following:

1 a description of the proposed development and its main purpose;

2 ° an analysis of potential effects of project activities on the environment;

3 ° an analysis of the possible impact of the project on the environment, particularly the impact on wildlife, plants, waters, air quality and changes in the morphology of the land and layout of the river;

4 ° measures envisaged for the protection of the environment, the limitation or elimination of pollution and ways to make them more effective;

5 ° an estimate of negative and positive impacts on the environment and the socio-economic, including the impact on environmental improvement;

6 ° a thorough analysis of possible changes to reduce environmental impact.

CHAPTER III. BACKUP PLAN OF ENVIRONMENT AND ENVIRONMENTAL IMPACT STUDY ON AN AREA OF MINING AND QUARRY

Article 5:

Analysis and approval of the plan to safeguard the environment

The application for an exploration license and looking for mines and quarries is accompanied by a plan to safeguard the environment in the area of mining and quarrying.

The plan should present the work of prevention and rehabilitation relating to areas that may be damaged.

The plan must also provide the cost of the work of prevention and rehabilitation relating to areas that may be damaged.

A deposit must be made in the form chosen by the applicant for the permit and in accordance with Rwandan law.

This plan is forwarded to the Ministry in mines and quarries within its remit for review and approval.

Article 6:

Analysis and approval of an Environmental Impact

Anyone intending to carry out a project Mining and quarrying develops an environmental impact study and submit to the Rwanda Development Board (RDB) for review and approval.

A copy of the approved environmental impact study is recorded in the file operating permit application for mining or quarrying which is sent to the Ministry in mines and quarries within its remit.

Article 7:

Environmental Report of the start of mining and quarrying

During the period of construction and startup of operations of mines and quarries, the operator shall forward to the Ministry in mines and quarries within his remit a monthly report detailing the management capabilities of each environmental impact identified in the study. This report also provides the means for managing environmental impacts during the preparatory work on the area of mining and quarrying.

Article 8:

Environmental Report for the period of mining and quarrying

During the mining and quarrying, the operator shall forward to the Ministry in mines and quarries within his remit a monthly report outlining how progressive management of environmental impacts as follows:

1 ° soil degradation that could cause erosion and affect the socio-economic activities;

2 risk of soil contamination;

3 ° prevention of contamination resulting from past activities;

4 risk of slope instability;

5 environmental risks resulting from seismic events.

Article 9:

Environmental report on the hydrogeology and surface water

During the mining and quarrying, the operator shall forward to the Ministry in mines and quarries within his remit a monthly report with the means to fight against pollution of groundwater and surface water as follows:

1 ° lowering of ground water by abstraction;

2 contamination of ground water;

3 potential socio-economic effects;

4 ° retained and abstraction of surface water;

5 ° contamination of surface waters.

Article 10:

Environmental Report on the use of land and mining infrastructure facilities

During the mining and quarrying, the operator shall forward to the Ministry in mines and quarries within his remit a monthly report on land use and mining infrastructure facilities as follows:

1 ° displacement of productive land use;

2 ° blocking mining operations or diversion of existing equipment;

3 ° the comings and goings impeding the work of exploitation.

Article 11:

Environmental report on air quality and weather impacts

The environmental report on air quality and meteorological impacts present the following:

1 ° the risks associated with dust during periods of construction and operation;

2 ° off-gases from the combustion in processing and smelting of ores and vehicles, which can pose risks to health or contribute to greenhouse gases.

Article 12:

Environmental Report on the socio-economic impacts

The environmental report on the socio-economic impacts present the following:

1 ° negative social impacts of population growth in the region.

2 ° positive impact on the lives of local communities located around the proposed development.

Article 13:

Environmental Report on the Ecology and Attractions

The environmental report on the ecology / heritage / tourist sites present the following:

1 ° and ecosystem impacts on protected species;

2 sites of degradation of historical and cultural value;

3 ° topographic effects on the character of interest, including the loss of their distinctive features.

Article 14:

Environmental report on the health and safety

The environmental report on the health and safety at work this work accidents, occupational diseases and occupational health.

The operator must present the estimated costs of operations management environment, including the rehabilitation program of the site.

Article 15:

Closure plan

If mining or quarrying is to close, a management plan for the closure of the site must be established.

The management plan developed during the operation will clear all activities related to such closure. The closure plan must specify:

1 ° the causes of the closure;

2 rehabilitation of areas of infrastructure;

3 methods of closure areas waste;

4 ° the closure plan of the underground excavations and dangerous;

5 ° The maintenance plan for areas closed until a closure certificate is delivered.

The closure plan of the site of operation is approved by the institutions responsible for mining and quarrying and the environment.

CHAPTER IV. REHABILITATION OF DEPOSIT OF THE ENVIRONMENT

Article 16:

Caution rehabilitation

The deposit for rehabilitation of the environment is a guarantee for the rehabilitation and site closure, but in case of insufficient funds for the final rehabilitation, the additional work shall be borne by the operator.

Article 17:

Determination of the bond for rehabilitation

The deposit for environmental rehabilitation is determined based on the duration of the operation, an amount calculated on the estimated budget for rehabilitation as provided by the study of environmental management, divided by the expected life of the operation in years. The estimated budget for rehabilitation with a frequency that does not exceed five (5) years. This reassessment may recognize a reduction in funds if final rehabilitation occurred on part of the deposit after acceptance of the rehabilitation work by the Offices of Mines and the Environment.

In the "impossibility of a proper assessment of the rehabilitation costs, the deposit will be calculated based on the gross sales at a rate between 0.3 and 1%. The deposit of rehabilitation can be provided by cash or other forms accepted by national legislation.

Article 18:

Rehabilitation satisfactory

When the exploration license, research or exploitation expires or is withdrawn or abandoned by its owner and that the successful implementation of the rehabilitation work was approved by the authority responsible for mines and quarries, the deposit is given to the rehabilitation the licensee.

If rehabilitation is not accepted by the authority, the rehabilitation works are taken up by the owner after the required conditions.

In case of failure of rehabilitation, the state uses the guarantee for the rehabilitation of damaged sites.

Article 19:

Repealing provision

All previous provisions contrary to this Order are hereby repealed.

Article 20:

Entry into force

This Order comes into force on the day of its publication in the Official Gazette of the Republic of Rwanda.

Kigali, on 14/09/2010

RWANDA VISION 2020

The Vision 2020 is a reflection of our aspiration and determination as Rwandans, to construct a united, democratic and inclusive Rwandan identity, after so many years of authoritarian and exclusivist dispensation. We aim, through this Vision, to transform our country into a middle income nation in which Rwandans are healthier, educated and generally more prosperous. The Rwanda we seek is one that is united and competitive both regionally and globally.

To achieve this, the Vision 2020 identifies six interwoven pillars, including good governance and efficient State, skilled human capital, vibrant private sector, world -class physical infrastructure and modern agriculture and livestock, all geared towards national, regional and global markets.

This Vision is a result of a national consultative process conducted between 1997 and 2000. These discussions and debates involved Rwandans from all walks of life, including leadership of all levels in the business community, government, academia and civil society.

It is important to emphasize the point that this Vision is not only for government. Vision 2020 is a shared purpose for all Rwandans. We need to constantly remind ourselves how our work – in our individual capacities, communities, business and public institutions – contributes towards realizing this Vision. Like all achieving societies whose success is generally inspired by a shared purpose, our Vision 2020 constitutes a bond that holds Rwandans as a people determined to build a better future.

I am certain that Vision 2020 will inspire us to achieve our goals, and that our vision is clearly and powerfully stated – thus setting in motion the vital energy and the sense of urgency needed for its realization. I thank all Rwandans and Friends of Rwanda who will play their part to making our Vision realizable.

PAUL KAGAME PRESIDENT OF THE REPUBLIC OF RWANDA (SÉ)

1. INTRODUCTION

How do Rwandan envisage their future? What kind of society do they want to become? How can they construct a united and inclusive Rwandan identity? What are the transformations needed to emerge from a deeply unsatisfactory social and economic situation? These are the main questions Rwanda Vision 2020 addresses.

This Vision is a result of a national consultative process that took place in Village Urugwiro in 1998-99. There was broad consensus on the necessity for Rwandans to clearly define the future of the country. This process provided the basis upon which this Vision was developed.

Today, Rwanda finds itself at a crossroads, moving from the humanitarian assistance phase associated with the 1994 genocide into one of sustainable development. Since 1994, the Government of Rwanda has stabilised the political situation, whilst putting the economy back on track with considerable assistance from development partners. However, the challenges remain daunting.

The Rwandan population is expected to double to around 16 million by 2020[1]. Given that the major aspiration of Vision 2020 is to transform Rwanda's economy into a middle income country (per capita income of about 900 USD per year, from 220 USD in 2000), this will require an annual growth rate of at least 7%. This will not be achieved unless we transform from a subsistence agriculture economy to a knowledge-based society, with high levels of savings and private investment, thereby reducing the country's dependence on external aid.

Economic growth, alone, is not sufficient to bring about the necessary rise in the standard of living of the population. To vanquish hunger and poverty, growth must be Pro-Poor, giving all Rwandan's the chance to gain from the new economic opportunities. Vision 2020 aspires for Rwanda to become a modern, strong and united nation, proud of its fundamental values, politically stable and without discrimination amongst its citizens.

In view of the aspirations and challenges outlined above, it is important to develop a new Vision for Rwanda and translate it into an achievable program based on the following pillars:

-Reconstruction of the nation and its social capital anchored on good governance, underpinned

by a capable state; -Transformation of agriculture into a productive, high value, market oriented sector, with

forward linkages to other sectors; -Development of an efficient private sector spearheaded by competitiveness and

entrepreneurship; -Comprehensive human resources deve lopment, encompassing education, health, and ICT

skills.aimed at public sector, private sector and civil society. To be integrated with

demographic, health and gender issues;

[1] Unless family planning improves, in which case the population is projected to reach 13 million.

-Infrastructural development, entailing improved transport links, energy and water supplies and ICT networks; -Promotion of regional economic integration and cooperation.

At all times, these will be affected by a number of cross-cutting issues including, gender equality and sustainable environmental and natural resource management , and ICT.

Vision 2020 is to be achieved in a spirit of social cohesion and equity, underpinned by a capable state. Rwanda's ongoing development will have, at its core, the Nation's principal asset - its people.

2. CURRENT SITUATION AND THE CHALLENGES

2.1. Historical Perspective

Although Rwanda has made significant progress from the devastated nation that emerged from the 1994 genocide, it still remains a severely under-developed, agrarian based economy with around 60% of the population living under the poverty line. In order to fully understand the present situation, it is important to appreciate Rwanda in a historical perspective.

Since the 11th century, Rwanda existed as a nation founded on a common history of its people, shared values, a single language and culture, extending well beyond the current boarders of the country. The unity of the Rwandan nation was also based on the clan groups and common rites with no discrimination based on ethnicity.

The colonial power, based on an ideology of racial superiority and in collaboration with some religious organisations, exploited the subtle social differences and institutionalized discrimination. These actions distorted the harmonious social structure, creating a false ethnic division with disastrous consequences.

The recent history of Rwanda can be summarised by the following key events: -The 1884 Berlin Conference placed the Kingdom of Rwanda under German rule as part of Deutsch Ostafrica (German East Africa);

-During the subsequent partition of Africa in 1910, a big part of Rwanda was annexed to neighbouring countries. This caused the loss of 1/3 of the Rwandan internal market and a large part of its natural resources;

-Following the 1st World War and the defeat of Germany, Rwanda was given to Belgium as a trustee territory under the authority of the League of Nations; -After the 2nd World War, the League of Nations became the United Nations and Rwanda became a UN Mandate trust territory, under Belgian administration, until 1962;

-During the colonial period, the Belgian administration applied contemporary Darwinian theories, thereby deeply dividing the people of Rwanda. This unfortunate development can be seen as laying the foundations for periodic mass killings even after independence was gained in 1962, culminating in the 1994 genocide.

-The RPF put an end to the 1994 genocide and thereafter formed the Government of National Unity (GNU) and the Transitional National Assembly (TNA) in coalition with other political parties to define a new future for Rwanda through democratic institutions.

This historical legacy goes some way to explain the challenges that Rwanda faces today. These will be examined individually in the following section.

2.2. Major challenges facing Rwanda today

The economy of Rwanda is currently characterized by internal (budget deficit) and external (Balance of Payments) macroeconomic disequilibria, alongside low savings and investment rates and high unemployment and underemployment (table 1). In addition, Rwanda's exports, composed mainly of tea and coffee – whose prices are subject to fluctuations on the international market – have not been able to cover imports needs.

Table 1: Rwanda's Macro -economic indicators from 1995 to 2000

Indicateurs		1995	1996	1997	1998	1999	2000
	CPI	48.2	13.4	11.7	6.8	-2.4	3.9
Inflation rate (%)	GDP Deflator	51.3	10.9	15.6	2.2	-3.5	3.3
Savings less investments	% GDP	-22.3	-20	-18.4	-17.4	-15.6	-16.3
	In billion RwF	-77.5	-85.4	-103.1	-110.1	-101.8	-115
Internal absorption (%GDP)		122.8	120.3	124.6	120.4	118.7	113.7
Overall budget deficit (% GDP)	Without grants	-13.3	-13.1	-9.9	-8.3	-9.7	-8.9
	With grants	-2.3	-5.7	-2.5	-3	-3.8	0.1
	Excl . official transfers	-20.5	-19.1	-17.6	-16.8	-17.1	-16.9
Current balance	Incl. Official transfers	4.5	-0.3	-4.9	-9.4	-7.6	-5.1
Real GDP per capita (USD) Debt service (% Exports)		185.6	204.3 20	216.8 14	202.6 17	252.5 26	227.7 25

Source : Rwanda Development Indicators Reports, BNR Reports

This overall situation can be best explained by reviewing a number of individual challenges.

(i) Diminishing agricultural productivity and arable land distribution

Agriculture, accounts for more than 90% of the labour force, yet remains unproductive and largely on a subsistence level. Distribution of arable land now stands at one hectare for every 9 Rwandans and is diminishing due to high birth rates. The obvious consequence is that a substantial number of rural families who subsist on agriculture own less than 1 hectare, which is too small to earn a living. Available pastureland is 350,000 hectares most of which is of poor quality. This results in intense exploitation of the land, with no simultaneous application of corrective measures, most notably through fertilizer use. The net result has been a decline in land productivity and massive environmental degradation, contributing to rampant malnutrition amongst the Rwandan population. Rwandans can no longer subsist on land and ways and means need to be devised to move the economy into the secondary and tertiary sectors.

(ii) Natural Barriers to trade

Rwanda is land-locked, with long distances from ocean ports; a factor that raises transportation costs for both exports and imports. The country lacks a link to regional railway networks, which means most trade is conducted by road. Poor road quality creates high transportation costs leading to inflated prices of domestically manufactured products, as raw materials used for manufacturing need to be imported. These natural barriers to trade hinder industrial and other forms of development.

(iii) Narrow economic base

It is clear that increases in the productivity and exports of Coffee and Tea alone, will not be sufficient to build the Rwandan economy. Therefore efforts need to be made to expand the economic base and especially exports. Although there are small pockets of various high value minerals in Rwanda, there is no single natural resource of sufficient quantity that will kick-start the economy. For several decades, the mining sector was largely based on the extraction and export of Cassiterite from several mines and numerous surface operations. Deposits of other minerals such as Wolfram, Colombo-tantalite and Gold do exist, but total reserves are not known. The country does have estimated reserves of 60 billion cubic metres of natural gas in Lake Kivu, but this sector has lacked investments both for effective exploration and profitable exploitation.

(iv) Weak institutional capacity

Governance, including the management of public resources remains insufficient due to lack of sound institutions and competent personnel. Rather than develop sound systems themselves, past governments continued to rely on foreign technical assistance that was both costly, largely indifferent to domestic long term needs and failed to build local capacities. A lthough great progress has been made on this front, it still represents a significant hindrance to effective governance.

(v) Low level of human resource development

The severe shortage of professional personnel constitutes an obstacle to the development of all sectors. Lack of adequately trained people in agriculture and animal husbandry hampers modernisation of this sector, whilst a shortage technicians and competent managers severely constrains the expansion of the secondary and tertiary sectors. Illiteracy is rampant both amongst the urban and the rural population with 48% of Rwandans unable to read and write. Addressing this situation is made more difficult by the prevalence of major diseases, such as malaria and HIV/AIDS, which together with malnutrit ion reduce the productivity of the population.

(vi) Public debt

Rwanda's public debt constitutes a major obstacle to its economic development. Public debt stands at about US$ 1.5 billion and is larger than current national GDP of US $ 1.3 billion (2000 data). About 75% of public debt is owed to the World Bank and other multilateral lenders. This has been accumulating at a rate higher than the country's capacity to generate wealth to service the debt. A return to sustainable level of debt, where existing debt can be serviced comfortably without jeopardising the country's growth prospects, is envisaged for 2015. However, continued debt relief and grant financing by donors will still be needed, at least in the medium term and a significant rise in export earnings is vital to avoid returning to the current situation.

(vii) Social and Economic Consequences of the Genocide

The 1994 Genocide devastated the Rwandan economy as well as its population. GDP was halved in a single year, eighty percent of the population was plunged into poverty and vast tracts of land and livestock were destroyed. The genocide also exacerbated a number of development constraints, which existed before 1994. The already poorly developed productive infrastructure was completely destroyed and the nation was robbed of a generation of trained teachers, doctors, public servants and private entrepreneurs. Thus, the consequences of genocide have devastated

Rwanda's social, political and economic fabric. Without successful reconciliation, politic al stability and security, private investors will not develop confidence in the country.

3. MAJOR OBJECTIVES OF VISION 2020

The VISION seeks to fundamentally transform Rwanda into a middle-income country by the year 2020. This will require achieving annual per capita income of US$ 900 (US$ 220 in 2000), a poverty rate of 30% (60.4% n 2000) and an average life expectance of 55 years (49 years in 2000). Appendix 1 shows, in more detail, the transformation we hope to achieve.

Taking into account Rwanda's extremely scarce resources, prioritisation and sequencing will be crucial. This section shows prioritisation in the short, medium and long run. It acknowledges the interdependencies and complementarities between different policies and developments. For example, industry and service sector development cannot be realised without a competitive stock of skills, infrastructure and financial services.

In the short run the key issues of stabilizing the economy, reducing aid dependency and developing exports will be vital. The following section will discuss these in detail.

3.1. The Short Term: Promotion of macroeconomic stability and wealth creation to reduce aid dependency

Rwanda will put into place macroeconomic stabilization policies that are conducive for private sector development. This, together with expanding the domestic resource base and increasing exports, is the only way to lessen aid dependence.

The imbalances highlighted in Table1 have been a source of macroeconomic instability and have led to an unsustainable debt burden and dependency on foreign aid. To reduce this dependency it will be crucial to develop effective strategies to expand the tax base, attract foreign investors and address the debt situation. Also, diversification and the development of non-traditional exports need to be promoted, as well as addressing the anti-export bias in public policies.

Envisaged policies, some of which are already being formulated and implemented include trade liberalisation, privatisation, tax reforms, competitive exchange rates and market driven interest rates. Government will desist from providing services that the private sector can deliver more efficiently and competitively. With these policies in place the economy will be able to take up the challenge of transforming from an agrarian subsistence economy into a sophisticated knowledge-based society.

3.2. The Medium Term: Transforming from an agrarian to a knowledge -based economy

Even if Rwanda's agriculture is transformed into a high value/high productivity sector, it will not, on its own, become a satisfactory engine of growth. There has to be an exit strategy from reliance on agriculture into secondary and tertiary sectors. The issue, however, is not simply one of a strategy based on agriculture, industry or services, but rather, identifying Rwanda's comparative advantage and concentrating strategies towards it. For instance there is a plentiful supply of cheap labour, a large multi-lingual population, a strategic location as the gateway between East and Central Africa as well as its small size, making it easy to build infrastructure (resources permitting). The industries established would need to address basic needs, for which there is a readily available market, as these products can satisfy local demand and even move towards export.

As for services, in the medium to long term, this sector will become the most important engine of Rwanda's economy. Since Rwanda is landlocked and has limited natural resources, the

Government should take a lead role in designing policies geared towards encouraging investment in services, to acquire and maintain a competitive edge in the region.

It should be noted that the elaboration of such policies will not be sufficient to achieve a knowledge based economy. Major infrastructural investment will be required in the areas of energy, water, telecommunication and transport to reduce costs, whilst increasing their quality and reliability. Improvements in education and health standards will be crucial for providing an efficient and productive workforce.

Figure 1: Transformation of economic activity 2000 -2020

3.3. LONG TERM: CREATING A PRODUCTIVE MIDDLE CLASS AND FOSTERING ENTREPRENEURSHIP

The developmental process and capital formation cannot – in the long run – be achieved by the state or by donor funds alone. While both of these must contribute, the backbone of the process should be a middle class of Rwandan entrepreneurs. Productive entrepreneurship must be fostered to perform its traditional role of creating wealth, employment and vital innovations through opportunities for profit.

Stimulating the private sector, particularly with regard to the promotion of exports and competitiveness is not achievable without broadening and deepening the financial sector such as banking, insurance and the application of information technology. Provision of high quality educational services in sciences and technology will be necessary for consolidating development gains made in the short and medium term. Rwanda should also aim to find a niche market in the region, for example, becoming a telecommunications hub. It is envisaged that with these reforms, Rwanda will transform from a subsistence agricultural economy to a knowledge-based society, with a vibrant class of entrepreneurs. The following section outlines the major stages of this transition.

4. THE PILLARS OF VISION 2020

Whereas section three focussed more on the timing of activities, we will now identify the key aspects of Vision 2020 that have been discussed so far and address them individually. The aspirations of Vision 2020 will be realised around six "Pillars" and will be interwoven with three cross-cutting issues. This section will examine the Pillars, whilst section 5 will address the crosscutting issues.

Table 2: Pillars of the Vision 2020 and its crosscutting areas

Pillars of the Vision 2020	Cross-cutting areas of Vision 2020
1. Good governance and a capable state 2. Human resource development and a knowledge based economy 3. A private sector-led economy 4. Infrastructure development 5. Productive and Market Oriented Agriculture 6. Regional and International Economic integration.	1. Gender equality 2. Protection of environment and sustainable natural resource management 3. Science and technology, including ICT

4.1. Good Governance and a Capable State

Rwanda will become a modern, united and prosperous nation founded on the positive values of its culture. The nation will be open to the world, including its own Diaspora. Rwandans will be a people, sharing the same vision for the future and ready to contribute to social cohesion, equity and equality of opportunity.

The country is committed to being a capable state, characterised by the rule of law that supports and protects all its citizens without discrimination. The state is dedicated to the rights, unity and wellbeing of its people and will ensure the consolidation of the nation and its security.

Social and economic transformation is as much about states as markets. In effect, the role of the state is indispensable for wealth-creation and development. However, currently in Rwanda the low capacity of the state hinders this transformation. This situation calls for rapid development and deployment of public sector skilled human resources, who grasp the needs of other sectors – in particular the private sector – and can translate them into sound policies and strategies. In short, we need a small but effective, flexible public sector that can lay the foundations for Rwanda to be competitive in the modern international economy.

The State will ensure good governance, which can be understood as accountability, transparency and efficiency in deploying scarce resources. But it also means a State respectful of democratic structures and processes and committed to the rule of law and the protection human rights in particular.

People's participation at the grassroots level will be promoted through the decentralisation process, whereby local communities will be empowered in the decision making process, enabling them to address the issues, which affect them, the most.

A reconstruction of the nation of Rwanda and its social capital, anchored on good governance and an effective and capable state is considered a minimal condition to stimulate a harmonious development of other pillars[2].

[2] It cannot be stressed enough however that the 6 pillars and 3 cross-cutting areas have to be developed in tandem – indeed that was the main message of section 3.

4.2. Human Resource Development and a Knowledge-based economy

Apart from raising the general welfare of the population, improvements in education and health services can be used to build a productive and efficient workforce. This will be essential for Rwanda to become a sophisticated knowledge-based economy.

(i) Education

Rwanda is committed to reaching "Universal Education for All", which is one of the most important Millennium Development Goals. However, there is clearly a need to educate and train people at all levels: primary, secondary and tertiary, with special attention paid to the quality of education. This has been declining, due in a large part to low calibre teaching staff and therefore, the government will organise intensive teacher training programs.

Major emphasis will be placed on vocational and technical training in the fields of technology, engineering and management. This will be targeted at secondary school leavers, as well as various sections of society (with particular emphasis on youth and women). To encourage skills development, micro-credit schemes will be promoted specifically to extend finance to self-employed young technicians. Special emphasis will be given to innovative, small-scale entrepreneurs. To promote efficiency and continuous upgrading of skills, appropriate programs will be launched in the national institutions aimed at on-the-job-training, in -service training and distant learning.

Rwanda lags behind in professional training, with the most acute deficiency being apparent in the fields of applied and natural sciences and ICT. Although the country will continue to rely on imported technology from advanced countries, well-trained, specialised nationals will be essential to run as well as maintain technological systems ranging from medicine and agriculture to industry and telecommunications.

Absolutely crucial for achieving Vision 2020 will be to properly link education policies, with sector development and labour policies. It is crucial to understand that the investment needed for the development of the secondary and tertiary sectors, will not be effective without a skilled labour force.

(ii) Health and population

The Rwandan population is estimated at about 8 million people in 2000 with one of the highest population densities in Africa and a high population growth rate close to 3% per annum. This demographic trend is one of the major causes of the depletion of natural resources and the subsequent poverty and hunger. The demographic dynamic is the result of a number of factors: (1) the high fertility rate of women, itself linked to (2) a pro-birth culture (3) diminishing child death rates and (4) the relatively low general mortality rate, due to a climate and topography unfavourable to diseases.

Rwanda considers its population as its fundamental resource and banks on it for its future development. With the success of current and future population policies, Rwanda projects to reduce the fertility rate within 20 years from 6 to 4.5 children and the population growth rate to 2.2%.

Although the state of health of the Rwandan population has improved significantly over recent years, it is still inadequate. The prevalence of malaria (40% of hospital consultations in health centers) and of HIV -AIDS (13% of the total population) is high and constitutes a major economic problem.

The objectives to be attained in the field of health within the next 20 years include: a reduction in the infant mortality rate from 107 to 50 per 1000 and the maternal mortality rate from 1070 to 200 per 100.000. Life expectancy will have increased from 49 to 55 years, malaria and other potential epidemic diseases will have been controlled and the AIDS prevalence will have been reduced from 13% to 8%.

To achieve these improvements, health policies must be targeted at the poorest members of the population to improve access to healthcare, the quality of that healthcare and to reduce its cost. Family planning is crucial for reducing both birth rates and the prevalence of HIV/AIDS. Envisaged and current population policies should go hand in hand with strategies to overcome problems in the health sector. Indeed, poverty remains a major cause of poor health and vice versa.

4.3. Private Sector-led Development.

For Rwanda's development the emergence of a viable private sector that can take over as the principle growth engine of the economy, is absolutely key. Not only will such a development be conducive for economic growth, but it will also ensure the emergence of a vibrant middle class of entrepreneurs, which will help develop and embed the principles of democracy. Although foreign direct investment will be encouraged, a local-based business class remains a crucial component of development.

The Government of Rwanda will not be involved in providing services and products that can be delivered more efficiently by the private sector. It is, therefore, committed towards a comprehensive privatisation policy that will help reduce costs and prices and widen consumer choice. The State will only act as a catalyst; ensuring that infrastructure, human resources and legal frameworks are geared towards stimulating economic activity and private investment.

The development of the financial sector will be crucial, as it is currently underdeveloped and poorly adapted to the economic needs of the country. The financial sector must be able to provide the necessary capital for private sector development. The government will also promote local business through the introduction of export processing zones, in which foreign operators could have local partners.

The development of Rwanda's private sector will not limit itself to the formal sector. The informal sector will also be developed, in such area as retail trade, repair workshops and garages, handicrafts and metal works.

Particular attention will be paid to the labour market. During the 40 years of colonialism, the Rwandan economy has been able to generate only 200,000 jobs outside agriculture. If family planning services impr ove, the population is still projected to reach 13 million by 2020, of which 7 million people will be earning a living on off-farm activities. Therefore, it will be necessary to create 1,4 million jobs outside agriculture. Given the trends of the Rwandan economy over the past decades, this is clearly a huge challenge, in which the private sector needs to play a pivotal role.

4.4. INFRASTRUCTURE DEVELOPMENT

The rehabilitation and development of infrastructure is a crucial aspect in lowering the costs of doing business in Rwanda, which will attract domestic and foreign investment.

(i) Land use management

Land use management is a fundamental tool in development. As Rwanda is characterized by acute land shortage, a land use plan is needed to ensure its optimal utilization in urban and rural development. Currently, Rwanda's land resources are utilized in an inefficient and unsustainable manner, which limits the profitability of land and infrastructure, whilst aggravating the national capacity to retain rainwater. To address this, a modern land law providing security of tenure and freedom of exchange will be instituted.

Rwanda will pursue a harmonious policy of grouped settlements based on economic activity. Rural settlements organized into active development centres will be equipped with basic infrastructure and services. This system of settlement will serve as an entry point into the development of non-agricultural income generating activities. Land will be reorganized and consolidated so as to create adequate space for modern and viable farming.

(ii) Urban development

Rwanda is characterized by low but accelerating urbanization. This has happened in a rapid and uncoordinated manner, meaning that social services and employment opportunities are lagging behind. From now until 2010, each town will have regularly updated urban master plans and specific land management plans. The country will develop basic infrastructure in urban centres and in other development poles, enabling the decongestion of agricultural zones. The proportion of those living in towns and cities will increase from 10% in 2000 to 30% in 2020 (from 5% in 1995). The income differential between towns and rural areas should remain within reasonable proportions, due to the decentralization of economic activities to the country.

(iii) Transport

Rwanda is landlocked with high transport costs to the ocean ports of Kenyan and Tanzania. Therefore, it is imperative to develop, alternative lower costs of transport to the sea, notably through a regional rail extension to Isaka, Tanzania and an extension to the Ugandan Railway system. A combined rail and water system that can link to the Banguela Railway will be considered. Furthermore, a second airport capable of serving, as a regional hub for the great lakes region will be developed. For the internal market, Rwanda has a reliable and safe transport network of feeder roads, however, this will continue to be extended and improved.

(iv) Communication & ICT

Telecommunication coverage in Rwanda is very low. The communication policy will take advantage of the small size of the country, its high population density and the single local language to attract investors so that the sector can be liberalised. By 2020, Rwanda projects to have internet access at all administrative levels, for all secondary schools and for a large number of primary schools. Telephone services will be widespread in rural areas and efficiency of public services will have increased through the application of e-government principles.

(v) Energy

Inadequate and expensive electricity supply constitutes a limiting factor to development. Wood is the source of energy for 99 % of the population, which leads to massive deforestation and soil destruction. Imported petroleum products consume more tha n 40% of foreign exchange. Rwanda will therefore increase energy production and diversify into alternative energy sources.

To achieve this, Rwanda has considerable hydroelectric potential, in addition to large deposits of renewable methane gas in Lake Kivu, estimated at 60 billion cubic metres. In rural areas direct solar energy or photovoltaic energy can be used, whilst up to 1/3 of 155 million tons of peat deposit is currently exploitable. Rwanda projects that by 2020, at least 35 % of the population will be connected to electricity (up from 2% in 2000) and the consumption of wood will decrease from the current 94% to 50% of national energy consumption.

(vi) Water

Only 52% of Rwandans have access to clean water. Daily consumption of water is estimated at 8.15 litres per person in rural areas, far below the international standard of 20 litres. The country is endowed with reserves that could provide enough water for both consumption and agricultural purposes. These include substantial rainfall (between 900 & 1800 mm per year) and the abundance of lakes, streams and watercourses. Furthermore, there is an abundant supply of high altitude water in the western part of the country, which may be used in providing water by gravity to the southern and southeastern regions of the country that face water shortages.

In order to achieve the goals for water set out in Vision 2020, the country will have to increase the rate of access to potable water by 2.5 percentage points, annually from the current rate of 52% so that the whole of the Rwandan population will have access to drinkable water by 2020.

(vii) Waste management

Access to drainage and sewage disposal services is 85% of the population, whilst 64% of latrines do not meet the required hygienic standards. Cons umption of dirty and unsafe water is at the origin of various water-borne diseases. The unplanned and disorganized construction of towns without a suitable drainage system exacerbates sanitary problems. Sewerage and rainwater can destroy public roads or stagnate, creating ideal breeding grounds for both human and animal diseases. Since most houses are situated on the summit and on the slopes of hills, water sources are in constant danger of pollution by domestic sewerage and other human activities carried by the stream of water. The environmental impact of deficient waste management is barely taken into account by human settlements and industrial installations

By 2020, the rural and urban areas are to have sufficient sewerage and disposal systems. Each town is to be endowed with an adequate unit for treating and compressing solid wastes for disposal. Households will have mastered and be practicing measures of hygiene and waste disposal.

4.5. PRODUCTIVE HIGH VALUE AND MARKET ORIENTED AGRICULTURE

Rwanda's economic policies since independence are said to have targeted agriculture as the main engine of economic growth. However, the agricultural sector has continued to perform poorly, with consistently declining productivity. It will be necessary to formulate and implement realistic developmental policies that move beyond past delusions of viable subsistence -based agriculture.

Contrary to conventional wisdom, the most important issue retarding Rwanda's agricultural development is not land size, but low productivity associated with traditional peasant-based subsistence farming. Agricultural policy orientation will have to be overhauled, promoting intensification so as to increase productivity and achieve growth rates of 4.5 % to 5% per year. This can only happen through the production of high value crops and modern livestock management. The vision aims to replace subsistence farming by a fully monetized, commercial agricultural sector by 2020.

The key policy areas that need urgent attention to bring about this transformation include the following:

-Institutional and legal reforms to ensure security of land ownership; -Development of a market in land assets; -Extensive research and extension services; -Investment in rural infrastructures; -Use of high yielding varietie s and intensive input use, especially fertilisers; -Promotion of agro-based manufacturing;

-Environmental control measures to halt the decline in soil fertility; -Rural Financing Schemes and Markets

As mentioned above, a viable economic strategy for Rwanda requires diversification away from the agricultural sector. Agriculture will have to be developed to permit spin-off effects, beginning with the development of agro-businesses that can then provide spill-overs into other sectors of the economy. Furthermore, it can be very much expected that the above priority policy areas will not only be supportive to agriculture, but will also benefit the whole of the rural economy.

4.6. Regional and International Integration

Rwanda considers regional economic integration as one of the crucial elements of achieving Vision 2020. To this end, it will be necessary to pursue an open, liberal trade regime, minimizing barriers to trade as well as implementing policies to encourage foreign direct investment. Furthermore, the need to adopt policies to promote competitive enterprises, exports and entrepreneurship rather than protecting failing industries cannot be over-emphasised. Economic zones for ICT based production will be crucial for enhancing competitiveness of Rwandan firms.

The vision of accessing larger regional markets will be accompanied through a program of investing in infrastructure to promote Rwanda as a communication and telecommunication hub. Furthermore, taking advantage of Rwanda's comparative strategic position should be exploited in terms of entrepot functions in trade and commerce. Export processing zones, coupled with the industrial reforms noted above, will enable the country to consolidate its niche in services and communication sectors and take advantage of growing regional co-operation in the Great Lakes/ Eastern African Region.

5. CROSS-CUTTING ISSUES OF VISION 2020

Next to the 6 pillars, there are the three cross-cutting areas of gender, natural resources & environment and culture, science & technolo gy. These issues will not only be affected by the economic transformation but will also play an important role in achieving the V ision's development goals.

5.1. Gender Equality

Women make up 53% of the population and participate in subsistence agriculture more than men. They usually feed and provide care for the children and ensure their fundamental education. But until recently, girls were the minority in secondary schools, women had little access to the opportunities available to men and they were poorly represented in decision-making positions.

In order to achieve gender equality and equity, Rwanda will continuously update and adapt its laws on gender. It will support education for all, eradicate all forms of discrimination, fight against poverty and practice a positive discrimination policy in favour of women. Gender will be integrated as a cross -cutting issue in all development policies and strategies.

5.2. NATURAL RESOURCES AND THE ENVIRONMENT

The major problem in the field of environmental protection in Rwanda is the imbalance between the population and the natural resources (land, water, flora and fauna and non-renewable resources, which have been degrading for decades). This degradation is observed through massive deforestation, the depletion of bio-diversity, erosion and land slides, pollution of waterways and the degradation of fragile ecosystems, such as swamps and wetlands.

The average population growth of 3% per annum during the 80's to 90's period was faster than that of agricultural production, estimated at 2.2%. This has led to the occupation of more and more marginal areas and to the rapid and continuous soil degradation of the fragile ecosystems of the country. These environmental problems are exacerbated by the poor location of indus tries and the direct evacuation of their waste, without any treatment, into waterways and lakes. In order to ensure sustainable development, Rwanda will implement adequate land and water management techniques, coupled with a sound biodiversity policy.

5.3. SCIENCE, TECHNOLOGY AND ICT

Rwandans are rightly proud of their cultural roots and the government will ensure that it takes advantage of this heritage in all facets of the development process. However, for this development process to be a success, Rwanda must embrace the future and exploit innovations in Science and technology to complement its cultural strengths.

In Rwanda, the rate of adoption and integration of science and technology in socio-economic life is very low and the shortage of technically qualified professionals is visible at all levels. From now until 2020, Rwanda projects to have adequate, highly skilled scientists and technicians to satisfy the needs of the national economy. There is a need to generate, disseminate and acquire scientific skills as well as technological innovations, in addition to integrating them into the social and economic development drive, detailed above.

In order for Rwanda to achieve this objective, it will have to develop the teaching of science and technology at secondary and university levels. It will facilitate the creation of high and intermediate technology enterprises and develop access to ICT down to the administrative sector level, in accordance with the national ICT plan.

6. THE ROAD MAP

This road map lays out how the Rwanda Vision 2020 will be realized through the country's planning process. It also establishes a set of yardsticks against which we can measure our progress towards achieving the targets. Macroeconomic projections and the underlying assumptions clearly showing the financing requirements to realize the Vision are also made.

6.1. RWANDA'S PLANNING PROCESS AND THE REALISATION OF VISION 2020

To ensure smooth implementation of the Vision 2020 and achievement of the aspirations described above, it will have to be reflected in the whole planning process and, particularly, medium and short-term instruments. Therefore, the long-term aspirations of the Vision will translate into medium -term programmes of the National Poverty Reduction Strategy (PRS) as well as the National Investment Strategy (NIS).

The PRS is operationalised through medium -term sector strategies that will inform provincial and district development plans. The sector strategies and the decentralised development plans will be implemented through the Medium-Term Expenditure Framework (MTEF); three-year fully integrated budgets that mainstream the Public Investment Programmes (PIP) of these agencies and translate into concrete action plans costed through annual budgets. The poverty reduction achieved through the MTEF will be monitored and will feed back into the elaboration of sector and provincial plans. See the chart below.

Figure 2: Converting Vision 2020 into a reality

NIS

Sector strategic planss

Provincial / District development plans

MTEFs

Annual action plans

Annual action plans

Annual budgets

6.2. Financing of Vision 2020: Macroeconomic Assumptions and Projections

The implementation of the Vision 2020 takes into account the necessity to achieve aspirations of the Rwandans. The assumptions for the macroeconomic perspectives over the period until 2020 can be summarised as follows:

(1)

The population growth rate is assumed to average 2.7% until 2020;

(2)

To transform into a middle income country – with per capita income of about 900 USD- Rwanda will need to achieve above 7% GDP annual growth rate over the period,

(3)

Based on the ICOR approach, the country needs to annually invest 30% of GDP in order to achieve the targeted economic growth of 7%;

(4)

Initially, agriculture is the major engine of growth representing more than 45% of GDP until 2010 whilst industry and services represent 20% and 37% respectively. Afterwards, the industrial and services sectors take over so that by 2020, services will contribute 42%, industry 26% and agriculture 33% of GDP.

(5)

Private investment would account for an average of 20% of GDP and public investment 8%;

(6)

The public capital expenditure is assumed to increase to Rwf 605 billion.

Table 3: Key Economic Variables of the Vision 2020

	2005	2010	2015	2020
Population (Million)	8.65	9.88	11.29	12.90
Population growth rate	2.7%	2.7%	2.7%	2.7%
Nominal GDP (Billion)	1,218.75	2,147.85	3,957.28	7,291.04
GDP Growth Rate	7%	8%	9%	9%
GDP per Capita (Rwf)	140,915.87	217,369.10	350,540.18	565,298.46
GDP per Capita (USD)	231.39	336.48	542.63	875.08
Agriculture(billion)	560.63	923.58	1,582.91	2,376.88
Agriculture (%of GDP)	46%	43%	40%	33%
Services (Billion)	439	795	1,504	3,048
Services (% of GDP)	36%	37%	38%	42%
Industry (Billion)	219	430	871	1,867
Industry (% of GDP)	18%	20%	22%	26%
Gross Domestic Investment (GDI)	321.75	614.29	1,131.78	2,085.24
Public	124.19	163.26	314.35	605.25
Private	197.56	451.02	817.44	1,479.99

Gross Domestic Investment (GDI) % of GDP)	26%	29%	29%	29%
Public	10%	8%	8%	8%
Private	16%	21%	21%	20%
Total Capital Expenditure	124.19	163.26	314.35	605.25

Figure 3: Contribution of Sectors in GDP (2000-2020)

2005 2010 2015 2020 Year

Nominal GDP (Billion)

Agriculture(billion)

Services (Billion)

Industry (Billion)

Rwf billion

8000 7000 6000 5000 4000 3000 2000 1000 0

Figure 4: GDP and Investment Projections for Vision 2020

Nominal GDP (Billion)

Gross Domestic Investment (GDI)

Total Capital Expenditure

Private

200320042005200620072008200920102011201220132014201520162017201820192020

This road map highlights the challenges, which Rwanda will face in realising the targets set out in Vision 2020. Specifically, we will have to streamline planning processes so that the Vision is translated into implementable plans, with strong linkages between set priorities and the allocation of resources. It also requires a mobilisation of a substantial amount of financial resources from the state, the donor community and the private sector. If these resources can be efficiently allocated through the planning process, the goals set in this Vision will become attainable.

6.3 Institutional Framework for the Implementation of the Rwanda Vision

The implementation of the Vision 2020 Vision within the ambit of all players: the state, the private sector, civil society, NGOs, decentralised authorities, grassroots communities, Faith-based organisations and development partners. The top most policy making body of Vision 2020 implementation is the Cabinet. The Ministry in charge of Economic Planning coordinates the implementation and monitoring and evaluation of the Vision. It also ensures that Vision 2020 based sector strategic plans and district development plans are developed by all sector ministries and districts. The Ministry will specifically:

-Coordinate all the activities related to the implementation of the Vision 2020 -Mobilise and allocate resources to Vision 2020 priority areas -Support the planning organs and other institutions in charge of implementation of the Vision -Ensure that Vision 2020 based sector strategic plans and district developments are prepared and

linked to the Medium Term Expenditure Framework and annual budgets -Ensure the establishment of a monitoring and evaluation framework for Vision -Regularly report to Cabinet on the status of achievement of Vision 2020 obje ctives and targets

The Vision 2020 National Consultative Committee will be established to over see and guide the implementation of the Vision and ensure that consensus building around Vision 2020 implementation is realized. The Consultative Committee is a mechanism for stakeholder coordination bringing together Government, Development partners, civil society, private sector and other relevant stakeholders and resource persons to dialogue on the Vision. The Committee will be coordinated and chaired by the Ministry in charge of Economic Planning.

Vision 2020 technical platforms will be established in line with the pillars of the Vision 2020. The rationale is to facilitate coordination of policies and actions of different sectors, and promote dialogue among all stakeholders in order to build consensus as they implement a shared vision.

The institutional framework for implementation of Vision 2020 is shown in the organization chart below.

Institutional Framework for Implementation of Vision 2020

The Cabinet

The Ministry in charge of Economic Planning will prepare detailed terms of reference and definition of tasks and responsibilities for the different technical platforms as well as the National Steering Committee involved in the management of the implementation of the Rwanda Vision 2020.

Conclusion

Vision 2020 represents an ambitious plan to raise the people of Rwanda out of poverty and transform the country into a middle-income economy. Some will say that this is too ambitious and that we are not being realistic when we set this goal. Others say that it is a dream. But, what choice does Rwanda have? To remain in the current situation is simply unacceptable for the Rwandan people. Therefore, there is a need to devise and implement policies as well as mobilize resources to bring about the necessary transformation to achieve the Vision. This is realistic based on the fact that countries with similar unfavourable initial conditions have succeeded. The development experience of the East Asian 'Tigers' proves that this dream could be a reality.

Annexes Annex 1: Key indicators of the Rwandan Vision 2020

Indicators	Situation In 2000	Target in 2010	Target in 2020	Inter-national

				level
1. Rwandan population	7,700,000	10,200,000	13,000,000	
2. Literacy level	48	80	100	100
3. Life expectancy (years)	49	50	55	
4. Women fertility rate	6	5.5	4.5	
5. Infant mortality rate (0/00)	107	80	50	
6. Maternal mortality rate for 100000 live births	1070	600	200	
7. Child Malnutrition (Insufficiency in %)	30	20	10	
8. Population Growth rate (%)	2.9	2.3	2.2	
9. Net primary school enrolment (%)	72	100	100	100
10. Gross primary school enrolment (%)		100	100	
11. Secondary school transitional rate (%)	42	60	80	
12. Gross Secondary school enrolment (%)	7	40	60	
13. Rate of qualification of teachers (%)	20	100	100	100
14. Professional and technical training centres		50	106	
15. The rate of admission in tertiary education (0/00)	1	4	6	
16. Gender equality in tertiary education (F %)	30	40	50	50
17. Gender equality in decision-making positions (% of females)	10	30	40	
18. HIV/AIDS prevalence rate (%)	13	11	8	0

19. Malaria -related mortality (%)	51	30	25	
20. Doctors per 100,000 inhabitants	1.5	5	10	10
21. Population in a good hygi enic condition (%)	20	40	60	
22. Nurses per 100,000 inhabitants	16	18	20	20
23. Laboratory technicians per 100,000 inhabitants	2	5	5	
24. Poverty (%< 1 US $/day)	60.4	40	30	
25. Average GDP growth rate (%)	6.2	8	8	
26. Growth rate of the agricultural sector (%)	9	8	6	
27. Growth rate of the industry sector (%)	7	9	12	
28. Growth rate of the service sector (%)	7	9	11	
29. Ginni Coefficient (income disparity)	0.454	0.400	0.350	
30. Growth national savings (% of GDP)	1	4	6	
31. Growth national investment (% of GDP)	18	23	30	30
32. GDP per capita in US $	220	400	900	
33. Urban population (%)	10	20	30	
34. Agricultural population (%)	90	75	50	
35. Modernized agricultural land (%)	3	20	50	
36. Use of fertilizers (Kg/ha/year)	0.5	8	15	
37. Financial credits to the agricultural sector (%)	1	15	20	
38. Access to clear water (%)	52	80	100	100

39. Agricultural production (kcal/day/person (% needs)	1612	2000	2200	
40. Availability of proteins/person/day (% of needs)	35	55	65	70
41. Road network (km/km2)	0.54	0.56	0.60	
42. Annual electricity consumption (kWh/inhabitants)	30	60	100	
43. Access to electric energy (% of population.)	2	25	35	
44. Land portion against soil erosion (%)	20	80	90	
45. Level of reforestation (ha)				
46. Wood energy in t he national energy consumption (%)	94	50	50	
47. Non-agricultural jobs	200.000	500.000	1.400.000	

Annex 2: The role of the State in Rwanda in a Historical Pe rspective

The role of the state	Pre-colonial era	Colonial era	From independence up to 1994	Post-genocide period
Internal peace and security	-Generally well ensured by the King's authority, - Periods of conflict expansion and relations with some neighbouring kingdoms	-Less regional wars, following the demarcation of colonial boundaries and the installation of the colonial administration.	-Pogroms caused by the ethnic divisions, - Permanent climate of insecurity.	-Fight against the 1996-2000 insurgency, -High level of internal security, - Pacification of the Great Lakes Region in process.
Nation Unity	-No internal problems and everybody contributed to defend the nation. However, there used to be voluntary exile by individuals or	Cracks in the social fabric of the nation: a) Exclusive schools for the chiefs' children in Nyanza in 1918 and Astrida in 1929 operated by white Fathers; b)	Development of divisive ethnic ideologies. Total disintegration of the social fabric following the 1990-1994 genocide.	-explicit political will and efforts for reconciliation, - National Commission for Unity and Reconciliation -anti-segregation legal framework including

	groups who had defied the royal authority. -The Rucunshu succession war in 1896 that resulted in the weakening of the royal regime.	Destitution of Hutu, modest Tutsi and Twa by the Belgians in 1926,		abolishment of ethnicity cards.
Justice				Efforts to separate the three powers, -Gacaca reconciliatory justice.
Human Rights	Poorly respected	Poorly respected	Not respected	Progress towards the rule of law
Decentralization	-Hierarchical and centralized policies.	The President concentrated the political powers in his hands, -Beginning of the concentration of the national economy into the hands of the State.	-Highly centralized economic and political powers.	Progressive decentralization of the political and economic powers, promotion of the private sector Establishment of a Common Development Fund for Decentralisation

27

The role of the state	Pre-colonial era	Colonial era	From independence up to 1994	Post-genocide period
Governance and	-Low level of social equity.	-loss of a third of the national	-poor governance by the state	-progressive im provement of
democracy	-all the leaders were nominated, -possibility of expression and questioning the authorit y	territory following the 1910 partition, -Low level of social equity. -no democracy but state control and coercion	party, -poor level of social equity -state party dictatorship	popular participation, -strategy to fight poverty, -Ombudsman institutionalized. -multipartism institutionalized, -law liberalizing the press, -consultation on National Constitution.

Regional and International Integration	-limited exchange with neighboring kingdoms, -no exchange with foreign countries (external world)	-opening of the country's boarders, -contacts with the world via the colonial state Belgium, - commodity products.	-further opening to international cooperation, - periodic problems with neighboring countries due to personal relations between the ruling classes.	-free entry and exit of citizens, -efforts to pacify the Great Lakes Region and for the policy of good neighborliness, - efforts towards multilingualism, - policy of regional integration and of openness.
Management of State (Public) affairs Diaspora	-monarchy. - limited	-efficient but coercive - exacerbation of waves of emigrants running away from the colonial yoke and ruthless rule, - close monitoring of indigenous administration.	-progressive improvement, -high level of corruption - negative role of the State in the forced emigration, - destabilization of the Diaspora in host countries.	-reforms and organs aimed at improving transparency, - fighting corruption. - double citizenship, - efforts towards good relations and contact, -easy entry and exit, - participatory approach and generalized consultation.

STRATEGIC ECONOMIC INFORMATION

The Rwandan economy is based on the largely rain-fed agricultural production of small, semi-subsistence, and increasingly fragmented farms. It has few natural resources to exploit and a small, uncompetitive industrial sector. While the production of coffee and tea is well-suited to the small farms, steep slopes, and cool climates of Rwanda and has ensured access to foreign exchange over the years, farm size continues to decrease.

Prewar population was growing at the high rate of 3% a year. By 1994, farm size, on average, was smaller than one hectare, while population density was more than 450 persons per square kilometer of arable land.

In the 1960s and 1970s, Rwanda's prudent financial policies, coupled with generous external aid and relatively favorable terms of trade, resulted in sustained growth in per capita income and low inflation rates. However, when world coffee prices fell sharply in the 1980s, growth became erratic.

Compared to an annual GDP growth rate of 6.5% from 1973 to 1980, growth slowed to an average of 2.9% a year from 1980 through 1985 and was stagnant from 1986 to 1990. The crisis peaked in 1990 when the first measures of an IMF structural adjustment program were carried out. While the program was not fully implemented before the war, key measures such as two large devaluations and the removal of official prices were enacted. The consequences on salaries and purchasing power were rapid and dramatic. This crisis particularly affected the educated elite, most of whom were employed in civil service or state-owned enterprises.

During the five years of civil war that culminated in the 1994 genocide, GDP declined in three out of five years, posting a dramatic decline at more than 40% in 1994, the year of the genocide. The 9% increase in real GDP for 1995, the first post-war year, signaled the resurgence of economic activity.

The Government of Rwanda posted a 13% GDP growth rate in 1996 through improved collection of tax revenues, accelerated privatization of state enterprises to stop their drain on government resources, and continued improvement in export crop and food production. It is estimated that in 1997 that food production levels will reach 81% of prewar levels, and should continue to improve as more returned refugees continue to put land back into cultivation.

Tea plantations and factories continue to be rehabilitated, and coffee, always a smallholder's crop, is being more seriously rehabilitated and tended as the farmers' sense of security returns. However, the road to recovery will be slow. Coffee production of about 15,000 tons in 1996 compares to a pre-civil war variation between 35,000 and 40,000 tons, while 1996 tea production reached 11,000 tons, compared to prewar production of about 13,000 tons. Rwanda's natural resources are limited. A small mineral industry provides about 5% of foreign exchange earnings. Concentrates of the heavy minerals cassiterite, columbite-tantalite, and wolframite are most important, followed by small amounts of gold and sapphires. Production of methane from Lake Kivu began in 1983, but to date has been used only by a brewery. Depletion of the forests will eventually pressure Rwandans to turn to fuel sources other than charcoal for cooking and heating, given the abundance of mountain streams and lakes, the potential for hydroelectric power is substantial. Rwanda is exploiting these natural resources through joint hydroelectric projects with Burundi and the People's Democratic Republic of the Congo.

Rwanda's manufacturing sector contributes about 15%-18% of GDP and is dominated by the production of import substitutes for internal consumption. The larger enterprises produce beer, soft drinks, cigarettes, hoes, wheelbarrows, soap, cement, mattresses, plastic pipe, roofing materials and textiles. By mid-1997, up to 70% of the factories functioning before the war had returned to production, at an average of 75% of their capacity. Investments in the industrial sector continue to mostly be limited to the repair of existing industrial plants. Retail trade, devastated by the war, has revived quickly, with many new small businesses established by Rwandan returnees from Uganda, Burundi, and the People's Democratic Republic of the Congo.

Industry received little external assistance from the end of the war through 1995. In 1996-97, the government has become increasingly active in helping the industrial sector to restore production through technical and financial assistance, including loan guarantees, economic liberalization, and the privatization of state-owned enterprises. In early 1998, the government will set up a one-stop investment promotion center and implement a new investment code that should create an enabling environment for foreign and local investors. An autonomous revenue authority should also begin operation, improving collections and accountability.

Possibilities for economic expansion, however, are limited by inadequate infrastructure and transport and the small available market in this predominantly subsistence economy. Existing foreign investment is concentrated in commercial establishments, mining, tea, coffee, and tourism. Minimum wage and social security regulations are in force, and the four prewar independent trade unions are back in operation. The largest union, CESTRAR, was created as an organ of the government but became fully independent with the political reforms introduced by the 1991 constitution. As security in Rwanda improves, the country's nascent tourism sector may expand. Centered around the attractions of a population of mountain gorillas and a game park, tourism has potential as a source of foreign exchange if the country's tourism infrastructure is improved.

In the immediate postwar period--mid-1994 through 1995--emergency humanitarian assistance of over U.S. $307.4 million was largely directed to relief efforts in Rwanda and in the refugee camps in neighboring countries where Rwandans fled during the war. In 1996, humanitarian relief aid began to shift to reconstruction and development assistance. The United States, Belgium, the Federal Republic of Germany, Holland, France, China, the World Bank, the UN Development Program and the European Development Fund will continue to account for the substantial aid. Rehabilitation of government infrastructure, in particular the justice system, is an international priority, as is the continued repair and expansion of infrastructure, health facilities, and schools.

Rwanda's government-run radio broadcasts 15 hours a day in English, French and Kinyarwanda, the national languages. News programs include regular re-broadcasts from international radio such as Voice of America and Radio France International. There is a fledgling television station. There are several independent newspapers, mostly in Kinyarwanda, that publish on a weekly, biweekly, or monthly basis. Several Western nations, including the U.S., are working to encourage freedom of the press, the free exchange of ideas, and responsible journalism.

DEFENSE

The military establishment is comprised of an army and a paramilitary gendarmerie. Defense spending continues to represent a disproportionate share of the national budget, largely due to continuing security problems along the frontiers with the People's Democratic Republic of the Congo and Burundi in the aftermath of the war. The government has launched an ambitious plan to demobilize thousands of soldiers. Under the International Military and Training program, the U.S. has provided professional training for Rwandan military officers, especially in civil-military relations and respect for human rights.

ECONOMIC SITUATION AND OVERVIEW

With little industry, no railroads, and few natural resources, Habyarimana was forced to depend heavily on foreign aid to prop up the economy and secure his regime. The President skillfully doled out the benefits of foreign aid to key sectors of society, insuring that elites would support him. Eventually, the influx of foreign aid created a privileged class of ministers, army officers, administrators, and local officials at precisely the time the economy declined in the 1980s due to a drastic fall in coffee prices.

The differences between privilege and poverty in Rwanda were readily apparent as only a few Rwandans were physically robust and even overweight. With coffee prices down, export earnings fell by more than half. In bad years, it was not unusual for fully a third of the population to be chronically malnourished. Almost all salaried employment was through the state, and because government positions require literacy and other skills, access to education was a key determinant of economic security.

Rwanda's economy, with an annual income of $260 per person, is almost completely based on agriculture, with only eight percent of the people living in cities. 93 percent of the population works in agriculture, three percent in industry, and four percent in services. Rwanda is only 10,169 square miles with about eight million residents, giving it a population density of 312 per kilometer, the highest in black Africa. The population growth rate is 3.5 annually, the highest in Africa, and the annual birth rate is 52 per 1,000. The average family has eight children. Half the population is under age 15, with a life expectancy of 49 for males and 52 for females. 40 percent of hospitals and clinics are administered by the Catholic Church, hence family planning is a delicate issue.

With one of the lowest urbanization rates in Africa-- only about 8% of the population lives in towns - the majority of Rwandans are subsistence farmers. There are a few coffee and tea plantations and processing plants in the northern part of the country, but these industries suffered looting and destruction in 1994. With economic aid from the international community, tea and coffee are being rehabilitated and have reached pre-1994 production levels. Coffee is Rwanda's main export, accounting for 60% of the countries foreign exchange earnings. Tea accounts for about 30%. Rwanda has a small industrial sector that only employs about 3% of the population. Other than agricultural processing, there is also a brewery. The industrial sector was hard hit by the recent turmoil and has just begun to recover.

The Rwandan economy was completely devastated by war in 1990-1994. The present government is trying to help the economy recover by adopting a neo-liberal approach. This includes trying to increase the revenue from exports of coffee and tea by privatizing large sectors of this government run industry. There is also an attempt to diversify the type of foreign exchange earning exports. One of the major problems that the Rwandan economy is facing is that energy imports use more foreign exchange reserves than exports.

Another approach is to cut government spending by reducing the number of civil service employees and selling government run parastatals. Another serious obstacle that the recovery of the economy faces is that in Rwanda, as a landlocked country, transportation costs are high. With assistance from donor countries, and in cooperation with the East African community, Rwanda is planning to improve its transportation infrastructure. Rwanda is a poor country with an economy based largely on subsistence agriculture. The scarcity of arable land and a rapid rate of population growth has severely strained the country's efforts to develop its economy. Since 1959 Rwanda's political and social instability has had serious economic repercussions.

Intense demographic pressure, the shortage of arable land, and lack of access to the Indian Ocean have been three critical problems in Rwanda's economic development. New challenges arose in 1994 when severalsocial problems brought on catastrophic changes to the country's economy. These included the murder ofhundreds of thousands of Rwanda's citizens in ethnic violence, the flight of over a million, and the return of large numbers of refugees who had fled the country.

Today, Rwanda is slightly more urbanized than in 1993. Kigali's population has increased by nearly 100,000 and has now reached 300,000. Seventy percent of this new urban population consists of arrivals from rural areas. Nonetheless, Rwanda remains one of the least urbanized countries in Africa. Only 8% of the population lives in towns, an increase of only 5% since 1965. Most Rwandans continue to work as subsistence farmers. Virtually all potential farmland has been brought under cultivation, though some land has recently gone fallow because farmers have fled or been killed.

The Belgian colonial government converted Rwanda to a cash-based economy by setting up enforced tea and coffee production. These two crops have remained the country's main exports ever since. A policy to diversify the country's export base was implemented recently under an IMF-sponsored Structural Adjustment Program (SAP) launched in 1990, but this program was abandoned in 1994.

Rwanda`s government is the nation's main employer. Since independence, the ruling party has allocated government positions primarily according to a patronage system that rewards party loyalty and regional origin. After the political crisis of 1994 and the flight of much of the civil service, the new government promised to end the patronage system and to introduce strict criteria for competent performance in state employment. It has also pledged to privatize most parastatals. Rwanda's two most profitable parastatals, Electrogas and Rwandatel, which control the energy and telecommunications sectors respectively, are soon to be privatized.

A government policy encouraging over-cultivation of arable land with the aim of keeping out refugees was an important factor leading to the 1990 invasion. It has subsequently been changed to allow returnees to re-acquire their land, but implementation of the new policy has been beset by complications. Other measures orienting the economy towards the free market have been undertaken by the government. Tariff bands have been reduced. The Rwandan franc now floats freely. There are numerous independent foreign exchange bureaus in Kigali. Depositors may maintain foreign exchange accounts; expatriates may repatriate their money, unless it comes from sales of tea and coffee. In this case, they must change 90% of their moneys at a Rwandan bank.

The World Bank works closely with the Finance Ministry in formulating economic policy; together they recently announced a new growth plan for low inflation, privatization and aid directed at infrastructural recovery rather than emergency relief. Agricultural policy is aimed at improving the production of subsistence and commercial crops. Rwanda is still heavily dependent on international aid for food, though land cultivation increased by 34% and the amount of food harvested by 6% between 1996 and 1997.

The total cereal and pulse deficit for 1997 reached 192,000 tons. The government lacks resources to increase production significantly, and so strives to create a stable political climate, to ensure that farmers suffer no major disruptions, and to enable aid agencies to carry on their work. The government has also sought help from international donors to increase commercial agricultural production.

Rwanda's major exports are coffee, tea, tin cassiterite, Wolfframite, and pyrethrum. Coffee makes up between 50% to 80% of the total export. Because of declines in export earnings and increased need for imports, Rwanda's policy has been directed at ensuring that net private and official transfers are sufficient to keep the current account deficit at acceptable levels. The government also has taken steps to ensure that tea, coffee and industrial production at least maintains pre-war levels. The government has loosened restrictions on foreign exchange in an attempt to stimulate nontraditional exports. It has established reasonably tight control of its border with Uganda in an effort to reduce smuggling. Rwanda was unable to import or export goods easily through Uganda until the RPF came to power in 1994. This route now functions well. An alternative route through Tanzania to Dar es Salaam is more arduous and costly, although Tanzania has facilitated the operation of this route in efforts to compete with Mombassa in Kenya. Political insecurity has disrupted much of the trade between Rwanda and the Congo. Trade with Uganda is booming, in part because of family and business networks operated by returned refugees. The same was true of Burundi until neighboring countries imposed sanctions in 1996.

Rwanda is a member of three regional trade organizations: the Common Market for Eastern and Southern Africa (COMESA), the Communauté Economique des États de l'Afrique (CEEAC), and the Communauté Economique des Pays des Grands Lacs (CEPGL). The country has also made a bid to join the East African Cooperation (EAC).

Rwanda's economy is almost exclusively agriculturally based. More than 90% of the population makes its livelihood by producing food crops or through industrial work involving the processing of crops. Agriculture contributes more than 40% of the nation's GDP. The most fertile agricultural areas in the country are the mountain regions forming the Congo-Nile watershed and the central plateau, where two crops can normally be harvested each year. Principal food crops include bananas, sweet potatoes, cassava, sorghum and beans.
Principal export crops include coffee, tea, pyrethrum, cotton and cinchona.

Cattle have played an important political and social role in the country under the Tutsi, whose dominance was traditionally based on the ubuhake (a feudal patron-client relationship based on possession of cattle). Most farmers have some livestock, though animal husbandry is generally considered a supplemental source of income.

Fishing in Rwanda is underexploited. Lake Kivu is well-stocked and could support an annual catch of 5,000 tons. The potential of Lake Ihema has also underutilized.

Manufacturing is a relatively minor source of Rwanda's revenue, employing about three percent of the labor force and contributing only about 17% of the nation's GDP. The small manufacturing sector is based on processing agricultural products and low-technology consumer items such as beer, matches, sugar, and soap. Industry suffered severe setbacks in 1994, when many skilled workers were put to death or were forced to flee. Half of the country's 120 working factories were damaged or looted.

DEBT REDUCTION PROGRAM

Rwanda stands at a critical point in its history. The country's people are seeking to rebuild a society shattered by war and a genocide in which one in eight Rwandans - Tutsi and Hutu opponents of the government's extremist policies - was killed, and which further led to the outflow of over one and a half million refugees. Since the 1994 conflict, poverty levels have increased dramatically, the health-care and education systems have collapsed, and the economic infrastructure has been shattered. Conflict in Rwanda continues to have enormous destabilizing effects on all the neighboring countries, including the Democratic Republic of Congo, Burundi, Tanzania, and Uganda. In turn, conflicts across the region affect Rwanda. There is an urgent need for peace, security, and poverty reduction.

Despite notable efforts to reconstruct the country, Rwanda remains in need of massive international assistance if it is to enjoy a peaceful and prosperous future. But aid alone is not enough. The present peace is partial and fragile, and Rwanda continues to face serious security concerns. Internally, conflict has been largely concentrated in the country's north-west. The security situation has improved in recent months but continues to cause concern. Rwanda has also been involved in the conflict in neighboring Democratic Republic of Congo, arguing that this has been necessary to defend Rwanda against attacks by the Interahamwe. Such conflict continues to threaten lives and livelihoods across the entire region. A renewed respect for human rights - economic, social, civil, and political rights - is needed, to break the cycle of violence, and to restore the rule of law.

Fifty years ago, political leaders in Europe and the US embarked on a concerted post-war reconstruction strategy, driven partly by the fear that failure to restore hope, and the opportunity for economic recovery, to a continent devastated by war would create the potential for a return to conflict. Today, Rwanda stands at a similar cross-roads - and it needs a similar sense of political purpose and integrated effort. Failure in the reconstruction project will exacerbate social tensions, increase poverty and insecurity, and raise the likelihood of intensified conflict not only in Rwanda, but across the region. The international community has a moral obligation to use all the means at its disposal to avert such a crisis. But it also has a self-interest in acting decisively now. As Rwanda's recent tragic history has underlined, crisis prevention is far less costly than responding to another humanitarian crisis.

THE PROTECTION OF BASIC RIGHTS

Peace cannot last, and recovery cannot be sustained until the basic human rights of all Rwandans are recognized and respected. Debt directly limits the provision of basic life necessities: thousands of people do not have access to clean water; children die of diarrhoea and other preventable diseases; many people do not have access to affordable health-care.

These are violations of human rights. This is not to suggest that debt is the only cause of human rights' violations. The conflict between the Rwandan Patriotic Army (RPA) and insurgent groups in Rwanda's north-west and DRC has resulted in the manipulation and abuse of civilian populations. Human-rights groups, including African Rights and Amnesty International, have reported that both the RPA and insurgent groups are responsible for the indiscriminate killing of civilians. Some people are subject to extra-judicial arrest. The failure to address all these human-rights abuses also threatens Rwanda's future. Although the Rwandan Government has legitimate security concerns, military expenditure threatens to eclipse social spending. The Government needs to ensure that its own policies do not jeopardize the reconstruction project.

POVERTY REDUCTION ACTIVITY

The fulfilment of basic rights in Rwanda will require a radical reduction in poverty. Rwanda is one of the world's poorest countries. Seventy per cent of all households live below the meagre poverty line. Not only are more Rwandans living in poverty now than at the start of the decade;

those living in poverty have also become poorer. Almost one in five children born this year will die before they reach their fifth birthday.

Half of the adult population is unable to read and write. These appalling indicators, and the human suffering that lies behind them, have steadily worsened in the wake of the catastrophic events of 1994. Violent conflict and the return of refugees in late 1996, have placed additional pressures on the country's under-funded social sector and ravaged infrastructure. Poverty reduction in Rwanda is not only an urgent priority in itself, it is also a necessary condition of social and political stability.

Despite this bleak picture of rising poverty and continued conflict in parts of Rwanda and across its borders, there is also cause for hope. Rwandans, with the support of the international community, have begun the painstaking reconstruction of their society and economy. The Rwandan Government has already made budget commitments to poverty reduction, in particular by increasing its social-sector spending for 1999.

But while donors have given substantial assistance to develop a framework for poverty reduction, their response to Rwanda's great and urgent needs has often been too slow, insufficient, and incoherent. Rwanda continues to spend scarce resources on debt-servicing, at a time when the pace of the reconstruction program appears to be slowing. Once the limits of recovery-based growth are reached, rapid, broad-based growth will depend on further resources being released for priority social investment.

THE COST OF INDEBTEDNESS

The facts of Rwanda's debt tell their own story. Debt stock has doubled over the past five years to more than US$1bn stock in nominal terms, over five times the value of Rwanda's exports. Repayments are absorbing almost one third of foreign exchange earnings and one quarter of government revenues. Using the debt-sustainability criteria adopted under the IMF-World Bank Highly Indebted Poor Countries (HIPC) initiative, Rwanda's debt is unsustainable. It will remain so until well into the next decade - Rwanda will not qualify for comprehensive debt relief under the HIPC framework until 2003, or later. Although bilateral creditors have reduced their claims, the impact has been limited, because multilateral debt accounts for over 80% of Rwanda's debt stock.

Rwanda's parlous position underlines the shortcomings of the HIPC framework, which has provided too little debt relief, too late. This delay results from the requirement that eligible countries must adhere to two consecutive IMF programs over a six year period. The limited benefits which have resulted for eligible countries reflect the fact that the debt-sustainability targets have been set at levels which are too high for heavily indebted poor countries. For a country such as Rwanda, which faces a combination of unsustainable debt and extreme reconstruction needs, the HIPC framework is grossly inadequate.

In the interests of stability and improved self-reliance, an immediate ceiling must be set on repayment levels, at no more than 10% of public spending levels; and the debt reduction framework must be accelerated. Early implementation of HIPC debt relief in 1999 could make available an extra US$31.8m for the Government budget, enough to finance an immediate phasing-out of user fees in health-care and education, as well as provide funds for training and better materials for schools and health centers. If a 'poverty window' were created which provided incentives for the Rwandan Government to invest savings in priority social sectors and basic infrastructure, such early treatment under the HIPC initiative could act as a catalyst for economic recovery and human development gains.

OVERCOMING ETHNIC CONFLICTA

As violent clashes continue to occur in Rwanda and beyond its borders, with reports of serious human rights abuses by all sides in those conflicts, and as many of Rwanda's people slip deeper into poverty, it is essential that the international community uses fast and deep debt relief as part of a wider strategy of building peace, reducing poverty, and fostering greater respect for human rights and international humanitarian law. This requires action on many fronts - by the Rwandan Government, donors, NGOs - and a form of contractual agreement about these actors' respective roles and responsibilities. At the heart of this approach is a strengthened dialogue between the international community and the people and Government of Rwanda.

Such a strategy will only be effective if, as a result of strengthened and sustained dialogue, all parties make commitments which they are prepared to be held accountable to. All parties should agree to a clear and costed poverty-reduction plan with explicit benchmarks and targets, as well as mechanisms to monitor performance. The plan should focus on outcomes, including targets for strategies to strengthen Rwandan judicial and human rights institutions, and ensure greater participation by Rwanda's people in the decisions that affect their lives.

Rwanda's involvement in the DRC conflict has threatened to scupper the possibilities for such dialogue, as donors' articulate concerns about the diversion of scarce funds to the war effort. There has been little political will among donors to provide Rwanda with the exceptional help it needs. Rwanda's people cannot afford such delays or diversion of resources. An end to the war in DRC and the speedy disbursal of aid are both important for the country. What is critical is that the Rwandan Government can assure donors that deeper, swifter debt relief will be effectively used for fighting poverty, not fomenting conflict. On their part, donors must be able to show Rwanda that assistance is a realistic prospect, ensure that:

- HIPC debt relief is provided during 1999-2000.

- A fiscal cap of 10 % is placed on debt-service claims.

- Increased funds are provided to reduce the burden of multilateral debt during the interim period.

- Donors make clear commitments to provide substantial human and financial resources for a poverty-reduction plan with clear targets on the increase of poor people's access to economic opportunities and basic social services.

- Disbursal should be calibrated with progress towards the benchmarks and targets agreed with the Rwandan government.

- All UN members co-operate more fully with UN Security Council resolution 978, which requires international action to arrest and extradite those suspected of genocide in Rwanda.

- Resources are directed at the continued rebuilding and strengthening of Rwanda's judicial system, and the establishment of an independent and impartial National Human Rights commission.

Rwandan Government should be urged to fulfill its stated commitments to reduce poverty, avert further conflict, and respect human rights by:

- Allocating resources from debt relief to a clear and costed poverty-reduction plan which has clear targets on increasing poor people's access to economic opportunities, education, and health-care.

- Ensuring that the overall policy and expenditure framework is coherent with the aims of poverty reduction and reconstruction. This requires that scarce Government resources are not diverted from health-care and education into military expenditure, and that all possible measures are taken to reduce military expenditure.

- Establishing full budget transparency, in order to demonstrate the use of debt relief for poverty reduction. The Government should fulfill its commitment under the 1998 Budget Law to consolidate all revenues and expenditure in the budget, and to prohibit extra-budgetary expenditure.

- Fulfilling commitments to involve non-government actors, such as civil society, in the scrutiny of expenditure and the assessment of expenditure against priorities.

- Establishing mechanisms for joint monitoring of the use of finance by the Government, donors, and Rwandan civil-society groups.

- Expediting the process of decentralisation to include civil society in decision-making, and to equip and entrust local government with the management of local development budgets, and rooting out corruption.

- Denouncing, investigating, and punishing all war crimes, extra-judicial killings, and violations of humanitarian law, regardless of the identity of the perpetrator.

Inevitably, there will be financial costs associated with this strategy. But these costs must be set against the potential for achieving human development gains and increased self-reliance. They must also be considered in the light of the threats posed to the entire reconstruction process by unsustainable debt.

REDUCING POWERTY

Seventy per cent of Rwandans live below the poverty line, and are in desperate need of equitable, broad-based economic growth. Yet economic recovery remains incomplete. Today, GDP is only 85% of its 1990 levels, and underemployment is threatening social stability in urban areas. Devising strategies for economic growth which provide viable opportunities for the poor to earn a livelihood is a priority. Export diversification will also be crucial to a convincing economic recovery. Yet the options are limited. Over 90% of
Rwanda's population work in agriculture, typically on small plots of deteriorating quality. Rwanda is overwhelmingly dependent on two primary commodities, tea and coffee, for its small foreign exchange earnings. International prices for both are highly volatile.

A PROFILE OF RWANDA'S DEBT

Like other HIPCs, Rwanda's heavy indebtedness is the result both of domestic policy failings, and of external events beyond Government control. In common with other African countries, Rwanda borrowed heavily in the late 1970s and early 1980s. While some of this borrowing was wasted, much of it was invested prudently in physical infrastructure and clean water systems. But the total stock of external debt rose rapidly after 1985, as regional recession and a collapse in world coffee prices hit the Government's earnings.

After 1990, Government revenue-raising capacity was further constrained by escalating conflict in the north of the country. Between 1990 and 1995, Government revenue as a percentage of GDP fell from 10% to 7%, one
of the lowest ratios in sub-Saharan Africa. At the same time, society became increasingly militarized as communal tensions and violence increased. Public spending on arms rose sharply, crowding out social sector budgets. Poverty levels rose, and investment fell. Against this backdrop, the Government soon found it was unable to meet the demands of creditors. Arrears rapidly accumulated, and the debt stock became increasingly unsustainable. Between 1985 and 1997, the stock of external debt more than doubled, from US$400m to over US$1bn. Rwanda also built up a large public domestic debt, reaching the equivalent of US$220m in mid-1997.

Rwanda's external debt indicators

Net present value/GDP	**65%**
Net present value/exports	**557%**
Debt service/exports	**32%**
Debt service/government revenues	**23%**

In common with other African HIPCs, the share of the multilateral creditors in Rwanda's external debt has steadily risen, as the debt crisis has progressed. Today, over 80% of Rwanda's debt is owed to multilateral creditors, the highest proportion of multilateral debt owed among the HIPCs. The HIPC initiative was designed to resolve the multilateral debt problem, by requiring for the first time that multilateral creditors reduce their claims in conjunction with bilateral and commercial creditors.

DEBT STOCK

At the end of 1997, Rwanda's external debt stood at US$1164m including arrears. This debt is large even by the standards of other HIPCs, and equivalent to 65% of Rwandan GDP. US$947m is owed to multilateral creditors; 48% of the total external debt - US$558m - is highly concessional debt owed to the International Development Association (IDA), the World Bank's 'soft loan' arm. A further US$203m (17% of the total external debt) is owed to the African Development Bank (ADB). Only 16% of the total external debt was owed
to bilateral creditors at the end of 1997, and 6% owed to the Paris Club. In descending order, the principal bilateral creditors at the end of 1995 were: France (US$54m), Saudi Arabia (US$27m), Kuwait (US$18m), China (US$14m) and Japan (US$14m). Private debt amounted to only US$18m, less than 2% of the total. Figure 1 illustrates the distribution of Rwandan debt at the end of 1997.

DEBT SERVICE

Debt-service repayments due in 1997 totaled US$35.78m, equivalent to 32% of Rwanda's export earnings. This represents more than the operational health-care and education sector expenditures combined. On 23 July 1998, 67% of Rwanda's Paris Club debts were rescheduled according to the Naples terms. This is a welcome measure, but it will have limited impact because of the small size of bilateral debt. While the application of Naples terms will reduce Government debt repayments to bilaterals by US$76m in 1998 - US$63m of it arrears - and by about US$15m in 1999 and 2000, scheduled debt-servicing is nonetheless set to rise steeply over the next three years.

In 2001, total scheduled debt service is set to reach US$60.6m, and it is projected to fall only slightly in 2003. More than a third of this increase is accounted for by IMF debt. This represents only 4% of debt stock, but one
fifth of debt-servicing, because the Fund's lending terms are less concessional than those of other multilateral creditors. Working even with the most optimistic economic growth projections,

Rwanda's crippling debt will not fall until well into the next decade, threatening to compromise reconstruction efforts in the process. On the basis of the optimistic export growth projections of the IMF and World Bank, conventional debt rescheduling by itself would leave Rwanda with a debt to export ratio of 360% in 2003.

MULTILATERAL TRUST FUND

Creditors have recognized that Rwanda will continue to carry a heavy debt burden before a sustained debt-relief strategy is in place, and that conventional treatment would be inadequate. Therefore a proposal has been made for a World Bank-managed Multilateral Debt Trust Fund (MDTF), which will aim to cover about one third of servicing on multilateral IDA and ADB debts over the next three years. The fund will support Rwanda's balance of payments and could help avoid a build-up of arrears with bilateral creditors and delay in the Government's reform program. It will also make available significant funds in the recurrent budget, which can be directed to priority sectors. But the US$17m a year on offer under the MDTF remains an inadequate sum compared to the amount of total external debt-servicing - US$197m payable through to 2001.

EFFORTS TO BECOME INDEBTEDNESS

Behind the figures and flow charts used to summarize debt problems, there are human faces. In Rwanda's case, they are the faces of children who are denied the opportunity to learn, because their Government is expected to prioritise debt repayment over education. They are the faces of the fifty thousand infants born this year who will die before their first birthday, most of them from diseases which could be easily prevented by the transfer of only a fraction of debt-service repayments to clean water and primary health-care provision.

Debt-servicing at current levels carries high social costs, especially in a country like Rwanda. As it is shown in the table below, child mortality, literacy, and nutritional indicators are extremely poor, and have deteriorated significantly since 1992. The health of Rwandans has suffered dramatically. Maternal mortality has almost quadrupled since 1990, and severe wasting of children has increased more than sevenfold. The genocide in 1994 and its devastating aftermath eroded the Government's revenue base and its capacity to deliver basic services. In 1997, the UNDP ranked Rwanda 174th out of 175 countries, using a composite of welfare indicators in its human-development index. Prior to the genocide, Rwanda's human-development indicators were better than the regional average.

With a predominantly rural population engaged in smallholder farming, and a small and poorly developed export base, the scope for raising additional revenues remains limited. In 1995, a year after the genocide, government revenues were only 7% of GDP, among the lowest in sub-Saharan Africa. While economic recovery has been rapid, it remains incomplete. Real GDP in 1997 reached only 85% of its 1990 levels. Per capita GDP amounts to only US$200.

Rwanda's deteriorating human development - 1992 and 1996

Indicator	1992	1996
GNP per capita (US$)	250	209
Infant mortality rate*	85	125
Child mortality rate*	141	185
Illiteracy - aged 10+ (%)	56	60
Severe wasting- under-fives (%)	0.7	5.3

* (per 10,000 live births) Source: UNICEF 1998

HEALTH AND EDUCATION

There is an urgent need for public investment in health-care and education, in water-provision and livelihoods projects, and in demobilization programs. Yet debt-service repayments continue to crowd out social-sector spending. Last year, for every Rwandan child, woman, and man US$5 were spent on servicing the external debt, but only 50 cents were spent for each Rwandan on the operational health budget, and US$2 per capita on capital investments. While the spending situation in education does not seem quite so dire as in health-care, Rwanda massively under-invests in its children, even in comparison with other sub-Saharan African countries. Rwanda allocates approximately US$12 to recurrent spending on primary education for each primary-age child, whereas the regional average is US$49. In this context, it is important to remember that per capita debt-servicing is set to almost double over the next three years.

BUDGET CONSTRAINTS

In effect, external debt problems are eroding the Rwandan government's capacity to direct domestic resources to where they are most needed. Last year, servicing the external debt absorbed US$35m, one quarter of the entire budget. This is equivalent to more than the health-care and education operational budgets combined.

Although social-sector expenditure is projected to rise by 30% this year, proportionately the burden of debt service repayments will remain heavy, since total debt service is rising. For ordinary Rwandans the costs of this resource diversion are high.

- Over 800,000 children of primary school age are not enrolled in school.
- Children who are in school often learn little, because almost half of all teachers have no training, and basic materials such as books, pencils, and school furniture are often lacking.
- 55% of primary health centers are in urgent need of physical rehabilitation.
- 120,000 unaccompanied children - most of them traumatized by violence - are in need of support services and appropriate education.
- Water supplies need rapid new investments. One third of all installations were damaged in 1994, and a quarter of people in rural areas are without access to potable water. Clean water for all would prevent over 6,000 child deaths annually from diarrhea, as well as improving the health of the wider population.

AID DEPENDENCE

The Government's Program d'Investissements Publics, (PIP), which ran from 1996-98, sought to address these reconstruction needs. One third of its budget was allocated to human resources and social development. But, while the US$52m earmarked for reintegration of refugees and displaced people, health-care and population planning, and for primary and secondary education, represented a valuable contribution to Rwanda's short- and medium-term needs, the PIP was almost entirely dependent on outside donors. Unsustainable debt has helped create a dependence on aid.

While ongoing aid, together with access to export markets, has a key role to play in Rwanda's reconstruction, current levels of dependence on external assistance for the social sectors raises serious doubts about the sustainability of interventions under the PIP, and subsequent programs. In education and in health-care, many of the social and economic benefits come through only in the longer term. The integration and reconciliation process programs like the PIP is intended to contribute to will require substantial resources for at least a decade, if poverty reduction and political stability are to become realities. But donor funding is unreliable, and it cannot be assumed that current levels of external assistance will be maintained beyond the next few years.

Substantial and quick debt relief would help to provide a far more sustainable financial basis for reconstruction than can be achieved by donor support alone. With commitments from government to use budget savings from debt relief to meet reconstruction targets, debt relief could provide a sustainable foundation for Rwanda's recovery into the next century. Imaginative incentives, rather than further conditionalities, must be created which provide the Rwandan government with opportunities to meet their poverty eradication targets.

DEBT RELIEF PROSPECTS UNDER THE HIPC INITIATIVE

Because of the structure of Rwanda's debt, the country urgently needs multilateral debt reduction. Even after receiving bilateral debt reduction on Naples terms, it will continue to spend close to one third of export earnings on debt-service in 2001. Unfortunately, under existing rules, Rwanda is unlikely to qualify for multilateral debt reduction for up to six years. Even then, it is far from certain whether it will receive a level of debt reduction commensurate with its needs.

The failure so far on the part of the creditor community to establish a closer link between debt relief and poverty reduction is one of the HIPC initiative's major shortcomings. Despite the changes made to the HIPC framework at the G7 summit in Cologne, access to HIPC remains determined partly by the debtor country's success in meeting conditions set under IMF programs, and partly by estimates of debt sustainability. These criteria for access to HIPC will probably result in Rwanda receiving too little debt relief, too late.

TIME FRAME

Part of the problem facing Rwanda derives from the eligibility criteria for entry to the HIPC initiative. Broadly, all candidates are required to complete two consecutive IMF programs over a six-year period. This arrangement is intended to avert problems of moral hazard, although an element of flexibility has been
introduced, whereby a country's past track record of compliance with IMF programs can be taken into account. Oxfam International believes that, in requiring Rwanda to wait for six years, insufficient weight is being attached to the country's track record.

The new Rwandan Government began a reform program in 1995, one year after the genocide, which was closely monitored by the IMF. The early stages concentrated on trade and fiscal areas, and, even though the new Government was faced with many pressures, the IMF and World Bank have judged their performance to be 'satisfactory'. In June 1998 the government signed up to a three-year Enhanced Structural Adjustment Facility (ESAF), which was soon followed by a flow rescheduling on Naples terms. The ESAF is a detailed
reform program, enforced by loan conditionality, which is designed to improve both resource mobilization and human development, while also accelerating public-sector restructuring. Privatization, improved social-sector performance, and further investment in the reconciliation process are being supported.

According to the IMF and the wider donor community, Rwanda's track record begins in 1998, with the new ESAF program. On this basis, Rwanda can expect to reach decision point in 2000 at the earliest, and may wait until 2001. Full debt relief under HIPC may not take place until 2004. Oxfam International takes the view that three years of track record have been established since 1995, and that the advent of the new Government, rather than 1998, should mark the start of this period of track-record accumulation. If this view is adopted, and if the creditor community recognizes the country's special needs, a decision on debt relief can
be made this year.

DEBT SUSTAINABILITY

Debt sustainability under the HIPC initiative is decided by applying a sustainability threshold of 150% for the debt to exports ratio (NPV/XGS), and a threshold of 15% for the debt service to exports ratio (TDS/XGS). These were lowered at the Cologne summit from 200-250% for NPV/XGS and from 20-25% for TDS/XGS. Since countries prior to Cologne received debt relief close to the bottom end of the sustainability band, the additional relief is likely to be either modest or negligible for most of the HIPCs.

There is little doubt that, even with the maximum amount of bilateral debt relief, Rwanda will qualify for HIPC on the export criteria. Between 1997 and 2004, the ratio of net present value debt (NPV) to exports is projected by the World Bank to fall only slightly from 393% to 358%. Moreover, this is a best-case scenario, arrived at by using the IMF's optimistic export projections indicated in the table below, which understate the extent of debt relief required. According to the Fund's projections, Rwanda's exports will grow by 65% in only seven years, from US$101m in 1997 to US$168m in 2004.

As a small, landlocked, overwhelmingly rural and low-skill economy, dependent on tea and coffee for an average of 80% of foreign exchange earnings, Rwanda will have to achieve rapid diversification into higher value-added manufacturing and services industries if these targets are going to be met. The IMF's projections also ignore the potential for continued low-level conflict and instability in the country, which will make growth precarious for some time to come. The IMF has projected that manufacturing's share of export earnings will increase from 14% in 1997 to 34% in 2004. So far, there are few signs of this happening, and foreign direct investment has been disappointing since the reform program began.

Past export-growth rates suggest more modest rates of export growth, with volatile prices and volumes for coffee and tea leading to marked fluctuations year on year. While the IMF has a 'downward projection' to account for the possibility of external shocks, their estimate remains extremely high, projecting a 57%
increase in export earnings over 1997-2004. In contrast, using a sample seven-year period from 1986-1993 gives a dramatically different picture of where Rwanda might be in 2004, especially with the debt-service ratio almost doubling (see Table 3). From the IMF's point of view, there are good reasons for systematically underestimating a country's debt burden, and minimising the costs to itself of HIPC debt relief. Yet without unprecedented export growth, Rwanda's debt-service ratio will rapidly become unsustainable, and further arrears will accumulate. Far deeper and faster relief than is currently provided for under the HIPC initiative is needed to avoid this outcome.

The debt-service ratio under IMF export projections, and less optimistic projection (US$m)

	Total exports	Debt service	TDS/XGS
1997	101.0	35.8	35.4%
2003/4 IMF upward projections	168.0	58.6	34.0%
2003/4 IMF downward projections	159.0	58.6	36.8%
past record projected*	106.5	58.6	63.4%

Source: IMF 1998

THE CASE FOR EARLY ACTION

Although Rwanda is highly likely to become eligible for special relief under HIPC on the export criteria, the track record conditions threaten to jeopardise the reconstruction process. While the Cologne initiative promises flexibility in interpreting track record, the IMF remains the arbiter of whether or not a country has performed exceptionally under ESAF. The fact that the Cologne initiative has further strengthened the IMF's role as gatekeeper in HIPCs does not inspire confidence. Two thirds of ESAF programs go off track as a result either of delay or interruption; while given that the strongest reformers under ESAF have already gone through the HIPC process, there is little reason to believe that Rwanda will not be required to meet the track record criterion of two uninterrupted ESAF programs.

This condition is designed to guard against 'moral hazard', on the basis that unless the preconditions of debt relief are sufficiently onerous, there is little incentive for countries to borrow responsibly in the future. Oxfam International agrees that there is a need for some form of track record. However, the process is unduly protracted, and linking eligibility to compliance with IMF programs has in practice slowed down the process further. Moreover, ESAF has proved to be a poor tool for promoting the international poverty reduction targets for 2015 to which the major IMF are committed. The failure to develop ESAF conditionalities
in the context of these poverty reduction commitments has resulted in a fragmented approach to conditionality, and in the subordination of long-term development goals to short-term macroeconomic criteria. Oxfam International believes that eligibility for HIPC debt relief should be determined on the basis of a more integrated approach, in which poverty reduction concerns are placed at the heart of macro-economic policy design.

Rwandans cannot afford to wait for debt relief from HIPC while creditors concern themselves with insuring against what they perceive as a 'moral hazard', least of all when the track record is based on as flawed a program as ESAF. Even with additional transitional measures such as the Multilateral Debt Trust Fund, Rwandans cannot afford to wait. The changes to HIPC announced at Cologne promise interim multilateral debt flow relief between decision and completion point, with the International Financial Institutions (IFIs) providing debt flow relief to match that offered by the Paris Club.

Potentially, this could generate significant gains for Rwanda, given the large portion of its debt stock owed to multilaterals. Yet there is cause also for skepticism. So far there has been no explicit statement on the level at which the IFIs will provide interim relief, and the benefits have therefore not been quantified. Oxfam believes that sufficient debt flow relief between decision and completion point should be provided to bring servicing down to completion point levels, freeing up significant additional resources for necessary investment in poverty reduction.

Indeed, without debt relief that goes beyond HIPC mechanisms, the reconstruction process will be slowed, risking a descent into further poverty and violence. Delay could incur a heavy cost in terms of human lives, as well as in terms of recurrent emergency interventions. Rwanda's experience points to the inadequacies of the existing HIPC framework for countries emerging from conflict in three respects.

First, any country which has experienced a widespread conflict, violent change of government, and the economic and social upheaval associated with sudden political change, is unlikely to have an uninterrupted track record of reform under IMF programs. Second, conflict leaves reconstruction needs which go beyond the normal challenges associated with debt in poor countries. Finally, excessive debt makes it more likely that post-conflict countries will fail to implement successful adjustment programs, and jeopardise their access to aid and debt relief in the process.

CONVERTING DEBT INTO DEVELOPMENT

In the case of Rwanda, early implementation of HIPC could generate significant budget savings. In 1999 alone, projected debt-servicing would be reduced by 69%, to about $16m, or 6% of revenue. The US$37.25m of funds thus released could finance an immediate phasing-out of user fees in health-care and education, as well as contribute to complementary qualitative interventions. This would help raise private demand for basic social provision, and extend access to the poorest households, for whom user fees are a major deterrent to medical care and school enrolment. If a 'poverty window' were created which provided incentives for the Rwandan Government to invest a major proportion of these savings in priority social sectors and basic infrastructure, perhaps through government sectoral plans of action, then early treatment under HIPC could act as a catalyst for economic recovery and human development gains.

Implementing HIPC in 1999 (US$m unless otherwise stated)

	NPV	TDS	XGS	NPV/XGS	TDS/XGS
1999 projections	724.1	53.6	109.0	664.3%	49.2%
After HIPC*	163.5	16.35	109.0	150.0%	15.0%
Reduction	560.6	37.25	- -	514.3%	34.2%

IMF 1998 * at NPV/XGS of150%, and TDS/XGS of 15%

Inevitably, each country emerging from conflict must be considered on its merits. But as a broad principle, Oxfam International believes that where post-conflict countries demonstrate a commitment to effective pro-poor spending, they should be provided with debt-relief arrangements which free resources at a level commensurate with needs. The alternative to early action on Rwanda's debt is an ongoing diversion of scarce resources away from reconstruction needs to creditors. Debt servicing is projected to increase to $60m in 2001, 60% of it owed to multilateral creditors. If debt relief was provided this year, rather than in 2004, it would release an additional $195m over five years; sufficient to almost double annual education spending in a country where on current trends 1.2 million children will be out of school in 2015.

Debt is not the only problem facing Rwanda, whose peace is partial and fragile. Resolving conflict in the north-west, adhering to the DRC cease-fire accord, reducing the diversion of scarce resources into military expenditure, and developing coherent policies for poverty reduction are among the necessary measures. This requires action on many fronts - by the Rwandan government, donors, NGOs, and civil society. Nor is debt relief the only solution for Rwanda's problems. But the debt problem, left unresolved, will contribute to wider pressures endangering Rwanda's development prospects. Rwanda's debt burden is a fundamental obstacle to the reconstruction and rehabilitation efforts of the Rwandan Government and members of the international community. It is diverting scarce resources away from priority social sectors and the infrastructure, and hampering economic recovery. The HIPC framework has so far proven inadequate in tackling the problems of unsustainable debt in a country emerging from conflict. The creditor community must develop more flexible mechanisms for substantial, and fast, debt relief as a matter of priority. Without a new debt agenda which focuses on basic rights, an opportunity for reconstruction and development will be squandered.

INTERNATIONAL ASSISTANCE TO RWANDA

ECONOMIC ASSISTNANCE STRATEGY

The Government of Rwanda is interested in ensuring proper donor co-ordination to enhance the several reforms it is undertaking. The best way to coordinate aid is through the budget reform where Government spending is reflected through a comprehensive, prioritized, programme and output oriented budget. Currently, the Government intends to move away from focusing on inputs and towards the delivery of goods and services and the outcomes of those services. Accordingly, the budget process will concentrate on ensuring:

Transparency

By having clearly defined sector objectives, outputs and activities; allowing participation of civic society in the budget process, and improving the management of the budget.

Comprehensiveness

By creating a consistent, predictable National Policy and Budget Framework and including all Government expenditure in an integrated (recurrent and development) budget.

Prioritization

By defining the role of Government and ensuring priority programmes and activities are allocated the required resources to execute that role.

Reliability

Through proper estimation of all resources, both domestic and external.

In order to achieve these objectives, the donor community has to assist the effort at each of these stages:

Transparency

By clarifying **all the activities they are undertaking in Rwanda.**

Comprehensiveness

By providing **full information on all the expenditure they are supporting** either within the Government budget or outside the budget.

Prioritization

Through ensuring that their **funding only goes to the Government determined priority sector/ programme/ project activities, and through the Government budget.**

Reliability

By providing information on the **amounts that will actually be disbursed** towards the activities of the Government of Rwanda **by specific time frames.** This will enable Government to make reliable resources forecasts over the years.

THE ROLE OF THE GOVERNMENT

Over the next three years, the Government will create a consistent, predictable National Policy and Budget Framework through which ministries are provided with reliable ceilings within which to achieve agreed upon outcomes (see MTEF Action Plan 2000-2002). This will entail developing a clear and concise national policy with a medium term (three-year) fiscal strategy. To move away from input oriented budgeting, the Government will also introduce missions, objectives and outputs for each ministry, which will be the basis for the ministries to design measurable output oriented budgets. Financial management will be improved by using a more computerized budget accounting and monitoring system, and provision of flash reports to donors. The coming into being of the Office of the Auditor General is also one aspect of improving accountability. The budget will be comprehensive by including all resources and all expenditures, using standard programme classification. Therefore projects financed outside the Government budget will have to be brought in.

The budget calendar, which reflects the specific activities to be undertaken, is given in Annual Buget Calendar, with highlights of some activities related to donor participation.

With regard to fiscal transparency, the Government of Rwanda has made a start in certain areas.The role of Government has been defined and will continue to be better defined in the exercise of developing specific ministry missions, objectives and outputs. Fiscal law is in preparation to govern the management of the budget. National Accounts will be published annually reflecting the outturn of the Government operations in any previous year, and accessible to the general public. With improved preparation and presentation of the budget, it will be possible to indicate the major/ priority activities that the Government is undertaking, in the Budget statements. A statement on the macroeconomic framework, through which the budget is framed, will be made. The macroeconomic framework is being developed using a multidisciplinary team of experts/ officials. A more computerized accounting and reporting system is being developed, and it is intended to include none financial data on achievements planned and accomplished. In all this, a timetable of activities will be produced.

THE ROLE OF DONORS

The Current Situation

In Rwanda, where externally financed budget support provides an important part ofrecurrent financing, the predictability of the budget is highly influenced by the nature of the financial agreements for this budget support. At present, most of these arrangements are annual rather than multi-year and typically subject to complex and often inter-locking conditions. In this context, it is very difficult, if not impossible, for approved budget allocations to be fully honoured by MINECOFIN on timely basis.

The management of external resources, which form a large proportion of the budget, is not harmonised.Also, a significant amount of external financial support to public sector activities is provided off budget and often with little, if any, information on disbursements remitted to MINECOFIN.

Consequences

As a consequence, off-budget funding reduces the comprehensiveness of the budget and, in the process undermines the ability of MINECOFIN (and indeed of Cabinet) to impose a hard-budget constraint on spending ministries. The “MTEF Contract” relies on a guaranteed firm budget ceiling being imposed on line ministries in exchange for the achievement of a pre-agreed set of output targets.

What Needs to be Done

If this situation is to change, it will be necessary:

To simplify the conditions for accessing budget support and ensure their mutual consistency;

To introduce multi-year rather than annual arrangements; and ideally

To introduce arrangements with an appropriate aid agency which might provide some sort of “funding of last resort” role to give “insurance” to budget allocations in the event of slippages in the disbursement of budget support or major external shocks to tax and customs revenues.

The long-term objective of the budget reform which has taken the form of a Medium Term Expenditure Framework (MTEF) is to develop integrated three-year estimates. This will be based on the planned outputs by each ministry, reflecting the predetermined objectives. Projects are one means of achieving objectives. Other activities carried out by ministries are also a means of achieving specific objectives. It is therefore essential to look at all the activities of a ministry and agree on the overall outputs to be produced and the objectives to be achieved.

The implementation of the budget depends on the availability of funds at the right time. The estimates of resources therefore need to be accurate and with a clear flow over the three-year period, as well as within each financial year. This can be achieved if donors provide the Government with reliable information on what levels of assistance they will provide over the three-year period and the possible flow during each year.As the budget process provides better information, with improved accountability and transparency, the need for specific project financing will fall away and be replaced by programme financing. The ultimate goal will be budget support. With clear objectives and specific outputs elaborated in the budget, monitoring will focus on the outputs and thus reporting will be standardised.

Currently, the Government is seeking from its development partners the following:

Off budget resources to be brought into the budget. The actual accounting for these resources may initially be different from the Government accounting system, but the aim is to bring these into the Government system.

If the inclusion of the off budget is seen as difficult to adopt immediately, information on the activities should at least be properly recorded and monitored. In this way, it can be factored into the definition of ceilings and corresponding output targets, even if the actual flow of funds is distinct from the normal budget.

As ministries develop objective and output based budgets, with clear **programmes** for the achievement of the objectives, projects will be a part of the overall activities within the programmes, and donors may consider shifting to programme financing rather than project financing.

Budget support is the ultimate goal in a working MTEF, and donors should start considering this. The Government will meanwhile be improving the preparation and presentation of the budget to ensure it is transparent enough for donor confidence to provide overall support.

THE WORLD BANK IN RWANDA

HISTORY

Rwanda is a small, densely populated, landlocked country in Central Africa, who became independ in 1962, after colonization by Germany (1899) and Belgium (1945). In 1961 its monarchical government was formally abolished by a referendum and the first parliamentary elections were held.

Ethnic conflicts between the Tutsis, who represent 15 percent of the population, and the Hutus who represent over 80% of the population, have engulfed the country for decades. These conflicts triggered the displacement of tens of thousands of Tutsis to neighboring countries in 1959, 1969, and 1972. This recurring ethnic strife, as well as a Government policy prohibiting the return of exiles, culminated in a large-scale armed invasion of Rwanda in October 1990 by the Rwanda Patriotic Front (RPF), composed mainly of exiled Tutsis. The RPF sought political reforms and the rights of all exiles to return to Rwanda; its army fought the Government's mainly Hutu army to a stalemate.

A peace agreement known as the Arusha Accords, mediated by the international community, was signed by the Government and the RPF in Arusha, Tanzania in August 1993. It provided for the formation of a united national government and the integration of the two armies. However, the implementation of the accord was delayed due to opposition by Hutu extremists. The subsequent deaths of the presidents of Rwanda and Burundi in a plane crash over Kigali sparked a well-organized Hutu extremist uprising. With the support of the army, Hutu extremists engaged in genocide, killing up to 800,000 people, mostly Tutsis and also moderate Hutus. The RPF responded by ousting the government and its army, and about 2 million Hutus fled Rwanda into refugee camps in neighboring countries.

A transitional Government of National Unity, formed along the lines of the Arusha Accords, was sworn in July 1994 under the presidency of Pasteur Bizimungu. The new government included representatives of the 5 major political parties, from both the Hutu and Tutsi ethnic groups. The dominant parties in the Government are the RPF, now chaired by vice-president Paul Kagame, and the "Mouvement Démocratique Rwandais" (MDR), now chaired by Prime Minister Rwigema. Following the installation of the new government, about 800,000 exiles from previous conflicts returned to Rwanda. Many of the 1994 Hutu exiles also returned to Rwanda in 1996/97 and have been resettled and reintegrated into the society and economy. The Government has adopted a transition program featuring national reintegration and reconciliation, and economic reform.

ECONOMY

The economy continued to recover rapidly in 1998. With a GDP growth of 10 percent in 1998, Rwanda exceeded the PFP projection of 6.7 percent. Inflation is abating, dropping from 12% in 1887 to 6.8% in 1998. A drop in government revenue has increased the primary deficit.

The international community has provided substantial assistance—in excess of US$2 billion since 1994—for the reconstruction of Rwanda. The World Bank has provided an emergency grant (US$20 million) and two emergency credits of US$50 million each since 1994. The International Monetary Fund (IMF) approved a Post-Conflict Reconstruction Program of about US$20.6 million in May 1997 to support Rwanda's emergency reconstruction and economic recovery efforts. An Enhanced Structural Adjustment Facility (ESAF) was approved by the IMF in June 1998. An Economic Recovery credit in the amount of $75 million was approved by the Bank's Board in March 1999 to support Rwanda's economic recovery and adjustment program. In light of satisfactory progress in the country's economic reform program, a second ESAF is being prepared and is expected to be presented to the IMF board in October 1999.

POLITICS

The Arusha Accords provided a five-year term for the Government of National Unity. The transitional Government includes members of both ethnic groups and different political parties. The five year transition period expired in July 1999, and has been extended for another 4 years. The implementation of the transition program has been delayed by the enormous task of dealing with the effects of the genocide and the massive displacements and resettlement of the population.

Rwanda faces the major challenge of bringing to justice the perpetrators of the genocide. About 130,000 persons are in prison awaiting trial on charges of genocide. The National Assembly has passed legislation to enable the trials of the accused persons and these trials are now taking place.

Internal security in the north-western and central parts of the country has improved since Rwanda has been successful in containing the ongoing insurgency from the neighboring DRC. A peace accord signed on July 10 between the Government of the Democratic Republic of Congo and other countries involved in the conflict (Rwanda, Angola, Uganda, Zimbabwe, Namibia) makes provisions for dealing with Rwanda's security concerns.

DEVELOPMENT PICTURE/DONOR COORDINATION

The most recent UNDP Roundtable meeting on Rwanda was held in June 1996. UNDP has the primary role for assisting the Government of Rwanda in donor coordination and mobilization of external assistance. The Bank was assigned lead role for economic management and budget support, and co-lead role for capacity building.

The Bank and Swedish authorities organized a special donors meeting held in Stockholm in June 1998 to mobilize resources for Rwanda's economic reform program and its multilateral debt service needs. About US$250 million was pledged, of which about US$55.2 million will be allocated to a multilateral trust fund established to service Rwanda's African Development Bank, IFAD and IDA debt for a period of three years, following which Rwanda is expected to qualify for debt relief under the HIPC initiative assuming its economic reform program remains on track. The United Kingdom (DFID) organized a special meeting held in London in July, 1999 to exchange views between donors and Rwanda on its reform program for the year 2000 and to discuss other donor coordination matters.

WORLD BANK ROLE

The World Bank is currently financing eight projects in Rwanda, with International Development Association (IDA) commitments of US$258.0 million. The Bank is providing 100 percent (net of taxes) financing for foreign expenditures for its projects, and the Government will provide counterpart funds for 5 percent of local expenditures.

Policy dialogue has concentrated on public resource management, public utilities, trade, infrastructure, private sector development and agriculture and rural development.

For Fiscal Year 2000, the Bank will be providing assistance through 2 projects, one in Agriculture, one in Rural Water for a total of $25 million. For fiscal 2001, the Bank will be providing assistance through 4 projects: one in Agriculture, one in Human Resources Development, one in Trade and Private Sector Development and a Leveraged Insurance Facility for Trade (LIFT), a regional facility to guarantee investment against sovereign –but not exchange rate- risk. The total amount of assistance for Fiscal Year 2001 is expected to be $125 million.

Under current rules, Rwanda should qualify for HIPC in 2001, provided that the reform program remains on track.

In 1998, the International Finance Corporation (IFC) made a loan to a company that produces roses for export and is exploring an investment opportunity in Rwandacell, the provider of cellular phone service in Rwanda.

Rwanda ratified the Multilateral Investment Guarantee Agency (MIGA) convention on October 27, 1987, but has not yet completed membership requirements.

Contacts

Mr. Emmanuel Mbi
Country Director
1818 H Street NW,

Washington DC 20433 USA
Phone: (202) 473-4953
Fax: (202) 473-8300
E-mail: embi@worldbank.org

Mr. Edward K. Brown
Resident Representative
Blvd. de la Revolution, SORAS Building, Kigali, Rwanda
Phone: (250) 72204
Fax: (250) 76385
E-mail: ebrown@worldbank.org

Mr. Chukwuma Obidegwu
Country Economist
Phone: (202) 473-9458
Fax: (202) 473-8466
E-mail: cobidegwu@worldbank.org

US ASSISTANCE TO RWANDA

In his 1998 visit to Rwanda, President Clinton reaffirmed the U.S. commitment to assist the Government of Rwanda (GOR) and its people in their recovery from the 1994 genocide and war and the subsequent political unrest and displacements. He acknowledged the United States' lack of timely response to the genocide to the Rwandan people. In so doing, USAID's program was dedicated to the transition which Rwanda is undergoing from meeting emergency needs to achieving sustainable development where justice, respect for human rights and accountability in governance prevail. Achieving a lasting peace in Rwanda is crucial to regional stability and is in the clear interest of the United States. The USAID program is fully consistent with Greater Horn of Africa Initiative principles.

THE DEVELOPMENT CHALLENGE.

Rwanda continues to make progress on political, social and economic fronts, but daunting problems remain. GOR battlefield successes in the northwest prefectures of Gisenyi and Ruhengeri, combined with the inability of insurgent forces to materially support the civilian population in the area, resulted in over 600,000 internally displaced persons (IDPs) between May and October 1998 as residents sought protection and security in commune centers. USAID led all donors in responding to this humanitarian and political situation through provision of food and material supplies.

By the end of 1998, the potential disastrous consequences of the sudden creation of large IDP concentrations were averted. The importance of stability and increased productivity in the northwest cannot be overestimated as the region contains Rwanda's most productive farmland and has been the stronghold of opposition to the current GOR. Social, political and economic stability in this region is essential to Rwanda's transition.

In the political arena, the GOR's Ministry of Justice (MOJ) continued to make remarkable progress in the formidable task of processing over 120,000 people detained and accused of genocide crimes. By the end of 1998, case files were established for almost half of all detainees, more than 3,000 detainees have been released, over 1,000 have confessed through the plea bargaining system established by the USAID-supported National Genocide Law, and 150 have been tried. Although trying the remaining detainees is still an impossible task, prospects are now improved for speedier resolution of cases including group trials. USAID assistance in cooperation with the U.S. Department of Justice will endeavor to improve caseload management. Improvements in the overall justice system will be expanded once Great Lakes Initiative (GLI) funding becomes available later in FY 1999.

Rwanda made progress in 1998 towards a more open and participatory political system. USAID's local governance efforts became a model for programs funded by the World Bank, the United Nations Development Program, and the Netherlands. The GOR developed plans for local elections which will enable communities to select representatives with increased authority to make local decisions.

Social indicators in Rwanda, the most densely populated African country with population figures over 7.7 million in a country the size of Maryland, are alarming. The population growth rate is in excess of 3% per year and infant mortality is at 130 per 1,000 live births with child mortality rates (children under 5) adding another 70 deaths. To effectively solve these problems, the Ministry of Health (MOH), with USAID support, continues to decentralize its resources to improve service delivery in an integrated primary health care system. Economic Support Funds (ESF) is requested in FY 2000 through the GLI to meet the U.S. Government's commitment to the Rwanda Multi-Donor Debt Relief Trust Fund will enhance the GOR's abilities to allocate national resources to social sector service delivery.

Rwanda's economy is dominated by an agricultural sector which has re-absorbed over two million people during the period 1995-1998. Nearly 95% of the population is engaged in subsistence agriculture for household consumption; however, per capita food production has declined steadily since the early 1980's and 25% of all households do not produce enough for their families to eat. USAID's program has now relinked the work of Michigan State University with the Ministry of Agriculture (MOA) to improve data management and planning capacities. USAID's expanded agricultural program will support food marketing, seed multiplication and the private sector distribution of agricultural inputs and the development of off-farm employment that secures sustainable livelihoods through agricultural processing and small and micro industry. Development programs are augmented by P.L. 480 Title II Monetization Program-funded support for critical food security interventions and OFDA assistance for emergency interventions.

OTHER DONORS.

A wide range of multilateral and bilateral donors are active in Rwanda and are closely coordinated by the Ministry of Finance and Planning's new unit for external assistance, CEPEX, The World Bank, International Monetary Fund and the European Union along with the full range of UN agencies provide the bulk of all project assistance and financial support. Bilateral programs are currently making the final transition into development assistance. Future funding levels have not be firmly established. Donors are coordinated by sector through thematic groups organized by UNDP. Overall coordination is the role the GOR and is still evolving.

PROGRAM.

USAID programs will continue to focus on three strategic objectives: 1) increased rule of law and transparency in governance; 2) increased use of health and social services and changed behaviors related to STI/HIV/AIDS and maternal and child health by building service capacity in target regions; and 3) increased ability of rural families in targeted communities to improve household food security.

Related to USAID's goal of strengthening democracy and good governance, Funds are requested to pursue achievement through: 1) strengthened capacity for administration of justice; 2) increased sense of security on the part of the general population by increasing capacity to demine productive areas, promoting civilian police protection and reintegrating former military into the productive sector; and 3) improved governance, accountability and transparency within a decentralized national structures. Resources will permit a rapid expansion of program support to genocide caseload management, reconciliation, and local elections.

Related to USAID's goal of stabilizing population growth and protecting human health and providing humanitarian assistance, Child Survival funds are requested to achieve: 1) increased availability of decentralized, quality primary health care (PHC) focusing on reproductive health; 2) improved knowledge, perceptions and practices related to reproductive health; 3) improve MOH financial and administrative accountability; and 4) increased GOR capacity to provide basic social support activities.

Related to USAID's overall goals of promoting broad-based economic growth and agricultural development and providing humanitarian assistance, DA resources are requested to achieve: 1) increase GOR capacity in the MOA to plan and implement sound food security policies and programs; 2) create and enhance broad-based economic growth through internal production-marketing chains; and 3) increase capacity of institutions to develop and disseminate agricultural technologies that can result in increased production and profitability.

SELECTED PROJECTS

PROGRAM: RWANDA
TITLE AND NUMBER: Increased Rule of Law and Transparency in Governance, 696-SO01
STATUS: Continuing
PROPOSED OBLIGATION AND FUNDING SOURCE: FY 2000: $2,400,000 DFA
INITIAL OBLIGATION: FY 1997; **ESTIMATED COMPLETION DATE:** FY 2001

Summary: Since 1995, USAID has been achieving results under this strategic objective (SO). The Ministry of Justice, the courts and prosecutorial system, the representative political institutions such as the transitional National Assembly, the Ministry of the Interior and the decentralized, local organizations coordinated by that Ministry, the National Demining Office, the two principal police institutions, and civil society non-governmental organizations (NGOs) have been partners and beneficiaries of USAID-supported activities. Current plans for FYs 1999 and 2000 are to continue and deepen gains related to these results. A major expansion of activities is foreseen when significant Economic Support Fund resources become available for programming and implementation under the Great Lakes Initiative).

All Rwandans will benefit from increased confidence in legal and governmental structures, decentralization and improved security of persons and property. Immediate and direct beneficiaries are the institutions which underpin administration of justice, rule of law and broad-based participatory development and political processes, including at least 350 civil servants in the areas of justice and local government, 190 law school students, 150 members and staff of the transitional National Assembly; 20,000 rural citizens in target communities; more than a total of 8,000 former soldiers in reintegration activities; 100 members of local NGOs committed to improving civil society; and 800 genocide survivor orphans who are attending secondary schools.

Key Results: Support through this SO will build the capacity to improve the administration of justice and decentralized local governance by providing the tools and the skills necessary to develop legal and governmental structures and civil society associations. In FY1999/2000, activities will focus on: 1) creating the institutional capacity for more timely and effective administration of justice; 2) increasing security of property and persons; and 3) building consensus for greater participation in decision making at the local and national level.

Performance and Prospects: USAID efforts during 1998 were directed towards establishing the basis for justice and good governance. Major accomplishments include: 1) Completion of law degree education for 120 Anglophone law students in 1999 at the National University thus addressing the critical shortages in legal expertise within the country; 2) material assistance in preparing dossiers for individuals accused of genocide crimes; 3) continued training for public safety officials at the community and national level in order to lay the institutional foundation for the rule of law and respect for human rights; 4) building a capacity through the National Demining Office (NDO) to identify and destroy land mines and unexploded ordnance; 5) in partnership with the Netherlands, enabling the Ministry of Internal Affairs (MOIA) to issue new identity cards, free of ethnic affiliation, nationwide, thus enabling freedom of movement while still maintaining security; and 6) supporting the establishment of a decentralization unit within the MOIA to build consensus for national policies that will transfer decision making to local communities

USAID assistance in improving the administration of justice will: 1) continue to train new legal professionals--(120 law students are scheduled to graduate in 1999) and produce legal materials in English; 2) fund placement of Rwandan journalists in Arusha to provide extensive reporting, in the local language, on the proceedings of the International Criminal Tribunal for Rwanda; 3) assist the Ministry of Justice (MOJ) to develop and implement an effective awareness campaign informing the population at large, and the detainees in particular, about the genocide law and duties and responsibilities of all citizens in a country governed by the rule of law; and 4) provide legal/prosecutorial expertise and caseload management advice to the MOJ; and 5) provide material and technical assistance to the newly authorized National Judicial Council, the body tasked with selecting and supporting judges.

To improve security, USAID will: 1) to train public safety personnel, including police trainers and new police officers, and equip public safety institutions to provide the basis for civilian law enforcement; 2) build the capacity and self-sufficiency of the NDO so that more land can be returned to productive use; and 3) support the Government of Rwanda (GOR) demobilization effort through participation in a multi-donor program, funded through the United Nations Development Program trust fund which would provide technical assistance to the National Demobilization Commission and skills training for demobilized soldiers. The scope and timing of the demobilization actions will depend on the situation in the Congo (DRC) and the current insurgency in the northwest of the country.

To improve accountability and transparency in governance, USAID will: 1) promote participatory processes at the community level that enable communities to plan for and allocate resources for rehabilitation activities; 2) assist the MOJ and the MOIA to develop sound financial management and accounting systems; 3) continue to support policy dialogue on decentralization to increase local ownership of communal government; 4) provide technical assistance and material support to develop and strengthen civil society through local non-governmental organizations (NGOs) that represent professional associations such as the Bar Association, human rights groups and other civil society organizations; 5) provide technical assistance to the National Assembly to improve technical staff's legislative analysis and drafting skills; and 6) contribute to the National Assistance Fund for Genocide Survivors to pay school fees for secondary school students orphaned in the genocide. These activities all play a key role in resolving the traumatic events of the past, and establishing a framework to mitigate future conflict as Rwandan society rebuilds.

Possible Adjustments to Plans: USAID is prepared to design and implement a major expansion of on-going activities when funds become available for the Great Lakes Initiative (GLI). Support to the Rwandan Prosecutor General's Office, the MOJ, the national court system, programs for healing and reintegration, and increased participation in democratic decision-making are all areas where activities can be expanded to meet the GLI objectives.

Other Donors Programs: The Netherlands and Germany are the major donors in the justice sector, each contributing more than the United States. UNDP has funded advisors with the MOIA and the MOJ. The World Bank and the Netherlands have provided $15 million to replicate decentralization activities based on the USAID Local Governance Initiative. Canada is supporting the local language publication of material on the work of the ICTR. Through an NGO, Belgium furnishes defense lawyers for genocide detainees. Demobilization and reintegration efforts will be a multi-donor funded activity through the UNDP Trust Fund with a total estimated budget of $39 million.

Principal Contractors, Grantees, or Agencies: The MOIA, the MOJ, the U.S. Department of Justice, the University of Quebec at Montreal, AFRICARE, SUNY, Chemonics, and Ronco are currently implementing activities.

Major Results Indicators:

	Baseline (1997)	FY 2000	Target (2000)
Increased availability of legal expertise.	40 lawyers working in Rwanda	250 lawyers	370 lawyers
Productive Land demined	600 sq km of land compro- mised by mines and UXOs	50% of compromised area cleared	projected completed in 2000)
Mechanism estab- lished for local resource allocation	All development resources allocated by central government	Mechanism estab- lished for local partici- pation in 12 communes	Local authorities in 12 communes access central funds

PROGRAM: RWANDA
TITLE & NUMBER: Increased Use of Health and Social Services and Changed Behaviors Related to STI/HIV/AIDS and Maternal and Child Health by Building Service Capacity in Target Regions, 696-SO02
STATUS: Continuing
PROPOSED OBLIGATION & FUND SOURCE: FY 2000: $3,500,000 CSD
INITIAL OBLIGATION: FY 1997; ESTIMATED COMPLETION DATE: FY2001

Summary: This Strategic Objective's purpose is to increase the utilization of quality primary health care (PHC) and basic social services in target regions and contribute to increased stability and strengthened development capacity. USAID work in the health sector has made excellent progress in the transition from emergency response to long-term sustainable activities. Much of the work in FY1997 met short-term needs, especially in re-establishing community level health services with a focus on STI/HIV/AIDS and maternal child health. However, in FY1998 and FY1999, the program shifted to working closely with an increasingly competent ministry and decentralized public health service delivery system on basic and long-term issues of quality of care and health sector finance. FY2000 will see a continuation and deepening of the shift to sustainable development activities.

Direct program beneficiaries are the general population of the prefectures of Byumba (772,500), Gitarama (858,800), Kibungo (671,000), the health districts of Nyagatare in Umutara (300,000) and Kigali (600,000) as well as 30,000 unaccompanied or orphaned children and their foster families. To improve service delivery, 300 Rwandans working in the public health delivery system and social service sector will be direct beneficiaries of professional training activities.

Key Results: USAID is implementing a set of activities in close cooperation with the Ministry of Health (MOH) and other partners which continues to rebuild delivery of key services and to build the long-term financial sustainability and quality of health care. Activities will: 1) integrate and improve planning, management and implementation of STI/HIV services within existing primary health care delivery systems in four pilot regions; 2) establish and expand sustainable quality assurance systems through greater quality design, control and improvement; 3) improve HIV/AIDS prevention through peer education program and increase capacity to produce and disseminate information, education and communication (IEC) messages to target groups about STI/HIV/AIDS; 4) develop comprehensive financial and administrative systems which will be used to budget and account for MOH resources; 5) to develop and pilot sound health care cost recovery systems to reinforce MOH efforts to deploy qualified health care providers, to develop the skills and confidence of health workers at all levels, and empower health districts to monitor service standards and performance, and identify training needs; and 6) increase the capacity of local communities to identify and address the needs of vulnerable people, including orphans and foster children.

Performance and Prospects: USAID assumed a leadership role in rebuilding Rwanda's health and social service capacity to serve Rwandans reintegrating into their communities after the genocide and war of 1994. Infrastructure assistance through the rehabilitation and refurbishing of health clinics and training facilities was complemented by technical assistance to improve management and accounting systems in the national health care system. The quality of health and social welfare services in target regions improved through better clinical practices, establishment of community-based education and communication networks, improved referral systems, technical training, and innovative STI/HIV communication interventions. In addition, USAID has strengthened the capacity of the public sector to provide basic child welfare services to the community while simultaneously mobilizing communities to meet the needs of unaccompanied and orphaned children, and other vulnerable individuals.

These activities build a public capacity to deliver quality primary health care (PHC) and social welfare services for children as well as strengthen existing community social, communication and economic networks and services. To increase the availability of decentralized PHC services in target areas, USAID provides technical assistance to improve primary health care planning, management and implementation with an emphasis on STI/HIV prevention and control interventions. USAID assistance is used to improve knowledge and perceptions related to reproductive health, emphasizing STI/HIV, through innovative peer education programs and aggressive education at the community level of political, religious and opinion leaders.

Technical assistance to the MOH to enhance sustainability of PHC services through improved financial, administrative and management systems and accountability at the central and regional levels has led to the establishment of a Finance and Administrative Division. This will improve reporting on donor accounts, produce greater decentralization of resource management, and create standard costs to be paid by customers for national health system services and pharmaceuticals. USAID support to basic social welfare services for children has resulted in a national action plan to decentralize such services and has mobilized community-based networks to assist families with foster children. Technical assistance and training will improve the capacity of social development committees at the prefecture and community levels to address the needs of vulnerable people.

Possible Adjustment to Plans: USAID has requested ESF funding to meet the U.S. Government commitment in October 1998 to the Multi-Donor Debt Relief Trust Fund. These funds will enhance the GOR's capacity to deliver social services in health and education.

Other Donor Programs: USAID and the World Bank jointly fund a Rwandan-managed national communications center. USAID and the World Bank also collaborate with the MOH to decentralize and improve STI/HIV services nationally. USAID and the United Nations Development Program share in the joint planning and financing of a community based comprehensive health and sanitation intervention program in northeastern Rwanda. USAID collaborates with the MOH to implement their national health policy and action plans and with the Ministry of Gender, Family and Social Affairs to strengthen coordination, develop policy and build a community capacity for the care and protection of children.

Principal Contractors, Grantees or Agencies: The MOH, the Ministry of Gender, Family and Social Affairs, and international non-governmental organizations (CARE International, Save the Children, Family Health International, Samaritan's Purse International, Population Services International), and contractors AbT Associates,and Johns Hopkins University.

Selected Performance Measures:

	Baseline (1997)	FY 2000	Target (2001)
Increased access to quality PHC services in five regions	50% with STI correctly diagnosed and treated	60% of clients with STI correctly diagnosed and treated	65% of clients with STIs correctly diagnosed and treated
Improved management of national health delivery system	Inability to provide USG funds to MOH	Central and regional accounting and administration systems acceptable to USAID	USAID funds provided directly to the MOH for approved programs
Reduction of children in institutions and residential centers	6,600 children	1,200 children	(program ends 2000)

PROGRAM: RWANDA
TITLE & NUMBER: Increased Ability of Rural Families in Targeted Communities to Improve Household Food Security 696-SO03
STATUS: Continuing
PROPOSED OBLIGATION & FUND SOURCE: FY 2000 $7,100,000 DFA; $1,516,000 P.L.480 Title II
INITIAL OBLIGATION: FY 1997; **ESTIMATED COMPLETION DATE:** FY 2002

Summary: The purpose of this objective is to increase access to agricultural inputs and staple foods for rural families through expanded production, better market access, an improved environment for small scale private enterprise, and through increased capacity to monitor and respond to those most affected by food insecurity. During 1997, USAID was instrumental in meeting the emergency needs of 1.5 million returnees with timely and effective use of humanitarian assistance. During 1998, USAID provided resources to meet the needs of approximately 600,000 internally displaced persons (IDPs).

Successful transition activities will help diversify economic opportunities for targeted poor rural households by increasing both agricultural production and purchasing power, thus reducing vulnerability to food insecurity. Beneficiaries include:

1) households and farmers in target communities who will benefit from growing trade with neighboring countries, increased availability of agricultural inputs at reasonable prices and improved rural market access;

2) an estimated 20 technical staff plus decision and policy makers within the Food Security Technical Unit (FSTU) and the Government of Rwanda (GOR); and

3) an estimated 700,000 persons acutely affected by food insecurity in Rwanda through effective monitoring and provision of appropriate assistance.

Key Results: Development Assistance resources for longer term capacity building are being combined with local currency from the P.L. 480 Title II Emergency Monetization Project which address immediate needs. Development Assistance will achieve the following intermediate results:

increase GOR capacity in the Ministry of Agriculture (MOA) to plan and implement sound food security policies and programs; 2) create and enhance broad-based economic growth through internal production-marketing chains; and

3) increase capacity of institutions to develop and disseminate agricultural technologies that can increase production and profitability.

P.L. 480 Title II emergency monetization proceeds will:

1) fund food security initiatives to address emergency needs including short-term causes of food insecurity in Rwanda;

2) reduce dependency on overall external food aid;

3) enhance local production and marketing capabilities; and

4) increase the GOR's understanding and ability to respond to the root causes of food insecurity in Rwanda. All activities aim to increase rural purchasing power by expanding agricultural production and off-farm employment and improving market services including agro-processing, storage facilities and trading networks with neighboring countries.

Performance and Prospects: In FY1997, approximately $29 million in U.S. food assistance (out of a regional total of $72.5 million) was provided to World Food Program (WFP), representing 40% of all food assistance to Rwanda. This assistance was distributed to vulnerable groups, through Food for Work programs; to promote agricultural recovery, build houses and rehabilitate basic infrastructure. OFDA assistance, totaling more than $26 million in 1997, provided life saving and rehabilitation assistance including clean water, sanitation, health supplies, seeds and agricultural tools, food distribution and emergency shelter assistance, as well as communication equipment furnished directly to the GOR. Small grants were directed to community based women's associations for restocking small ruminants and income generation opportunities in the amount of $350,000.

During FY1998, USAID was instrumental in meeting the emergency needs of about 600,000 IDPs in Rwanda's northwest with timely and effective use of humanitarian assistance. During this period, U.S. assistance totaled over $5 million. An additional $1.4 million was provided in FY1999 for emergency activities in the northwest. P.L. 480 Title II monetization in the amount of $400,000 provided seeds and tools to restart agricultural production in this, the country's most productive zone.

Over $100,000 were provided to Northwest communities reaching 140 womens' association. As emergency needs at the household level and national levels are met, USAID's programs will address rehabilitation and development requirements by shifting assistance to promoting productive activities and private marketing channels that lead to long-term food security. It is encouraging to note that overall agricultural production has reached just over 90 percent of its pre-genocide levels but still represents a major decline in per capita food availability which has decreased 33 percent since 1984.

Possible Adjustments to Plans: No major adjustments are anticipated for this Strategic Objective.

Other Donor Programs:USAID will work with: (1) the MOA and Michigan State University to restore the agriculture statistical data base in the MOA and provide policy development assistance; (2) the United Nations Development Program (UNDP), the European Union (EU) and the World Bank to enhance broad-based economic growth by empowering farmers' associations, cooperatives and formal private sector to respond to market demand and improve investment in rural sector production; and (3) the Ministry of Commerce, Cooperatives and Industry (MCCI), the MOA and International Institute of Tropical Agriculture to increase capacity of ISAR to develop and disseminate agriculture technologies which will improve production and profitability with the help of IARCs and their research network.

Principal Contractors, Grantees, or Agencies: The MOA and the MCCI are USAID's principal partners in these endeavors. Contractors and grantees include Michigan State University, the International Institute for International Agriculture, World Vision for Rural Development, International Refugee Committee, Save the Children (UK), Food for the Hungry International, Catholic Relief Services, and Concern International, RONCO Inc., ACDI/VOCA, and other U.S., Rwandan and international non-governmental, international and organizations and private sector firms.

Selected Performance Measures:

	Baseline (1997)	FY 2000	Target (2001)
Increased GOR capacity and to implement sound agricultural practices.	FSTU not yet functional	FSTU functional data collected and analyzed	FSTU analysis used to develop policy
Increased household food security in targeted areas	25% of the population, or 2 million, are food insecure	5% reduction in food insecure persons in targeted areas	10% reduction in food insecure persons in targeted areas
Increased off-farm enterprise.	Post-genocide period rural enterprises are minimal	Rural enterprises created in targeted areas	Rural enterprises provide off-farm in targeted areas

U.S. AGENCY FOR INTERNATIONAL DEVELOPMENT REBUILDING RWANDA'S DEVASTATED FARMING COMMUNITIES

Rwanda is a fertile country, but the devastating 1994 war almost destroyed the country s farming base. Land was left to grow wild, homes were destroyed and tools stolen. A season's growth was lost and returning farmers lacked the seed stock and tools they desperately needed to rebuild their lives. USAID has responded to the crisis and is partnering with the private voluntary organization World Vision to provide hundreds of thousands of peasant farmers tools and seeds and to help reorganize farm associations.

- Many of Rwanda's families are headed by widows with no means of support. More than 85,000 families are headed by children -- sometimes as young as 11. These families want to get their lives together again, but had nowhere to start. Now they have help.

- USAID and World Vision have been providing families with "ag-paks," consisting hoes, seeds and other items for small- scale farming. USAID is also funding a World Vision program to give essential help to the most recent returnees and others who have fallen on hard times. This program is providing support to 20 percent of Rwanda's vulnerable families.

- A total more than 86,000 households in 32 communes are being assisted. More than 86,000 hoes, 458 tons of beans, 68 tons of Maize and nearly 10 million sweet potato cuttings have been distributed through the program.

HELPING WOMEN FARM PINEAPPLES

In some areas of Rwanda, two-thirds of farm workers are women, bringing booth unique opportunities and problems, according to fruit crop coordinator and trainer Felicite Nyashuti. Ms. Nyashuti has been working to help farmer associations cash in on lucrative pineapple farming.

"There are techniques which are important to learn if you want to be successful, said Felicite. We are able to help these associations a great deal -- there is a great need for training that they can understand.

" There is also a serious shortage of pineapple shoots to start growing, and even if these farmers could find them they wouldn't be able to afford them. " Felicite and her colleagues search out as many pineapple shoots as they can, and provide them to farmer associations. In return, each association promises to return a larger number of shoots to World Vision at the end of the season. These shoots will be used to kick-start another association's pineapple plantation in a different area.

- On a typical training trip, Felicite finds a large group of representatives from four associations keen to study what she had to teach them. Using photocopied sheets with photographs and clear diagrams, real fruit and shoots and bags of fertilizer, she carefully outlines the right spacing needed for a good plantation, the way to prepare and plant shoots and the best way to fertilize and water the plants to get the biggest, tastiest fruit.

The audience is not all women. The associations' biggest problems are the difficult labor involved at the planting stage, and the need to protect the developing crop from theft. To help with this, each group can allow up to a third of its members to be men -- but women retain the leadership.

"They did try to employ men to work for the associations, but the men made their labor very expensive because they wanted to join," explained Felicite. "Men are so scarce in this region that we can't form male associations, so this is actually a good solution for them, too."

In the neighboring commune of Gashora there are four women's associations supported through the program who already have fields of pineapples. One of them, called Cyambere Mutagarugati -- "Women should be first in everything" -- has seven women members. They have no husbands, and there are no men available to work for them, either.

- "We came together in may 1995," explained president Bampurineza Virginie. "This is the first time we have tried pineapples, but it is working well.

- "Between the seven of us we have about 40 children, and our agriculture is the only thing we have to support them. We feed the children some of the fruit, and we sell the rest at the market to raise money for school fees, medicine and other needs. "

"There is always the possibility of something going wrong, like a bad season or a drought," said Virginie. "It is encouraging for us that there are people like Calixte and Felicite whom we can ask for help. "

ECONOMIC DEVELOPMENT REGULATORY FRAMEWORK

RWANDA AID POLICY

The elimination of poverty is one of the biggest challenges facing the Government of Rwanda. Whilst we have come far since the war and genocide of 1994, we still have further to go in ensuring that all Rwandan citizens lead prosperous lives, free of the burden of poverty.

A decade ago, most aid to Rwanda came in the form of emergency humanitarian assistance, responding to Rwanda's most immediate needs. Ten years on, Rwanda has embarked on an ambitious path to longterm sustainable development. This shift in Rwanda's needs must be accompanied by a change in the way in which both the Government and its development partners conceptualise aid, so that together we ensure that assistance to Rwanda has maximum impact on the lives of the Rwandan citizen.

Last year, Rwanda signed the Paris Declaration on Aid Effectiveness along with its bilateral and multilateral development partners, with the aim of stimulating increased efficiency and efficacy in the provision and management of external aid. The present document has been developed in the context of the Declaration, and sets ambitious goals that respond to Rwanda's situation and needs. It is the outcome of extensive consultation with stakeholders from across the Government of Rwanda, donor organisations, civil society and the private sector, and will act as a guiding framework for the management of aid in Rwanda.

Whilst the Government of Rwanda makes important efforts to realise a gradual reduction of dependence on external aid, it sees high quality aid as crucial to Rwanda's development in the mediumterm. Rwanda reached the Highly Indebted Poor Countries (HIPC) completion point last year but the need for assistance in the form of grants delivered in an effective manner cannot be emphasised enough. With sufficient high quality aid in the medium term, the Government of Rwanda can deliver efficient services to its citizens, stimulating economic development and poverty reduction.

BACKGROUND AND RATIONALE

1.1. At a global level, increasing attention has been accorded to the issue of aid effectiveness. The Rome and Paris Declarations – to which Rwanda is a signatory – set a basis for the development of partnerships that will improve the way in which development assistance is delivered and utilised.

1.2. Rwanda has made significant achievements in its recovery from the genocide and war of 1994, and in promoting peaceful and equitable social and economic development. External assistance has played a crucial role in Rwanda's progress over the last decade, and will continue to do so in the years to come. Whilst external assistance a decade ago came predominantly in the form of emergency humanitarian assistance, the gradual restoration of order, stability, and national institutions ensued, and the Government is now in a position to assert genuine ownership and leadership in development activities – and the external resources on which they rely – in Rwanda. This document sets out the Government of Rwanda's vision for improved aid management, and those policies which will turn this vision into reality.

OVERVIEW OF PROBLEMS

1.3. Despite moves towards better coordination and dialogue on the part of both the Government and its development partners, a number of problems remain. These problems continue to limit the efficiency and effectiveness with which assistance is delivered, and weaken the Government's case for the scalingup of assistance in the shortto mediumterm.

Capacities

1.4. The Government of Rwanda continues to suffer from capacity problems. This is in part a legacy of the genocide of 1994, and the fact that Rwanda has moved from a period of emergency assistance through a period of transition, to a new period with an ambitious development agenda. The GoR's ability to attract and retain highly qualified and skilled staff remains limited, and this affects planning and negotiation and can result in poor coordination and implementation.

1.5. The lack of clear process in some cases leads line ministries and decentralised entities to negotiate assistance directly with donors, thus undermining the role of MINECOFIN in the management and coordination of assistance.

Predictability

1.6. Politicisation of aid remains an issue in Rwanda. Excessive conditionality arises, and this may result in problems of predictability in terms of the volume, quality and timing of aid, which in turn halt or slow down implementation of propoor programs. Project support is in many cases characterised by implementation delays rather than lack of predictability as such.

Transaction costs

1.7. In common with many developing countries, the costs to Rwanda of receiving assistance are often high, and whilst it is difficult to quantify these in a meaningful manner, it is clear that high transaction costs lower the real value of assistance received. Donors continue to place significant demands on government in terms of time, reporting needs, and use of other resources through numerous missions and meetings. This is in some instances the result of a lack of delegation of authority to local offices by donor organisations, and this burden consequently exacerbates the capacity problems faced by the Government of Rwanda.

Information on aid flows

1.8. Incomplete reporting of ODA (including that provided through some NGOs) to the government reduces transparency, and hinders the ability of government to monitor and manage the assistance Rwanda receives. This information is critical to planning and budgeting processes, as well as the execution of the development budget. It is difficult to obtain a complete picture of external assistance to Rwanda, as some donors are unwilling or unable to meet the government's requests for information. This reduces levels of transparency and accountability in the delivery of assistance.

1.9. At the same time, it is clear that the Government of Rwanda may in some areas place unstructured demands on development partners for information, with different ministries and implementing bodies making requests for information, and then failing to share such information effectively.

Alignment

1.10. Too frequently donors continue to promote their own, often political, objectives at the expense of government ownership. Much assistance remains offplan and offbudget[1], reflecting a lack of alignment with government priorities and systems. Some of the problems surrounding lack of alignment are a symptom of weak (or nonexistent) strategies in some sectors, this often being the result of weak capacities in planning. At the same time, some donor agencies remain constrained by their own institutional arrangements.

1.11. The existence of large vertical funds, whilst beneficial to development in some areas, may have a distortionary effect in the allocation of resources across sectors and subsectors. For example, higher salaries in certain subsectors may draw qualified and experienced personnel from other subsectors, hindering service delivery in these areas.

1.12. Technical assistance is not always effective, and in some instances is perceived to undermine local capacities rather than improving them.

Volume of Assistance

1.13. Whilst Rwanda's attainment of completion point under the enhanced HIPC initiative is a significant achievement, the challenge now is to ensure that Rwanda's external debt is maintained at sustainable levels. At the same time, significant investment is required if Rwanda is to become a middle income country by 2020, as set out in the government's Vision 2020 document. In order to increase investment whilst ensuring that debt remains at

[1] For the purpose of this policy document, assistance is considered offplan where no link with the relevant strategic plan is identified. Offbudget assistance is that assistance which is not reflected in the government's budget.

sustainable levels, the Government of Rwanda must mobilise significant additional resources in the form of grants.

RATIONALE FOR AN AID POLICY

1.14. Historically, the Government of Rwanda has lacked clear structures and guidelines for the mobilisation and management of external assistance, exacerbating the problems described above. As a signatory to the Paris Declaration on Aid Effectiveness, Rwanda is committed to increasing the effectiveness of the assistance it receives. It is intended that the present document will act as a strong foundation for improvements, on the part of both Government and development partners. Increased aid effectiveness is particularly important in improving service delivery to the Rwandan citizen and accelerating the implementation of the Economic Development and Poverty Reduction Strategy.

1. This document clarifies what Rwanda wants to achieve with its assistance, preferences in terms of mobilisation and management of assistance, and the changes necessary in order to reach these goals.
2. By providing clearly articulated policy statements and action points, this document has two ultimate goals. These are (a) to increase the effectiveness of external assistance to Rwanda, and (b) to provide a basis on which the additional aid required by Rwanda to meet its shortto midterm investment needs can be mobilised.

OBJECTIVES AND GUIDING PRINCIPLES

IMPROVING AID EFFECTIVENESS

2.2. The Government of Rwanda and all of its major development partners are signatories to the Paris Declaration on Aid Effectiveness. The Declaration binds both the Government and its development partners to implement policies and strategies that will increase the effectiveness of the assistance received by Rwanda, and as such the principles set out in the Declaration form the basis of the Government's definition of effectiveness.

2.3. Within the overall aim of improving aid effectiveness, the following objectives have been identified:

(a) Operational development strategies	There are clear linkages between the Poverty Reduction Strategy (PRS), sector strategies, budget, Medium Term Expenditure Frameworks (MTEFs), and district development plans, facilitating donor alignment to government priorities.
(b) Reliable country systems	Rwanda's public financial management (PFM), procurement, and reporting systems are strengthened.
(c) Alignment of aid flows on national strategies	All aid flows are reported on the Government's budget and in line with strategic plans.
(d) Strengthening of local capacities by coordinated support	Technical assistance is focussed on knowledge transfer through coordinated programmes consistent with Rwanda's priorities.
(e) Use of country systems	All assistance is delivered through Rwanda's PFM and procurement systems.
(f) Avoiding parallel PIUs	The stock of parallel project implementation units (PIUs) is reduced.
(g) Aid is more predictable	Assistance to Rwanda is disbursed as scheduled,

and medium term projections are reliable.

(h) Aid is untied	Reduction in the volume of assistance to Rwanda that is tied.2
(i) Use of common arrangements	Significant increase in the proportion of assistance delivered in the context of sectorwide approaches.
(j) Joint missions and analysis	Joint missions and analytical work between donors becomes increasingly prevalent.
(k) Resultsoriented frameworks	Harmonisation of conditionalities is achieved and performance indicators are commonly defined.
(l) Mutual accountability	Independent monitoring mechanism in place.

MOBILISING INCREASED ASSISTANCE

2.4. Whilst the Government of Rwanda aims ultimately to reduce its dependence on external assistance, it is clear that in the medium term, simply increasing the effectiveness of the aid Rwanda currently receives will be insufficient to enable the levels of investment required for Rwanda to meet its development objectives (as set out in Vision 2020 and the Millennium Development Goals).

2.5. It is recognised that the Government's case for the scaling up of aid is dependent on its ability to manage current volumes of external assistance effectively.

2.6. In attracting additional external resources, the government will seek to ensure debt sustainability, as set out in paragraphs 3.12 to 3.14 below.

GUIDING PRINCIPLES

2.7. Country ownership is of prime importance. The Government of Rwanda will continue to set its own development objectives and policies, and will seek to ensure that these are the outcome of broad dialogue and consultation across government, the private sector, and civil society.

2.8. This document is a statement of Government policy, and as such its content is 'owned' by the Government of Rwanda. In order to ensure country ownership, the government will seek to mobilise external assistance in forms that do not undermine its autonomy. The importance of consultation and dialogue with development partners is recognised, and to this end the government has sought to consult with its partners throughout the development of this Policy.

2.9. In order to maximise the effectiveness of external assistance to Rwanda, it is important that this and any subsequent statements of policy be inclusive in their nature. This document is therefore intended as a statement of government policy towards all

[2] In this context, tying is taken to mean the imposition of restrictions relating to the source or nature of goods or services used.

official development assistance (ODA) received by Rwanda.[3] Whilst ensuring that an inclusive approach is adopted, the Government of Rwanda has sought to recognise the diverse nature of its development partners and their differing roles in Rwanda's development.

2.10. Where external assistance is mobilised in a manner that strengthens GoR ownership and capacities, this not only renders that external assistance more effective, but it further strengthens the government's ability to manage all of its resources effectively, further enhancing service delivery to the Rwandan citizen.

2.11. This statement of policy is intended as a living document, and it is envisaged that revisions will be made in the future, as the needs of the government and its development partners evolve over time, and as the government's capacities to implement reforms are strengthened.

[3] The GoR adopts the definition of ODA endorsed by OECD DAC (see DAC Working Party on Statistics, Is it ODA? – Note by the Secretariat, 22 May 2001).

POLICIES ON THE VOLUME AND EFFECTIVENESS OF ASSISTANCE

3.1. This section of the document sets out the Government of Rwanda's position on a number of issues relating to the volume and effectiveness of external assistance provided to Rwanda. Each subsection describes a policy, along with the rationale behind it and, where relevant, those steps taken to ensure adherence to policy.

PLANNING AND ARTICULATION OF GOVERNMENT PRIORITIES

3.2. The Government of Rwanda's longterm vision for development is set out in its Vision 2020 document. The forthcoming Economic Development and Poverty Reduction Strategy (EDPRS) identifies and articulates national priorities in the medium term, and all assistance should ultimately be aligned with this.

3.3. Strong strategic plans are essential in all sectors if alignment of donor funds to national priorities is to be achieved. Some existing sector strategic plans and policies must be improved to strengthen donor alignment, and to this end the Government will take steps to ensure that these contain clear objectives and targets, which are consistent with plans at the national level, and are the outcome of a consultative process involving development partners. All external assistance packages in a sector should be identified in an updated annex to the sector strategic plan, with sectors ultimately developing a comprehensive sectorwide approach (SWAP).

3.4. The Government seeks to ensure that all external assistance is aligned with priorities identified in the EDPRS and sector strategic plans. To this end, MINECOFIN has a role in monitoring the Government's total aid portfolio and it will, in collaboration with line ministries, decentralised entities and MINAFFET, encourage donors to channel their resources in a manner that is consistent with the principles of this Policy. Paragraphs 3.26 to 3.46 set out the process through which this is to be achieved.

PREFERRED AID MODALITIES

3.5. The Government of Rwanda recognises that maintaining a 'mixed' portfolio in terms of the modalities through which assistance is delivered can be beneficial. It is however concerned that certain types of assistance bring with them limited benefits, as the costs of accepting such assistance are often high. Project support is often poorly aligned to government priorities, and often carries with it high transaction costs. Such project support too often bypasses – and therefore undermines – government systems rather than strengthening them.

3.6. Where budget support is provided, the government is concerned that earmarking of funds distorts the allocation of government spending across sectors. This in turn undermines the government's role in determining priorities, and means that resources cannot be channelled to meeting the government's objectives as effectively as it would like.

3.7. The Government of Rwanda's preferred modality for external assistance is unearmarked budget support. Excessive requirements on additionality would undermine the government's role in determining priorities and allocating resources as identified in 3.2 above.

3.8. The government recognises that not all donors are able to provide support in the form of budget support. Furthermore, it recognises that project support brings with it particular benefits in some areas (for example, where the work being undertaken is innovative or pioneering in its nature). Before accepting such assistance however, the government must be satisfied that the assistance is being delivered in an effective and efficient manner in line with GoR priorities, and that the costs to Rwanda of accepting such assistance are minimised.

3.9. After unearmarked budget support, the GoR prefers sector budget support followed by standalone projects, which must be onbudget and onplan[4]. Further, the GoR prefers that donor resources be pooled rather than earmarked for individual projects.

3.10. Where the primary beneficiaries of development assistance are decentralised entities, the GoR prefers that such assistance be channelled through its Common Development Fund (CDF). The GoR is in turn able to ensure an equitable distribution of development resources across such entities. Where a donor is unable to channel resources through the CDF, the GoR's preference is for financing of decentralised entities through mechanisms that seek to achieve equity in the allocation of resources across districts. In all cases, alignment of assistance with district development plans must be demonstrated.

3.11. The Government will decline any or all offers of assistance where it considers transaction costs to be unacceptably high, alignment to government priorities to be insufficient, or conditionalities to be excessive. Where assistance is offered in the form of standalone projects, the Government may also decline proposals that are not shown to be sustainable. Transaction costs should be considered in the broadest sense, as defined in 1.7 above, to include the opportunity cost of allocating scarce (human and financial) government resources to activities and their followup.

EXTERNAL DEBT

3.12. Having successfully attained completion point under the Enhanced HIPC initiative, the Government of Rwanda is concerned that any increase in its debt burden must be sustainable. To this end, strong preference is given to assistance offered in the form of grants.

3.13. Assistance in the form of loans will only be considered where the terms (interest and maturity) of such a loan are highly concessional, and subject to the provisions made in

3.11 above.

3.14. The Government of Rwanda currently has a framework for the management of external debt to ensure that this is maintained at sustainable levels in the future. Given that a significant proportion of the assistance Rwanda receives is in the form of concessional loans, the Government continues to pursue a holistic and consistent approach in the management of all external finance.

[4] In the context of this policy, resources are deemed to be onbudget where they are reflected in the government's budget. Resources are onplan when clear alignment with a strategic plan is demonstrated.

TECHNICAL ASSISTANCE

3.15. The Government of Rwanda receives a large volume of technical assistance (TA), much of it in the form of experts appointed on both shortand longterm contracts. All such assistance should be aimed at the building of local capacity. TA has been criticised for failing to transfer capacity to local staff in an organised manner, often adopting an adhoc 'gapfilling' role instead.

3.16. All TA provided to the Government of Rwanda must be concerned primarily with the transfer of capacity to the government by building the skills and capabilities of local staff and/or developing systems and procedures and codifying these in an accessible manner for use by local staff. All terms of reference for TA must recognise these as the ultimate objectives of such assistance.

3.17. The donor and government body with primary responsibility for a TA project will undertake regular appraisals and on the basis of these will seek to strengthen plans to ensure that 3.16 is fulfilled.

3.18. All technical assistance is overseen by the Human Resources and Institutional Capacity Development Agency (HIDA), and to this end the Government shall encourage the pooling of donor resources in financing this initiative.

NONGOVERNMENTAL ORGANISATIONS

3.19. The GoR recognises the important and diverse roles played by both local and international NGOs active in Rwanda. Where NGOs assume a service delivery role, the government is concerned that such assistance should be provided in line with national and sectoral plans as identified in 3.2 above.

3.20. In order to ensure better coordination and to avoid duplication of efforts, the GoR requires that NGOs undertaking a service delivery function provide it with concise and timely information on all such activities. The forthcoming laws regulating the activities of national and international NGOs set out the Government's information requirements in this respect. Procedures for the collection and dissemination of such data will be set out in the manual of procedure referred to in 5.5 below.

3.21. The GoR recognises that many NGOs play a complementary role to that of the government in promoting the interests of Rwandan citizens. The government continues to facilitate an environment which enables and empowers NGOs to fulfil their objectives alongside those of the state.

3.22. The GoR retains a fundamental duty to ensure that all such organisations – regardless of whether their activities are financed by ODA – act in a manner that is transparent and accountable to the Rwandan citizen. The GoR's regulatory role in this respect is detailed in its Laws regulating the activities of national and international nongovernmental organisations operating in Rwanda.

VERTICAL FUNDS

3.23. The Government of Rwanda is concerned that whilst vertical funds – that is, large volumes of external finance that are delivered in structures parallel to that of the government – can provide important assistance in the implementation of programmes, they may hinder the effective allocation of resources to priority areas, undermine government ownership, and in the worst cases create distortions in service delivery.

3.24. The Government requires that information on all activities financed under such arrangements be communicated to MINECOFIN and line ministries or other government bodies working in the same sector(s) / subsector(s). Without timely and comprehensive information, the government is unable to manage its own resource allocations so as to ensure maximum fit with national priorities.

3.25. The Government expects flexibility on the part of vertical funds to align with sector plans and bring such assistance onbudget. It will also influence the areas of activity of other, more flexible donors, to prevent excessive financing of a small number of subsectors. The GoR will seek to develop guidelines on the acceptance and management of such resources with the aim of ensuring that assistance provided by vertical funds does not create the undesirable distortions highlighted in 1.11 above.

RESPONSIBILITIES IN THE MOBILISATION AND MANAGEMENT OF RESOURCES

3.26. The lack of explicit procedures for the mobilisation, negotiation and management of external assistance has had a number of undesirable effects. The ability of MINECOFIN to coordinate external assistance and ensure that it is aligned to government priorities has been weakened. The role of MINAFFET has often been unclear, with communication between MINAFFET, MINECOFIN and implementing authorities being poor or nonexistent. Donors do not know to whom to address proposals and offers of assistance, and with whom these should be negotiated.

3.27. MINECOFIN shall have a lead role in coordinating external assistance and ensuring its efficient allocation to activities in line with the national planning processes outlined in

3.2. At the same time, the Government wishes to see implementing ministries, districts or other government entities retaining ownership of externally financed activities and their implementation.

3.28. The Government recognises that the political aspects inherent to many bilateral relationships require specialist input and coordination from MINAFFET. MINAFFET is thus responsible for maintaining broad policy dialogue with donor organisations through its foreign missions, pursuing the interests of the Government of Rwanda and keeping MINECOFIN and other organisations with a role in soliciting and managing aid updated on relevant developments abroad. MINAFFET will cooperate with MINECOFIN in the identification of potential new donors and the mobilisation of resources from them.

3.29. The GoR agrees that the definitions of roles and processes contained in paragraphs

3.30 to 3.46 below shall constitute the procedures to be adopted in the soliciting, negotiation and management of all external assistance. These procedures will be codified in the form of a manual of procedure, as identified in 5.5 below.

Scoping and Initial Conception

3.30. Where a line ministry, district or other government body has identified a clear need for external assistance and this is consistent with its strategic plan, it may engage in initial discussions with interested partners with a view to developing such an idea and examining its viability.

3.31. MINECOFIN will provide advice on potential development partners, and may initiate discussions between line ministries/districts/other bodies and such partners.

3.32. At this initial stage, the government body concerned shall not enter into negotiations with a donor, nor does it sign agreements of any sort.

Proposals

3.33. The line ministry, district or other body seeking to mobilise assistance writes to the Minister of Finance and Economic Planning to outline the nature of the proposal, its fit with relevant strategic plans, and the details of any initial discussions with or expressions of interest from development partners.

3.34. Quality assurance in terms of the technical soundness of a proposal remains the responsibility of the line ministry or government body seeking to implement a package of assistance.

3.35. The Minister of Finance and Economic Planning, in his or her capacity as coordinator of external assistance, examines such documentation to ensure a proposal's fit with national priorities and policies (including those set out in this document), before writing to potentially interested donors to invite a proposal for assistance.

3.36. All correspondence and details of any relevant discussions are copied to the appropriate line ministry, district or other body rapidly, and also to MINAFFET where a bilateral donor is being approached. At this stage MINAFFET has the opportunity to raise objections.

Negotiation

3.37. Once written communication of a development partner's interest in financing or cofinancing a programme, project or other activity has been received by the Minister of Finance and Economic Planning, (s)he will communicate this to the relevant line ministry or other government body (and MINAFFET if implicated in 3.36 above).

3.38. Technical meetings with the line ministry or other government body will be initiated by the External Finance Unit in MINECOFIN with a view to assessing a proposal and agreeing the position to be adopted in meetings with donors. Where a package of assistance comprises or is likely to comprise a loan element (any sum which the government will be required to repay in the future), the Director of Treasury must, in his/her role as coordinator of national debt, be consulted on this.

3.39. MINECOFIN will, through its External Finance Unit, and in association with the relevant MINAFFET desk, lead meetings with line ministries and donors aimed at negotiating an assistance package. In this way, MINECOFIN's skills and experience in negotiation are utilised to communicate and seek consensus around the details already discussed with line ministries and other bodies as described in 3.38.

Agreement

3.40. Where the outcome of negotiations meets with the satisfaction of both the Minister of Finance and Economic Planning and the government body which will be primarily concerned with the implementation of an assistance package, this is recorded in writing (in the form of a Memorandum of Understanding or similar agreement). The Minister of Finance and Economic Planning will, in his or her capacity as coordinator of all external assistance, normally sign such documentation for and on behalf of the Government of Rwanda.

3.41. Where it is a donor requirement that such agreements be signed by the Minister of Foreign Affairs and Cooperation, documentation will be forwarded to MINAFFET for this purpose. MINAFFET will sign agreements with donors only once agreed in writing with MINECOFIN. Copies of agreements with bilateral donors will be retained by both MINAFFET and MINECOFIN.

3.42. MINECOFIN is responsible for overseeing the fulfilment of loan agreement effectiveness.

3.43. Data relating to the agreement is recorded using the governments systems as specified in 3.52 and 3.53.

Implementation

3.44. The line ministry or other government body designated as the primary recipient of an assistance package is responsible for the implementation of investments or other expenditures agreed. It will engage in regular dialogue with MINECOFIN through CEPEX on aspects of implementation requiring attention, for example where delays to disbursements pose a problem or where there are delays to implementation.

Evaluation

3.45. Where assistance is provided in the form of project support, the line ministry or other implementing body shall work with CEPEX to ensure adequate followup of project implementation.

3.46. Where assistance is provided in the form of budget support, the implementing line ministry or government body is usually responsible for the collection, aggregation and dissemination of data relating to targets and performance indicators agreed with the donor(s). Such information shall be provided to MINECOFIN for use in the Annual Progress Review process, which will in turn be communicated with donors.

FINANCIAL OVERSIGHT AND ACCOUNTABILITY

3.47. The Government acknowledges that continued strengthening of public finance management (PFM) is necessary to ensure that resources – both internally and externally sourced – are used effectively, and in pursuit of the policy of increasing the proportion of assistance delivered as budget support. Weaknesses remain, with poor linkages between budget and MTEF processes, limited budget execution by some sectors, weak integration of the recurrent and development budgets, and weaknesses in auditing and accounting.

3.48. In a move towards improved PFM, the GoR and donors have adopted a harmonised Public Expenditure and Financial Accountability (PEFA) mechanism, and the GoR shall continue to work with these partners to improve its performance.

3.49. Steps are currently being taken to strengthen procurement, auditing and accounting functions in government. The GoR's preference is for assistance that uses these procurement, auditing and accounting systems.

MONITORING, EVALUATION AND REPORTING

3.50. In line with its aim to reduce the transaction costs involved with receiving external assistance, the Government of Rwanda encourages its development partners to move towards use of the national monitoring and evaluation system, thus simplifying monitoring, evaluation and reporting, and ultimately reducing the burden on both government and donors.

3.51. The government lends its full support to joint missions and analytical work. Joint sector reviews should report on targets agreed in strategic plans, namely the link between expenditures and results, with the outcomes of this feeding into the following year's policy actions. The GoR seeks to facilitate these and other forms of joint and/or delegated cooperation between development partners.

3.52. Improved reporting of donor activities to the GoR is essential if aid management is to be improved. At the same time, the GoR recognises that for donors to provide comprehensive, timely and accurate data, the data collection process must be simplified.

3.53. Pursuant to 3.52, MINECOFIN has put in place a Development Assistance Database (DAD), which will act as an interface between donors, NGOs and government for the collection, verification and basic analysis of data pertaining to all external finance to Rwanda. The system is to be integrated with the GoR's SmartGov system, and MINECOFIN is responsible for communicating information to, and training, both donors and line ministries in the use of systems necessary for the monitoring of external finance once the tools are operational.

3.54. In order to ensure transparency and accountability in its relations with development partners, the GoR will make freely available data on its external finance from the systems described above.

MECHANISMS FOR DIALOGUE AND COORDINATION

3.55. The GoR is supportive of the development of sectoral and crosssectoral clusters (fora comprising donors and government bodies active in a particular area), and it will seek to work with its partners to 'provide clear views on donors' comparative advantage and how to achieve donor complementarity' at country and sector levels, as mandated in the Paris Declaration.

3.56. The GoR favours further development of delegated cooperation ('silent partnerships') in clusters, whereby authority is delegated to such donors for the execution of programmes, activities and tasks where a donor's comparative advantage is clear. At the same time it is recognised that a pragmatic approach must be adopted in guiding donors towards this given the requirements imposed on some donors by their headquarters.

3.57. The GoR is concerned that at present some multilateral and bilateral donors are highly centralised with limited delegation of authority to their local representatives in ways that would allow them to play a full role in aligning behind Rwanda's priorities and harmonising their activities. To this end, it will pursue discussions with such donor organisations with a view to rectifying the situation.

3.58. Where forms of assistance (such as budget support) are inherently reliant on a high degree of trust between the GoR and its partners, the GoR will seek to develop clear rules with its partners, outlining the processes to be adopted in the resolution of disputes. These should include agreement on the level and nature of consultations to be undertaken, a period of time within which efforts should be made to resolve difficulties, and agreement not to withdraw assistance in the financial year in which the dispute arises. This is intended to ensure that assistance is not interrupted, delayed or withdrawn unexpectedly, resulting in an adverse impact on service delivery.

3.59. The GoR reaffirms its commitment to the Development Partners Coordination Group (DPCG) as the highestlevel body responsible for overseeing aid coordination in Rwanda. The DPCG consists of representatives from both the GoR and its development partners, and it will continue to serve as a forum for dialogue on coordination of aid to Rwanda, harmonisation of donor support, strategic planning and the alignment of donor resources to GoR priorities. The DPCG oversees the operation of other fora mandated with moving forward the aid coordination, harmonisation and alignment agenda (such as clusters), and it advises the Cabinet on the creation, dissolution, and amendments to the mandates of such fora. The DPCG also reviews progress made in the fulfilment of commitments identified in the Paris and Rome Declarations[5].

1. The Government is committed to agreeing with its development partners on the principle of an independent mechanism for regular monitoring of the performance of both the government and its partners against accepted criteria.

2. The Government of Rwanda recognises that no volume of external assistance can stimulate sustained economic growth and poverty reduction without a stable and supportive social, political and economic climate.

[5] Paris Declaration on Aid Effectiveness, 2005; Rome Declaration on Harmonisation, 2003.

GOR COMMITMENTS

4.2. The Government remains committed to promoting the longterm development of the economy alongside the reduction of poverty, as identified in its Vision 2020 document. The Economic Development and Poverty Reduction Strategy sets out the GoR's strategy medium term strategy for realising these objectives. This will be achieved through private sector development, supported by an active state, trade openness, and continued maintenance of macroeconomic stability.

4.3. Reform of the public sector will ensure that Rwanda has efficient and effective organisations fit to push forward the development agenda over the coming decades. Continuous review of organisational objectives and structures will facilitate the definition of the roles and responsibilities of civil servants in a way that meets Rwanda's current and future needs, rather than those of the past.

4.4. The GoR remains committed to pursuing policies of decentralisation, transferring powers, responsibilities and resources to decentralised entities and in doing so increasing local ownership of development activities.

1. In the interest of mutual accountability, the GoR is committed to developing contracts with development partners in which rights, mutual obligations and accountabilities are identified clearly. These contracts will take the form of memoranda of understanding signed by the GoR and donor agencies.
2. Whilst sections 3 and 4 of this document set out the Government's policies and commitments, this section outlines how these statements will be translated into action on the part of the government and its development partners.

IMPLEMENTATION OF THE AID POLICY

5.2. The GoR is keen to ensure that the implementation of externally financed projects and programmes currently underway is not adversely affected by the adoption of this Policy. Disruption to such assistance may reduce, rather than increase, its real value. It is therefore intended that a phased approach be adopted in the implementation of this Policy, which will not be applied retrospectively.

DEVELOPMENT OF AN ACTION PLAN

5.3. Upon adoption of this policy by the Cabinet, MINECOFIN will be tasked with the drawing up of an action plan for the effective implementation of this policy. This plan will prioritise actions on the part of government bodies, taking into account the government's capacities to implement change. The action plan will comprise a number of components, as identified in 5.4 to 5.13 below.

Communication strategy

5.4. A strategy for sensitising stakeholders at both central and decentralised levels to the content and implications of the present Policy will be devised and implemented. This will ensure that all GoR employees involved in the negotiation and management of external assistance are able to fulfil their roles as implementers of the Policy.

Manual of procedures

5.5. A manual providing detailed advice on the processes of negotiation and management of aid will be devised, in order to ensure adherence to the division of responsibilities set out in 3.26 to 3.46 above. This document will provide clear guidance on the responsibilities of different government actors at each stage in the process, the necessary documentation, and timeframes within which requests must be actioned.

Vertical funds

5.6. In order to address the potentially undesirable effects of vertical funds as set out in

3.23 to 3.25 above, research will be undertaken to ascertain the extent to which such mechanisms for the delivery of assistance may be problematic in Rwanda, and clear guidelines for the negotiation and acceptance of such assistance will be developed on the basis of this evidence.

Strengthening of GoR capacities for aid management

5.7. An assessment of capacity needs to facilitate the management of aid will be undertaken, and on the basis of this, a prioritised capacity building plan will be devised and implemented, to include capacities in central and local government, as well as other bodies managing externally sourced resources.

5.8. Training in the use of government systems relevant to the management of aid will be undertaken as mandated in 3.53. Steps will be taken to ensure that comprehensive information on the activities of international NGOs is collected, as set out in 3.20 above.

5.9. Steps will be taken to ensure that the present Policy is implemented in a manner that is consistent with the principles set out in Rwanda's policies on decentralisation.

Donor commitments

5.10. This document sets out how the GoR intends to fulfil its commitments made at an international level to increase aid effectiveness. The GoR will proceed to communicate this with its donors and will invite them to provide clear statements on how they each see themselves implementing those commitments in Rwanda. Subsequent to this, a joint proposal to support the implementation of this policy will be invited.

5.11. Pursuant to 2.9 above, international NGOs active in Rwanda will also be invited to set out how they intend to respond to the government's adoption of this Policy.

Independent monitoring

5.12. Discussions will be initiated with the aim of establishing an independent monitoring mechanism, as provided for in 3.60 above.

Dispute resolution

5.13. Pursuant to 3.58, discussions will be held with a view to agreeing on clear rules for the resolution of disputes with donors.

OVERSEEING IMPLEMENTATION

5.14. An Aid Policy Implementation Committee will be mandated by Cabinet to oversee the effective implementation of this policy, the chair reporting to Cabinet on a regular basis on the progress made in implementation.

5.15. The External Finance Unit within MINECOFIN is mandated with, amongst other tasks, overseeing the Government's activities in the area of aid coordination, harmonisation and alignment.

5.16. The External Finance Unit will act as the secretariat to the Implementation Committee identified in 5.14 above, and will provide technical input to the Committee in the implementation of this Policy.

MINISTRY OF FINANCE AND ECONOMIC PLANNING (MINECOFIN)

The Ministry of Finance and Economic Planning (MINECOFIN) was formed in March 1997 from the joining of the Ministry of Finance and the Ministry of Planning. This was done in order to improve the co-ordination between the functions of finance and planning.

In the ministerial re-structuring of February 1999, the Ministry took on the function of development co-operation from the Ministry of Foreign Affairs.

The building on the left was used by the old Ministry of Finance, and now houses the Minister of Finance and Economic Planning, the Departments of Budget, Treasury and Administration and Finance, and CEPEX.
Similarly, the building on the right [to be inserted] was used by the old Ministry of Planning, and should now be visited for the Minister of State, the Secretary General, the Documentation Centre, the Departments of Statistics and Strategic Planning, the Privatisation Secretariat and CEPEX.

MISSION

The Mission of the Ministry is as follows:

Develop policy and initiate programmes for raising and managing the State's financial resources;

Supervise the national budget;

Elaborate guidelines and the framework of national and sectoral development plans and programmes;

Coordinate and harmonise sectoral policies and programs as well as monitor their implementation and effectiveness;

Develop and coordinate programmes of external cooperation and support.

OBJECTIVES

Rwanda has embarked on an ambitious program of transition from conflict and emergency to peace and sustainable development. The overall objectives of the transition program are to lay the basis for national reconciliation, sustainable economic growth, human resource development, and the improvements of the standard of living of the Rwandans.

Macroeconomic and structural reforms, improvements in justice and political governance, sustainable reintegration of the population, poverty reduction, and transformation of the economy are at the heart of this ambitious program. Given Rwanda's circumstances and recent history, the transition is complex. In June 1998, the Government adopted an economic reform program elaborated in the first post-genocide policy framework paper (PFP), prepared in collaboration with the staffs of the World Bank and the IMF. The program received strong support from multilateral institutions and some bilateral donors.

The performance of this program so far can be judged as satisfactory. Rwanda successfully implemented and concluded the first-year ESAF with the midterm review completed in March 1999. This document focuses on the Government's program of policy and institutional reforms for the three-year period July 1999 to June 2002.

NATIONAL STRATEGY

The strategy for the next three years will put emphasis on national reconciliation and poverty reduction through:

Consolidating the progress made in the areas of reintegration, justice, governance, and transparency;

Revitalizing agriculture and the rural economy;

Focusing on human resource development;

Maintaining macroeconomic stability;

Improving public resource mobilization and management;

Enhancing the institutional framework to help develop private sector activity and promote external competitiveness;

Strengthening institutional and administrative capacity;

Promoting the diversification of exports and Rwanda's access to the sea; and

Improving transport services and energy supplies and reducing housing shortages.

MACROECONOMIC FRAMEWORK AND STRATEGY

The main elements of the medium-term macroeconomic program are to:

Achieve annual average real GDP growth rate of 5-6 percent a year;

Keep inflation at below 5 percent a year; and

Maintain the external current account deficit (excluding official transfers) at about 17 percent of GDP

Maintain the level of gross official reserves at a level of at least four months of imports c.i.f.

Whereas the high growth rate in real GDP in 1995–98 was achieved by bringing existing capacity back into use, henceforth, sustained growth at the targeted rate would require a significant increase in investment, from 152 percent of GDP in 1998–99 to 192 percent in 2001–02. With government investment projected at about 9 percent of GDP, an increase in private investment from 82 percent of GDP in 1998–99 to more than 10 percent in 2001–02 would be needed, as well as similar increase in private savings. Increases in investment and savings levels will depend on continued progress in restoring confidence in the economy, which, in turn, depends on the progress in national reconciliation, domestic and regional security, and structural reforms. Significant foreign aid, including assistance to reduce the external debt burden, will remain essential to enable Rwanda to achieve high and sustainable growth.

CONTACT DETAILS

Postal Address
Ministry of Finance and Economic Planning, BP 158, Kigali, Rwanda.

E-mail Address
mfin@rwandatel1.rwanda1.com

Telephone and Fax

250 is the international code for Rwanda.
Ex-Finance building: 77994
Ex-Planning building: 75113

Contact	Telephone	Fax
Minister	75756	77581
Minister of State	74785	75719
Secretary-General	75113	75719
Director of Budget	72272	77581
Director of Treasury	75239	77581
Director of Macro Policy	71605	77581
Director of Strategic Planning	75776	75719
Director of Statistics	78937	75719
Director of Admin. & Finance	74568	75719

RWANDAN ECONOMY: STRATEGIC ANALYSIS AND REFORMS

The Rwandan economy is at the crossroads. It has to urgently address structural challenges while simultaneously dealing with the consequences of the 1994 genocide. Support from its external partners has provided a breathing space to develop the productive apparatus, but these cannot be counted upon in the future. As aid flows decline throughout Sub-Saharan Africa, the country must create and maintain an environment conducive to private sector activity and that replaces the aid flows by increased Foreign Direct Investment (FDI).

World market prices of coffee and tea, Rwanda's main exports, declined by about 30% and 14% respectively between July 1998 and July 1999, and are not expected to recover in the medium term. World petroleum prices have risen from under US$ 12 per barrel to over US$ 23 per barrel over the year. The increased petroleum prices had to be passed on to the consumer. In addition, the imposition of axle weight limits in neighbouring countries has increased transport costs that were already high due to Rwanda's distance to the sea and dependence upon road transport.

The integration of the Rwandan economy into the larger East Africa/Great Lakes regional market could enhance the access of Rwanda's goods and services to these markets. Rwanda belongs to COMESA and has been accepted as a member of the East African Co-operation Council. Rwanda is also participating in the Cross Border Initiative (CBI).

The Rwandan economy suffers from a number of structural problems. These date back over the last 30 years, but have been exacerbated by the events of 1994. At the moment, they have been masked by external inflows of aid, grants and concessional loans. The main structural problems include: (i) Structural trade deficit (ii) Structural imbalance between Government revenues and expenditures (iii) Incidence and depth of poverty (iv) Expensive land transport (v) Negative savings and low investment (vi) Environmental degradation.

INDUSTRIAL SECTOR

The economy showed signs of stagnation in 1999, partly due to a general slowdown in demand associated with the phasing down of activities after the post-1994 emergency period. Real GDP growth, which was projected at 8%, is now estimated to be only 5% in 1999.

Agriculture constitutes over 40% of GDP, and provides 91% of employment and 80% of exports. Food crop production has increased, but a food deficit is still projected. Furthermore, whilst production improved in the northwest, the spectre of drought and famine became a real possibility elsewhere in the country. With respect to traditional export crops, the performance of tea and coffee remained subdued. Coffee revenues are at its lowest in 8 years due to decline in value and volume.

The industrial sector registered the fastest growth, but its impact is limited given its relative size. Imported raw materials and semi-finished goods are lower, largely on account of transport and slackened demand. Beer and cigarette production is also down as manufacturers and consumers adjust to changes in excise taxes. The retail and wholesale trade have fared well. However, the transport sub-sector has suffered from the axle weight limits.

The economy as a whole suffers from institutional, financial and sectoral constraints to growth. However, various measures can and are being taken to remedy them.

FISCAL PERFORMANCE

The 1999 revenue performance shows an improvement over 1998. However, in view of adverse exogenous factors as well as delays in tax administration reforms, the Government's revenue targets were revised downwards. Tax revenue is projected to increase from 10.5% in 1999 to 10.7% Of GDP in 2000.

Given the expected revenue shortfall, the Government decided to reduce non-social recurrent expenditures during the second half of 1999. Social spending objectives, including exceptional social spending programmes, are within targets set and the social sector is protected from expenditure cuts.

The primary fiscal deficit has been projected at 4.5 billion RWF (0.7% of GDP) to virtually zero in the year 2000.

Foreign financed capital expenditure is estimated at 60.5 billion RWF of which 63% is expected in the form of capital grants. The rate of execution of externally funded projects remains relatively weak due to limited implementation capacity.

Fiscal reforms introduced in the course of 1999 included: (i) the lowering of the maximum import tariff rate from 40% to 25%, the middle rate from 20% to 25% and the lowest rate from 10% to 5%; (ii) revised increases of excise duties on cigarettes, wines and spirits, beer, petroleum products and soft drinks; (iii) introduction of a withholding tax; (iv) abolition of the coffee export tax; (v) imposition of an import surcharge on selected imports and (vi) VAT.

The objective of the Government for the year 2000 is to consolidate progress made over the last five years in macroeconomic stability and structural reforms. Accordingly, the fiscal policies will aim at improving the primary fiscal balance, while increasing the allocation of resources to the social sectors.

MONETARY SECTOR AND PRICES

After sluggish growth in 1998, money demand continued to remain subdued in 1999, reflecting faster growth of the non-monetised sectors of the economy. The increase in net foreign assets of the BNR was much lower than programmed, while domestic credit to the private sector grew by about 13% compared to 22% in 1998. In the first half of 1999, deposit and lending rates fell slightly, but in the face of declining inflation, remained positive.

The rate of inflation is expected to decline from 3% in 1998 to 2% in 1999. Monetary and credit policies will aim at keeping the annual inflation rate at below 5%.

EXTERNAL SECTOR

The current account deficit is expected to be significantly reduced from 20% of GDP in 1998 to 16% in 1999. However, this is not due to a rise in exports but rather a fall in imports. Total export earnings are only projected to rise slightly, as increases in tea and coffee volumes are offset by declines in world prices. Imports are declining in response to higher transport costs and lower demand.

Gross official reserves are expected to rise to 7.4 months of imports by the end of 1999, compared to 6.1 in 1998.

Rwanda's external debt situation is likely to remain very difficult in the medium term. The external debt stock for 1999 is estimated to remain at US$ 1.2 billion. Bilateral debt relief is being pursued following the Paris Club Agreement with Rwanda in July 1998. A Multilateral Debt Fund with expected donor contributions of about US$56 million has been established under the World Bank auspices. Based on its track record under the ESAF – supported program the Government will seek qualification for debt relief under the Heavily Indebted Poor Countries (HIPC) initiative.

The exchange rate continues to be market determined. In confirmation of the Government's commitment to a regime free of controls, the Government has accepted the obligations under Article VIII of the IMF's Articles of Agreement.

SOCIAL EXPENDITURE AND THE CHALLENGE OF POVERTY

Rwanda's social indicators are considerably below the Sub-Saharan African (SSA) average. Life expectancy is 48 years compared to 51 in SSA, and infant mortality is 131 per thousand compared to 91 for SSA. Social expenditure is also below the SSA average.

The Government is committed to raising the allocation of resources to the social sector, safeguarding social spending in the execution of the budget, and to closely monitor social sector performance. Recurrent social expenditure has steadily increased from 2.8% GDP in 1998 to 3.7% GDP in 1999. It will be further increased to 4% in 2000.

Despite such increases, from the results of the social expenditure review in 1998, it is clear that Government resources alone cannot cover the cost of the programmes and projects needed to improve the living conditions of the majority of the population. Some of the Government's social targets include: universal access to primary health care; universal primary education by 2005; raising access to potable water from 50% and 60% of the population; and the elimination of discriminatory laws and practices that limit the access of women to education, employment, land and credit and; strengthening of the HIV/AIDS control program.

With regards to exceptional social spending the Government established a Victims for Genocide Fund to which by law it allocates 5% of domestic recurrent revenue.

Poverty has been a structural problem in Rwanda for decades, but it was worsened dramatically by the genocide of 1994. The proportion of households below the poverty line has risen from 53% in 1993 to an estimated 70% in 1996. Furthermore, the characteristics of poor households have changed dramatically since the war: female- and child-headed households have increased considerably and are particularly vulnerable.

The Government is in the process of formulating a National Poverty Reduction Strategy. Key priority areas include revitalisation and recapitalisation of the rural areas, increasing access to the basic social services of health, education, water and sanitation; and improving roads and marketing infrastructure. The Government will further strengthen the monitoring of key poverty and social performance indicators.

INSTITUTIONAL REFORMS

The Government of Rwanda recognises that to deliver its programmes, it has to build and reorganise public administration to improve its efficiency, effectiveness, transparency and accountability. This is being pursued through the adoption of new organisational structures for ministries, a new job classification and grading system for all civil servants, the removal of ghost workers, and the retrenchment of remaining unqualified staff with an appropriate severance and retraining package.

The Rwandan Demobilisation and Reintegration Programme will continue to demobilise a substantial number of RPA and ex-FAR soldiers, successfully integrate them into civilian life, and enable them to contribute to national reconciliation and economic recovery. Despite the achievements of its first phase, it suffers from a shortfall in donor disbursement.

In an effort to rebuild the social fabric, various Good Governance commissions have been set up to foster the conditions for peaceful coexistence of all Rwandans: the Commission for National Unity and Reconciliation; the Human Rights Commission; and the Commission on Legal and Constitutional Affairs.

PRIVATE SECTOR DEVELOPMENT AND PRIVATISATION

The Government is determined to actively promote the private sector so that it can become the engine of economic growth and development in Rwanda. The primary means by which it is doing this, is by creating a supportive business environment. A new investment code has been passed to facilitate the flow of private investment into the country. This includes the setting up of the Rwanda Investment Promotion Agency that will act as a 'one-stop centre' for new businesses and investments. Tariff and financial reforms are also intended to improve the business environment.

Significant progress has been made in the privatisation of public sector enterprises. As of July 1999, 22 enterprises have been privatised and another 15 are being offered for sale. Forthcoming large privatisation include the tea factories, Electrogaz, the electricity, water and gas utility, and Rwandatel, the national telecommunication monopoly.

TOWARDS ECONOMIC GOVERNANCE AND TRANSPARENCY

Public accountability is being improved through the creation of the National Tender Board in 1998 and the Office of the Auditor General in 1999. The Government has also put in place two procedures for monitoring Government expenditure: quarterly expenditure targets and indicators, and a flash reporting system.

As part of the Government's effort in orienting economic and social policy towards reducing poverty in the country, a poverty-monitoring unit will be set up in the Ministry of Finance. Through this unit and in collaboration with the social ministries data will be analysed and information provided on the impact of poverty related policies. A household living standards survey is being undertaken. The Government plans a population census in 2001.

The post-1994 emergency period made donor co-ordination difficult. Uncoordinated projects and programmes proliferated. In an effort to remedy the situation, the Government is in the process of establishing more effective aid co-ordination mechanisms. The Ministry of Finance and Economy Planning has been assigned responsibilities for development co-operation. In order to assist it fulfil this role, it is setting up the Central Projects and External Finance Bureau (CEPEX) to improve the co-ordination and management of projects. Furthermore, the Government is encouraging donors to increasingly direct resources through the national budget, by providing mechanisms to ensure accountability (see Aid Coordination Through the National Budget).

In order to ensure that resources are better allocated according to Government priorities, the medium term expenditure framework (MTEF) approach to budgeting and planning is being introduced. This contains the following features: (i) Medium-term sector/ministry ceilings based upon estimates of domestic and external resources; (ii) Integration of the recurrent and development budgets at the programme level;

Poverty worsened dramatically due to the genocide of 1994. The proportion of households below the poverty line,1 estimated at 40 percent in 1985, rose to 53 percent in 1993 and 70 percent in 1997. While the population has increased by more than 50 percent since 1985, the number of poor households, as defined in 1985, has more than doubled. The roots of poverty in Rwanda are fourfold: (i) the stagnation of the economy during 1986–94; (ii) the decline in agricultural productivity in the context of a rising population and diminishing land resources; (iii) the low level of human resource skills; and (iv) the impact of the genocide in 1994 that decimated the human resource base, confidence, and the economic and social infrastructure.

Given the massive destruction of life and human resources and the predominance of rural poverty, a radical policy of human resources development and the revitalization of agriculture and the rural economy are necessary for tackling poverty in Rwanda. In the long term, creating nonfarm employment in rural areas and industrial and service jobs in urban settings, empowering the poor and vulnerable, increasing their access to social services, and protecting their human and legal rights are central to sustainable poverty reduction. The Government fully adheres to this agenda.

Since 1998, priority in budget allocations has been placed on basic social services and reintegration programs. However, certain economic services are also essential to increase the productivity and incomes of the poor and should be priorities in any anti-poverty program. Raising agricultural productivity and developing a market-based agricultural economy are key elements for improving rural incomes. Agricultural field services, particularly research and extension, to enable farmers adopt improved inputs and farming practices, are essential to raising agricultural productivity. Poor infrastructure is increasingly isolating the poor from the markets for their goods and services and hindering the development of a market-based agriculture. Poor people's participation in the development process and access to basic policing, the judicial system, and capacity building would contribute significantly to reducing poverty. With local elections successfully held in March 1999, the Government intends to deepen the democratic process, strengthen decentralization and support the grassroots initiatives. The Government will ensure that budget allocations to these key subsectors and activities receive priority and adequate funding from the budget.

During 1999, the Government, in collaboration with the UNDP, initiated work on the elaboration of a national poverty reduction strategy. This work will be accelerated, with the involvement of other development partners, including the World Bank, and wide consultations with civil society. Meanwhile, the Government is setting up a *Poverty Observatory* in the Ministry of Finance and Economic Planning that will work closely with other social sector ministries, including the Gender and Women in Development and the Social Affairs ministries, to monitor progress in meeting the targets on poverty and basic social indicators.

HUMAN RESOURCE DEVELOPMENT

The acute lack of human capacity and poor health standards are major constraints to the effort to eradicate poverty in Rwanda. The Government is therefore putting very high priority on building the human resource base, with emphasis on education, capacity building, health, the development of women, and HIV/AIDS prevention. Debt relief from bilateral creditors (on Naples terms) and through the Multilateral Debt Trust Fund (MDTF) has made it possible to allocate more domestic budgetary resources to these priority sectors. Under the enhanced HIPC Initiative, Rwanda hopes to benefit from a significant further reduction in its debt burden, and allocate the resources thus freed to the social sectors and other pro-poor priorities.

EDUCATION AND CAPACITY BUILDING

The genocide caused a heavy loss in human resource capacity and the destruction of social capital. It is urgent to educate and train Rwandese in order to meet the country's development challenges. However, low rates of access, poor quality, lack of trained teachers, inadequate teaching materials, and outdated curricula largely devoid of scientific and technical subjects characterize all levels of education. The illiteracy rate was estimated at 40 percent in 1996. The objectives for the education sector are to: (i) increase the net primary school enrollment ratio from the current 70 percent to 80 percent in 2000; (ii) achieve universal primary education by 2005; (iii) increase the transition rate from primary to secondary education from the current 20 percent to 30 percent in 2000 and to 40 percent in 2005, in particular by increasing access to secondary education in rural areas; and (iv) improve the quality and practical relevance of education at all levels, including through a stronger focus on education in science, technology, management, and vocational skills. The Government places priority on building capacity at all levels with emphasis on formal and nonformal continuing education, including adult education, particularly for women and rural dwellers.

To achieve these objectives, the Government intends to progressively raise the proportion of the budget allocated to education, including adequate funding for school infrastructure and for the provision of learning materials. The recently established Kigali Institute of Education (KIE), the Kigali Institute of Science and Technology, the establishment of teacher training colleges and the plan to establish one science-focused secondary school in each prefecture will further enhance these efforts.

KIE graduates will teach in secondary schools and teacher training colleges, which will accelerate the training of primary school teachers. New curricula emphasizing the acquisition of relevant basic skills are being introduced into primary and secondary schools. To help assess the achievements of primary school children, a system of national examinations has been introduced. These efforts are in addition to ongoing programs to rehabilitate and staff primary, secondary, and tertiary institutions and thereby enhance access. The Government intends to adopt cost-recovery policies where possible, including through a system of student loans for tertiary education to be introduced in late 2000. Following a social sector expenditure review undertaken in 1998, work is under way to prepare a comprehensive sector strategy and an expenditure framework that will ensure the efficient use of the increased budget allocations.

HEALTH

In the decade preceding the events of 1994, health standards had deteriorated as a result of the rapidly rising population, underfunding of public health programs, increasing incidence of drug-resistant malaria and AIDS, and growing food insecurity and malnutrition. Since the genocide, a functioning system of decentralized primary health care services delivery, a national drug distribution system and a flexible system of cost sharing have been put in place. Furthermore, community participation, information sharing, and education are being used to facilitate the delivery of primary health services, with special emphasis on public hygiene and other preventive practices.

As the emergency interventions by donors and NGOs are being phased out, the Government has been increasing the budget allocations to the health sector to meet the priority needs of the population within its limited resource envelope. The sector priorities are to strengthen the delivery of primary health care—vaccination, nutrition, water supply and sanitation, and prevention of malaria, AIDS, and other infectious diseases—and improve access to quality health care throughout the country. A key constraint in the health sector is the lack of adequately trained medical and nursing staff, especially in rural areas; the recently established Kigali Institute of Health (KIH) will provide training to health workers. In 1998, the Government carried out a health sector expenditure review; a health sector financing study is under way and an expenditure review of water and sanitation is to be carried out in late 1999. The results of these studies will be used to elaborate further the framework for the health, water, and sanitation sectors.

GENDER AND THE ROLE OF WOMEN

Women, who constitute about 54 percent and 60 percent of the population and labor force, respectively, continue to face substantial constraints on their participation in the economy and society. They receive relatively poor rewards from economic activities due to discriminatory laws and practices that limit their access to education and training, formal employment, land, and credit.

The Government's program for the development of women consists of (i) eliminating all discriminatory legal provisions and institutional practices; (ii) improving water supply, health care, and home energy supply to reduce the constraint on women's participation in the labor market; (iii) raising access to formal and informal education, including training to build entrepreneurial capacity, and adult education and training programs for women in rural areas; (iv) strengthening women's organizations at national and grassroots level to take a lead role in educating women and defending their rights; (v) ensuring the participation of women in decision-making structures at all levels; and (vi) changing perceptions of women's role in the society through education and training. Effective participation by women in the design of these programs will give greater assurance that the long-term interests of women are protected.

The Ministry of Gender and Women in Development is charged with the mandate to bring about a positive change in attitude toward women and promote community-based organizations and programs that facilitate the empowerment of women. At the national level, the ministry is to ensure that the Government's programs and national laws reflect the interests of women and are consistent with the policy of empowering women. A review of the legal and other constraints to the development of women is under way. Specifically, a revised civil code, adopted by the National Assembly in July 1999, will provide for new matrimonial regimes that help to eliminate gender discrimination on inheritance and property rights. The proposed land law will also reinforce the rights for women to inherit and own land. Public education programs to ensure compliance with the revised civil code will be undertaken from late 1999.

HIV/AIDS

The problem of HIV/AIDS, initially regarded as a health issue, has become, for countries like Rwanda, a major development constraint. Since the discovery of the first cases of AIDS in Rwanda in 1983, the infection has spread throughout the country. In Rwanda as elsewhere, AIDS prevalence is not uniformly distributed, with high rates among females between 25 and 34 years of age (20 percent infected), males between 40 and 49 years (18 percent), female prostitutes, people with sexually transmitted diseases, and military personnel. AIDS is far less prevalent than malaria or measles but its socioeconomic impact is greater. It affects primarily adults in their economically most productive years and creates large numbers of widows and orphans who become impoverished and a burden to society.

Despite the Government's efforts during the last 12 years—with support from its external partners—to monitor and stem the spread of AIDS, progress has been slow. This is in part due to the low level of human, material, and financial resources allocated to the health sector. However, to a large extent, slowing the transmission of HIV resides outside the realm of health services, and requires behavioral changes and the active involvement of many other actors. The Government will prepare a comprehensive multisectoral strategy and action plan for a renewed fight against AIDS and begin implementation of the plan by mid-2000. Meanwhile, the Government will further strengthen the AIDS Control Program and intensify the public education campaign on AIDS prevention, with active participation of civil society.

POPULATION

Rwanda's population, estimated to be 8.1 million in 1999, is projected to grow to 11.3 million in 2012, an annual average growth rate of 2.6 percent, compared with the current growth rate of 2.9 percent. This projection assumes that the total fertility rate will decline from 8.3 in 1997 to 4.5 in 2012. The main elements of the Government's strategy for reducing the population growth rate are information, education, and communication (IEC); promotion of education and access to social and economic opportunities for females; and improving the availability of contraceptives. The Government plans to conduct a population census in 2001.

AGRICULTURE AND NATIONAL RESOURCES

INCREASING PRODUCTIVITY IN AGRICULTURE

For over a decade, agricultural productivity has been declining. This decline has demographic, environmental, and policy dimensions. The high population growth led to a rapid exhaustion of arable lands and the fragmentation and excessive use of farmlands.

The degradation of the environment, the very limited use of modern inputs, and the loss of soil fertility reduced yields. Weak research and extension services and a policy environment that was not conducive to the development of agricultural markets contributed to the stagnation of the sector. The Government has now developed an agricultural sector strategy that will move farming from a subsistence activity to a market-based enterprise. The main elements of the strategy are to: (i) promote security of land tenure, improve land use, and encourage land markets; (ii) develop private sector-led markets for both inputs (such as fertilizer and seeds) and products; (iii) improve soil conservation and management; (iv) improve farming methods through research, extension and information services, and intensification of the use of modern inputs; (v) promote rural credit and other financial mechanisms for rural-based activities; (vi) promote the formation of farmers' groups and professional associations; and (vii) improve storage, markets, and farm-to-market roads.

In line with the strategy, a land law to ensure the security of land tenure, improve land use, and provide the framework for land markets to develop, is under preparation. To promote the adoption of modern inputs by farmers, the Government adopted, in 1999, a policy framework for market-based distribution of agricultural inputs, including fertilizer and seeds, and exempted agricultural inputs from sales taxes. The Government will adopt regulations for the distribution of inputs provided by donors and NGOs to avoid distorting the markets and ensure that the market-based input distribution system is sustained. On rural credit, the revised banking law authorizes the BNR to issue and amend prudential regulations for banks and nonbank financial institutions. This allows the BNR to enhance the regulatory framework for rural cooperative savings and loan associations.

Regarding infrastructure, the main and rural access roads have experienced a marked deterioration during the last four years due to excessive loads by relief-related vehicles and severe damage by flooding, more recently associated with the El Niño-weather pattern. Many households and communities, including new settlements, are thus isolated from the services and markets needed to improve their productivity and market their goods. The Government recognizes that the rehabilitation of roads and local market infrastructure would reduce isolation and link up these communities to larger markets.

RENEWING NATURAL RESOURCES

The natural resource base of Rwanda—land, forests, wildlife, and water—has been an important source of household and national income, providing the basis for farming, fishing, energy production, and tourism. These resources have been degraded by excessive demand for them for agriculture and household energy, owing to high population growth rates and the lack of effective policies to preserve biodiversity. Environmental degradation has been a major factor in the decline of agricultural production. The genocide and the subsequent efforts to resettle displaced populations have accelerated the destruction of natural resources.

The Government believes that resettlement must be carried out in a way that does not further damage the resource base, and it attaches a high priority to resource restoration, protection, and effective management. In this light, it has recently established the Ministry of Lands, Human Resettlement, and Environmental Protection. The Government's strategy includes the creation of conditions for increasing nonfarm employment to relieve the pressure on the land and forests; the adoption of a land law that encourages efficient land use; the undertaking of environmental impact assessments of major sectoral projects; and the promotion of national consciousness on environmental issues. This strategy will be integrated into the review and update of the National Environmental Action Plan scheduled for 2001.

PRIVATE SECTOR DEVELOPMENT

BUSINESS ENVIRONMENT

The strategy of the Government for private sector development is based on the following elements: (i) maintaining a stable macroeconomic framework and eliminating distortions in incentives; (ii) establishing a liberal and transparent legal, labor, trade, and tax framework for the private sector; and (iii) reducing business costs through the provision of infrastructure and public utility services at competitive costs. The Government is reviewing and revising business-related laws with a view to facilitating private business activity and improving the functioning of a market economy. Laws under revision include the labor code, the internal trade act, and the insurance law. A framework for a structured dialogue between the private sector and the Government is also being developed. In early 1999, the Investment Promotion Act became law, providing for the establishment of the Rwanda Investment Promotion Agency as a 'one-stop-center' for facilitating investments and establishing new businesses.

Small- and medium-size enterprises in urban and rural areas are likely to be effective employment generators. The Government is therefore taking specific steps to promote these enterprises through the restructuring of the rural savings and loans cooperatives, improvements in markets and transport infrastructure (particularly in rural areas), and the simplification of the licensing and taxation requirements.

PRIVATE ENTERPRISES AND PRIVATISATION

The Government aims at a smooth and transparent privatization process while drawing lessons from experiences with public enterprise reform elsewhere. In the course of 1998, the implementation of the privatization program was accelerated and, as of September 1999, 20 enterprises have been privatized, 3 are under liquidation, and another 14 have been offered for sale. During 1999–2000, the Government intends to sell, bring to the point of sale, liquidate, or sell its minority shares in a cumulative total of 46 enterprises out of a divestiture program of 69. The main enterprises remaining to be privatized are the 9 tea factories and estates, the telecommunications monopoly (Rwandatel), and the energy/water/gas utility (ELECTROGAZ). The World Bank is providing assistance for the privatization of these enterprises. Specifically, the Bank has assisted the Government to prepare the regulatory framework for the telecommunications sector. Work is under way, with the assistance of the Bank, to prepare a restructuring plan for ELECTROGAZ, separating it into electricity, water, and gas companies, and to privatize certain functions during 1999–2001. The legislation to put in place the regulatory frameworks for the telecommunications and energy/water sectors will be presented to the National Assembly in the course of 2000.
To ensure the transparency of the privatization process, the Government will continue with the extensive advertising of enterprises for sale, public opening of bids, and intensive media campaigns to inform the public about the privatization process. The privatization of public enterprises is hampered by the lack of qualified manpower and resources to deal up front with the labor consequences. The Government also sees the need to widen and increase ownership by Rwandese. For these two reasons, the Government proposes to put in place a scheme to reintegrate retrenched workers and set up a Privatization Trust Fund to enhance wide ownership of privatized firms.

EXPORT DEVELOPMENT

The Government is concerned that the current macroeconomic stability is based on increasing external aid and not growth in exports. With export receipts that cover only about 20 percent of imports and an external current account deficit at about 17 percent of GDP, Rwanda is highly dependent on external aid. A rapid expansion of exports is needed to reduce this dependence. The Government's medium-term strategy for export expansion is to revive traditional exports, encourage foreign and domestic investment in high value-added export production, and reduce international transport costs.

The Government has initiated substantial reforms in the tea and coffee sectors, with a view to increase production for exports and enhance rural cash incomes. The producer price of tea was increased by 37 percent in February 1999. The privatization of the tea factories and estates managed by OCIR-Thé2[2]will begin by end-1999. The Government will also adopt by March 2000 a new regulatory framework for the tea sector, including a revision of the legal mandate of the Rwanda tea board (OCIR-Thé), converting it into an entity responsible for regulating, promoting, and monitoring the performance of the tea sector. The coffee export tax was eliminated in early 1999, removing a major impediment to growth and investment in the sector.

The Government is actively consulting with the stakeholders (coffee farmers, farmers associations, traders, processors, and exporters) to draw up a comprehensive strategy to revive the coffee sector. This will include the reform of the Rwanda coffee board (OCIR-Café)1[3] into an industry-based organization, with its mandate limited to regulation, monitoring, and promotion, including research and possibly the provision of extension services. The Government will encourage the formation of coffee farmers associations to facilitate communication with farmers and enhance the distribution and adoption of improved seedling and other inputs in remote regions.

Rwanda has a good potential for nontraditional exports, including manufactures for regional markets, mineral products, and high-value horticulture. The Government recognizes that the diversification of exports will require sustained efforts to create a friendly environment for private investment. The establishment of the Rwanda Investment Promotion agency, to promote and facilitate investment, exports, and business development, is expected to give a boost to the export sector. The mining code is being revised to attract investment to the sector and boost its exports. The eventual acceptance of Rwanda into the East African Community, comprising of Kenya, Tanzania, and Uganda, will hasten the integration of the Rwandese economy into the larger COMESA regional markets.

CAPACITY BUILDING AND PUBLIC SERVICE REFORM

The Government of Rwanda recognizes that to deliver its programs it has to reorganize the public administration in order to improve its efficiency, effectiveness, transparency, and accountability. In February 1999, the ministerial tasks were regrouped, increasing the number of ministries from 18 to 21, to emphasize key development priorities (land reform and resettlement, gender and women issues, energy and natural resources, and decentralization and local government). In October 1999, the Government adopted new organizational structures for all ministries, in line with their respective missions, as well as a new job classification and grading system for all civil servants. This will provide the basis for the rationalization of positions in the civil service, ensuring that responsibilities are consistent with qualifications and grading. The authorities - with technical assistance from UNDP - will finalize the job descriptions and assign all eligible staff to positions in the new structure, consistent with their qualifications by end-1999.

In late 1998, a census of civil servants was undertaken to help complete the process of removing ghosts from the payroll and provide the database for the further rationalization of functions, posts, and remuneration of the civil service. The Government will, in the course of 1999/2000, retrench any remaining unqualified staff with an appropriate severance and retraining package and selectively recruit qualified staff, consistent with an overall target of 9,500 for the core civil servants (excluding teachers) and with the need for meeting priority needs in the health and justice sectors. The Government fully realizes the social consequences of retrenchment and is looking for donor assistance to finance the reintegration of retrenchees into the labor market and business activities.

Regarding payroll management, the Government has recently regularized the status of about 7,700 civil servants (mostly teachers) without proper contracts and therefore not on the payroll. A central computerized civil service database—a key instrument for effective control of the size of the civil service and payroll management—was established in April 1999, with technical assistance from UNDP. A similar system for maintaining employee career records will be set up by March 2000. To increase the capacity of the institutions charged with public accountability and fiscal transparency (i.e., the National Tender Board (NTB) and the Office of the Auditor-General), the Government is receiving a World Bank grant to support the NTB and is seeking support from bilateral donors for the Office of the Auditor-General.

The next stage of reforms of public administration will concentrate on sustaining and deepening the efficiency improvements, including contracting out noncentral civil service functions to the private sector, and carry out institutional reforms to establish a civil service that operates on the principles of competency, accountability, transparency, and is outward looking and service/goal/results oriented. The Government will develop in 2000, and in consultation with civil society, a vision for the next stage of reforms of public administration.

IMPROVING INFRASTRUCTURE

TRANSPORT AND TELECOMMUNICATIONS

Rwanda's geographical location and poor transport facilities constrain its participation in the regional and global economy. Transport costs are very high because of the distance to the sea, as well as to inefficiencies and structural inadequacies in the current transportation arrangements. The recent introduction of axle-load weight limitations in Kenya and Uganda has drastically raised import costs and adversely affected import volumes. To bring down transport costs, enhance Rwanda's integration into the regional and global economies and develop its role as a regional trade center, the Government intends to privatize utilities and transportation facilities and diversify the routes to the sea, particularly through the central and southern corridors. The Government is considering a number of options including a railway from Kigali to the Tanzania rail terminus at Isaka and/or to Lake Tanganyika.

On the domestic infrastructure, it is increasingly urgent to deal with the marked deterioration of main arteries and rural roads damaged in the last four years. The Government will seek donor assistance for the rehabilitation of the main and feeder roads, which are essential for agricultural and trade development. It will promote an efficient private sector-based rural transport system and, in this context, encourage the reestablishment of transport cooperatives in rural areas. As previously noted, the Government will privatize Rwandatel and establish a regulatory framework that would liberalize the telecommunications sector and attract private investment. The Government, given its capacity constraints, is considering a multisector regulator to avoid a proliferation of industry-specific bodies.

WATER AND SANITATION

Access to potable water was identified by both rural and urban dwellers as the highest priority public service. Women, many of whom have become household heads, spend a large part of their day in obtaining water, which considerably constrains their time available for income-earning employment. The Government's strategic framework for water supply in rural areas requires strong community participation in water delivery. It gives priority to capacity building to enhance community participation and the technical skills of operators, and to reinforce planning and management by the municipalities and central administration.

For water supply in the urban areas, the break-up of ELECTROGAZ, leading to a privately managed water supply and sanitation company, is a priority. For urban sanitation, the priority is to build the institutional capacity of urban administrations to effectively manage sanitation services. The Government seeks to improve the population's awareness of the importance of water conservation and sanitation through information and educational programs.

ENERGY

The objectives of the Government in the energy sector are to expand and diversify energy supplies at competitive costs, promote the efficient utilization of Rwanda's energy resources, and minimize the potential adverse environmental impacts. The immediate priorities in the energy sector are to (i) rehabilitate key power facilities; (ii) restructure and privatize the part of ELECTROGAZ that supplies and distributes electricity and gas so as to improve its operational efficiency; (iii) build capacity for policy development and investment planning in key subsectors such as gas, hydropower, petroleum products, rural electrification, and renewable energy; and (iv) promote the regeneration of forest resources damaged during the emergencies in the country.

The Government is preparing a strategic and regulatory framework to address both urban and rural energy needs and to encourage private sector energy provision and distribution. This strategy will emphasize the efficient use of sustainable energy sources based on natural resources. Therefore, it envisages the reduction of the use of wood, particularly in urban areas, including by encouraging the use of more efficient stoves. The Government aims to promote private investment for harnessing the methane gas reserves in Lake Kivu. For that purpose, it has just created a Natural Gas Promotion Unit in the Ministry of Energy. The expansion and regeneration of forest resources is also an important element of the strategy. The Government, in collaboration with the World Bank, will carry out, in 2000, a review of the energy situation in Rwanda, with particular emphasis on rural energy needs and supplies.

HOUSING AND URBAN DEVELOPMENT

Providing assistance for permanent shelter to returnees ("old-case" and "new-case" refugees), victims of genocide, and other vulnerable persons remains a priority. In the rural areas, the assistance will enable the affected populations to construct and/or rehabilitate their own houses. The housing and social services shortage in urban areas is acute. The population in Kigali and other urban centers has more than tripled since 1994 and demand for housing and other urban services has increased dramatically, overtaxing the ability of the urban administrations. The Government is placing priority on strengthening the capacity of urban communities to provide social services and facilitate the provision of housing by the private sector. A cadastre and land-titling system will be developed to improve the functioning of land and housing markets in urban areas. The Government will also prepare and adopt a Land Use Master Plan, including a sites and services program, for Kigali and other urban areas, and will design and implement water supply and sanitation systems with an appropriate institutional structure to ensure sustainability.

TAXES FOR GROWTH AND DEVELOPMENT: BASIC REGULATORY FRAMEWORK

BACKGROUND

The Rwanda Government announced the idea of setting up the Rwanda Revenue Authority in February 1997 as a major tax modernization initiative to try and redress the detrimental impact on the revenue collecting capacity of the Departments of Tax and Customs shattered by the events of the 1994 war.Rehabilitation of these, therefore, is the background to the formation of the RRA in the quest to restore procedures and controls by the Government of Rwanda.Parliament, having reviewed changes to fiscal policy in 1997, made preparations, and on 1st January 1998, the autonomous Rwanda Revenue Authority was launched.The RRA is a central body for the assessment and collection of specified tax revenue, for administration and enforcement of the laws relating to such revenue, as well as accounting for all the revenue to which those laws apply.The RRA is also required to advise the Government on policy matters relating to revenue whether specified or not.

MISSION

We contribute to the National Development by maximising revenue collection at minimum cost, while providing a high quality, courteous and equitable service to taxpayers.

OBJECTIVES

The RRA has the task of financing the national budget through revenue mobilization so as to:

1. Finance development activities and alleviate poverty in the Rwanda society;

2. Aim at empowering the Government of Rwanda to fund its own essential expenditure.

ORGANISATIONAL STRUCTURE

Board of Directors

The RRA is governed by a Board of Directors under a Board Chairperson who is appointed by the Prime Minister with the recommendation of the Cabinet. It is responsible for the formulation and implementation of the day to day policies of the RRA.

The eight members of the Board include: the Chairperson, the Commissioner General, the Secretary General of the Ministry of Finance and Economic Planning, the Secretary General of the Ministry of Commerce and Industry, and three other distinguished members in the field of accountancy, law, economics or other relevant fields appointed by the Prime Minister with the recommendation of the Cabinet.

COMMISSIONER GENERAL

Mr. Edward Larbi Siaw.

REVENUE DEPARTMENT

Customs and Excise

Commissioner: Mr. Simon Ntare

Outputs: The primary strategy of the Customs and Excise Department is to maximise and sustain revenue collections while facilitating trade and protecting the country's economy. The Departments responsibility involves prompt assessment and collection of customs taxes, specifically all import duties.

TAX

Commissioner: Mr. Appolinaire Murangira

*Outputs:*The primary aim of the Tax Department is to maximise and sustain revenue collections. The department also aims to improve revenue collection processes and procedures, increase tax compliance, combat tax evasion and avoidance, and develop and implement cost effective strategies to expand the tax base. The Department's responsibility involves prompt assessment and collection of all direct taxes as well as arrears due to the Authority.

Audit and Investigations

Commissioner: Mr. Xavier Mbarubukeye

Outputs:

SUPPORT DEPARTMENT

Divisions:

Taxpayer Services
Finance and Administration
Human Resources and Training
Board Secretariat (Legal)
Information Systems and Technology
Management and Tax Information
Commissoner General's Office

CONTACT DETAILS

POSTAL ADDRESS

Headquarters: Rwanda Revenue Authority, BP 3987, Kigali, Rwanda

Customs Department – Gikondo and Kanombe: BP 718, Kigali, Rwanda

Tax Department – Muhima: BP 42, Kigali, Rwanda

STREET ADDRESS

Headquarters: Opposite the Post Office, Boulevard de Paix, Kigali

E-MAIL ADDRESS

siaw@rwandatel1.rwanda1.com

TELEPHONE AND FAX

250 is the international code for Rwanda.

Contact	Telephone	Fax
Reception	78487	78488
Commissioner General	73608	78488
Commissioner of Customs and Excise	75166	75166
Commissioner of Tax	74920	74920
Commissioner of Audit and Investigations	75198	75198
Director for Taxpayers Services	71741	71741
Revenue Protection Services	71439	71439

Customs Department - Gikondo	78088	78088
Customs Department – Kanombe Airport	87043	87043
Tax Department - Muhima	74916 / 74919	74916

PRIVATIZATION PROCESS IN RWANDA: PROGRAM AND THE REGULATORY FRAMEWORK

PRIVATIZATION PROGRAM IN RWANDA

Rwanda 's Government of National Unity has embarked on a program of comprehensiveeconomic and social reforms necessitatedby the tragic genocide which befell the country in 1994 .

Recognizing that the principal of economic growth in Africa and elsewhere has been the private sector, Rwanda felt it should not be left behind and has put in place an ambitious privatization program of its state-owned enterprises. It started with a declaration by his Excellency President Bizimungu on April 11, 1996, a Privatization and Public Investment law enacted, which gave the Government powers to liquidate, hire out, restructure and divest partially or wholly any public enterprise, depending on the legalities of its creation.

In August 25 1996, the Government directed that 46 enterprises be privatized as soon as possible and government shares in an additional 18 enterprises be ceded to the private sector. The Privatization Programme started to be implemented in October 1997 and since then, 20 enterprises have been sold, four are under liquidation, and the process of selling another five is almost complete.

Privatization in Rwanda, like everywhere else, carries with it a number of challenges and opportunities. The way the players in the field respond to these challenges will determine Rwanda's economic future.

On the other hand, the range of opportunities for investors runs the gamut from acquiring a growing business to increasing efficiency through better management of the acquired enterprise.

A crucial underlying assumption is that privatization is not an end in itself, but can be an instrument for making the government more efficient and the economy more productive when it is part of broader social reforms.

Ultimately, the success of privatization depends on developing a fully functioning market economy.

Rwanda will continue its liberal economic policies and our privatization policy will remain consistent, predictable and transparent.

OBJECTIVES

Privatisation was adopted by Governmentto meet the following main objectives:

Relieve the Financial and Administrative Burden of Government

It is meant to relinquish commercial management to the private sectorand leave the Government free to concentrate on sovereigntyfunctions of maintaining law and order and providing support for achieving growth and social objectives.

Improve Efficiency and Productivity

This would be promoted through several means such as introduction of competition, doing away with civil service rigidities and the introduction of incentives for employees.

High efficiency and profits will enable the Government to gain additional revenue especially in the form of corporate tax to finance projects under its socio-economic development plan

Reduce the Size and Presence of the Public Sector in the Economy

Thegradual disengagement of the state from economic activities through privatisation will reduce the public sector which will allow the economy to be increasingly led by the private sector.

Broadening the Ownership Base

PROCEDURES

The implementation of the Privatisation Programme is carried out in a series of Annual Work Plans which set out the priority activities for the year and the enterprises which will be handled during that time. In executing the annual work plan, the following activities are carried out in respect of the enterprises to be privatised:

Performing Financial and Legal Audits of Enterprises

A properly conducted legal audit informs the Privatisation about who owns the company and that the company has authority to sell the company or its assets.

The financial audit informs the commission about the financial condition of the Enterprise. It gives a fair indication of the enterprise's value as a going concern.

Valuation of Enterprises

The Public Enterprises are valued in order to ensure transparency and public accountability. The valuation is done before they are advertised for sale.

Bidding Preparations

The pre-bidding preparation involves assembling all the relevant information on each enterprise to produce a memorandum for each enterprise being offered, preparation of terms of reference for the bidders, the procedures and qualifications for bidding on the Enterprise.

Invitation for Bids

A Public Enterprises slated for sale is sufficiently advertised in the press. The advertisement includes a profile of the Enterprise to enable prospective buyers undertake preliminary evaluation of the business before detailed valuation and submission of bids.

The bid documents inform the prospective bidder about the following :

Bid fees - the bidder shall be required to pay a certain sum based on the size of the Enterprise to the Secretariat

Technical capabilities statement - This has to demonstrate the bidder's competence to effectively manage the business of the concerned enterprise. The capability statement is required only when pre-qualification process has not been carried out.

Business Plan - The bid document has to spell out the required elements of the business plan especially those which will form the basis of evaluation.

Bid Price - The bidder must submit his best price, in the currency specified by the terms of reference, and the payment terms.

Bids Opening and Evaluation

At the bid opening, each bid is publicity opened and read out aloud. This entails mentioning the names of the bidder, his or her address and how much money they will have offered for the items being divested.

The Privatisation officials and the Inter-Ministerial Bids evaluation Committee analyses the merit of each bid against the criteria set down in terms of the Tender.

Report of the Bids Evaluation Committee to the Cabinet

The outcome of the Bids Evaluation exercise and the recommendations are forwarded to the Cabinet for a final decision.

Negotiations with the Successful Bidder

Negotiations are carried out with the successful bidder and an agreement has to be reached on all important clauses which have to go into the sales contract. It is the Final sales contract that is signed by Hon. Minister of Finance and Economic Planning representing the Government and the new owner of the Enterprise.

Post Divestiture Monitoring

The Post-Divestiture Monitoring is mandated to make sure that the business plan presented by the successful bidder is adhered to by checking on the dates of achieving specific and other relevant performance targets.

PRIVATISATIONS FOR 2000

The following enterprises are planned to be privatised during 2000:

RWANDATEL

Telecommunication being the economic sector of the 21st century, RWANDATEL has taken up the challenge to follow the developments closely and keep in touch with modern technology.

ELECTROGAZ

As the national company for the the production, transport, marketing and distribution of electricity, water and gas, ELECTROGAZ has some major projects for the future: rehabilitate and upgrade the electricity net, assure self- sustainability in water, extraction of methane gas from Lake Kivu.

Tea Factories and Plantations

Tea is one of the main export products of Rwanda. Several tea factories and plantations which have a bright future are for sale.

Hotel Izuba

The ideal place for tourists wishing to visit the gorillas, for conference participants or people wanting to relax in a quiet environment. Located in a park of 10,000 m^2 the hotel has 68 rooms and offers a wide range of facilities.

Hotel Akagera

Overlooking the scenic lake Ihema, this hotel serves as an open gateway to the Akagera National Park. With its 60 rooms, conference rooms and swimming pool, the hotel has a great potential.

REDEMI

The *Régie d'Exploitation et de Développement des Mines*, a state-owned mining company, has big potential. While several mines and part of the infrastructure has to be rehabilitated, mining in Rwanda is rapidly expanding.

IMPRISCO

With a monopoly in printing and supplying schoolbooks and educational work, this state-owned printers also wants to explore the market of commercial printing.

TABARWANDA

With a market share of 74% in 1998 and a turnover of 1,860,517,760 Frw (1997), TABARWANDA is the most important producer of cigarettes in Rwanda. The Rwandan state has 23.5% of its shares.

RWANTEXCO

Specialised in the production and marketing of fibres and textiles, this company (50% state-owned) is very ambitious to get going again.

RWANDEX

The main activities of RWANDEX are the exporting of hids and coffee, as well as importing of primary goods and computer equipment. In 1998, the company exported 49% of Rwandan coffee. Through OCIR-Café, the Rwandan State has an interest of 49% in RWANDEX.

MAGERWA

The Magasins Généraux du Rwanda, that runs several warehouses, has adapted itself easily to container transport, and is now the major player in the Rwandan storage market. The Government has 6.25% of the total shares.

Rice Mills

At this moment, the various rice mills in the country - the one in Rwamagana (Kibungo), in Gkonko (Butare) and Bugarama (Cyangugu) - are not exploited at their full capacity. While most of the infrastructure is in place, this sector has big potential.

ETIRU

15% of the capital of this company specialised in flour-milling is owned by the Rwandan State.

ONATRACOM

This is the national transport company, and is in charge of about 10% of the public passenger transport system. It owns 30 Isuzu buses and 15 Nissan buses.

FUTURE PRIVATISATIONS

The Government has also decided to sell its shares in the following enterprises:

SOPAB - Animals Feeds Factory

SONAFRUITS - Fruit Juice Bottling
SORWAL - Match Company
BCR - Commercial Bank of Rwanda

BRD - Rwanda Development Bank

BK - Banque de Kigali – Commercial Bank
SORWATHE - Tea Company
SONARWA - Insurance
BRALIRWA - Beer and Soft Drinks

THE REGULATORY FRAMEWORK

Rwanda 's Government of National Unity has embarked on a programme of comprehensiveeconomic and social reforms necessitatedby the tragic genocide which befell the country in 1994 .

Recognizing that the principle of economic growth in Africa and elsewhere has been the private sector, Rwanda felt it should not be left behind and has put in place an ambitious Privatization Programme of its state-owned enterprises. It started with a declaration by his Excellency President Bizimungu on April 11, 1996, that enacted a Privatization and Public Investment Law which gave the Government powers to liquidate, hire out, restructure and divest partially or wholly any public enterprise, depending on the legalities of its creation.

MISSION

The Privatisation Secretariat is charged with the day to day management and coordination of the activities of the Technical Privatisation Commission in its implementation of the Privatisation Programme.

OBJECTIVES

The objectives of the Secretariat are:

1. To formulate the Privatisation Programme's Work Plan and submit the same to the Technical Committee for adoption;
2. To prepare public enterprises for privatisation, including carrying out financial and legal audits to remove impediments to privatisation;

3. To advertise the enterprises for sale and receive the bids from interested buyers;

4. To assist the Technical Committee to carry out the evaluation of bids received;

5. To carry out public education campaigns about the Privatisation Programme to explain its objectives and benefits to the general public, as well as to encourage private sector investment in privatised enterprises; and

6. To carry out post-privatisation facilitation and monitoring exercises to ensure that the investors' obligations are being fulfilled; that the Government's objectives for each enterprise are achieved; and to provide assistance to the investors, where possible.

ORGANISATIONAL STRUCTURE

The Privatisation Secretariat is comprised of the following:

- **Executive Secretary**
- **Financial Audit and Valuation Unit**
- **Advocacy Unit**
- **Public Enterprises Monitoring Unit**
- **Legal Unit**
- **Administration Unit**

CONTACTS

Postal Address
Executive Secretary, Privatisation Secretariat, BP 158 Kigali, Rwanda.
E-mail Address
pvs@rwandatel1.rwanda1.com
Telephone & Fax
Tel: (250) 75383, 70989, 70991, 70992

Fax: (250) 75384

INVESTMENT CLIMATE: US GOVERNMENT ASSESMENTS

STRATEGIC OBJECTIVE GRANT AGREEMENT

The Government of the United States, through the US Agency for International Development (USAID) and the Government of Rwanda have today 21st June signed three grant agreements (called Strategic Objective Grant Agreements) which commit an additional U$ 15.1 million in economic and social assistance to Rwanda for fiscal year 2000.

The Funds will be made available to continue and expand USAID's on going programs in three strategic assistance areas : rule of law and transparency in governance, health and social sector assistance, and food security and agricultural based economic growth. With today's commitments, the total amount of USAID Funded assistance since 1997 will reach U$ 25. 4 million in the rule of law and governance Sector, U$ 19.3 million in health and social services sector and U$ 19.1 million in the food security area.

With the funds being committed today, USAID will have provided about U$ 485 million in overall assistance to Rwanda since 1994. Including almost U$ 450 in food assistance.

INVESTMENT CLIMATE ASSESMENT

Rwanda is a small, densely populated, landlocked central African nation with an estimated population of over 8 million. The country is recovering the genocide of 1994 which resulted in the destruction of the country's social fabric, its human resource base, institutional capacity, and economic and social infrastructure. Over 800.000 people were killed, about two million fled to camps in neighbouring countries, and another one and one-half million were displaced internally. As a result, economic activity in the country declined by about 50%.

In July 1994, the Rwanda Patriotic Front (RPF) drove out the previous government and formed a government of national unity with four other political parties. Since then, peace has been restored to most of the country , and the internally displaced and returned old-and new caseload refugees, including those who fled in 1994, are being resettled and reintegrated into society. The Government of Rwanda has made it a priority to shift the focus from emergency assistance and rehabilitation to sustainable development and private sector growth. They intend to return the economy to pre-genocide levels by the year 2000 through appropriate macroeconomic policies and to reinforce public sector capacity and private sector skills. In the summer of 1998, Rwanda signed a three-year arrangement with the international Monetary Fund (IMF) under the Enhanced structural adjustment Facility (ESAF). The IMF is expected to give Rwanda a positive report from the first mid-term review expected out in February 1999. However, even with improved economic policies, Rwanda will continue to depend on foreign aid for up to 75% of its budget requirements for the foreseeable future, only slowly expanding its productive capacity.

REGULATORY ENVIRONMENT

In 1995, a fully liberalized and market-determined exchange rate system was established and 20 foreign exchange bureau's were licensed. All lending and deposit interest rates were liberalized and administrative controls abolished. Exporters are permitted to sell their foreign export earnings freely on the domestic exchange market or to retain them in accounts with domestic banks. The exchange rate for the Rwandan Franc fluctuates freely, and payments and transfers for current international transactions are easily made. Special provisions apply to receipts from Rwanda's two major exports, coffee and tea:90% of these export earnings have to be sold to commercial banks. The average market reference exchange rate, as reported by the National Bank of Rwanda, applies to these transactions.

In 1998, the Government of Rwanda established the Rwandan Revenue Authority (RRA). The RRA has had a difficult first year and the staff has been restructured several times. However, their tax collection is slowly improving with special attention being paid to collection of customs duties. Customs duties on imports have been simplified and lowered, using a three-tier system with a maximum rate of 40% and a minimum rate of 0%. Rwanda is moving towards a value added tax system, to be established in the year 2000.The import licensing system is simple and fast, but customs clearance on imports is still fraught with corruption and bureaucratic hurdles.

The Rwandan Parliament approved a new investment code in December 1998. In early 1999.

The GOR plans to open an investment Promotion Agency or "one stop center" to assist foreigners investing at least USD 100,000 in Rwanda. There will be additional incentives for investors operating in a free export economic zone to be established in 1999. The agency will register new investment projects and assist registered enterprises in security all required approvals, certificates, work permits and land for their projects. Business enterprises registered with the agency will automatically be entitled to three work permits for expatriate employees. These expatriate employees will be exempt from import duty and sales tax for the importation of a vehicle and personal and household effects.

The Government of Rwanda's two year-old National Tender Board continues to function with authorizing legislation. The Tender Board was established to issue and manage procurement rules, regulations, guidelines and policies, but is currently serving as the procurement agency for most government purchases as including those made by parastatals and international donors. The government established an Auditor General's office to carry out a continuous audit of adherence to fiscal controls. A revised labor is being reviewed by the Parliament to be passed in 1999.

INVESTMENT POSSIBILITIES

Private investment since the 1994 genocide has been minimal. However, with the passage of the investment code and creation of the Investment Promotion Agency, the Government of Rwanda hopes to promote more aggressively investment opportunities in Rwanda for foreign investors. The major investment opportunities within the next year or two will be in the tea and coffee sectors. Privatization will also open up the market for investment in telecommunications and provision of gas, electricity and water. There are also investment opportunities in tourism, in the transportation and petroleum sectors, and in small industries, such as food processing, beer and soft drink production, flower production, other forms of agribusiness, and mineral processing.

SALES OPPORTUNITIES

Used clothes are Rwanda's largest import from the US sales opportunities also exist in bulk staple foods,4-Wheel drive vehicles, trucks, communications and computer equipment, cosmetics, and consultant services.

PROJECT OPPORTUNITIES

The best project opportunities are in projects funded by the World Bank, African Development Bank and the United Nations Development Program in road expansion, water supply and agriculture.

DOING BUSINESS

Business in Rwanda is conducted in both English and French. The business community imports most of its products from neighboring African countries, Europe, and Dubai.

However, there is a strong interest within the business community in establishing contact with American companies and importing American products. Cargo transportation costs are high.

Customs processing in Rwanda can be bureaucratic and corrupt. The Rwandan Revenue Authority strengthened their efforts to collect customs taxes in late 1998 and these efforts are expected to continue. It would be helpful to have a local agent to facilitate customs and other regulatory procedures.

CONTACT ADDRESSES

Interested parties are encouraged to contact the Economic/Commercial Officer at the U.S. Embassy in Kigali, Rwanda :

Fax : 011-250-72128

E-mail: amembkigali@hotmail.com

Mail:B.P.28,kigali,Rwanda.

PUBLIC INVESTMENT PROGRAM

IMPORTANCE OF THE PUBLIC INVESTMENT PROGRAMME (PIP)

Within the framework of its policy of liberalisation of the economy and the conclusion of the Enhanced Structural Adjustment Facility (ESAF) with the Bretton Woods institutions in 1998, the Government is reducing its role in direct productive activities and most of the public enterprises are being privatised. However, there is still need for the Government to plan its own activities, particularly when the private sector is not yet well developed and the Government is still the main initiator and investor in the country.

The Public Investment Programme (PIP) is an important document for defining the development strategy of the Government and making budgetary forecasts. It covers a rolling period of three years, and serves equally as one of the central documents for discussion with Rwanda's development partners.

CONSISTENCY OF THE PIP WITH NATIONAL ECONOMIC POLICY

The PIP is consistent with national economic policy, being based upon the objectives, policies and budgetary ceilings of the macroeconomic framework of the ESAF for 1999-2001. Section 3 below therefore shows the major macroeconomic objectives and policy framework of the PIP. The total budgetary ceiling for public investment for the period 1999-2001 is RwF 234.4 billion which is divided over three years as follows : 71.7 for 1999 ; 77.2 for 2000 ; and 85.5 for 2001. The PIP 1999-2001 respected these ceilings.

CONSISTENCY OF PROGRAMMES AND PROJECTS WITH SECTORAL POLICY

The PIP 1999-2001 adopts a 'Programme Approach'. The sectoral programmes were identified from the sectoral strategies, which themselves emanated from the sectoral objectives. The projects in the PIP were in turn identified from the programmes. This programme approach is an important part of the selection and prioritisation process which helps to ensure that the scarce resources available are devoted to programmes and projects which are in tune with national and sectoral objectives, policies and strategies. Projects earmarked for the PIP were screened against the programmes according to project screening critieria (see main document Chapter 10 p.63 for a list of these).

THE PROCESS OF THE PREPARING THE PIP 1999-2001 DOCUMENT

The process of preparing PIP involved the following steps :

1. The preparation and presentation of guidelines to the ministries to guide them in the preparation of PIP.

2. A workshop was held from the 17th – 23rd November 1998, whereby each ministry presented its draft PIP 1999-2001 document. The ministries' PIP documents were discussed and recommendations to improve the documents were made.

3. The ministries corrected their PIP documents according to workshop recommendations.

4. MINECOFIN (CEPEX) analysed and consolidated the sectoral PIPs into the final PIP document.

The preparation of the PIP has not been smooth and has met many difficulties and constraints. The most important constraints are :

- Unclearly defined national development priorities ;
- Lack of sectoral and ministerial budget ceilings ;
- Unclearly defined sector policies and strategies ;
- Incomplete database on projects and software not adapted ;
- Insufficient preparation and evaluation of projects ;
- Weak planning capacity at the sector level ;
- Weak involvement of line ministries in the process of developing the PIP.

To improve the process of preparing the PIP, the following actions must be taken :

- Define clearly the national development policies and priorities ;
- Determine sectoral and ministerial budget ceilings and carry out sectoral reviews within the context of the Medium Term Expenditure Framework (MTEF);
- Clearly define sectoral priorities;
- Ensure the establishment and strengthening of planning and monitoring activities in the ministries;
- Improve the planning of projects and the project information system.

SECTOR OBJECTIVES AND POLICIES FOR THE PERIOD 1999-2001

The sectoral policies and strategies allow among other things :

- Assuring the consistency of programmes and projects with objectives and macroeconomic policies ;
- Assuring the rationalisation of resource allocation on the basis of priority sector policies and strategies ;
- Guidance to donors and other investors in their interventions ;

The allocation of the resources of the PIP must be coherent with sectoral objectives, policies, strategies and programmes. The policies are defined from objectives and strategies from policies. Subsector programmes are also defined from strategies. Part II of the main PIP document indicates the objectives, policies, strategies and priority programmes.

The sector policies and strategies have been defined by sub-sector. These sub-sectors are grouped into specific sectors, which in turn are grouped into the four major sectors as follows:

- Productive sector which comprises: Agriculture, Livestock, Fishing, Forestry, Fish-farming, Environment, Cottage Industry, Industry, Mines, Trade, Tourism and Co-operatives;
- Service and Economic Infrastructure sector which covers: Town Planning, Transports, Communications, Water and Sanitation and Energy;
- Social sector that comprises: Education, Health and Population, Social Welfare and Youth, and Sports and Culture;
- Finance and Administration that covers: Justice, Defense and Security, Local Administration, Economic and Financial Management and Foreign Affairs.

SUMMARY OF INVESTMENT EXPENDITURE STATUS FROM 1996 TO 1998

The investment expenditure for the years 1996, 1997 and 1998 (127,718.48 millions FRW) were realised at a rate of 48.47%. In 1996, the realisations were valued at 33,303.15 millions FRW or 43.02% of the provisional estimates of 77,418.58 millions FRW. In 1997 they amounted to 46,054.24 millions FRW for the estimated 108,343.61 millions or a rate of realisation of 42.51%. In 1998 the amount of realisations was 48,361.11 or 62,21% of the provisional estimates of 77,743.52 millions.

SECTORAL BREAKDOWN OF EXPENDITURE FROM 1996 TO 1998

The sectors of Human Resources and Social Development, Infrastructures and Administration and Finance registered high expenditure during the period, with 39,92%, 22,85% and 21,02% respectively, of the total expenditure. In comparison to what had been planned initially, it was the sectors Administration and Finance and Human Resources and Social Development that achieved the highest performance, at a rate of 68,10% in Administration and Finance, and 55,71% in Human Resources and Social Development.

TABLE 1: SECTORAL BREAKDOWN OF INVESTMENT EXPENDITURE FROM 1996 TO 1998 (IN MILLIONS OF RWF)

Sector	1996/1998 forecasts		Estimates of Realisations 1996/1998		
	Amount	% Total	Amount	% Total	Rate of Realisation
Productive	50 243,56	19,07	20 691,46	16,20	41,18
Infrastructures	82 043,16	31,24	29 188,33	22,85	35,46
Human resources	91 522,80	34,73	50 987,94	39,92	55,71
Administration & Finance	39 426,30	14,96	26 850,75	21,02	68,10

Total	263 235,82	100,00	127 718,49	100,00	48,47

The weak performance of the Productive sector as well as the Infrastructure sector is due essentially to delays in the starting up of projects. These are caused firstly by difficulties in fulfilling implementation conditions of credit agreements or financing conventions, secondly by the complexity of donor procedures and especially modalities of tenders and fund disbursements. Some projects for which some funds were programmed have been closed before their end, and their funds have been allocated to other activities that were not necessarily realised : this is among others the case for the Energy Restructuring Project (PRSE), the Agricultural Services Project (PSA) etc...

The low level of realisation (48,47%) is due several factors, including:

- Weak institutional capacity of the technical services responsible for the implementation and the follow-up of development projects which are often not in a state of execution;
- Slowness in the take-off of projects because of difficulties faced by technical ministries in fulfilling the conditions for the implementation of credit agreements and financing conventions;
- Complexity of intervention procedures by various donors especially the modalities of pledging, contracts and disbursement of funds
- Accumulation of debt arrears which led to the freezing of interventions by certain partners;
- Delay of the Budget vote by Parliament for the 1996 and 1997 budgets, and the weakness of the system of planning leading to the overestimation of expenditures.

ANALYSIS OF INVESTMENT EXPENDITURE REQUIREMENTS OF MINISTRIES FOR THE 1999-2001 PERIOD

In conformity with the principle of coherence between the Public Investment Programme and economic and financial policies defined by the macroeconomic framework, the allocation of resources to programmes and projects must respect the budgetary ceilings determined according to financial constraints and sectoral policies. This chapter makes an analysis of the total expenditure requirements for the years 2000 and 2001 as formulated by the line ministries before the Government reshuffle of 8 February 1999, and aims to show the distance between needs and available resources.

The investment needs expressed by the ministries amount to RwF 342,148.89 million, (or the equivalent of US$ 1,0793.33 million at an exchange rate of 317.0 RwF for 1 US$). They are spread over the three years as follows : RwF 71,700.01 million in 1999 i.e. 20.96% of the total amount ; RwF 149,985.26 million in 2000 i.e. 43.25% and RwF 122,463.62 million in 2001 i.e. 35.75%. The breakdown of requirements by ministry is contained in Table 5 of the main document of PIP.

SECTORAL ANALYSIS OF EXPENDITURE REQUIREMENTS FOR THE PERIOD 1999-2001

As shown in table 2 below, the Infrastructures sector requires the largest part of the resources and comes first in ranking with RwF 130,794.73 millions i.e. 38.23% of the total requirements. The Human Resources and Social Development sector should occupy the second rank with RwF 98,272.06 million or 28.72%; the Productive sector comes in third place with RwF 77,965.41 million or 22.79% of the global requirements, before Administration and Finance sector which should benefit from an allocation of RwF 35,116.69 million i.e. 10.26%.

TABLE 2: ANNUAL AND SECTORAL BREAKDOWN OF INVESTMENT REQUIREMENTS FOR THE PERIOD 1999/2001 (IN MILLION RWF)

Year	1999/2001		1999		2000		2001	
Sector	Amount (MRWF)	%	Amount (MRWF)	%	Amount (MRWF)	%	Amount (MRWF)	%
Productive	77,965.41	22.79	19,484.73	27.18	29,371.80	19.85	29,108.89	23.77
Infrastructure	130,794.73	38.23	13,533.81	18.88	66,711.47	46.43	48,549.45	39.64
Human Res. & Social Dev.	98,272.06	28.72	28,061.70	39.14	38,074.62	25.73	32,135.73	26.24
Administration & Finance	35,116.69	10.26	10,619.78	14.81	11,827.36	7.99	12,669.55	10.35
Total	342,148,98	100.00	71,700.01	100.00	147,985.26	100.00	122,463.62	100.00

ANAYSIS OF THE FINANCIAL PROGRAMMING OF THE PIP 1999-2001 ON THE BASIS OF THE ESAF CEILINGS

The requirements of the ministries have been adjusted to respect the ESAF budgetary ceilings. Therefore, the programming of the financing being negotiated has been postponed to 2000 and most of the financing to be sought has been programmed from 2001 on.

After these adjustments, the PIP 1999/2001 amounts to RwF 234,400.0 million (or the equivalent of US$ 739.43 million at an exchange rate of 1 US$ for 317.0 RwF), against RwF 226,037.41 million for the PIP 1998-2000. This ceiling encompasses 498 projects grouped into 106 sector programmes (see Annexes 6 and 7 in the main PIP document). It registers a slight increase of 3.7% in relation to the previous PIP. The total represents 10.51% of GDP over the 1999-2001 period, whereas the total of the PIP 1998-2000 represented 10.13% of estimated GDP for 1998-2000.

NATURE OF THE 1999-2001 PIP EXPENDITURES

The categorization of projects according to the nature of expenses in Table 3 below, allows us to note that 76.34% of the 1999-2001 PIP expenditures may be considered as being investments linked to the creation of gross fixed capital, while 13.49% constitute recurrent expenditures, and the rest of 10.13% constitute technical assistance and pre-investment expenditures. This categorization remains a summary and should be further developed for the future PIPs in order to determine with more precision what the real investment expenditures are, and their implications in terms of recurrent costs which must be borne by the recurrent budget.

TABLE 3: BREAKDOWN OF EXPENDITURE ESTIMATES OF THE PIP 1999-2001 BY NATURE OF EXPENDITURE (IN MILLION RWF)

Year	1999		2000		2001		Total	
Type	Amount	%	Amount	%	Amount	%	Amount	%
TA	4,779.70	6.67	4,629.37	6.00	2,861.03	3.35	12,270.10	5.23
REC	10,535.27	14.69	10,730.83	13.90	10,348.24	12.10	31,614.37	13.49
INV	55,012.97	76.73	57,513.84	74.50	66,408.41	77.67	178,935.21	76.34
PRE	1,372.04	1.91	4,325.96	5.60	5,882.31	6.88	11,580.31	4.94
Total	71,700.00	100.00	77,200.00	100.00	85,500.00	100.00	234,400.00	100.00

(TA = Technical Assistance, REC = Recurrent, INV = Investment, PRE = Pre-investment)

SECTOR-BASED ANALYSIS OF THE 1999/2001 PIP EXPENDITURE ESTIMATES

In accordance with the priorities set out in the Policy Framework Paper for the Enhanced Structural Adjustment Facility, high priority must be given to the sectors of agriculture and infrastructure. Also, resources allocated to the human resources sector must be substantially increased. In this perspective, while allocating resources for the present PIP and especially for the years 2000 and 2001, a particular attention has been given to health and education in order to increase the resources of the Human Resources and Social Development sector.

As shown in Table 4 below, the sectoral breakdown of resource allocation under PIP 1999-2001 reflects the top priority given to the sector of Human Resources and Social Development with a share of RwF 82,452.75 million, representing 35.18% of the total resources planned for the period under consideration. The Productive sector comes second with RwF 64,256.68 million, or 27.41%, followed in third place by the sector of Infrastructure with RwF 58,873.51million, or 25.12%, and finally the sector of Finance and Administration, which is allocated RwF 28,817.06 million, or 12.29 % of the Programme's resources.

One notes that the adjustment of expenditure requirements allowed to contain the PIP amount 1999-2001 within the ESAF budgetary ceiling and to obtain a sector priority in conformity with the sector allocation recommended in the Policy Framework Paper.

TABLE 4: ANNUAL SECTORAL BREAKDOWN OF PIP EXPENDITURE 1999-2001 (IN MILLIONS OF RWF)

Year	1999/2001		1999		2000		2001	
Sector	Amount	%	Amount	%	Amount	%	Amount	%
Production Sector	64,256.68	27.41	19,484.73	27.18	20,703.36	27.28	24,563.65	28.73
Infrastructure	58,873.51	25.12	13,533.77	18.88	19,852.87	25.85	23,927.29	27.99
Human res. & Social dev.	82,452.75	35.18	28,061.73	39.14	29,518.38	37.64	23,825.45	27.87

Administration & Finance	28,817.06	14.16	10,619.78	14.81	7,125,39	9.23	13,183.61	15.42
Total for all sectors	234,399.99	100.00	71,700.00	100.00	77,200.00	100.00	85,500.00	100.00

In comparison with PIP 1998-2000, one notes an increase in resources allocated to the sector of Human Resources and Social Development, especially to the sub-sectors of Education and Health. This sector's share in resource allocation increased from 29.89% of the total PIP 1998-2000 resources to 35.18% of the new PIP, while the Infrastructure sector's share is being reduced from 32.77% to 25.12% under the new PIP. The Productive sector's allocation is also being slightly increased from 23.19% to 27.41%, while that for the Administration and Finance sector is going down from 14.6% to 12.29%.

FINANCING OF THE PIP 1999-2001

The financing of the PIP 1999-2001 is estimated on internal resources of RwF 21,000.00 million or 8.96% of the total amount, and on external resources of 213,400.00 million RwF or 91.04%. The acquired finance of RwF 155,634.49 million represents 72.93% of the total external finance for the three year programme. This acquired external finance is primarily destined to the Human Resource sector, which receives 31.37%, while the Productive sector receives 22.08% and Infrastructure 12.68% (see Annex 4 of the main document).

TABLE 5 : BREAKDOWN OF EXTERNAL FINANCE OF PIP 1999-2001 BY SITUATION AND SECTOR (IN MILLIONS RWF)

Situation	Total		PROD.		INFRASTR.		HUMAN RESOURCES		ADMIN.& FINANCE	
	Amount	%	Amount	%	Amount	%	Amount	%	Amount	%
AQ	155.999,93	73,10	47 089,81	78,70	27.048,28	51,64	66.906,09	84,02	14.955,75	69,41
TBS	33.191,09	15,55	9.226,95	15,42	10 737,57	20,50	8.723,87	10,95	4 502,70	20,90
BN	24.208,98	11,34	3.518,26	5,88	14 597,19	27,87	4.005,06	5,03	2 088,47	9,69
Total	**213.400,00**	**100,00**	**59.835,02**	**100,00**	**52.383,04**	**100,00**	**79.635,01**	**100,00**	**21.546,92**	**100,00**

(AQ = Acquired, BN =Being negotiated, TBS =To be sought)

The funds to be found or in negotiation are estimated at RwF 57,400.07 million, or 26.90% of total external PIP funding. The largest amount of RwF 19,296.86 million or 33.68% is destined for Infrastructure, with RwF 16,965.47 million or 29.61% for Human Resources and Social Development, and RwF 12,745.21 or 22.24% for the Productive sector.

PRIORITY PROGRAMMES OF THE PIP 1999-2001

In order to better identify the priority areas of intervention in the sectors of the PIP, 106 priority programmes were defined which are divided as follows : Productive sector 40 programmes ; Infrastructure sector 27 programmes ; Social sector 24 programmes ; and Administration and Finance 15 programmes. The list of these priority programmes by sector with their financial requirements is contained in the Annex. The analysis of this Annex shows that resources have been allocated to programmes in accordance with current priorities for sectors and sub-sectors.

SELECTED LAWS & REGULATIONS

CONSTITUTION

PREAMBLE

The National Council for Development, meeting as Constituent Assembly on 30 May 1991;

Trusting in God Almighty; In view of the liberation action of the people of Rwanda accomplished by the social revolution of 1959; Concerned about defending the republican form of government;

Born of the will of the people on 28 Jan 1961 and confirmed by referendum on 25 Sep 1961; Resolved to safeguard the national indep recovered on 1 July 1962 as well as the acquisition moral revolution 5 July 1973;

Faithful to democratic principles and concerned about ensuring the protection of human rights and promoting respect for fundamental freedoms, in accordance with the 'Universal Declaration of Human Rights' and the 'African Charter of Rights of Humans and People';

Wishing to adapt to national realities the constitutional principles established on 24 Nov 1962 and 20 Dec 1978 and to safeguard the national acquisitions for the purpose of reinforcing democracy;

Convinced of the necessity to achieve effectively national unity, peace, social justice, and respect for human rights based on liberty, equality, and fraternity for all members of the Rwandan community;

Resolved to guarantee to present and future generations the benefits of liberty, prosperity, and fulfillment for each person;

Resolved to pursue efforts made towards the development and prosperity of the country; Resolved to contribute to maintaining the peaceful coexistence of nations, reinforcing cooperation between peoples, and developing African unity; In revision of the Constitution of 20 Dec 1978 and in accordance with Article 91 thereof; Does establish and adopt this Constitution for the Republic of Rwanda:

TITLE I THE REPUBLIC

Article 1 State

(1) Rwanda shall be a democratic, social, and sovereign Republic which shall take the name 'Republic of Rwanda'.

(2) Its Principle shall be: "Government of the people, by the people, and for the people."

Article 2 Republic

Monarchy shall be abolished and cannot be restored.

Article 3 Flag, Seal, Anthem

(1) The national flag shall consist of bands of red, yellow, and green color, starting from the pole, and with the letter 'R' in black in the center of the yellow band. The Motto of the Republic shall be "Liberty, Cooperation, Progress."

(2) The Seal of the Republic shall be composed of ideograms of a dove and olive branch, a hoe and billhook, a bow and arrow, respectively symbolizing peace, work, and the defense of democratic liberties, in addition to the name and the motto of the Republic, all of it being framed by two National Flags placed opposite each other.

(3) The National Anthem shall be determined by law.

Article 4 Languages

Kinyarwanda shall be the National Language. Kinyarwanda and French shall be the official languages.

Article 5 Citizenship

Rwanda nationality and conditions for obtaining naturalization shall be defined by law.

Article 6 Sovereignty

(1) All power shall originate from the Nation.

(2) National sovereignty shall belong to the people of Rwanda which shall exercise it through representatives or by means of referendum.

Article 7 Political Parties

Political parties fulfilling the legal conditions shall concur to the expression of suffrage. They shall be formed and shall exercise their activities freely provided that they respect democratic principles and not infringe upon republican form of government, national territorial integrity, and the security of the State.

Article 8 Suffrage

Suffrage shall always be secret; it may be direct or indirect.

Article 9 Electoral Rights

Any Rwandan citizen, having attained majority and not being in any exclusion case prescribed by law, may be an elector within the conditions established by law.

Article 10 Consultation

The law shall determine the conditions and means of consultation of the people.

Article 11 Prefectures, Communes, Capital

(1) The Republic shall be divided into prefectures, endowed with their own juridical identities. A prefecture may be divided into sub-prefectures.
(2) Each prefecture shall be divided into communes, endowed with their own juridical identities.
(3) The law shall determine the number, limitations, organization, and operation of the prefectures, sub-prefectures, and communes.
(4) The Capital of the Republic shall be determined by law.

TITLE II PUBLIC LIBERTIES

Article 12 Human Dignity, Personal Freedom

(1) The human being shall be sacred.

(2) The liberty of the human being shall be inviolable; no one may be prosecuted, arrested, imprisoned, or convicted other than in the cases prescribed by the law in effect at the time of the perpetrated act and within the forms prescribed by that law.

(3) No infraction may be punished by penalties which were not prescribed by law before it was committed.

(4) Any person shall be presumed innocent of the charges as long as a definite conviction has not taken place.

Article 13 Security Measures

No one shall be subjected to security measures except in the cases and forms provided by law, for reasons of public order or State security.

Article 14 Criminal Responsibility

Criminal responsibility shall be personal. Civil responsibility shall be defined by the law. Defense shall be an absolute right at any state or level of the proceedings.

Article 15 Asylum, Extradition

(1) Asylum rights shall be recognized within the conditions defined by law.
(2) Extradition shall be authorized only within the limits prescribed by law.

Article 16 Citizen Equality

All citizens shall be equal in the eyes of the law, without any discrimination, especially in respect to race, color, origin, ethnic background, clan, sex, opinion, religion, or social status.

Article 17 No Slavery

Any form of slavery or bondage shall be prohibited.

Article 18 Religion, Expression

Freedom of religion and the public exercise thereof, liberty of conscience, as well as liberty of expressing one's opinion about any subject, shall be guaranteed, except for the punishment of infractions committed during the exercise thereof.

Article 19 Association

Freedom of association shall be guaranteed within conditions determined by law; prior authorization may not be prescribed.

Article 20 Assembly

(1) Freedom of assembly in peaceful and unarmed meetings shall be guaranteed within the limits determined by law.

(2) Prior authorization may be prescribed only by law and solely for outdoor meetings, on public streets, or in public places, and inasmuch as required by reasons of safety, peace, or health.

Article 21 Moving

Any citizen shall have the right to move and settle freely on the national territory, as well as to leave it or return to it; the exercise of this right may only be limited by law for reasons of public order or State security.

Article 22 Privacy

(1) The private lives of individuals snall not be infringed upon in any way.

(2) The privacy of correspondence and communications by post, telegraph, telephone, or by any other means shall be guaranteed; any restriction shall be determined by law only.

(3) Domiciles shall be inviolable. No house search may take place, except in the cases and manner prescribed by law.

Article 23 Property

Private property, whether individual or collective, shall be inviolable. No infringement shall take place except for the reason of public utility, in the cases and manner established by law, and in return for fair and prior compensation.

Article 24 Family

(1) The family, which is the natural basis of the Rwandan people, shall be protected by the State.

(2) Parents shall have the right and duty to raise their children.

Article 25 Marriage

(1) Only monogamous marriages shall be recognized within the conditions and forms prescribed by law.

(2) The conditions and forms of divorce shall be defined by law.

Article 26 Education

Liberty of teaching shall be guaranteed, except for the punishment of infractions committed in the exercise thereof. The organization of subsidized official and free education as well as recognition of diplomas and certificates issued by private institutions, shall be regulated by law.

Article 27 Mandatory Education

Subject to the enforcement of Article 24 (2), primary education shall be mandatory and free, according to the methods established by law.

Article 28 Service

National, civil, or military service shall be organized by law.

Article 29 Excessive Punishments

Excessively punishing hard labor shall be prohibited.

Article 30 Work

Any person shall have the right to work, to freely choose his work, and to have quitable and satisfying working conditions.

Article 31 Union Action

Any worker may protect his rights by the means of union action, except for the punishment of infractions committed within that action.

Article 32 Strike

The right to strike shall be exercised within the laws by which it is regulated. It may not infringe upon the freedom to work.

Article 33 Judicial Power

Judicial power, as the guardian of public rights and liberties, shall ensure the respect thereof within the conditions prescribed by law.

TITLE III POWERS

Chapter 0 General Provision

Article 34 Separation

The separation and collaboration of executive, legislative, and judicial powers shall be consecrated and regulated by this Constitution.

CHAPTER I EXECUTIVE POWER

Section 0 General Provisions

Article 35 President, Government

Executive power shall be exercised by the President of the Republic, assisted by the Government, composed of the Prime Minister and Ministers or Secretaries of State.

Article 36 Remuneration

The law shall establish compensation, pensions, and other material benefits pertaining to the presidential and ministerial duties.

Article 37 Economic Incompatibility

(1) The President of the Republic, the Prime Minister, Ministers, and Secretaries of State may not take advantage of their offices in order to acquire or dispose of any State property, nor exchange their personal property for a State property.
(2) Their duties shall be incompatible with the exercise of any other compensated professional activity.

Article 38 Immunity

(1) The President of the Republic, and except in case of flagrante delicto, the Prime Minister, Ministers, and Secretaries of State may be prosecuted or arrested for crimes or misdemeanors only upon accusation voted on, in secret ballot, by the National Assembly with a majority of three-fourth of its members.

(2) They shall be subject to the Court of Cassation which shall rule, all chambers assembled, as the first and final resort.

(3) They may be subjected to civil imprisonment only upon authorization by the

NATIONAL ASSEMBLY.

Section I The President of the Republic

Article 39 Functions

1) The President of the Republic shall be the Head of State. Through his arbitration he shall ensure the regular operation of higher level institutions of the Republic as well as the continuity of the State.

(2) He shall be the guarantor of national independence and unity, as well as territorial integrity.

Article 40 Election, Term

(1) The President of the Republic shall be elected by direct universal suffrage by an absolute majority of votes, according to the procedure prescribed by law.

(2) Candidates to the Presidency of the Republic must be at least thirty-five years of age.

(3) The President of the Republic shall be elected for a five year mandate.

(4) The President may be reelected. However, he may not exercise more than two successive mandates.

(5) The law shall determine the necessary means to be at the disposal of former Presidents of the Republic.

Article 41 Oath

Before taking office, the President of the Republic shall take an oath before the Constitutional Court and the National Assembly, in the following terms:

"I, ... , in the name of God Almighty, do solemnly swear to the Nation to faithfully carry out the duties entrusted to me, to be faithful to the Republic of Rwanda, and to promote the interests of the people of Rwanda with all respect to the Constitution and the law."

Article 42 Resignation, Replacement

(1) The President of the Republic may resign; his resignation shall be accepted by the National Assembly.

(2) In the event of impediment or temporary incapacity to express his will, the President of the Republic shall be temporarily replaced by the President of the National Assembly.

(3) In the event of resignation, death, or when impediment or incapacity shall be declared definitive by the Constitutional Court consulted by the Government, the President of the Republic shall be replaced by the President of the National Assembly until the election of the new President of the Republic, which must take place within 90 days.

(4) In the cases mentioned in the above Paragraph, the Prime Minister, Ministers, and Secretaries of State shall be considered as resigning and shall assume, each in his own right, the carrying out of the present affairs until the new Government is formed.

Article 43 Second Replacement

In the event the President of the Republic and the President of the National Assembly happen to be simultaneously placed in one of the cases prescribed in Article 42, the duties of the President of the Republic shall be carried out by the Prime Minister in the conditions prescribed in the said article.

Article 44 Functions

The President of the Republic:

1) shall appoint the Prime Minister and shall terminate his duties; upon the recommendation of the Prime Minister, he shall appoint the other members of the Government and shall terminate their duties;

2) shall preside the Council of Ministers;

3) shall make appointments to judicial positions as well as higher level civil and military posts established by law;

4) shall appoint and accredit ambassadors and extraordinary envoys abroad and shall terminate their duties; ambassadors and extraordinary envoys shall be accredited to him;

5) shall represent the Republic in his relations with foreign states;

6) shall negotiate, conclude, and ratify all international treaties, conventions, and agreements, whether of public or private law, and send them to the National Assembly as soon as allowed by the State's interest and security. However,

- peace treaties,
- alliance treaties,
- treaties that may bring modifications to the national territorial borders or affect sovereignty rights,
- treaties concerning the Republic's relations with one or several other States, as well as
- treaties, conventions, and agreements involving financial implications not anticipated in the budget, shall be enforceable only following approval by law. The federation of the Republic of Rwanda with one or several other democratic States must be approved by means of a referendum;

7) shall declare war and sign armistices upon authorization by the National Assembly;

8) shall sanction and promulgate laws within 15 days after the constitutionality ruling;

9) shall have the right to oppose a suspension veto to the laws passed by the National Assembly. When exercising this right, he must return the law to the National Assembly within 15 days for a second reading. If the law returned to the National Assembly within 15 days is passed after a second reading and is not subjected to a constitutionality ruling, it must be sanctioned and promulgated;

10) shall give the orders necessary for the execution of laws, without ever being able to suspend the laws themselves or exempt them from execution;

11) shall have the right to address messages to the Nation and, without causing debates, to the National Assembly;

12) may suspend for a maximum of 15 days the work of the National Assembly; however no suspension may be repeated in the course of one session;

13) shall exercise the right of pardon;

14) shall have the right to coin money.

Article 45 Commander-In-Chief

The President of the Republic shall be the Supreme Chief of the Armed Forces.

Article 46 Bound by Law, Indictment

(1) The President of the Republic shall attend to the observance of the Constitution.

(2) In case of violation of the Constitution by the President of the Republic, his indictment may only be decided upon by the National Assembly, ruling by a majority of four-fifth of its members and by secret ballot.

(3) If the case arises, the President of the Republic shall be subject to the Constitutional Court which alone shall be qualified to order his forced resignation.

Article 47 Referendum

The President of the Republic may, on the advice of the Government and the National Assembly, submit to a referendum any bill or any other matter.

Article 48 Siege, Emergency, Danger

(1) The President of the Republic may, when the situation requires it and after consultation with the Government, with the Constitutional Court and with the Bureau of the National Assembly, proclaim a state of siege or a state of emergency. States of siege and emergency are regulated by law.

(2) When the Republic's institutions, the Nation's independence or prime interests, territorial integrity, or the execution of its international commitments are threatened in a grave and imminent manner, and when the regular governmental services are interrupted, the President of the Republic shall take the measures required by these circumstances, after consultation with the Government, with the Bureau of the National Assembly, and with the Constitutional Court.

Article 49 Countersignatures

The actions of the President of the Republic shall be countersigned by the Prime Minister, as well as the responsible Ministers and Secretaries of State.

SECTION II THE GOVERNMENT

Article 50 Power

(1) The Government shall determine and conduct the Nation's policies.

(2) It shall have at its disposal the administration and the armed forces. It shall be accountable to the National Assembly according to the conditions and procedures prescribed in Articles 81 and 84.

Article 51 Prime Minister

The Prime Minister:

1) shall present to the National Assembly the Government's program and the ministerial cabinet in charge of the execution thereof;

2) shall direct the Government's action;

3) shall determine assignments for Ministers and Secretaries of State and the nature and competence of the departments under their authority. Ministers and Secretaries of State shall receive authority from the Prime Minister for affairs relevant to their departments; the Prime Minister shall determine the extent of this authority;

4) shall make appointments to civil and military posts, except for conflicting legal provisions or regulations;

5) may replace the President of the Republic to preside a Council of Ministers by virtue of express authority and for a specific agenda;

6) shall countersign laws adopted by the National Assembly and promulgated by the President of the Republic;

7) shall execute laws and regulations by means of decrees when he is in charge thereof.

Article 52 Countersignatures

The Prime Minister's actions shall be countersigned by the Ministers in charge of their execution.

Article 53 Ministers and Secretaries of State

Ministers and Secretaries of State shall execute laws and regulations by means of decrees, when in charge thereof.

Article 54 Accountability

The Prime Minister, Ministers, and Secretaries of State shall be accountable to the President of the Republic; moreover they shall be accountable to the National Assembly within the conditions defined by this Constitution.

Article 55 Mandatory Consultation

Upon convocation and presided by the President of the Republic, the Council of Ministers obligatorily shall be consulted about:

- bills of law and proposals of statutory orders;
- proposals of presidential decrees carrying execution of laws or statutory orders;
- proposals of presidential decrees relating to higher level government positions;
- dissolution of the National Assembly.

Article 56 Oath, Resignation

(1) The Prime Minister, Ministers, and Secretaries of State shall show solidarity with the President of the Republic.

(2) Before taking office, the Prime Minister, Ministers, and Secretaries of State shall take an oath before the President of the Republic and the National Assembly, in the following terms: "I, ..., in the name of God Almighty, do swear to the Nation that I shall loyally carry out my duties, be faithful to the Republic of Rwanda and the Head of State, and promote the interests of the Rwandan people with all respect to the Constitution and the law."

(3) Resignation or termination of the Prime Minister's duties for whatever reason, shall bring about the resignation of the Government.

(4) Each Minister or Secretary of State may, of his own accord, tender his resignation to the President of the Republic; this resignation shall be definite only if it is not withdrawn or refused by the President of the Republic within eight days.

CHAPTER II LEGISLATIVE POWER

Section 0 General Provision

Article 57 Power

Legislative power shall be exercised collectively by the President of the Republic and the National Assembly.

SECTION I THE NATIONAL ASSEMBLY

Article 58 Election

(1) The National Assembly shall be composed of members designated as 'Deputies to the National Assembly.' Deputies shall be elected for a five year mandate by universal and direct suffrage.

(2) Deputies may resign from their mandate.

(3) No person may be a Deputy to the National Assembly unless he is a Rwandan citizen, at least 21 years of age, and is able to fulfill any other conditions prescribed by law.
(4) The law shall establish electoral conditions, regulations for incompatibility, the number of Deputies, as well as compensation and other material benefits pertaining to the duties of Deputies.

Article 59 Independence

Any required mandate shall be invalid; the Deputies' right to vote shall be personal.

Article 60 Oath

1) At the beginning of each legislative session, the first meeting shall be dedicated to the swearing in of the Deputies and to the election of the Bureau of the National Assembly. It shall be presided by the President of the Republic.

(2) Before taking office, Deputies shall take an oath before the President of the Republic, in the following terms: "I, ... , in the name of God Almighty, do swear to the Nation that I shall loyally carry out my duties, be faithful to the Republic of Rwanda and the Head of State, and promote the interests of the Rwandan people with all respect to the Constitution and the law."

(3) The National Assembly shall form its Bureau by electing a President, two Vice-Presidents, and a Secretary.

Article 61 Presidency

The National Assembly shall be directed by its President and, in case of the latter's incapacity, by one of the Vice-Presidents.

Article 62 Internal Order

The National Assembly shall determine by internal order the regulation of its organization and the procedure according to which it shall carry out its assignments.

Article 63 Sessions

(1) The National Assembly shall hold, by right, each year two ordinary sessions and when required by circumstances, extraordinary sessions. Ordinary sessions shall respectively start the third Tuesday of the month of October and the third Tuesday of the month of April. However, for the first year of the legislature, the first ordinary session shall start, by right, 8 days after the legislative elections. (2) The National Assembly shall be convened by its President. It may be convened as an extraordinary session upon the initiative of the President of the Republic, its President, the majority of its members, or upon the request of the Prime Minister. When meeting in extraordinary session, the National Assembly may only address matters that motivated its convening.

Article 64 Place

(1) The National Assembly shall meet in the Capital except in case of absolute necessity.

(2) Any deliberation, whatever its subject, held without convocation or agenda, or held outside the session period or outside the premises noted on the convocation act, shall by right be invalid.

Article 65 Publicity, Minutes

(1) The National Assembly meetings shall be public; records of the debates shall be made public.

(2) However, upon the request of the President of the Republic, its President, a third of its members, or the Prime Minister, the Assembly may decide by an absolute majority to meet in camera.

Article 66 Indemnity, Immunity

(1) Deputities may not be prosecuted or accused because of opinions or votes expressed by them in the exercise of their duties.

(2) Except in case of flagrante delicto, Deputies may be prosecuted or arrested for other acts, or be subject to civil imprisonment only by authorization from the National Assembly passed by secret ballot by a majority of three-fourths of its members.

(3) Prosecution or imprisonment resulting from flagrante delicto or from authorization from the National Assembly shall be suspended during the session period if required by the National Assembly by a majority of three-fourths of its members and by secret ballot, except in case of a definite conviction.

(4) Deputies shall be subject to the Court of Cassation which shall rule, all chambers assembled, as the first and final resort.

Article 67 Dismissal

(1) No Deputy shall be dismissed from office unless he is met with a cause for ineligibility.

(2) If the case arises, the dismissal shall be by right and it shall be certified by the Council of State at the request of the Bureau of the National Assembly or the Government.

Article 68 Sleeping Mandate, Property

(1) When a Deputy is appointed to the Government or any other public office and he accepts, he shall immediately cease his duties as a Deputy and shall be replaced by his substitute.

(2) He shall resume his duties as soon as the reasons for incompatibility have disappeared, and as long as the legislature to which he has been elected is still in session.

(3) No Deputy may take advantage of his office in order to acquire or dispose of a property of State, or exchange a personal property for a property of State.

SECTION II ELABORATION OF LAWS

Article 69 Rule of Law

(1) Leqislative power shall be exercised by means of laws.

(2) The law shall supremely intervene in any matter; in no case shall regulations contravene the provisions of the law.

Article 70 Statutory Orders

(1) In case of emergency or when the National Assembly is unable to meet, the President of the Republic shall temporarily legislate by means of statutory orders adopted in the Council of Ministers.

(2) Unless they are confirmed by the National Assembly in the course of the next closest session, statutory orders shall lose any mandatory effect.

Article 71 Initiative

(1) Initiative for laws shall belong to Deputies and the President of the Republic concurrently.

(2) Deputies and the President of the Republic have the right to amend them.

Article 72 Spending Bills

Bills and amendments formulated by Deputies and the adoption of which could bring about either a decrease of public resources or the creation or increase of public expenses, must be accompanied by a bill to augment revenue or savings of equal value.

Article 73 Majorities

(1) Laws shall be passed by an absolute majority of Deputies to the National Assembly; laws to which the Constitution imparts the character of organic laws shall be passed by a majority of three-fifths. The provisions of an organic law may not be dispensed with by another law.

(2) No law may be adopted except after having been passed article by article.

(3) Votes shall be expressed verbally or by sitting and standing positions; as a whole, a law shall be voted upon calling out names and answering verbally. Ballots shall be secret when mention is made of individuals and in the cases established by internal order regulations.

Article 74 Urgent Examination

(1) Urgent examination of a proposal or bill may be requested by a Deputy or by the President of the Republic.

(2) When it is requested by a Deputy, the National Assembly shall decide upon the urgency.

(3) When it is requested by the President of the Republic, it shall always be granted.

(4) In all cases when emergency is granted, the examination of the law in question shall have priority over the agenda.

Article 75 Constitutional Court Ruling

(1) Before promulgation, laws and statutory orders must be sent to the Constitutional Court which shall give a ruling on their constitutionality within eight days or, in case of emergency, within four days.

(2) If the Court gives a ruling of incompatibility, it shall return the text to the National Assembly or the President of the Republic as the case may be.

Article 76 Financial Laws

(1) The National Assembly shall vote upon the financial laws which establish the resources and expenses of the State within the conditions prescribed by an organic law.

(2) Any budgetary transfer must be authorized by law.

Article 77 Budget

(1) Each year, the National Assembly shall rule on the financial accounts and pass a balanced budget, a bill for which shall be filed before the opening of the first ordinary session.

(2) If it has not been passed within forty days after the opening of the first ordinary session, or if it has not been passed as balanced, the budget bill shall be adopted by means of a statutory order at the latest on 31 Jan of the year of its execution.

(3) If the budget bill for a specific fiscal year has not been presented on time to be passed and promulgated before the opening of that fiscal year, the Prime Minister, upon authorization from the National Assembly, shall propose by presidential decree, deliberated upon in the Council of

Ministers, the opening of the provisional twelfths of the budget based upon the budget of the previous fiscal year.

(4) The same presidential decree shall authorize the collection of revenue in accordance with the law by which it is regulated. Thus shall it be each month until the adoption of the budget.

Article 78 Tax Laws, Monopoly

(1) No taxation may be established, modified, or abolished except by law; no exemption or reduction may be granted except in the cases prescribed by law.
(2) No monopoly may be granted except by law and for a specific duration.

Article 79 Authentic Interpretation

Authentic interpretation of the laws shall be the prerogative of the legislative power.

CHAPTER III RELATIONS BETWEEN THE NATIONAL ASSEMBLY AND THE GOVERNMENT

Article 80 Information, Participation

(1) The President of the Republic and the Prime Minister must be informed of the agenda for the meetings of the National Assembly and its committees.
(2) The Prime Minister, Ministers, and Secretaries of State may, if they so desire, attend the National Assembly meetings; they shall speak whenever they wish; if need be, they may be accompanied by technicians of their choice.

Article 81 Control

(1) The National Assembly's means of information and control with regard to governmental action shall be:

- oral questions;
- written questions;
- committee hearings;
- committees of inquiry;
- interpellations.

(2) Conditions and application procedures thereof shall be prescribed by law.

Article 82 Motion of Censure

(1) The National Assembly may call into question the responsibility of the Government, as well as of any Minister or Secretary of State, by passing a motion of censure.

(2) Such a motion shall be admissible only after interpellation and only if signed by at least one-fifth of the National Assembly members in the case of a Minister or Secretary of State, and by one-third in the case of the Government.

(3) Voting may only take place at least 48 hours after the motion is registered, and the latter may be adopted only by secret ballot and by an absolute majority of Deputies.

(4) The closing of ordinary or extraordinary sessions shall be by right delayed in order to allow the application of the provisions of the present article if necessary.

Article 83 Vote of No Confidence

(1) When a motion of censure is adopted against a Minister or Secretary of State, the latter shall be required to tender his resignation to the President of the Republic.

(2) When this motion is adopted against the Government, the Prime Minister shall tender the resignation of the latter to the President of the Republic.

(3) If the motion of censure is rejected, the signatories may not present a new one in the course of the same session.

Article 84 Revenue Court

(1) The Revenue Court shall be in charge of examining, liquidating, and settling accounts for all public services.

(2) It shall submit to the National Assembly a report on the regular performance of the general accounts of the State.

(3) The Revenue Court shall be organized by an organic law.

Article 85 Dissolution

(1) The President of the Republic may, after consultation with the Council of Ministers and the Bureau of the Nation Assembly, order the dissolution of the National Assembly. However, in the course of his mandate, he may not order a second dissolution without this action bringing about his own resignation.

(2) Elections to the legislature shall take place within 90 days in accordance with

Article 58. If need be, the election to the Presidency of the Republic shall take place within 90 days in accordance with Article 40.

(3) The National Assembly may not be dissolved in the course of the exercise of the exceptional powers mentioned in Article 48.

CHAPTER IV JUDICIAL POWER

Article 86 Independence

(1) Judicial power shall be exercised by courts, tribunals, and other jurisdictions; it shall be independent from the legislative and executive powers.

(2) The President of the Republic shall guarantee the independence of the judicial power.

(3) Justice shall be dispensed in the name of the people.

Article 87 Magistrates

(1) Magistrates shall be appointed and dismissed by the President of the Republic on the proposal of the Minister of Justice and upon conforming advice from the Supreme Council of Magistrates.

(2) The Supreme Council of Magistrates shall be composed of magistrates elected by their peers according to procedures prescribed by an organic law. The Minister of Justice shall be a member by right.

(3) During the first session presided by the President of the Republic, the Supreme Council of Magistrates shall elect in its midst its President, Vice-President, and Secretary.

(4) An organic law shall establish regulations for competence, organization, and operation of the Supreme Council of Magistrates.

Article 88 Court Hierarchy

(1) Juridictions of the following order shall be recognized and sanctioned by this Constitution:

- canton courts,
- courts of the first instance,
- courts of appeal, and
- the Court of Cassation.

(2) Except when prescribed by law, the Court of Cassation shall not have cognizance of the substance of the cases.

Article 89 Council of State

(1) When consulted, the Council of State shall be competent to express a justified opinion about the text of any law proposal, bill, or amendment to this proposal or bill, any statutory order proposal, as well as any proposal of execution order. It may propose drafting modifications as judged necessary.

(2) The Council of State shall have cognizance of appeals for invalidation against regulations, orders, and decisions of the administrative authorities; it shall control the regular operation of popular consultations.

(3) The Council of State shall be organized by an organic law.

(4) Lower administrative jurisdictions shall be created and organized by an organic law.

Article 90 Constitutional Court

The Constitutional Court, composed of the Court of Cassation and the Council of State assembled, shall be in charge of controlling the constitutionality of laws and statutory orders; it alone shall be competent to order the forced resignation of the President of the Republic in the conditions prescribed by Article 46.

Article 91 Organic Law Establishment

(1) No other jurisdiction may be established except by an organic law.

(2) The organization and competence of any juridiction shall be defined by an organic law.

Article 92 Constitutional Judge

No one may be removed against his will from the judge assigned to him by law.

Article 93 Publicity

Jurisdiction hearings shall be public, except for in camera cases ordered by a judgement when publicity may endanger public order or morals.

Article 94 Public Rulings

Any judgment or ruling shall be justified and pronounced in a public hearing.

Article 95 Constitutionality

Jurisdictions shall apply orders and other regulations as long as they are in accordance with the Constitution and the law.

TITLE IV REVISION OF THE CONSTITUTION

Article 96 Amendments

(1) Initiative for revision of the Constitution shall belong to the President of the Republic and the National Assembly concurrently.

(2) No revision bill or proposal may be taken into consideration if it infringes upon the republican form of government, national territorial integrity, or democratic principles ruling the Republic.

(3) Any revision proposal by the National Assembly must be presented by at least two-thirds of its members.

(4) Any revision must be adopted by a majority of three-fourths of the members of the National Assembly.

TITLE V GENERAL AND TRANSITIONAL PROVISIONS

Article 97 Promulgation Effects

(1) Laws and regulations may not take effect unless they have previously been published within the conditions established by law.

(2) No one should be ignorant of regularly published laws.

Article 98 Applicable Old Law

(1) Starting from the promulgation date of this Constitution, any legislation which is not constrained by it, shall remain applicable inasmuch as it is not modified, repealed or replaced by the new laws or regulations.

(2) Custom shall remain applicable inasmuch as it was not replaced by laws or is not contrary to the Constitution, laws, regulations, public order or morals.

Article 99 Oaths

Without prejudice to provisions in Articles 41, 56 and 60, no oath may be imposed except by a law which shall establish the wording and the procedure for taking this oath.

Article 100 Foreigners

Any foreigner shall enjoy the protection granted to persons and property, as well as the civil rights recognized by this Constitution, except in cases prescribed by law.

Article 101 Continuation of Offices

(1) The President of the Republic and the Deputies to the National Council for Development presently in office will continue to exercise their duties until the next

(2) The dates for these elections will be determined by the President of the Republic.

Article 102 Old Constitution

(1) This Constitution shall revise and replace the Constitution of 20 Dec 1978.

(2) It will take effect on the date of its promulgation by the President of the Republic.

MULTI SECTOR REGULATORY LAW

OBJECTIVES

The principal objectives of the Law are:

1. To support private sector investment in Rwanda;
2. To create the Regulatory Board, which will be the regulator for the utility sectors in Rwanda;
3. To provide the Regulatory Board with administrative and enforcement support for all aspects of utility regulation by the creation of the Regulatory Agency;
4. To provide for a flexible law which will allow further sectors to be added to the remit of the Regulatory Board as and when the Government decides;
5. To address the sensitivity of moving from regulation by central Government to independent regulation by defining the individual roles of the regulator and the relevant Government Ministers;
6. To provide for the regulation of competition in the utilities sector.

FEATURES

In substance, the draft Law meets the Government's requirements in the following ways:

ENCOURAGEMENT OF PRIVATE INVESTMENT IN RWANDA

Private investors will be encouraged to invest in Rwanda if they can see both a modern effective legal code for the utility sector in which they wish to invest and a strong independent regulation of that sector. This law establishes the latter element.

CREATION OF A REGULATORY BOARD

The draft law provides for the creation of a five person Regulatory Board to act as the utility regulator for Rwanda. One person will be a full-time managing director who will oversee the daily running of the Regulatory Agency. Four persons will be part-time members. Considerable measures have been taken in the draft Law to ensure both the integrity and independence of the Board members.

CREATION OF A REGULATORY AGENCY

The Regulatory Board cannot handle all of the many issues with which regulation is concerned (e.g. granting licences, enforcing the law, dealing with anti-competitive activity, implementation of technical standards) and the many utility sectors with which it will be involved. It has to be supported by professional and administrative staff.

This Law provides for the creation of the Regulatory Agency to provide such support. It has been drafted so as to provide for independence. It is not a state institution within the meaning of décret-loi n° 39/75.

FLEXIBILITY

It is known that telecommunications, water and electricity will come under regulatory control in the near term. In the longer term, gas and transport may be added. The Law has been drafted so as to give the Government flexibility to add new sectors. This has been done by setting out very general duties for the Regulatory Board in the Law (e.g. encouraging competition, protecting the interests of users) and then stating that the regulatory duties will be spelled out in the individual sector law. In this way, the issues pertinent to a particular sector remain with that sector's law (e.g. environmental control and pollution may be relevant to water regulation, but not to telecommunications).

For example, the Telecommunications Law is supported by a Presidential decree setting out very detailed duties for the regulator, many of which are amplified in the Telecommunications Law.

GOVERNMENT CONTROL VERSUS INDEPENDENCE

The Law tries to meet the very real concern that many people have, namely that considerable powers are being vested in an independent body rather than central Government. Therefore, this Law provides that:

a) The independence of the Regulatory Board and Agency have to be respected but without detracting from the overall power of the relevant Minister to make policy and enact laws for his or her sector.

b) The annual budget for the Agency has to be prepared with independent scrutiny from a firm of accountants.

c) Accounts have to be audited annually

d) A report on the activities of the Agency has to be presented annually and a Ministerial decree sets out what is required in each report. The Agency is therefore fully accountable.

e) The decisions of the Regulatory Board are subject to scrutiny by the courts. Measures have been taken to ensure that the court does not become an alternative regulator.

However, the regulator must not be seen to be subjugated to a Minister. The Law therefore provides that the regulator investigates, terminates and applies sanctions in respect of anti-competitive activity in utilities on behalf of the Minister of Commerce. This recognises that a) there is not, currently, the opportunity to draft a new Competition Law covering all commercial activities and not just utilities, and b) the Regulatory Board may well be closer to daily activity in the utility sectors, as it has a foot in four camps: Government, user, operator and international community.

COMPETITION

There appears to be no fully developed competition law in Rwanda. Hitherto, most major economic activities have been concentrated in Government hands, so it has been unnecessary to have such a law. Law N° 35/91 concerning the organisation of national commercial activity, seems to contemplate regulation of competition and prices in terms of general commercial activity e.g. the buying and selling of goods on wholesale, intermediary, and resale terms. Further, some of the sanctions are inappropriate to utility regulation (e.g. small fines which would not trouble a significant private investor, and the ability to close down a business, where the ordinary citizen would suffer). Other aspects also suggest that this is an inappropriate law for utility regulation.

If private investors in these major businesses are to be encouraged into Rwanda, the law must present a more recognisable code, which leaves a wider discretion with a regulator, and which provides for very significant sanctions. For example, the regulator should have the discretion to decide that, although an activity is, on the face of it, anti-competitive, if it is allowed to continue, the consumer may benefit in the longer term. Sanctions (in the form of fines) are expressed as a percentage of world-wide turnover of the defaulting utility.

SOURCES USED IN DRAFTING THE LAW

In preparing this Law, the consultants have drawn down the detailed regulatory provisions which were originally inserted in the Telecommunications Law and made these more general in their application. The advantage of this is that the Telecommunications Law had been approved in substance by the relevant Ministry (the Ministry for Public Works, Transport and Communications) together with independent legal adviser, M. Frédéric Mutagwera, the Chairman of the Rwanda Bar Association.

However, they have also consulted the Ghanaian Public Utility Regulatory Act (in relation to utility regulation), and the GATT and COMESA provisions (in relation to competition). The Ghanaian law was the only relevant law which could be identified in the time scale allowed for this project.

The consultants have also been conscious of the work of Booz Allen and Hamilton (BAH) which has been retained to advise on the restructuring of ELECTROGAZ. They have read the BAH document on the proposed regulatory framework for the sectors in which BAH is advising. Gratifyingly, there is a strong similarity in the themes raised by BAH for multi-sector regulation and those previously drafted by the Adam Smith Institute.

Finally, they have consulted a number of statutes which relate to water, gas and electricity regulation in the UK in order to gain a perspective on their regulation in one liberalised market. In view of time pressures to complete this work, they have been unable to consult any further laws.

SUMMARY

The Law is written in 8 Chapters and 33 Articles. References in brackets are to the individual article numbers.

Chapter 1 sets out the definitions to be used in the Law.

Chapter 2 provides for the creation of the Regulatory Agency (2). It sets out its location and the right to set up local offices (3). (4) defines the status of this body and that part of the Government to which it is responsible. General powers for its existence are given by (5), and (6) states that the Regulatory Board will manage the Agency as well as being the regulator for utilities in Rwanda.

Chapter 3 introduces the Regulatory Board, qualifications for appointment, and the means by which the Regulatory Board members are appointed (7). Implicit in this is that corporations are not to be members of the Board. (8) determines how long Board members will serve and their rights to subsequent re-election to the Board. It is expressly stated that these persons act in the interests of the Agency. Provisions as to remuneration etc. are set out in (9). (10) defines the circumstances in which an individual is required to resign as a member of the Board and also gives him or her the right to resign. (11) sets out the general "high level" duties of the Board and requires it to act in an open and even-handed manner. Of particular note is the cross reference to the individual laws on utilities in which the detailed regulatory duties will be set out.

(12) sets out the responsibility of the Board to manage to Agency and (13) defines the conduct of the Board's meetings. The Board is expressly given the right to co-opt persons to advise it and to form committees to investigate any matter in depth and report to it. (14) is the important section which attempts to spell out the relationship between the Board and each of the utility sector Ministers. (15) emphasises the independence of Board members by preventing them from holding office in situations which might put them in conflict with their responsibilities to the Board. (16) requires the Board to report on their activities and those of the Agency each year and underscores the accountability of the Agency for the work it does.

Chapter 4 (17) defines the requirement of the Board to prepare and manage its own budget in consultation with retained accountants. The Agency is to be a non-profit making entity and to be self-financing.

(18) defines the sources of revenue for running the Agency and (19) the right to call upon Government funds. There is no obligation on the Government to vote these funds but if it does, they are described as a loan. Fines levied in the execution of its duties are to be paid to the Treasury (20).

(21) requires the preparation of annual accounts and their publication in the Official Gazette as well as presentation to the responsible Minister.

Chapter 5 provides for the Regulatory Board to maintain and promote effective competition, including investigation and termination of anti-competitive activity and the application of sanctions (22 – 25). Organisations are required to give supporting information to the investigation and there are penalties for failure to do so. (26) The application of very severe fines are open to the Regulatory Board for anti-competitive activity.

(27) is a more general power requiring all utilities to provide information about their activities. Failure to do so attracts a fine. The Board is expressly permitted to enter premises to gather

information. The reason for this provision is that the Board is required as part of its general duties to ensure compliance by utilities with the law relating to that utility.

(28) specifies what are dominant organisations for the purposes of the competition provisions.

Chapter 6 This gives a right of appeal to the court from the Board's decisions and at the same time sets out measures to ensure that the court does not become a second regulatory body (29). (30) gives the Board express powers for implementation and enforcement of each utility law and defines the status of Board Members as law enforcement officers.

Chapter 7 This sets out sanctions (31)(32).

STRATEGIC SPEACHES AND MATERIALS

ADDRESS TO THE NATION BY H.E. PAUL KAGAME, ON HIS INAUGURATION AS PRESIDENT OF THE REPUBLIC OF RWANDA

April 22, 2000

Your Excellency Frederick CHILUBA, President of Zambia,
Your Excellency Benjamin MKAPA, President of Tanzania,
Your Excellency Pierre BUYOYA, President of Burundi,
Your Excellency Specioza KAZIBWE, Vice-President of Uganda,
Your Excellencies, Representatives of Eritrea, Ethiopia, Kenya and South Africa;
Your Excellency the Representative of the Secretary General of the Organization of African Unity (OAU);
Your Excellency the President of the National Assembly,
Your Excellency the President of the Supreme Court,
Your Excellency the Prime Minister;
Honourable Ministers;
Honourable Members of Parliament;
Honourable members of the Diplomatic Corps and Representatives of International Organizations in Rwanda;
Distinguished Guests,
Friends of Rwanda,
Ladies and Gentlemen.

I would like, first of all, to thank the distinguished guests who have come from various countries and international organizations, to be with the Rwandese people during the ceremony of my inauguration as President of the Republic of Rwanda. Your attendance is a clear manifestation of the friendship and solidarity existing between Rwanda and your countries and the international organizations you represent.

I would also like to thank all the leaders of the recognised political parties in Rwanda, and the Rwandese people, who overwhelmingly supported my candidature for the post of President of the Republic of Rwanda; and who have come in big numbers to witness my inauguration as their President. I would also like to thank the ministers and members of Parliament who showed their trust and confidence in me with their votes.

In a very special way I would also like to thank RPF – Inkotanyi who fought for a change in the leadership of Rwanda. The RPF fought for and achieved a new political dispensation in Rwanda that has made this day possible.

I would also like to thank the leaders who have worked together with RPF-Inkotanyi to rebuild Rwanda since 1994. In particular, I would like to thank the outgoing President, His Excellency Pasteur Bizimungu.

Your Excellencies Heads of State,
Distinguished Guests,
Friends of Rwanda,
Ladies and Gentlemen;

This is the first time in the history of Rwanda that there is peaceful change at the highest office in the country - without the spilling of blood or mourning.

This demonstrates to us the tremendous steps taken by the Rwandese people toward political maturity so soon after the end of the era of bad politics in our country.

However, even though the Rwandese people have developed political maturity, there are some people who have failed to understand Rwanda's new politics. These people lack an appreciation of the tremendous strides taken by post-genocide Rwanda, and instead peddle rumours about the resignation of President Bizimungu and speculate about the spilling of more blood. Some of them went as far as saying that if the new President is not Hutu things will get out of control.

This demonstrates that there are some people who still think that the Rwandese are still a divided people. These people do not realize that most Rwandese people have abandoned the politics of division. We shall not stop explaining the achievements that we owe to the new political dispensation in our country.

When you analyse the manner in which the elections at grassroots level were conducted, the way the elections of the President of the Republic were held, and the way the Rwandese people welcomed the results, you realize that most Rwandese no longer judge the value of a person on the basis of his ethnicity or origin. Value is attached to an individual on the basis of their actions and behaviour. We would therefore like to request our foreign partners not to lag behind in this crusade to change our way of thinking and working, lest you impede our progress.

Your Excellencies Heads of State,
Distinguished Guests,
Friends of Rwanda,
Ladies and Gentlemen.

Today we should all leave this place with a determination to take a new step forward in the life of our country. But before we take this step, it is necessary to ask ourselves whether we are convinced that we are capable of taking that step.

We should also look back and see where we have come from, where we are now, and whether we have the capacity to enable us to take that step into the future. Furthermore, we cannot take the step without knowing where we are going. It is therefore necessary that we leave this place armed with the knowledge of where we are going as a nation.

There are many Rwandese who are convinced beyond any doubt whatsoever that our country, Rwanda, will become a country governed by the rule of law, where democracy and the respect for human rights have a place and where people are happy to live. A country where there is no political, social or economic injustice, a country where development is sustainable. I am among those Rwandese people with these aspirations and convictions. I appeal to all the Rwandese people to rise up so that together we may build such a country. We should avoid being discouraged by those among us who thrive on being prophets of doom.

If after decades of genocide and massacres, we were able to live on; if we were capable to start the process of reconciliation and unification of the Rwandese people; if we were able to rehabilitate what had been destroyed and develop; there is no reason why we should, at this juncture, lack the drive to continue what we have already started.

However, in order to look to the future with confidence and courage, we need to be able to look back to where we have come from and the difficulties we have encountered so as to be able to rise to the challenges that lie ahead for us.

Your Excellencies Heads of State,
Distinguished Guests,
Friends of Rwanda,
Ladies and Gentlemen.

The last time we had a similar event of the oath of office by the President of the Republic Rwanda was on the 19th July 1994. At that time, the RPF-Inkotanyi had just stopped the genocide and massacres which had been planned and executed by the MRND leadership.

The genocide resulted in the deaths of more than one million Rwandese, and one million more were orphaned, became widows or were handicapped. Many became criminals. Hundreds of thousands were forced into camps either inside the country or as refugees in neighbouring countries. They left behind a deeply scarred and traumatized people, either because of the evil acts they suffered, or the crimes they committed. They also left the country without leadership. The authors and planners of the genocide left the country after looting all they could take with them and destroying whatever they could not carry. They also carried with them all the military hardware they needed to continue their evil plan of annihilation of all Tutsi and Hutu opposed to their politics. This is the country that the Government of National Unity inherited in 1994.

Although the country was in such a bad shape, we, the Rwandese people did not get discouraged. A lot of progress has been made. Rwandese and friends of Rwanda should all be proud of the progress so far made.

We set up a government comprising all Rwandese from all the political parties, all ethnic groups and regions of Rwanda. Today, all the Rwandese people are represented at all levels of Government.

Peace and security have returned to the whole country. Nearly all Rwandese who had been displaced or evicted from their properties during the war and the genocide have returned to them. More than three million refugees have returned and have been resettled in different parts of the country.

The Government has done what it can to establish a judicial system to try those who perpetrated the genocide, although because of the big numbers of those involved, the prisons are full to the extent that people may get the impression that the trials are too slow. We are setting up other methods of dealing with this large caseload. The Gacaca courts will speed up the trial and sentencing process while involving the population in the trial process, a vital ingredient to reconciliation.

The Rwandese people have willingly adopted orphans and the children who had been separated from their relatives during the genocide. As a result, the number of orphans living outside their extended family unit has fallen from three hundred thousand to less than five thousand. The government has set up a special fund to support genocide survivors. Every year 5% of its national budget is contributed to this fund. Last year the contribution stood at 4 billion Rwandese francs.

The local government and grassroots democratic leadership have been established to bring decision-making closer to the people.

We also set up organs to fight against corruption and lack of transparency. The National Examination Council, the National Tender Board, the Auditor General's Office and the Rwanda Revenue Authority, have all been established by the government of national unity to ensure transparency.

Development infrastructure that had been destroyed has been repaired and new infrastructure constructed. Since Rwanda's most important resource is its people, the government has invested a high proportion of government expenditure on the provision of education to its people. We have established new schools at all levels (primary, secondary and higher institutions) as well as reopening and redeveloping old ones. We have sent many young Rwandans to study abroad so as to equip them with the knowledge that will help Rwanda develop.

We live at peace with other African countries and with those outside Africa. Rwanda enjoys a good relationship with International Organizations all over the world, as is exemplified by the representation of distinguished guests here with us today.

The people of Rwanda live together in more peace and security than ever before. We set national commissions for unity and reconciliation and for Human Rights, whose objectives are to promote unity, understanding and tolerance in Rwanda.

When we look back, we realize that we have achieved a lot in our struggle, indeed so much so that we can build on this to make many steps forward.

Your Excellencies Heads of State;
Distinguished Guests;
Friends of Rwanda;
Ladies and Gentlemen;

Where should we be going today? As your President I would like to tell you where I think we should be heading. And I would like to request our friends here present and other friends of Rwanda to accompany us in this crusade. Do not continue to regard Rwanda as a nation torn apart by ethnic rivalry and hatred, poverty and dependence.

I would like us to rise up together and build a new Rwanda where unity, mutual understanding and respect are the foundation on which we will build everything else. Thus the Rwandese people will feel, once again, that they have a common destiny, a shared hope in life and death, equal access to the country's wealth and resources and equal rights for all. The Rwandese people should feel that anything detrimental to a section of the community is detrimental to the whole country and should therefore be fought by all.

I appeal to every Rwandese to rise up and fight against anything that divides the our people. We must also fight injustice against our people. Current and future legislation will ensure that the state has its full weight behind the fight against division and injustice.

I would like call on every Rwandan to be his brother's keeper. Only when we commit ourselves to helping guarantee the security of others can we enjoy maximum security as a nation.

It is in this spirit that I appeal to all Rwandese who are still living in self-imposed exile, whether in Africa or outside Africa, to come back home so that we can rebuild our country together.

I appeal to those Rwandese people still in Congo and elsewhere who still have the desire to fight and terrorize the people of this country, to stop, and return to Rwanda to participate in the reconstruction of their motherland. There are many of them who gave up this way of fighting, and when they came back we welcomed them and we helped them to resume normal lives. Some were absorbed into the national army.

We shall support the Unity and Reconciliation Commission and the Commission for Human Rights because if they are effective, they will enable Rwanda realize achieve its full potential as a nation.

Rwanda needs to be seen as country governed by the rule of law, and all the Rwandese people to be equal before the law. I would like to request leaders, at all levels, to respect the law. Let there be no Rwandese buying or paying a bribe for his rights, so that he who is not able to pay for it, is deprived.

It is in this context that I would like to appeal to all the Rwandese people to fight against corruption. They should never accept a situation where they are made to buy those things that are theirs by right. Those leaders who will be found guilty of corruption will be severely punished.

I would like to request those working in the judiciary to always be fair in their judgements. They must never accept bribes to influence their decisions. When in a country, the person who is unfairly treated does not hope to receive fair treatment, and the one who is meeting out unfairness is not punished, sooner or later the country perishes. The people of Rwanda shall therefore not tolerate a judiciary bent on destroying the very fabric or our society.

I would like to call upon all sections of society to return any property that is being illegally occupied. Those who might be reluctant to return property to their rightful owners should be prepared to face justice.

We must also rise and fight against the culture of impunity that has been rampant in the country for a long time, culminating in the genocide. We would like to appeal to all Rwandese to actively participate in the Gacaca courts and to tell the truth because what we build on lies will not last. This is one of the ways that will help us to reestablish unity and reconciliation in Rwanda and to solve the problem of trying the many cases of the people accused of having committed genocide.

I would also like to request all the Rwandese people to respect and handle public property with care. In Rwanda, you find that public property is regarded as belonging to no one in particular, and whoever has it handles it in whatever way they think fit. This culture should be uprooted and discarded in Rwanda forever.

In the spirit of fighting against lack of transparency and corruption, we shall continue to support the National Examination Council, the National Tender Board, the Auditor General's Office and the Rwanda Revenue Authority; we will establish other organs as and when need arises. In particular, we shall enact a leadership code of conduct, which will requiring leaders to make declarations of their assets.

It is my sincere hope that on the expiry of the term of office, I would have bequeathed to you a country inhabited by people who see no value in injustice and corruption.

Your Excellencies Heads of States,
Distinguished guests,
Friends of Rwanda,
Ladies and Gentlemen.

Many Rwandese are very poor. Many of them do not have places of abode worthy of a human being. Many do not have access to clean water, and they do not eat food with enough nutrients. Many of them do not know how to read and write and do not have jobs that can sustain them. The sick do not have access to health services, essential drugs or competent doctors. There are many children who do not go to school and those who do, do not go beyond the first six years of primary school.

Furthermore, Rwanda does not have plenty of natural resources in its soil. We do not have oil, nor do we have precious stones. We do not even have access to the sea, so much that even the things we export or import turn out to be very expensive. In addition to all this, Rwanda is a heavily indebted country.

Despite all this, I do not believe that we should lose hope and surrender ourselves to lives of poverty. If we can utilize the resources that God has given us to good effect, we can eradicate poverty.

The most important resource we have is our people. That is why it is our policy to invest whatever resources we have at our disposal in them.

We would like to urgently appeal to the Rwandese people to work. As the bible says: "he who does not work should not eat". I would like to request every Rwandese in whatever trade they are involved in, to work with dedication and diligence. If we adopt this culture of working diligently, we will be able to create more jobs for our people.

Furthermore, the limited resources at our disposal will be applied to building schools for science and technology, especially in the modern field of information and communication technologies. This way we shall be able to start new jobs.

We shall also continue to invest money in public utilities like electricity, telephones, water, and roads, which are essential to creating a good environment for foreign investment in Rwanda.

We plan to use the ethane gas in Lake Kivu to provide some basic services. It is in this context that we shall establish the Rwanda Investment Promotion Agency in order to encourage and facilitate foreign direct investment into Rwanda.

Rwanda is a very beautiful country. We intend to make the world aware of Rwanda's unspoiled beauty, thereby encouraging them to visit the country. We would also like them to visit Rwanda and see for themselves the tremendous progress being made to develop the country after the genocide. We plan to make tourism a major source of earning for the country.

Though small, Rwanda is well endowed with rainfall and fertile soils. I am convinced that if we used the land in the most productive way possible, we would not only banish hunger from our country, but also produce enough for export.

In Rwanda, women and the youth comprise more than 75% of the entire population. It is among women and the youth that we find the most poverty, unemployment, ignorance and illiteracy. The government of national unity has placed women and the youth at various levels of responsibility, where they can be empowered to spearhead the development of their peers. We shall continue to support and empower disadvantaged groups to participate, through the national assembly and other fora, to finding lasting solutions to our many challenges.

The AIDS scourge remains among the serious challenges facing our country today. The efforts of the liberators of this country and the government will come to naught if the nation's youth are claimed by this dreadful disease. As I said earlier, Rwanda's most important resource is its people. Our efforts and dreams for development will come to naught for as long as the youth, who are the most productive section of society and are also best qualified to acquire knowledge in information and communication technologies, are dying from the disease daily.

I therefore appeal to all Rwandese people, leaders in local or central government and the civil society, to come together and fight the AIDS scourge. I appeal to leaders to seize whatever opportunity they can get to caution people about AIDS. Our people must change their sexual habits so as to avoid the disease.

Your Excellencies Heads of State,
Distinguished Guests,
Friends of Rwanda,
Ladies and Gentlemen,

We have had a transitional government for five and a half years. I would like to point out that this was necessary because our country has had bad leadership for such a long time. The post-independence leadership sowed seeds of discord, division and hatred resulting in many Rwandese people being killed, while others were excluded from schools, work and politics. The culmination of this was the terrible 1994 genocide. It is quite clear therefore, that after the country had been subjected to bad politics for such a long time, it would be imprudent to immediately plunge into competitive politics.

However, our efforts are geared towards ushering a truly democratic dispensation in Rwanda, where respect for the human rights of all, peace, unity and tolerance are the cornerstones. The future politics of Rwanda will be deeply rooted in these principles.

It is in this context that we shall set up a Legal and Constitutional Commission. The commission will solicit the views of the Rwandese people both inside and outside Rwanda. This way, we will have the first ever 'peoples constitution'. The constitution will lead the country out of the transitional period. The process will help make the people more aware of their basic rights as stipulated under the constitution.

We shall continue to empower the people and educate them about choosing leaders on the basis of their programmes and plans rather than on basis of their tribes, regions or religions.

When one analyzes how the political ideas of the Rwandese people are developing, one is hopeful that by the end of the transitional period, Rwanda will have settled down in security, peace, unity and reconciliation – an excellent basis for free and fair elections.

Your Excellencies Heads of State,
Distinguished Guests,
Friends of Rwanda,
Ladies and Gentlemen,

I would like to take this opportunity to tell the Rwandese people and friends of Rwanda, that we would like to enjoy peace and cooperation with all the countries of the world, but in particular with our neighbours. We shall therefore do whatever we can to live in peace with the countries of the region. However, we cannot attain all these objectives without peace and security in the country.

Let me repeat it here today, both to the Rwandese people and our friends that, the fact that Rwanda has troops in the brotherly country of Congo is not because the Rwandese like fighting, nor is it because Rwanda would like to be a great power in this region, or acquire Congo's wealth, or annex part of its territory.

I would like to remind you that the reason why our troops are based in Congo, is because some Rwandese who perpetrated the 1994 genocide were remobilized and retrained in the DRC Congo with the intention of causing instability in Rwanda, and completing the genocide.

We would like to take this opportunity to state openly that, if the rebels based in the DRC agree to abandon their evil plans to kill, destroy and loot, and they resolve to return to the country and cooperate with their fellow Rwandese citizens to build their motherland as we have so often appealed to them to do, we will have no further concerns in Congo that would justify our troop presence.

But while our soldiers remain in Congo, I would like to appeal to the Rwandese people to support them because the peace and security we are enjoying today has been achieved as a result of their sacrifice.

We once again assure the Rwandese people and friends of Rwanda that we will do all we can to ensure that there is peace in this region. We shall continue to give maximum support to the Lusaka Agreement which we believe offers an excellent framework for peace in the region.

Your Excellencies Heads of State,
Distinguished Guests,
Friends of Rwanda,
Ladies and Gentlemen,

I would like to take this opportunity once again to assure all the Rwandese people, both those present and those who could not be present, that I will do everything in my power to carry out the responsibilities you have entrusted in me. I will regularly consult you, and those at various levels of local or central government, so that together we can begin a new crusade.

We shall consult and explain government policies, so that you may accompany us on the crusade, well aware of where we are going. We shall also explain things to our friends and development partners, so that they too can join in and support our efforts.

Finally, as we looked at ourselves trying to find the confidence to take the new step that I called on you to take, we should look back to where we are coming from and also look around to see what we have that can help us to take that new step forward. I would like to request you also to look upward and pray to God to bless us in the new era for our country; one in which the Rwandese people will live in unity, mutual understanding, respect and cooperation; a country in which there is real democracy, justice, peace, security and development.

Thank you. May God bless you all.

ADDRESS TO THE GOVERNMENT STRATEGY WORKSHOP[3]

Your Right Honourable Prime Minister,
Honourable Ministers,
Secretaries General,
Distinguished Guests,
Ladies and Gentlemen,

I wish to welcome you to the Workshop on "Prosperity Creation and Improved Governmental Performance" for Rwanda's Cabinet Ministers and Secretaries General.

I wish to first of all, thank all the facilitators for this Strategic Workshop, namely:

- Mr. Mike Fairbanks, Ms Kaia Miller, Ms Mickey Mericle, and Mr. Malik Fal, of Monitor Company, from the United States;
- Sir Bhinod Bacha and Mr. Dan Bundhoo, from the Republic of Mauritius;
- Professor James Katorobo, and Dr. John-Mary Kauzya, UN System;
- Local resources persons from our ministries and other institutions.

Distinguished Guests
Ladies and Gentlemen

Today we begin an intensive week of discussions regarding creating prosperity opportunities for Rwanda. In undertaking this important exercise, let us bear in mind the context and challenges that face our country, including the following factors:

- Land-locked status
- High population density, and a predominantly peasant agriculture
- Lack of viable natural resources
- Unskilled human resources
- Limited capacity of the state and public sector
- Low level capacity of the private sector
- Decades of conflict and bad governance culminating in the 1994 events
- Post-conflict status in an unstable region

These constraints pose a challenge to us in terms of how to circumscribe them or turn them into opportunities. In this sense then, we are called upon to engage in deep reflection on how to develop an agenda, as well as capacities to carry forward that agenda of turning constraints into prosperity.

Let me add here that creating opportunities for our people requires that we address our challenges in both national and global contexts. Our domestic challenges notwithstanding, we must recognize the vast opportunities in the unfolding global economy. Markets around the world are becoming more liberalised; advances in information technologies are changing the very nature of communication, innovation, and competition. Businesses are becoming economic engines of national economies, and are playing the leading role in employment-creation for citizens. It is evident, furthermore, that in these innovations and prosperity-creation processes, the potential of the human mind is limitless. Little wonder that human resources have in fact become the greatest national assets - with the right strategies.

[3] H.E. PAUL KAGAME, President of the Republic of Rwanda 21st June , 2000

It is time for us in Rwanda to make the choices that are to thrust us into the global economic arena as active participants, as opposed to bystanders.

Ministers Distinguished
Guests Ladies and Gentlemen

Rwanda has come a long way since 1994 in the social, economic, political, as well as in the peace and security fields. An enabling environment is slowly getting in place, permitting us to become part of the global change. Despite 40 years of inward looking policies, our Government is fully committed to an open economy. This is demonstrated by an increasingly liberalised economy as reflected in different sectors.

Despite the noted progress, however, much remains to be done. We Rwandans have shown remarkable resilience; we have to recognize the urgent need for further change. We are now called upon to tackle the next developmental phase - that of prosperity creation. It is therefore not by accident that "prosperity creation" is the theme of this Workshop involving political and technical leaders of our Government, namely, Cabinet Ministers and Secretaries General.

Let me hasten to add four key points:

- First, Government cannot spearhead prosperity creation alone. Our success in creating prosperity will depend in large part on our ability as Government to provide an enabling environment, to promote domestic private sector, foreign investors and international trade. Thus, expanding dialogue far beyond the walls of Government - into the private sector and civil society of our country - is an imperative that should not become underestimated.
- Second, the right agenda without adequate capacity and a vehicle to carry it through runs the risk of remaining an unrealised dream. Our challenge is how to ensure that, within the resources constraints, the state machinery, the private sector, and civil society can carry forward this agenda. To do this more efficiently and effectively, we all must endeavour to build and strengthen institutions that are both transparent and accountable.
- Third, as has become an almost universal practice, I intend that we become a 'learning government'. In addition to our existing knowledge-base, we must continuously acquire new skills, in line with the changing regional and global circumstances.
- Four, we ought to strengthen, and engender a culture of teamwork in the execution of our governmental tasks and duties. Our Ministers and Secretaries General should constitute a single team, one that should inspire and lead their institutions, as they pursue their policy objectives.

Ladies and Gentlemen
Distinguished Guests

Let me take this opportunity to recall that this is not the first time Government Leaders have undertaken a strategy retreat. Three years ago, from 31 March to 05 April 1997, our Cabinet conducted an exercise on how best to re-organise our administrative structures.

This time, we are moving to a higher level of posing the issue of how best we can move Rwanda forward within the constraints and opportunities I have referred to, and how best to render our Government machinery effective to carry out these goals.

I intend that the exercise of bringing together our policy-making leaders to develop a common agenda, becomes an annual event. Indeed, these strategic workshops should be encouraged and adopted by other national institutions, to permit broader and consistent dialogue on how our country is to become properly situated in the challenging global economy.

Distinguished Guests
Ladies and Gentlemen

am convinced beyond any shadow of doubt that Rwanda can succeed in its quest for transformation. The constraints we face are real, but we should think and act bold. Forty years ago, a well-known economist Gunnar Myrdal published a book entitled "The Asian Drama". Four decades later, we are talking of "The Asian Miracles". Many small nations have transformed themselves into "Tigers". Rwanda may not become a Tiger in one generation, but we can, and will certainly lay the foundations for a profound social and economic transformation.

In conclusion, let us assign ourselves specific objectives that we must achieve in this Workshop:

- A long-term focused vision on how our country should transform;
- Strategy for rendering our Government machinery effective and efficient in pursuit of the focused vision
- Realistic action plans and benchmarks in regard to the implementation of our vision.

H.E. PAUL KAGAME, PRESIDENT OF THE REPUBLIC OF RWANDA THE SWEAR-IN CEREMONY

of: - The New Minister of Energy , Water and Natural Resources ; - The Vice-Preident of Supreme Court and President of the Gacaca Courts ; - The New Members of Parliament

27th June , 2000

Your Excellency the President of the Transitional National Assembly ;
The Right Honourable Prime Minister ;
Honourable Ministers and Ministers of State ;
Honourable Members of the Transitional National Assembly;
Your Excellencies Members of the Diplomatic Corps and Representatives of International Organizations ;
Distingushed Guests;
Ladies and Gentlemen;

I would first of all like to congratulate those who have just taken their oaths of office, namely:

- The Minister of Energy, Water and Natural Resources;
- The Vice-President of the Supreme Court and President of the Gacaca Courts;
- And the new Members of the Transitional National Assembly.

You have all held various positions in public service in the past. I would like to thank you for your continued service to the nation, and to appeal to you to discharge your new responsibilities with as much diligence as your previous assignments.

Government will continue to provide you with all the assistance and facilitation necessary to effectively discharge your new duties.

Your Excellency the President of the Transitional National Assembly,
The Right Honourable Prime Minister,
Honourable Ministers,
Honourable Members of the Transitional National Assembly,
Ladies and Gentlemen:

I would like to take this opportunity to highlight some of the challenges that lie ahead for the newly sworn-in office holders. Energy, whether it comes from hydro-electric power or from any other source, it is a basic and essential tool for the development of a country. The challenge for the new Energy, Water and Natural Resources Minister is to address Rwanda's Energy problem, which is an essential prerequisite for faster economic growth and development and increased foreign direct investment into our economy.

There is also the challenge of better and more optimal energy use. We need to ensure that our people use what energy they have at their disposal in the most optimal and economical manner, so as to maximise productivity from each unit of energy consumed.

We also need to urgently address challenge of rural electrification. As a result of our failure to provide rural areas with a more environmentally friendly energy source, our people continue to rely on firewood for energy, resulting in destruction of forests and soil cover, environmental degradation, hence low productivity and greater poverty.

The Ministry of Energy should look seriously into providing energy for domestic and general economic use in Imidugudu across the country.

With regard to water, we face another serious challenge: providing clean water for domestic use and for farming. Water is another resource which I fear we are not utilising optimally. Yet during dry seasons, our people suffer from hunger and low agricultural productivity because of a lack of water. We need to ask ourselves how we can conserve and use our water resources more optimally.

The new Minister and his staff should work together with the other Ministries concerned with the use of natural resources, like the Ministry of Agriculture and Livestock, so as to find ways for the Rwandese people to make the best use of their limited natural resources. How can we use our lakes, rivers and pastureland more profitably? Can we conserve rain water for use during the dry season? Experts and specialists say that it is possible and that it is done in other countries. So why can't we do it too?

Among the people who have just taken their oath of office is the President of the Gacaca Courts, the community courts we are establishing to deal with certain categories of genocide offences.

The 1994 genocide was devastating to our society because it destroyed confidence within and between communities and led to massive loss of life and property. The challenges we face in the aftermath of the genocide calls upon us to search for more comprehensive and inclusive solutions that embrace our entire population.

The Gacaca Courts are in part aimed at this. We aim to involve the entire community in the process of investigation, the trials, sentencing, punishment and forgiveness. This is no longer a process that involves a handful of legal experts. It will involve all Rwandans. It is our hope and prayer that this will be a therapeutic exercise in which, through community participation, we can collectively deal with the 1994 genocide as a community and build a solid new dispensation in which tolerance and respect for human rights and the rule of law have a central place.

I wish the new President of the Gacaca Courts every success in the discharge of her duties, and express the hope that she will continue to work with diligence, wisdom and justice.

Ladies and Gentlemen,

Four new Members of the Transitional National Assembly have taken their oath today. I would like to congratulate them on their new appointments. Together with the other two new public office holders, they represent the three arms of state, which we aim to strengthen so that they can better meet their day-to-day challenges. I also call upon you to improve your methods of work and acquire new knowledge and expertise instead of clinging to old and out-of-date methods of work.

Last week, we held a workshop for Government Ministers and Secretaries-General. In that workshop we learnt a lot of useful things. I would like to request all the levels of leadership to organise similar workshops, even at the Commune and Sector levels, so as to focus the attention of leaders at all levels on our national vision and the way forward. But we should be prepared to enforce the decision that will emerge from such workshops.

I would like to end by thanking all those who have just taken their oaths of office for answering the call to serve their country, and wish them every success in the discharge of their new assignments.

Thank you and May God bless you.

H.E. PAUL KAGAME, President of the Republic of Rwanda

36TH OAU SUMMIT OF HEADS OF STATE AND GOVERNMENT

10-12 July 2000

Mr Chairman,
Your Excellencies Heads of State and Government,
Heads of Delegation,
Secretary General, OAU,
Distinguished Delegates;

Allow me first and foremost, Mr Chairman, to express my personal satisfaction, and that of my delegation, to have you in the Chair, to guide our deliberations at this session, and indeed the affairs of the OAU for the forthcoming year. I am convinced that your wisdom and experience will be of great value to all of us. May I also extend my appreciation for the very warm hospitality extended to myself and my delegation by HE President Gnassingbé EYADEMA, the Government and people of the Republic of Togo.

Mr Chairman,
Your Excellencies Heads of State and Government,
Heads of Delegation,
Distinguished Delegates:

I now wish to direct my remarks on the question of security and stability on our continent. Let me first state that Rwanda, as a founder member of the Organisation of African Unity (OAU), is a firm believer in the principles of the OAU, particularly in regard to peace and development. We note, however, that peace and development cannot thrive amidst strife, conflict, and insecurity. Development can only occur in a secure and stable environment, all which largely continue to elude our continent.

Mr Chairman;

We believe that insecurity and instability on our continent stems from bad governance and the accompanying denial of fundamental rights, such as:

- The right to individual dignity as a human being;
- The right to equal opportunities in society;
- The right to a fair share of national resources;
- The right to freedom of expression; and most importantly,
- The right to life itself;

Mr Chairman,
Your Excellencies Heads of State and Government,
Heads of Delegation,
Distinguished Delegates;

The consequences of bad governance and the denial of the fundamental rights have had devastating impact on our continent, as demonstrated by, among others, sectarian practices, corruption, mass poverty, refugees, wars, and conflicts of one type or another. In our own case in Rwanda, bad governance and the denial of fundamental rights culminated into horrific events of the 1994 Genocide, an episode that subsequently spilled over into broader Great Lakes Region. Six years later after this grotesque episode, energies that should be focussed on prosperity-creation and development are still drained by security preoccupations which stem from the misdeeds of yesteryear.

Mr Chairman,
Your Excellencies Heads of State and Government,
Heads of Delegation,
Distinguished Delegates;

Let me emphasise, however, that we are not here to engage in gloom and doom regarding the future of our continent. Rather, we are calling for concerted efforts in confronting the root causes of insecurity and instability. Only then can we seriously concentrate on prosperity-creation for African people. We should, in resolving conflicts and building peace purposefully and timely, become guided by our desire for African social and economic transformation - the basis for our African Renaissance.

Mr Chairman,
Your Excellencies Heads of State and Government,
Heads of Delegation, Distinguished Delegates,
Ladies and Gentlemen;

Two days ago, the International Panel of Eminent Personalities established by the OAU to investigate the 1994 Rwanda genocide presented its report. The Rwanda Government welcomes the report, which we hope will help shed more light on how these heinous crimes were conceived, planned and executed while the world folded its arms and allowed one million of our people to perish.

On behalf of the Government and people of Rwanda, I would like to register our sincere appreciation to the Panel of Eminent Personalities who authored the report, particularly His Excellency Sir. Ketumile Masire who very ably led the Panel.

On behalf of the Government and people of Rwanda, I would also like to express our sincere appreciation to His Excellency Prime Minister Meles Zenawi of the Federal Democratic Republic of Ethiopia, for initiating the idea of setting up the International Panel of Eminent Personalities to investigate the 1994 Genocide and surrounding events. The Government of Rwanda strongly supported the initiative in all its stages.

I would also like to register our sincere appreciation to the OAU General Secretariat, and particularly His Excellency Dr. Salim Ahmed Salim, who worked tirelessly in support of the Panel and its work.

Permit me to conclude my remarks on security and stability on our continent by acknowledging a pioneering conference on "Women as Partners for Peace" held in Kigali, Rwanda from 25th - 30 June 2000. I was very touched by these women who came from almost all corners of the globe, with the objective of calling for equal participation in decision-making processes on peace and development. This and other such initiatives help to remind us that African civil society, particularly women and children, have borne the brunt of wars and genocide. Therefore Your Excellencies, we should endorse such initiatives as "Women as Partners for Peace", and assist in bringing African civil society into the mainstream of peace building and development of our continent.

H.E. PAUL KAGAME, President of the Republic of Rwanda

PRESENTATION ON SONARWA'S SILVER JUBILEE

August 2nd , 2000... Kigali, RWANDA

Excellency President of National Assembly,
Excellency Prime Minister,
Excellency President of Supreme Court,
Chairman of the Board and Management of SONARWA, Honourable Ministers and members of Parliament,
Secretary General of COMESA,
Distinguished invited guests,
Ladies and gentlemen,

I am pleased to be the guest of honour on SONARWA's Silver Jubilee. I congratulate SONARWA on their contributions not only to the development of insurance sector in Rwanda, but also their mobilisation of savings and investments in the social sector in the past 25 years. I congratulate the Chairman of the Board and Management of SONARWA, who have skilfully steered this institution to productivity over the past several years, during challenging times for our country. Let me also take this opportunity to welcome SONARWA's guests from outside Rwanda, who have come to celebrate SONARWA Silver Jubilee.

Distinguished Guests
Ladies and gentlemen,

The issue of savings is of considerable importance if we are to transform our economy and improve the standard of living of the Rwandan people. We all know that there can be no growth without investment and no investment without savings. The resources mobilised by insurance companies, namely, pension, life and medical funds, are all very crucial because they are long-term and stable. It is stating the obvious that our country, as the rest of developing countries, is highly indebted and over-dependent on outside funding. Substantive mobilisation of domestic savings and investments by insurance companies, such as SONARWA, would permit us to become less dependent on external financing, and to increasingly rely on domestic resources.

To effectively mobilise savings and make them responsive to financing needs of our economy, our country has to develop a competitive and efficient insurance sector with viable, solvent companies that are capable of fulfilling their key roles of saving and associated norms and responsibilities. Further, in the face of globalisation, domestic insurance companies must not only be competitive locally, but ought to take advantage of open markets and compete on regional markets. This calls for efficient and modern financial and human resource management coupled with aggressive marketing. In other words, SONARWA and other Rwandan insurance companies should look and operate beyond the borders of Rwanda.

Excellencies
Distinguished guests,

Our Government attaches importance to Rwanda's service sector. Without any substantive natural resources, we have identified the service sector as the lead sector in social and economic transformation of our country. The realisation of our transformation goals requires developing our human resources, who will, in turn, actively make Rwanda a financial and information technology hub for our region. I cannot over-emphasise the central role of the insurance sector and other financial services, in this quest.

SONARWA and other companies in the insurance sector must therefore widen their products and services to accommodate the needs of your clientele, and make them affordable. To date there are various financial instruments on the global market that are not developed in Rwanda. You must strive to facilitate investment by providing the relevant securities needed. To achieve these objectives, we must draw clear working guidelines governing the relationship between the state as an entity to provide incentives and to regulate, and the enterprise as the key player in the economy. There are several important issues to emphasise in this regard:

1. We must enact modern laws and regulations in line with the profound changes in the international financial system through which solvency of insurance companies can be monitored and the interests of the insured and contract beneficiaries are protected. I am aware that currently the Ministries concerned are looking into this.

2. We must insist on an efficient and diligent judicial system to help ensure equitable and rapid settlement of claims.

3. We shall encourage incentives to promote long-term classes of insurance business, e.g., life funds, and pension funds.

4. You as companies must employ modern financial management and be competitive on the global market. We must always strive to expand our market beyond our geographical borders.

5. Insurance companies must involve a bigger majority of our population to realise the insurance principle of the law of large numbers. Today insurance and other services are concentrated in the towns; yet over 90% of our population are located in rural areas.

6. Our financial institutions, insurance companies inclusive, must address their products and services to the needs of the clientele. Credit insurance, life insurance and agricultural insurance must be further developed and made affordable to the consuming public.

On Government's part, we believe in a strong private sector, which should become the principle agency of creating prosperity in our country. We are committed to providing an enabling business environment and to keep in constant dialogue with the private sector, to render the latter effective. In this regard, we have put up important organs such as the Rwanda Investment Promotion Agency (RIPA) and the Presidential Commission charged with the economy. What remains, therefore, is to form active, consistent and concerted partnership between the stakeholders to address the task of resources mobilisation and development.

Ladies and gentlemen,
Distinguished guests,

Finally, let me note that SONARWA has entered the international insurance arena. The company is a shareholder in COMESA affiliates, namely, the PTA Reinsurance Company, and the African Reinsurance Company; it is in this context that SONARWA acts as the national facilitator of the COMESA Yellow Card. We strongly encourage these relations as they are in line with the Government policy of regional co-operation and integration. We fully support COMESA and its institutions; our companies will always be encouraged to co-operate with their COMESA counterparts. Once again, I congratulate SONARWA on their Silver Jubilee.

ON THE OCCASION OF THE OFFICIAL LAUNCHING OF PROCESS FOR THE PREPARATION OF THE POVERTY REDUCTION

H.E. PAUL KAGAME, President of the Republic of Rwanda

1s June , 2000

Your Excellency the President of the National Assembly, Your Excellency the Prime Minister,
Your Excellency the President of the Supreme Court, Honourable Ministers,
Honourable Members of Parliament,
Your Excellencies Members of the Diplomatic Corps and Representatives of International Organisations in Rwanda,
Distinguished Guests,
Ladies and Gentlemen,

We are gathered here today to launch what I believe is a very timely and relevant programme for the Preparation of the Poverty Reduction Strategy Paper for Rwanda. However, in launching the programme, we need to be mindful of the fact that poverty is not new to Rwanda. Indeed it has been a major feature of the life of our country. Despite many public and privately funded poverty reduction projects, today 69% of our people live in poverty.

The genocide played an important part in aggrevating an already desparate situation. One million, mostly economically productive people, were killed in their prime during the genocide. Many were Teachers, Doctors or enterprising Businessmen and women. Almost the entire population of our country was displaced between 1994 and 1996, either internally or in neighbouring countries. Apart from this human cost, property worth hundreds of millions of dollars was looted or destroyed. This includes public infrastructure like roads, telecommunications and electricity.

Consequently, although Rwanda was already among the poorest countries in the world before 1994, the tragedy of the genocide worsened the already dire situation. For example; in 1985 about 45% of the Rwandese people lived on incomes of less than one dollar (350 RWF) per person per day; in 1993 they were about 55% ; while in 1999, as a result of genocide and displacement, the figure had risen to 69%.

Rwanda's social indicators are evidence of the gravity of the poverty situation. For example, the average life expectancy at birth for Rwandans is 49 years; for every 1,000 children born, 131 die before the age of 5; about 52 % of the Rwandese population above the age of 15 are illiterate; about 91% of the population still use traditional, non-productive methods of farming; of the children between the ages of 7-12, only 61% go to school and many people still have no access to safe drinking water.

Distinguished Guests,
Ladies and Gentlemen,

It is time for us to seriously examine the poverty situation in Rwanda and come up with a common policy and programme for poverty reduction. It is an exercise which calls for the full participation of all Rwandans since it is our collective concern. Poverty cannot and will not be reduced by Government initiative alone, nor from the efforts of donors. We believe in popular, grassroot participation in issues which, like poverty, affect the entire country. It is a problem that affects all Rwandans, so solutions must come from every village, hamlet and parish of our country.

It is encouraging that, despite the many challenges we face, we have been able to reach, and in some cases surpass, pre-1993 levels of production in a very short time. However, structural problems inherent in our society need to be urgently addressed, providing solutions for the serious poverty that affects our country. The problems of low household incomes, traditional, non-productive farming methods and production with no added value requires our special attention.

Distinguished Guests,
Ladies and Gentlemen:

For a long time now, our society has suffered as a result of poor leadership. Poor leadership leads to many other problems, most important of which are ; a low level of manpower development both among leaders and the general population; a poor work ethic and attitude to work ; laziness ; sectarianism ; abuse of human rights and poor health. Under these conditions, a society cannot develop.

We need to work hard together to ensure that the problems of the past which resulted directly from poor leadership do not have a place in today's Rwanda.

Distinguished Guests,
Ladies and Gentlemen:

There are some people who think that Rwanda is, and will always be, poor. They think that a small country like ours without any natural resources like gold and oil, is doomed to perpetual poverty. Such people are resigned to the a life of dependence on foreign aid.

All I can say to skeptics like this is that with the right policies and hard work, we will overcome poverty. There are numerous examples of countries developing without natural resources, or rainfall in the same abundance as that of Rwanda. However, with good leadership, foresight and the right policies, these countries are wealthy, prosperous and respected members of the international community. Why can't we achieve the same in Rwanda?

We need to make a correct analysis of our problems, and let this analysis inform the strategies we chose to get us out of poverty. Let the support of friends from outside Rwanda only complement our own efforts, not be centre of our strategies.

Distinguished Guests,
Ladies and Gentlemen:

It is with this in mind that today we are setting up a programme to elaborate on the poverty reduction strategy paper for Rwanda . We plan to conduct discussions and consultations with all stakeholders so that everyone can be part of the process to elaborate a strategy to reduce poverty. The United Nations, of which we are an active member, aims to reduce poverty by 50% by the year 2015. It will be commendable if we can meet this target in Rwanda, though we should aim to surpass it.

Distinguished Guests,
Ladies and Gentlemen:

Despite the many challenges we face in Rwanda, the Government of National Unity has registered some significant successes in creating an enabling environment for economic growth and development, investment and trade. There is now peace and security throughout the country ; refugees have been repatriated and resettled ; we have made efforts to promote and develop agriculture ; we have had an average annual economic growth rate of 6% since 1994 ; there have been improvements in infrastructure particularly roads, schools and hospitals. We have achieved a lot in the last six years, yet there still remains so much to do.

As I said earlier, 69% of the Rwandese people live in extreme poverty. In order to reduce poverty by 50% we need to have an annual economic growth rate of 8% for the next 15 years.

This will not be an easy task. We will need to adopt certain measures which will help us achieve our target. Some of them are :

- The need to fight ignorance and adopt a system of education relevant to our realities. We need to invest more in our people, because they are Rwanda's only source of wealth and development.

- We need to modernise agriculture, and add value to our exports and increase our national income.

- We need to fight the ills of corruption, laziness and sectarianism. - We need to promote the private sector and develop a culture of hard work and self-sustainance.

- We need to promote national unity, the rule of law and promote harmony and cooperation among all our people.

- It is important to empower women and the youth for they are a great source of development and hope in this country .

- We must work with our neighbours and partners regionally and internationally to foster the common ideals and aspirations we have for our peoples.

- We need to improve our policies on land use, settlement and the environment.

- We need to attract investment and create an conducive environment for investors in Kigali and beyond.

- Government needs to build the necessary infrastructure (roads, schools, hospitals, clean water, electricity, markets, etc), as a measure to encourage more production and trade.

- As a nation we also need to rally together to fight AIDS and other killer diseases, because an unhealthy population is an unproductive population.

Distinguished Guests,
Ladies and Gentlemen,

The programme we are launching today requires our full support and participation so that we can develop a well thought-out, relevant and integrated poverty reduction strategy paper.

These consultations for a poverty reduction strategy paper are timely, especially because the Government has began the process of decentralisation to the lower levels of government. I hope you will make every effort to consult as widely as possible with local leaders in the process of developing this strategy paper.

I would therefore like to call upon leaders at all levels in the country, to begin consultations and dialogue with the people, so that this can be a truly peoples strategy, representing their concerns, their hopes and their dreams.

I conclude by thanking all of you for having come to attend this official launching. I would like to particulary thank the donor community who are with us today. I would like to assure you of full government support to make this programme a success. Finally, it gives me great pleasure to declare the Programme for the Elaboration of the Poverty Reduction Strategy Paper for Rwanda officially launched.

Thank you and may God bless you all.

JOINT PRESS CONFERENCE PRESIDENT KAGAME OF THE REPUBLIC OF RWANDA AND PRESIDENT MUSEVENI OF THE REPUBLIC OF UGANDA

At the end of a two-day official working visit to Uganda by the Rwandan President, Their Excellencies Presidents Paul Kagame of Rwanda and Yoweri Kaguta Museveni of Uganda addressed a joint press conference at the Imperial Botanical Beach Hotel in Entebbe.

Proceedings were as follows:

Hon. Amama Mbabazi, Uganda's Minister for Regional Cooperation Your Excellency, President Yoweri Kaguta Museveni,

Your Excellency, President Paul Kagame, you are welcome to this press conference where we have assembled both local and international press representatives. We shall read the joint communiqué first, and this will be followed by questions from the press to Your Excellencies. If you have no objections to this proposed agenda for this meeting, Your Excellencies, I will go ahead to read the joint communiqué.

JOINT COMMUNIQUE

1. At the invitation of H.E. President Yoweri Kaguta Museveni of the Republic of Uganda, H.E. President Paul Kagame of the Republic of Rwanda paid a two-day official working visit to Uganda.

2. The two Heads of State met in a cordial atmosphere, reflecting the historical brotherly relations existing between the peoples of Uganda and Rwanda.

3. The two Heads of State held fruitful discussions and reviewed areas of mutual interest including bilateral, regional and international issues.

4. On bilateral issues, the two Heads of State stressed the need to consolidate further the relations between the two countries. They agreed on the need to explore new ways and means to further strengthen and deepen relations.

5. The two Heads of State held extensive discussions on the problems affecting the region. On the Democratic Republic of Congo, they reiterated their strong commitment to the implementation of the Lusaka Ceasefire Agreement and resolved to work together for its full and expeditious implementation.

6. On the recent clashes between the UPDF and RPA, in Kisangani, the two leaders regretted these unfortunate developments which were a setback to the Lusaka Ceasefire Agreement. In this regard, the two Heads of State reaffirmed their commitment to the demilitarization of the city of Kisangani and called on other parties to the Ceasefire Agreement to reciprocate and not take advantage of Rwanda and Uganda's withdrawal from Kisangani.

7. The two Heads of State called upon the United Nations to fully deploy MONUC observers to support the Ceasefire Agreement and to provide necessary and adequate resources to the facilitator of the National Dialogue and to the JMC to enable them discharge the important tasks assigned to them under the Ceasefire Agreement.

8. At the end of his visit, President Paul Kagame expressed gratitude to President Museveni and the people of Uganda for the warm reception and cordial hospitality extended to him and his delegation during their stay in Uganda.

9. President Kagame extended an invitation to President Museveni to visit Rwanda. The invitation was gladly accepted. The dates will be communicated through diplomatic channels.

Thank You.

Questions and Answers.

Rugenera Pierre-Desire, Rwanda TV News:
(Question translated into English from Kinyarwanda) After what happened in Kisangani, and what has transpired over the last two days between Your two Excellencies, what can you tell the people of Rwanda is the way forward.

President Paul Kagame
(Answer translated into English from Kinyarwanda)
What is important is that President Museveni and I met for talks with the intention of reaching a conclusion on how to iron-out the problems that caused the fighting in Kisangani. The talks have gone well. We have discussed the issues exhaustively. We have acknowledged that the problems did exist and we have agreed on solutions for them. But most significantly, we have been looking forward to how our two countries can once again revive the excellent relations that existed before these difficulties emerged. Rwandans and Ugandans should be confident and hopeful because we are committed not to allow these problems to happen again.

Ali Mutasa, BBC Kiswahili:
People are dying to know, those I have spoken to about the Kisangani question, and everybody you ask, either on the street or other places, they say only two people know what happened in Kisangani: President Museveni and President Kagame. Now what really happened in Kisangani? What was the cause of this fight between two allies?

President Museveni
What we agreed in the meeting here, was that in this meeting we would not spend our time doing post-mortems. The post-mortem will be done by a committee led by Ministers and some Army Officers. We just concentrated on the way forward, as the President was saying. The way forward is the important thing, while not forgetting the post-mortem.

Reuters:
Looking to the future, what assurances can you give us that we will never again see Uganda and Rwanda fighting each other in Congo.

President Kagame

The assurance is in the fact that we have been able to have a good meeting between the two of us. We have discussed at length the importance of overcoming these difficulties that caused the tensions in the past. We have focused on moving forward and we have also asked people to look into what happened in the past that perpetuated this kind of situation for the time it was there. We have also suggested that there be mechanisms in place to address any future problems before they develop into any form of clashes or violence such as those that took place in Kisangani. I think we have reinforced our commitment and the belief that the two brotherly countries should continue to work together, and I have no doubts that our commitments will be fulfilled.

Linus Kaikai,

SABC Your Excellencies how do you explain the fact that the fighting between your two countries occurred in a third country? What does this say of your mission in Congo? Has the mission and interest changed maybe to commercial perspectives?

President Museveni

We regretted fighting, not only in a third country, but between our two countries was regrettable. So that is why first of all the post-mortem will be done by our people. That is A of our meeting. B, is the way forward. The way forward which is clear, and with a clear mechanism for handling things. So you can't go into the details now of whether it was commercial or whatever causes without doing a post-mortem. That will be pre-judging the issue.

Tamale Mirundi, The Voice Newspaper:

Media reports say that we lost the case in The Hague. I would like to know what this implies for the future of our presence in Congo.

President Museveni

That was a lie. We actually won the case. But The Monitor is The Monitor. You don't have to waste your time with it.Hon. Wapakhabulo is the Lawyer, he can answer the question better.

Hon. James Wapakhabulo

The case against Uganda in the International Court of Justice in The Hague was that 1. Uganda should withdraw immediately its troops from Kisangani and Congo as a whole, and 2. Pay reparations for damage caused. These were to be in form of interim orders pending the determination of the earlier case which Kabila filed against Uganda last year.

However, the International Court decided that yes, Uganda should withdraw from Congo, but in accordance with UN resolutions, which means they sent the case back to Lusaka because the Security Council decided last week that Uganda and Rwanda should withdraw from the Congo in accordance with the Lusaka timetable. So in effect, there was a status quo, we won.

Richard Mulondo, Radio Sanyu:

According to your communiqué you say that you agreed on a number of issues. I am interested in the specifics. Your Excellency President Yoweri Museveni, you are on record as having said that the differences between Uganda and Rwanda at that time were on strategy. I would like to know whether in your new way forward, you have harmonized your positions.

President Museveni

We harmonized all issues, but you see unfortunately we don't always work for the press. You know we are working for the solution, not for the press. So, it is not possible to talk about all those in detail. The communiqué is good enough for now. Thank you very much.

Entebbe. 2nd July, 2000.

PAUL KAGAME: INTERVIEW TO WEST AFRICA MAGAZINE

In an exclusive interview granted to West Africa magazine Editor, Adama Gaye, Paul KAGAME, the Rwandan President who was in London this week, spoke on a range of burning issues.

WA : Often when your name is mentioned it is associated with evil. Are you a devil or an angel ?

PK : *Those who created the negative impression should be the ones to explain it. There is nothing that I have done that should have created it. I think the opposite should be the case.*

WA : Who is Paul KAGAME ?

PK : *Well, currently, he is the President of the Republic of Rwanda. He is a freedom fighter who fought hard to liberate his country and restore the rights of many Rwandans, both those who were inside the country long ago and those who were refugees in the neighbouring countries and beyond.*

WA : You have acted behind the scenes until your recent move to your current position of President. Why this move now ?

PK : *I have never been behind the scenes. I was the Vice President and I held the portfolio of Minister of Defence. If anything, that is being at the forefront.*

WA : Why have you accepted to be President now ?

PK : *Circumstances keep changing. There is always dynamism as things happen in different situations. This dynamic situation created that I became the President. I look at that as a matter of carrying a heavy responsibility for my country. I was carrying a responsibility anyway before. This time, it adds more responsibility and I am not a person who runs away from challenges that are created by having to do more for my country.*

WA : What do you say to those who believe that the removal of the Hutu President Pasteur BIZIMUNGU means further marginalisation of the Hutus?

PK : *It is not the truth. Unless they mean that since, initially there was a Hutu President, the Tutsis were sidelined. The issue is about being Rwandese, not being a Hutu or a Tutsi. In Rwanda there are three ethnic groups : the Batwa, the Bahutu and the Batutsi. They should all have equal rights. We don't treat any of those as secondary citizens.*

WA : As President of Rwanda what is your core goal, ambition and vision for the country?

PK : *We have to start rebuilding the country. We have to unite the people. We have also to reconstruct the country because it has been devastated by the events that took place in 1994 and the mismanagement that was prevailing in the political affairs years before that. We have to offer Rwandans equal rights and make sure that Rwanda contributes to the development of Africa.*

WA : These are lofty goals but how could you achieve them if the 1994 genocide has not been healed ?

PK : *Healing takes a process. It's not an event. In terms of reconciliation, we have set up commissions to look into how it can be carried out. We are looking at how justice relating to the 1994 events has been carried out so far. We have made progress in fighting poverty. You can't address reconciliation or political issues without addressing the actual things that affect our people. There are policies and programmes that will allow us move forward.*

WA : Your government wants justice done. How is the situation moving on that front ?

PK : *Justice has to be done. So reconciliation has got to take place. So democratisation has also to take place. It's a combination of all sorts of efforts. We have been able to put in place infrastructures to deal with the justice challenges that we face. It took a long time to rebuild the courts, to train lawyers, prosecutors and others. We have also been able to get the support from the international community. It has been a daunting task but I think in six years we have made quite remarkable progress.*

WA : Do you include the United Nations Tribunal for Rwanda as part of what you call a remarkable progress ?

PK : *Yes. We have at present a good cooperation between our Justice administration and the United Nations Tribunal for Rwanda.*

WA : Are you implying that this tribunal is no longer slow in the way it delivers justice as your govenment used to say ?

PK : *We can still talk of some weaknesses…*

WA : What are they ?

PK : *They have been very slow in handling cases. In other cases there had been mishandling of justice. But I think we have had good interactions. We raised our concerns. They have told us about the difficulties they have told us about the difficulties they are confronted with to get the suspects or the support of ther governments. On the basis of positive criticisms, we have been able to move forward.*

WA: Now, with hindsight, could you tell how all this crisis in Rwanda started ?

PK : *Some link it with the downing in April 1994 of the plane of the late Rwandese President, Juvenal Habyarimana. First of all, the downing of Habyarimana's plane couldn't have created a genocide. There had been before leaders who have died in different circumstances and that didn't lead to extermination of big sections of people. For exemple, in our case, during our struggle, we lost Fred Rwigyema, President of our Movement, the Rwandese Patriotic Front (RPF) who was killed by Habyarimana's forces. But the RPF didn't go on rampage to kill the population because their leader had died. So, it is very nonsensical that whatever could have led to the death of Habyarimana had justification for the extermination of about one million people.*

WA : You have not yet told me who downed his plane ?

PK : *It is a matter that really the United Nations should have come out to tell the world about, since they are the ones in charge of that situation. The other people who could have told the world what happened were the French forces or their government. When it happened they took control of the scene. Those who were in power in Rwanda at the time could also be a good source. The areas where it happened were under their control.*

WA : In short, your movement is not involved in the downing of Habyarimana's plane ?

PK : *Not at all !*

WA : Tells us now what are the causes of the Rwandan crisis…

PK : *Well, the genocide has a long history, if you know a bit of what happened in 1959 alone. There was a civil strife which led to many refugees moving out of the country in hundreds of* *thousands and tens of thousands of people being killed. More or less, genocide started around that time. There had been other genocides in 1963, 1967, 1973 and 1993 while we were negotiating a peace agreement in Arusha (people living in the north west of the country were exterminated by the then government forces). So you can see that genocide is not just a result of the downing of Habyarimana's plane. It has been taking place for quite a long period. A section of our population has always been targeted by the government and its forces. Huge sections of the population were wiped out from different parts of our country. This had been going on over thirty years. The history of that has a lot to do with the make up of our society. There were divisions in our society with three ethnic groups. But despite the fact that we were one people sharing a lot of things together, with one culture, the colonialists and the politicians who took over from them at independence tried to build on the artificial or superficial division in our society to entrench themselves. That led to the tragic situation of 1994. That has brought refugees in the diaspora who have been in exile for over 30 years in various parts of the world to fight for their rights, i.e.to return to their country. But the then government refused and said the country was too small to accommodate them. This refusal sparked off the war when other avenues had failed to have the problem resolved.*

WA : Given the rebellion of some Hutus, do you think that your country has overcome the genocide syndrome ?

PK : *Well, we have to ensure that it's over and that all Rwandese have equal opportunities and rights. We have to encourage that kind of politics. We have to democratise our society on that basis. As for the rebellion, it is not a serious one. Let me give you an example to clarify the situation : we have had over two million refugees following the events of 1994. They were scattered in the Democratic Republic of Congo, in Burundi, in Tanzania. In 1996 and 1997, we made sure that all these refugees returned and got settled in the country. We have only some remnants who got involved in 1994 genocide who are still loitering in the Democratic Republic of Congo and in some areas. They are the ones who still have a genocide ideology. But the rest of the refugees are back in the country. The remaining people cannot even claim they are fighting for the rights of Hutus. And their rebellion doesn's make sense. It cannot succeed.*

WA : How can you democratise a society that is divided along strict ethnic lines ? Don't you run the risk of having an ethnocracy, not a democracy ?

PK : *That is a danger and we consider it as such. In our democratisation process, we are being very careful. We have allowed the debate to take place for people to examine what went wrong with our history and what divided our society. So the conclusion generally being made today is that Rwandese should have a democracy but they should associate along national, political and rational issues rather than looking at themselves as belonging to an ethnic group. I think this is taking root. It is very rewarding for example that during the elections we had last year people elected their leaders not along ethnic lines. You had Hutus being elected by both Tutsis and Hutus and a mix of leaders coming up one the basis of merit. I believe this is a sign that we are succeeding in our process.*

WA : When you came to power in the 1990's along with other "young" leaders, like Uganda's Museveni, Congo's Kabila and Eritrea's Afewerki, people said this new leadership would promote an African Renaissance. Now, most of these leaders, including yourself, are involved in conflicts. Is this not a failure?

PK : *I think there are two aspects to it. One is success and the other one is failure. On a positive note, if you look at different countries, like Eritrea, Ethiopia, Uganda or Rwanda, there have been some good processes in terms of economic reforms. And in other countries there have been democratic reforms and political reforms taking place. There has been hope in terms of improvement in the living standards of the people of Africa. People should not ignore that or* *rubbish it because of other developments, which are indeed negative but which should and can be worked on to be resolved. The conflicts in the Horn between Eritrea and Ethiopia can also be resolved. It should not totally nullify the progress that has been made, both in Eritrea and Ethiopia. I think progress has been made but the negative tends to destroy the good things that have been achieved.*

WA : Why did you fight with Kabila ?

PK : *It's a long history. One has to look at it in terms of how Kabila came to power. That happened as a result of many things. One is that there was a seaech for security and peace for our country. At that time we had genocidal forces operating in Zaire, then under Mobutu, and being supported by Mobutu. Once the international community failed in its obligations to make sure that Rwanda did not continue to be destabilised by those who were in refugee camps in the Congo, Rwanda had to take the responsibility to create peace and security for its own citizens. That's what resulted in our forces crossing the border in 1996 and dismantling the camps in the Congo. Over one million of our people were returned home, and then the fighting that surrounded all that continued but also this time generated the rebellion against Mobutu, who was eventually overthrown, and that is how Kabila eventually came to power. Later on it was very unfortunate that, for all sorts of complex reasons which are very difficult to understand, Kabila, or his officials, became involved in almost the same things that Mobutu was involved in at the time when he was causing us problems. And again, in search of peace for us, we mentioned to Kabila that clearly he was the result of a process in which peace and security in the Congo was at issue. At the same time, we told him he could not be the same person causing us similar problems. If that didn't stop, then we might have a repeat of what we had in 1996 and in which Mobutu saw his exit, but the main target was to resolve that security problem. And that's how it happened. So what has been happenening in the DRC since 1998 is happening for the same reasons in Zaire in 1996.*

WA : You met Kabila recently, have the problems been resolved ?

PK : *They haven't been sorted out fully but I think we had the opportunity to discuss the details of what happened and discuss also the need to have peace. Peace in Rwanda, peace in the Congo and peace in the region. I think the meeting might have helped to push forward the peace agreement which we already have in place, which was brokered in Lusaka.*

WA : If your security concerns are addressed, are you likely to stop backing the rebellion against Kabila ?

PK : *There is no question that our only interest in that situation in the DRC is about security. If that is addressed we can only encourage the Congolese to be together. They have their own internal problems and should try to find a solution for their internal problems.*

WA : Why are you also having problems with Uganda's Museveni ? People do not understand..

PK : *I cannot blame them if they cannot understand. Even some of us who are directly involved don't really fully understand it. It's a very difficult situation we find ourselves conflicting in different ways. All I can say is that we are trying to look into it and look at the causes and try to find a solution. But it is quite difficult to understand.*

WA : What is the cause of this problem ?

PK : *I think the problem is that maybe Rwanda needs to be left to handle its own affairs. We are not interested in having other people run our affairs, be it in Rwanda, or in our presence in the*

Congo. We would rather deal with our internal affairs, we have the right and the will and the capacity to do that.

WA : Are you suggesting that perhaps Museveni is meddling in your country's affairs ?

PK : *Well, that could be part of the problem.*

WA : What role does the UN and the OAU play in all this ? Do you see them as partners in fixing the problems ?

PK : *I think that part of the problem we can fix ourselves. Between the Rwandans and the Ugandans we are able to understand one another and give respect to one another. We can fix it. I don't think it is an issue where a third party would be extremely useful. But some people have been very useful especially when the fighting developed, like in Kisangani. The UN has been useful. But overall, I think the two countries can sit down and discuss this issue and bring it to an end.*

WA : Do you think the UN peacekeeping group that is to be set up for the DRC can resolve the Congolese problem ?

PK : *It cannot fix it alone. It can help. The UN peacekeepers' presence is certainly very useful. They can tell the world who is doing what. In terms of monitoring what is going on, they would be very useful.*

WA : When he visited your country three years ago, Kofi Annan, the UN Secretary-General was not well received.Has your relationship with him improved?

PK : *Of late, it has changed and there has been progress. At that time, I think what happened was understandable. People were really very bitter about the failures of the UN and the lack of the UN's recognition of their failure. I think that since his visit a lot of other things have been taking place. Things have improved.*

INTERVIEW WITH NEW AFRICAN MAGAZINE

During the month of June, Rwandan President Paul Kagame was interviewed by Regina Jere-Malanda on a wide range of domestic, regional and international issues. Below are some of President Kagame's responses.

On why Rwanda went to the Democratic Republic of Congo and Kisangani in particular, President Kagame said:

"The situation in Kisangani is a complex matter which I find hard to explain, and it is difficult to justify everything.

"We were aware of the sovereignty issues involved, but we are not necessarily apologetic for taking over Kisangani. The security situation for us was bad - there were former soldiers (ex-FAR), armed Interahamwe and others who can invade our country from Congo. We have captured some of them and they have told us how they have been trained by Kabila's forces. We either had to let the same people invade our country and carry out another Genocide, or alternatively cross the border to deal with the problem there but at the expense of violating another country's sovereignty. We decided to be selfish, rather than having another Genocide. We had to breach the sovereignty issue in order to deal with another major problem. These are the facts and this is why we went to the DRC, and we challenge them to prove us wrong on this.

"If the security situation is resolved and we are still in the Congo, then people can be right to accuse us of being there for something else. Those talking about us being there to exploit the wealth of Congo should know that to exploit minerals is an expensive exercise, you need money to do this, which we don't have."

On the Eldoret meeting with DRC President Laurent Kabila, President Kagame said:

"My meeting with President Kabila has to be looked at in the context of the bigger picture. Our primary interest is that of peace - the issues of the Interahamwe, the camps, security or lack of it, genocide and so on, we will need peace from Kabila, Museveni and myself. So at this meeting we looked at this bigger picture.

"Our ultimate goal is not to remove Kabila, but that he should be part of the solution and not part of the problem. During our meeting in Kenya, he agreed to this. He did ask if I could withdraw our forces, and I said that we have no objection to this, but it has to be under certain conditions."

On Habyarimana's death, the Genocide and the assertions of a discredited charlatan named John Paul Mugabe, President Kagame said:

"First of all Mugabe was not an RPF intelligence officer but a mere journalist who expected to be appointed an Ambassador, and when he didn't get this he became disappointed and bitter, fled the country for greener pastures then claimed to have been persecuted to get political asylum in America. What he has been saying lately is simply not true. Even if it were true, Mugabe would not have been the person to be privy to such classified information. He would not even have been present at any meeting where such things could have been discussed.

"About the shooting of Habyarimana's plane, the area where it came down was in total control of Habyarimana's forces. They had taken over a whole village in the area, it was settled by Presidential Guard forces. It would have been difficult for anybody to infiltrate or penetrate the area and conduct an exercise of downing a plane then get out. Before the incident, Habyarimana himself felt so threatened that he took his army chief to the Arusha conference because he was under suspicion.

"When the incident took place, the area was cordoned off by the Presidential guard and the French troops. They prevented even the UN forces from entering. The RPF was about 15 kilometres away, (in the opposite direction) and they were surrounded by UN troops. Mugabe's story is just being told for political and other reasons.

"But Habyarimana's plane crash had nothing to do with the genocide that followed. It is immoral for people to give it that kind of justification. These are two separate issues. Genocide in Rwanda has its own history, it goes back a long time. Genocide started in 1959, then 1963, 1966, 1967, 1973, 1993, 1994 - it has no link to the downing of the plane.

"As to who and why the plane was brought down, the answer will be a guessing game. It is open knowledge that Habyarimana was considered too soft with the RPF, he was told he could not be allowed to have the RPF as part of the government. As of now, we don't have clear evidence of who did it, but it's not due to a lack of will that the evidence is not forthcoming."

RELATIONS WITH KENIA[4]

QUESTION: Since 1994, your relations with Kenya have been chilly. In recent months, however, they have improved dramatically, with President Moi visiting Rwanda and yourself coming to Kenya twice. Looked at the timing, some observers think the rapidly improving ties are not unrelated to the problems Rwanda has been having with Uganda in the Democratic Republic of Congo.

ANSWER: *Friendship or no friendship is not something that is permanent. It can be nurtured, worked on. Rwanda and Kenya have had a history of good relations. There were hiccups here and there, which have been overcome by reaching an understanding that the most important thing is to retain the friendship. As far as our government is concerned, the warm relationship between Rwanda and Kenya started before our problems with Uganda began. Remember I visited this country in 1998 when Kenya handed over the genocide suspects to the Arusha Tribunal. That was way before any problems had cropped up between us and Uganda. Whatever is happening in the Congo might not be related.*

QUESTION: What exactly were your differences with Uganda in Kisangani? Have they been resolved?

ANSWER: *Well, I wouldn't want to dwell on that because some of the problems that developed in the eastern parts [of DRC] have been resolved. I think we should now be looking forward rather than backward.*

QUESTION: What is the status of your application for membership in the East Africa Co-operation? What is holding it up?

ANSWER: *We have lodged our application. Over a year has passed now. Indications are that we might be accepted. I think a lot will depend on how the question of new applicants is handled, alongside the process of consolidating the East African Co-operation.*

QUESTION: Mombasa port is naturally a major priority for Rwanda. Beyond that, what other areas of cooperation are you seeking with Kenya?

ANSWER: *There are many things a country like ours can do with Kenya in areas of trade, business and more specifically, within the framework of regional cooperation.*

QUESTION: Have you managed to put behind you the quarrel over Interahamwe sympathisers said to be still resident in Kenya? Did you raise the matter with your Kenyan hosts?

ANSWER: *It is important to note that the government of Kenya cooperated with the International Tribunal in Arusha. Some of those people who were in this country were handed over to the Tribunal [in 1998]. There are other countries that have done the same. But there are some people still at large who have managed to escape the hand of justice.*

QUESTION: Restitution for the genocide victims remains a central issue in your country. Countless numbers of ordinary Rwandese are known to have participated in one way or another. Are you concerned about inadvertently leaving a permanent guilt complex on a particular segment of the population?

---

[4] Visiting Rwandese President Paul Kagame has many things he would like to see done, changed or tried in his country and in the East African region. Here are excerps of what he told writer GITAU WARIGI in an interview.

ANSWER: *First of all, we have to resolve problems with due regard to realities. Trying to ignore things as they have taken place can drive you into making even more serious mistakes. The fact is, the genocide took place. It was not accidental. It was planned. All the same, we are being very careful. We have not generalised guilt. We have tended to single out the people responsible. That has enabled us to come out with a categorisation of responsibility; starting with the authors of the genocide, the perpetrators, and others with lesser crimes. The aim is to be able to focus on specific characteristics in terms of those who committed genocide.*

QUESTION: Then there is the problem of the huge judicial backlog over which the RPF has been occasionally criticised. How are you resolving this matter?

ANSWER: *We have instituted a number of measures. There is no way out; if we don't process all the cases properly it can lead to other serious problems, including people taking the law into their own hands. There is a judicial process that has been taking place. Evidently, we have not been able to carry it out more quickly. The persons being tried are representative of a very small number.*

Secondly, we have been releasing the old people, children, an those with terminal illnesses. Others whose case files are not concrete to the extent of putting up a case in court, have also been released.

The third measure we are taking is to carry out justice at community level. It is not the classic form of the judicial process. It is an improvisation, where people with lesser cases can be taken to their home Communes and have their cases handled there. It will work along the lines of our traditional system of justice in Rwanda called Gacaca. This is a justice system at the community level overseen by village leaders. The formal justice system will, however, be close by to monitor, take appeals and ensure nobody is unjustly convicted.

QUESTION: From outside, the problem in Rwanda is often looked at in ethnic terms, as a Hutu-Tutsi divide. How are you tackling that perception?

ANSWER: *We have people who think we are condemned to that divide, unlike other countries. Maybe we have to look at why this divide has caused us so many problems. In our case, you have to recognise certain realities, especially to do with our history, with our heritage, which have made the divide such a serious one. We have to go back and examine what happened so as to build a society based on equality and respect for human rights.*

QUESTION: Ultimately, you have promised a new constitution which all the players in Rwanda are confident with. What features would you want to see in this constitution?

ANSWER: *Democratisation should be seen in terms of a process, not an event. Deliberate steps have been taken to make sure that we take into account our history that has caused so many divisions. We have recognised the existence of various political parties and these have been brought to play in terms of a broad-based system. At the same time, we are aware of the problems associated with ethnic divides, parties and so forth.*

We have been moving systematically and deliberately, making sure we lay a firm foundation. We have started on grassroots elections but these have not been on party lines because political party operations have been suspended during the transition period. We have five parties in a power-sharing arrangement within the transitional government. We have parties represented in the transitional national assembly.

We've also started a grassroots process of constitution-making. This new constitution should be built on a good understanding of all our problems. All concerns and political opinions will be taken into account. We hope that once the constitution is drafted, it will be debated and go through a referendum. It should embrace all the people's concerns and interests.

TRAVELING TO RWANDA

US STATE DEPARTMENT SUGGESTIONS

COUNTRY DESCRIPTION: Rwanda is a landlocked country in central/east Africa. It is recovering from a civil war and genocide in which as many as one million Tutsis and moderate Hutus were killed. Hotels and guesthouses are adequate in Kigali, the capital, and in major towns, but limited in remote areas.

ENTRY REQUIREMENTS: A passport and evidence of yellow fever immunization are required. Visas are not required for American citizens entering Rwanda for less than 90 days. U.S. citizens planning on working in Rwanda should apply for a work permit at the Department of Immigration as soon as possible after arrival in Rwanda. Detailed entry information may be obtained from the Embassy of the Republic of Rwanda, 1714 New Hampshire Avenue, N.W., Washington D.C. 20009, telephone 202-232-2882, fax 202-232-4544, Internet site: http://www.rwandaemb.org/rwanda/. Overseas inquiries may be made at the nearest Rwandan Embassy or Consulate.

Travelers who wish to travel to the neighboring Democratic Republic of the Congo (DROC) with visas and/or entry/exit stamps from Burundi, Rwanda, Uganda or Zimbabwe may experience difficulties at the DROC airport or other ports of entry. Some travelers with those visas or exit/entry stamps have been detained for questioning in DROC.

AREAS OF INSTABILITY: Most of Rwanda has been calm since the war and genocide ended in July 1994. Insurgents opposed to the current government launched attacks against Rwanda from bases in the DROC beginning in early 1997. While the government has largely brought the insurgency under control, sporadic attacks continue to occur in the northwest. U.S. citizens should avoid travel to the following communes (zones) in the northwest: Ndusu, Gatonde, Giciye, Kinigi, Mutura, Kidaho, Nyamyunba and Kayove. Unexploded ordnance still remains a danger off well-traveled roads in the northwest.

The Government of Rwanda has recently reopened the Parc National des Volcans (translation: Viruga National Park) and will be providing military escorts for those individuals with official passes to track gorillas. Visitors to the park risk being the target of extremist attacks. U.S. citizens are advised not to stay overnight in the park.

U.S. citizens are urged to avoid travel to the border areas between Rwanda and Burundi because of the unstable security situation in Burundi.

REGIONAL TERRORISM: One of the many Hutu rebel factions in the Great Lakes region has committed, and continues to threaten, violence against American citizens and interests. This faction was responsible for the March 1999 kidnapping and murder of several Western tourists, including U.S. citizens, in neighboring Uganda. A Hutu rebel faction was responsible for the kidnapping of four foreign nationals in August 1998 in a region of the DROC which borders Rwanda. Hutu rebel factions are known to operate in northeastern DROC and surrounding areas, including sections of Rwanda, Uganda, Tanzania and Burundi.

CRIME INFORMATION: Pick-pocketing in crowded public places is common, as is petty theft from cars and hotel rooms. The loss or theft of a U.S. passport should be reported immediately to local police and to the nearest U.S. Embassy or Consulate. The pamphlets A Safe Trip Abroad and Tips for Travelers to

Sub-Saharan Africa provide useful information on personal security while traveling abroad and on travel in the region in general. Both are available from the Superintendent of Documents, U.S. Government Printing Office,
Washington D.C. 20402, via the Internet http://www.access.gpo.gov/su_docs or http://travel.state.gov.

MEDICAL FACILITIES: Medical facilities are limited. Some medicines are in short supply or unavailable. Travelers generally bring their own supplies of prescription drugs and preventive medicines. A missionary hospital run by Americans is located in Kibogora, in the southwest of Rwanda, and has some surgical facilities.

MEDICAL INSURANCE: Doctors and hospitals expect cash payment for services. The Medicare/Medicaid program does not provide for payment of medical services outside the United States. Check with your own insurance company to confirm whether your policy applies overseas, including provision for medical evacuation. Ascertain whether payment will be made to the overseas hospital or doctor or whether you will be reimbursed later for expenses you incur. Some insurance policies also include coverage for psychiatric treatment and for disposition of remains in the event of death. Useful information on medical emergencies abroad, including overseas insurance programs, is provided in the Department of State, Bureau of Consular Affairs brochure Medical Information for Americans Traveling Abroad, available via its home page and automated fax service at (202) 647-3000.

OTHER MEDICAL INFORMATION: Malaria is prevalent in Rwanda and there are periodic outbreaks of meningitis. Information on vaccinations and other health precautions may be obtained from the Centers for Disease Control and Prevention hotline for international travelers at 1-877-FYI-TRIP (1-877-394-8747); fax, 1-888-CDC-FAXX (1-888-232-3299); or by visiting the CDC Internet home page at http://www.cdc.gov.

TRAFFIC SAFETY AND ROAD CONDITIONS: While in a foreign country, U.S. citizens may encounter road conditions that differ significantly from those in the United States. The information below concerning Rwanda is provided for general reference only and may not be totally accurate in a particular location or circumstance.

Safety of Public Transportation: Poor
Urban Road Conditions/Maintenance: Fair
Rural Road Conditions/Maintenance: Poor
Availability of Roadside Assistance: Poor

Excessive speed, careless driving and the lack of basic safety equipment on many vehicles are a hazard. Drivers frequently have unexpected encounters with cyclists, pedestrians and livestock. Nighttime driving is particularly hazardous and discouraged. Roadways are often not marked and lack streetlights and shoulders. While the main roads in Rwanda are in relatively good condition, during the rainy season many side roads are passable only with four-wheel drive vehicles. Travelers may be stopped at police roadblocks throughout the country, where their vehicles and luggage may be searched. Service stations are available along main roads. Public transportation can be dangerous due to overloading, inadequate maintenance and careless drivers.

CIVIL AVIATION OVERSIGHT: As there is no direct commercial air service at present, or economic authority to operate such service, between the U.S. and Rwanda, the U.S. Federal Aviation Administration (FAA) has not assessed the Rwandan Civil Aviation Authority for compliance with international aviation safety standards. For further information, travelers may contact the Department of Transportation within the U.S. at 1-800-322-7873. The U.S. Department of Defense (DOD) separately assesses some foreign air carriers for suitability as official providers of air services. For information regarding the DOD policy on specific carriers, travelers may contact DOD at 618-256-4801.

COMMUNICATIONS: Telephone communication to and from Rwanda can be unreliable. Cellular phones and Internet connections are available in Kigali and are generally reliable.

CURRENCY REGULATIONS: The Rwandan franc is freely exchangeable for hard currencies in banks and Bureaux de Change. Several Kigali banks can handle wire transfers from U.S. banks including Western Union. Credit cards are accepted at only a few hotels in Kigali and only to settle hotel bills. Travelers should expect to handle most expenses, including air tickets, in cash.

CRIMINAL PENALTIES: While in a foreign country, a U.S. citizen is subject to that country's laws and regulations, which sometimes differ significantly from those in the United States and may not afford the protections available to the individual under U.S. law. Penalties for breaking the law can be more severe than in the United States for similar offenses. Persons violating Rwandan law, even unknowingly, may be expelled, arrested or imprisoned. Penalties for possession, use, or trafficking in illegal drugs in Rwanda are strict and
convicted offenders can expect jail sentences and heavy fines.

CHILDREN'S ISSUES: For information on international adoption of children, international parental child abduction, and international child support enforcement issues, please refer to our Internet site at http://travel.state.gov/children's_issues.html or telephone 202-736-7000.

REGISTRATION/EMBASSY LOCATION: U.S. citizens who plan to travel to Rwanda are urged to register with the U.S. Embassy and to obtain updated information on travel and security in Rwanda. The U.S. Embassy
is located at Boulevard de la Revolution; the mailing address is B.P. 28, Kigali, Rwanda, telephone 250-75601/75602, fax 250-72128.

PRACTICAL INFORMATRION FOR TRAVELERS

REQUIREMENTS FOR U.S. CITIZENS TO ENTER RWANDA

TOURIST TRAVEL

- U.S. Passport must be valid 3 months beyond intended stay
- Tickets and Documents for return or onward travel
- Visa not required for stay up to 3 months. Eff. Aug 1 1999
- Vaccination: International Certificate of Vaccination for Yellow Fever required.

BUSINESS TRAVEL

- U.S. Passport must be Valid 3 months Beyond Intended Stay
- Tickets and Documents for Return or Onward Travel

- Visa not required for stay up to 3 months. Eff. Aug 1 1999
- Vaccinations - International Certificate of Vaccination required for Yellow Fever.

EMPLOYMENT OR STUDY TRAVEL

Contact the nearest Embassy or Consulate

REQUIREMENTS FOR NON U.S. CITIZENS TO OBTAIN VISA TO ENTER RWANDA

Tourist Visa

- 1. Your valid, signed, Passport
- 2. 2 Application forms, fully completed and signed
- 3. 2 Passport-type photographs required
- 4. International Certificate of Vaccination for Yellow Fever
- 5. Copy of round trip airline tickets or itinerary, or letter from travel agent

Business Visa

- 1-4. As Above
- 5. A business letter of responsibility is required, to be typewritten on your company letterhead and addressed to:
- **Embassy of Rwanda, Visa Section, Washington DC**
- **The letter must explain all of the following**
- Nature of business to be performed
- Name and address of reference to be visited
- Guarantee of return transportation and sufficient funds for the visit.
- The letter should be signed by an officer of the company other than the applicant.

Processing Instructions

- Please forward the completed requirements detailed above to:

TRAVEL DOCUMENT SYSTEMS, INC. 734 FIFTEENTH ST N.W. SUITE 400 WASHINGTON D.C. 20005

- Your application will be checked and hand carried to the Embassy, and is usually processed in 72 hours (4 business days).

FEES

- Include one (1) check or money order payable to "TDS Inc." for the TDS service Fee per visa, Embassy Consular Fee per visa, and return postage or Federal Express.
- Tds handling fee: $30.00 per visa
- Consular fee: $30.00 per visa

RETURN POSTAGE

- U.S. Registered Mail: $ 6.50 (Up to 3 passports)
- Federal Express: $15.50 (Up to 3 passports) /Saturday Delivery $10 extra

VISA INFORMATION

- The RWANDA tourist or business visa is usually valid for three months from date issued, for a stay according to the dates specified on your application, not to exceed 90 days.

Information and Fees are Subject to Change. Revised 8/99

GETTING THERE

Diplomatic ties have been restored between the United States and Rwanda. Passport and visa are required. Multiple-entry visa (extendable) for a stay of up to 1 month requires a US$30 fee (cash, check or money order), two application forms, two photos and immunization for yellow fever. Exact date of entry into Rwanda is required with application. Include prepaid envelope or $1.50 postage for return of passport by certified mail.

At the height of the hostilities, when DP asked about entry permission, a spokesperson replied, "We know nothing." Later, after things had calmed down, it seemed the embassy staff had developed a sense of bureaucratic humor. When we asked if there were any Americans in jail in Rwanda, we were told, "We have none; they have been behaving so far." You should know the first of the 12 conditions for entry and stay in Rwanda is that "proper attire and conduct are required of persons staying in Rwanda." The embassy maintains that it is safe to travel in Rwanda.

EMBASSY LOCATIONS

U.S. Embassy in Rwanda
Boulevard de la Revolution
BP 28, Kigali
Tel [250] (7) 5601/2/3
FAX [250] (7) 2128

Embassy of the Republic of Rwanda

1714 New Hampshire Avenue, N.W.
Washington, D.C. 20009
Tel (202) 232-2882

Canadian Embassy in Rwanda

Rue Akagera, BP 1177
Kigali
Tel 73210, FAX: 72719

Rwandan Embassy in Canada

121 Sherwood Drive
Ottawa, Ontario, Canada K1Y 3V1
Tel (613) 722-5835/722-7921
FAX (613) 729-3291

Permanent Mission of Rwanda to the U.N.

124 East 39th Street
New York, NY 10016
Tel (212) 696-0644/46

Consulate General in Chicago

Tel (708) 205-1188
Consulate General in Denver
Tel (303) 321-2400

GETTING AROUND

Rwanda has a total road length of 3036 miles; a mere 286 of them are paved. There are neither railways nor ports. There are eight airfields in the country, three of them with a permanent surface.

Air Rwanda flies internally from Kigali to Gisenyi and Kamembe. Occasionally, you can fly between Gisenyi and Kamembe. Due to the amount of foreign aid into the country, Rwanda's road system isn't too bad. As in neighboring Burundi, the roadways are served by a fleet of relatively late-model Japanese minibuses. The buses leave most towns when they are full. Larger government buses also traverse Rwanda's roads, although they are fewer and farther between. They cost less than the minibuses, but take longer to get to their destinations.

ACCOMMODATION

Hotels: Found mostly in Kigali; they are expensive. Missions with dormitory accommodation are recommended, particularly in remote districts and smaller towns. Ruhengeri and Gisenye mission station hotels are excellent.

Guest-Houses: Outside the main towns there are guest-houses, which are generally cheaper than hotels. There is a guest-house at the edge of the Kagera National Park at Biumba in the northeast of the country.

Camping: This is now forbidden. Rest huts are available on the expedition route in the Virunga Volcanoes.

NATIONAL PARKS

The main touristic attractions of the country, the Akagera and Volcanoes national parks possess a fauna and flora of incomparable wealth.

1. The Akagera National Park

The Akagera national park lies in the North East of Rwanda. It covers an area of 250,000 hectares along the river bearing the same name which is also the main inflow to Lake Victoria. Created 1934, the Akagera national park is characterized by a mosaic of grass, bush and tree savannas where such big mammals as lions, lepards, zebra, buffaloes, hippopotamuses and many species of antelope live.

The scenery of the Park, so varied in its ranges of hills and deep valleys, lakes and marshes, is a true delight to the eye. The avifauna too is extremely diverse and more than 500 species of birds can be found. The Akagera National Park possesses large families of mammals, 4 species of vultures.

2. The Volcanoes National Park

The Volcanoes national Park lies in the North-West of the country and covers an area of about 125 square kilometers. In addition to the special attraction of its magnificient mountains, the Volcanoes national Park is known to be one of the last sanctuaries of the rare mountain gorilla (Gorilla Beringei) of this planet.

In this park which was created in 1925 also live mqny elephants, monkeys, mountain buffaloes and antelopes as well as an endemic flora interestingly divided into five vegetation zones.

Birds are also of special interest for nature lovers who are attracted by some of the rare species in regions of higher altitude, especially with the Touraco living in the mountain and the most beautiful Francolin (Francolins nobilis).

3. THE NYUNGWE FOREST

The Nyungwe forest is an important water reserve for the country. It is found in the South-West region of higher altitude along the Nile-Zaire ridge. The Nyungwe forest is located at an altitude between 1700 and 2500 m. It covers an area of 970 square kilometers. The Nyungwe forest which is the largest and one of the latest mountain primary forests, is not only a large botanical reserve but also a favourable place for wild animals. The scenery of the Nyungwe forest is extremely beautiful.

4. LAKES

Twenty-eight lakes nestle in this country of a thousand hills. The most spectacular and the largest is Lake Kivu. It lies in the West of Rwanda at the foot of the Virunga volcanoes, mountains known even to ancient Greeks as the "Mountains of the Moon".

BUTARE, A UNIVERSITY TOWN

The town of Butare was created in 1920. At that time, it was called "Astrida", a name deriving from Astrid, the queen of Belgians. Butare was the capital city of the former Rwanda-Urundi territory under the Belgian supervision. It is now the second town in Rwanda after Kigali, the Capital city.

Butare town is located in the Urban commune of Butare Prefecture (see map of Rwanda). Ngoma commune has an area of 38 km2. Its relief is essentially made of hills and valleys which characterize the central plateau to which it belongs.

Butare is known for its contribution in the promotion of education. The National Univerisity of Rwanda is found in Butare together with many secondary schools:

- Le Groupe Scolaire Officiel de Butare (GSOB)
- L'ecole sociale de Karubanda
- L'ecole agricole et veterinaire de Kabutare
- Le Petit Seminaire de Butare
- Le Petit Seminaire Baptiste
- L'ecole secondaire des parents (CEFOTEC)
- L'ecole autonome de Butare

Besides these schools, the Institute for Technological and Scientific Research is also found. It has three research centres:

- The Pharmacopoeia centre
- The energy centre
- The centre for Rwandese studies

Some touristic attractions:

- The National Museum of Rwanda is important as far as archelogy and ethnology are concerned;
- The Ruhande arboretum has many local and exotic species;
- Gihindamuyaga at about 10 km in the North of Butare town is important for its handicracft workshop; goldsmith's, gift-shops and its local jam factory.

NATIONAL MUSEUM OF RWANDA

The National museum of Rwanda is located in Butare town. It is one of the wonders of Rwanda.

Inaugurated on September 18th, 1989 and opened to the public the following day, The National museum of Rwanda is built on a 20 or more hectares plot. The buildings themselves occupy 2500 m2. The remaining free space has been arranged for gardens and trees which makes the place more interesting. It is essentially the collections and the architecture of the buildings which attract visitors.

The structure of the museum symbolises the expression of the quality of life. Both the internal and external parts of the building express the Rwandan culture.

2. COLLECTIONS

Collections are essentially historical, ethnographic, artistic and archeological. They comprise items inherited from the ancient museum of Rwanda and others which have been collected since 1990. These collections can be subdivided in two categories: the first category is kept in two store-rooms and the second one has items used for the decoration of 7 exhibition rooms.

The first room has a counter and a shop where various handicraft items, photos, brochures, etc... are sold. At regular basis, the museum organises temporal exhibitions in the same room, about precise themes in order to arouse an awareness of a given situation or a particular event.

The second room is for maps, photos and graphics which provide more information about the relief of the country, its ever growing demography, the linguistic inter-relationship between Rwandans and other tribes in the region.

Rooms III and IV display items and tools used in various economic activities such as agriculture, cattle-breeding, bee-keeping, hunting, fishing, the making of the fire and transport. These objects are in wood, basketwork and ceramics.

Room V presents the various aspects of the Rwandan architecture, the way of living and the social organisation. An entirely reconstituted traditional hut can be found in the center of the room. Its upper part belonged to a former sous-chef in 1957.

Room VI is essentially dedicated to traditional dressing and its description. The material, the techniques used to make them, the samples of skins, barks of trees, wood fibres, clothes and a large variety of decorations in metal or plants ...are displayed.

Room VII reconstitutes some features of the Rwandan history. It presents the guidelines of the prehistory and shows the chronological succession of kings (Bami) based on oral tradition and written documents since the arrival of Europeans. It also provides some explanations about some traditional religious practices and marriage. Most of the sample copies are made in basketwork.

Basketwork constitutes the most familiar artistic expression to foreigners. It expresses the fineness and aesthetic value of the whole assembly, that of elements combination and decorative motifs in particular. Basketwork is of an indeniable aesthetic beauty. It is often used in interior decoration and domestic works: in the kitchen, luggage and people transportation, fishing, building, wall partitions and enclosures.

3. MISSIONS

The National Museum of Rwanda has four major missions:

- The gathering, the conservation and the restoration of collection for a faithful transmission to future generations. In this line, the museum stands for a consultative technical instance as far as the setting up and implementation of legal measures are concerned , aiming at protecting the national and world partimony. The museum collaborates with legal authorities in forbiding illegal export of cultural heritage.
- The scientific study of this cultural heritage and data facilitates the understanding and cultural links. Despite the various functions of the National museum of Rwanda, researches are carried out in various domains at the levels of the museum and in the villages . The museum is an ideal place for students, researchers from national and international scientific institutions.

- The museum is available to the people. Knowledge is transmitted for a double purpose: to teach and delight. The museum is a scientific and cultural center whose impact is to reach the whole. It actively contributes to the educative process at all levels.
- The museum contributes to the promotion of artistic and intellectual creativity in Rwanda. The museum contributes to the cultural development as:

- A meeting place for scientists, artists and people's exchanges;
- Information and documentation centre;
- Center for cultural entertainment

4. APPROCHES

In the line of preserving traditional techniques and promoting art and handicraft, the National Museum of Rwanda has adopted the following approaches:

- The study of creation techniques and their diffusion through occasional expositions and works publications;
- The creation of a ballet and a craft learning centre constitute the dynamic aspect of the museum. The centre comprises 80 young boys and girls with 5 workshops: basketwork, pottery, smithy , the making of pearl and postcards.

The ballet presents folkloric entertainments to the public. These may be organised either in or outside the museum.

5. CONTACTS

For more information, contact:

Director: KANIMBA Celestin
Phone: (250) 530586
Fax: (250) 530211
P.O. Box 630
E-mail: museum@nur.ac.rw
Butare/Rwanda

RWANDA- LARGEST HOTELS

DES MILLE COLLINES HOTEL

PO Box 1322
Kigali
Kigali
Rwanda

Tel No: 76 530/36
Fax No: 76 541
Number of Rooms: 112
Single Room Prices From: 159.85 US Dollars

Pleasant 1970 downtown hotel situated in the business centre of the city. All rooms come with bath, minibar, cable TV and phone; some with balcony. Suites. Bar, snack bar, restaurant, nightclub. Disabled access. Outdoor swimming pool. Free parking. Renovations took place in 1994.

Facilities

Car Parking
Conference Facilities
Disabled Facilities
Swimming Pool

Location Information

Airports: Kigali 100 kms, Gregoire Kayibanda Int'l 11 kms

Meridien Umubano Hotel

Po Box 874
Kigali
Rwanda

Tel No: 82176
Fax No: 83361
Number of Rooms: 92
Single Room Prices From: 133.4 US Dollars

1979 hotel located 5km from city centre. 12 suites, comfortable rooms. 2 restaurants, coffee shop, bar, meetings to 200, safaris arranged. Telex: 22561 HOMER RW ATT: MERIDIEN UMUBANO.

Facilities

Conference Facilities
Golf
Swimming Pool
Tennis

Location Information

Airport: Kigali 8 kms

MONEY

Currency: Rwanda Franc (FRw) = 100 centimes. Notes are in denominations of FRw5000, 1000, 500 and 100. Coins are in denominations of FRw50, 20, 10, 5 and 1.

Credit cards: Accepted at only a few hotels in Kigali. MasterCard is most widely accepted, with more limited use of Diners Club. Check with your credit card company for details of merchant acceptability and other services that may be available.

Traveler's checks: Generally not recommended.

Exchange rate indicators against Sterling and the US Dollar: The following figures are included as a guide to the movements of the Rwanda Franc against Sterling and the US Dollar:

	May'97	Aug'97	Mar'98	Oct'98
£1.00=	496.52	490.10	575.93	525.78

$1.00= 303.22 304.24 348.48 311.03

Currency restrictions: The import and export of local currency is limited to FRw5000. The import and export of foreign currency is limited to the amount declared on arrival.

HOLIDAYS

Jan 1New Year's Day.
Jan 9 Eid al-Fitr (End of Ramadan).
Jan 28 Democracy Day.
Apr 24 Easter Monday.
May 1 Labour Day.
Jul 1 National Holiday.
Jul 4 Independence Day.
Aug 15 Assumption.
Sep 25 Kamarampaka Day.
Oct 26 Armed Forces' Day.
Nov 1 All Saints' Day.
Dec 25 Christmas.

DANGEROUS PLACES

The entire country of Rwanda can be considered unsafe. Travelers are regularly the victims of theft, petty crime and murder. Sporadic violence is a problem in Kigali as well as in the interior. Fighting caused thousands of refugees to flee into neighboring Burundi as well as other countries in the region. In 1996, Paul Kagame ensured the safety of returning refugees and a trickle began returning to Rwanda, many to find their land and dwellings seized by squatters. The northwest has recently swelled with extremist Hutus, many returning from refugee camps in Zaire. This area is becoming a hotbed for insurgent activity. Travelers should use extreme caution everywhere in Rwanda. Do not travel into the troubled areas of Kigali or anywhere in or near Gisenyi. Do not travel after dark.

HEALTH INFORMATION FOR TRAVELERS TO EAST AFRICA

Burundi, Comoros, Djibouti, Eritrea, Ethiopia, Kenya, Madagascar, Malawi, Mauritius, Mayotte, Mozambique, Reunion, Rwanda, Seychelles, Somalia, Tanzania, Uganda

NOTE: Please check the Outbreaks section for important updates on this region, including information on the Epidemic of Meningococcal Disease in Addis Ababa, Ethiopia.

Several cases of African trypanosomiasis (African sleeping sickness) have been reported from this region recently, including cases among tourists visiting game parks. For more information and recommendations on trypanosomiasis, see Travelers' Health Information on African Trypanosomiasis.

Food and waterborne diseases are the number one cause of illness in travelers. **Travelers' diarrhea** can be caused by viruses, bacteria, or parasites, which are found throughout the region and can contaminate food or water. Infections may cause diarrhea and vomiting (E. coli, Salmonella, cholera, and parasites), fever (typhoid fever and toxoplasmosis), or liver damage (hepatitis). Make sure your food and drinking water are safe. (See below.)

Malaria is a preventable infection that can be fatal if left untreated. Prevent infection by taking prescription antimalarial drugs and protecting yourself against mosquito bites (see below). Most travelers to malaria risk areas in this region should take mefloquine to prevent malaria. You can be infected with malaria in all areas of this region except the cities of Addis Ababa, Ismara, and

Nairobi, the islands of Reunion and Seychelles, and in highland areas above 2,500 meters. For more detailed information about the risk in specific locations, see **Malaria in East Africa**.

A certificate of yellow fever vaccine may be **required** for entry into certain of these countries. For detailed information, see Comprehensive Yellow Fever Vaccination Requirements.

Dengue, filariasis, leishmaniasis, onchocerciasis, trypanosomiasis (sleeping sickness), and Rift Valley fever are diseases carried by insects that also occur in this region. Protecting yourself against insect bites will help to prevent these diseases.

Schistosomiasis, a parasitic infection, is found in fresh water in the region, including Lake Malawi. Do not swim in fresh water (except in well-chlorinated swimming pools) in these countries. (For more information, please see the Swimming Precautions on the Making Travel Safe page.)

Because motor vehicle crashes are a leading cause of injury among travelers, walk and drive defensively. Avoid nighttime travel if possible and always use seat belts.

CDC Recommends the Following Vaccines (as Appropriate for Age):

See your doctor at least 4–6 weeks before your trip to allow time for shots to take effect.

- Hepatitis A or immune globulin (IG).
- Hepatitis B, if you might be exposed to blood (for example, health-care workers), have sexual contact with the local population, stay longer than 6 months, or be exposed through medical treatment.
- Meningococcal (meningitis) vaccine, if you plan to visit the western half of Ethiopia (see meningitis map) from December through June.
- Rabies, if you might be exposed to wild or domestic animals through your work or recreation.
- Typhoid, particularly if you are visiting developing countries in this region.
- Yellow fever, if you travel anywhere outside urban areas.
- As needed, booster doses for tetanus-diphtheria, measles, and a one-time dose of polio vaccine for adults. Hepatitis B vaccine is now recommended for all infants and for children ages 11–12 years who did not receive the series as infants.

To Stay Healthy, Do:

- Wash hands often with soap and water.
- Drink only bottled or boiled water, or carbonated (bubbly) drinks in cans or bottles. Avoid tap water, fountain drinks, and ice cubes. If this is not possible, make water safer by BOTH filtering through an "absolute 1-micron or less" filter AND adding iodine tablets to the filtered water. "Absolute 1-micron filter" are found in camping/outdoor supply stores.
- Eat only thoroughly cooked food or fruits and vegetables you have peeled yourself. Remember: **boil it, cook it, peel it, or forget it.**
- If you travel to an area where there is risk for malaria, take your malaria prevention medication before, during, and after travel, as directed. (See your doctor for a prescription.)

- Protect yourself from insects by remaining in well-screened areas, using repellents (applied sparingly at 4-hour intervals) and permethrin-impregnated mosquito nets, and wearing long-sleeved shirts and long pants from dusk through dawn.
- To prevent fungal and parasitic infections, keep feet clean and dry, and do not go barefoot.
- Always use latex condoms to reduce the risk of HIV and other sexually transmitted diseases.

To Avoid Getting Sick:

- Don't eat food purchased from street vendors.
- Don't drink beverages with ice.
- Don't eat dairy products unless you know they have been pasteurized.
- Don't share needles with anyone.
- Don't handle animals (especially monkeys, dogs, and cats), to avoid bites and serious diseases (including rabies and plague). (For more information, please see the Animal-Associated Hazards on the Making Travel Safe page.)
- Don't swim in fresh water, including Lake Malawi. Salt water is usually safer. (For more information, please see the Swimming Precautions on the Making Travel Safe page.)

What You Need To Bring with You:

- Long-sleeved shirt and long pants to wear while outside whenever possible, to prevent illnesses carried by insects (e.g., malaria, dengue, filariasis, leishmaniasis, and onchocerciasis).
- Insect repellent containing DEET (diethylmethyltoluamide), in 30%–35% strength for adults and 6%–10% for children. Unless you are staying in air-conditioned or well-screened housing, purchase a bed net impregnated with the insecticide permethrin. (Bed nets can be purchased in camping or military supply stores.)
- Over-the-counter antidiarrheal medicine to take if you have diarrhea.
- Iodine tablets and water filters to purify water if bottled water is not available. See Do's above for more detailed information about water filters.
- Sunblock, sunglasses, hat.
- Prescription medications: make sure you have enough to last during your trip, as well as a copy of the prescription(s).

After You Return Home:

If you have visited an area where there is risk for malaria, continue taking your malaria medication weekly for 4 weeks after you leave the area. If you become ill after your trip—even as long as a year after you return—tell your doctor where you have traveled.

SUPPLEMENT

RWANDA DIPLOMATIC MISSIONS

Belgium

Ambassade de la République Rwandaise
1, Avenue des Fleurs
1150 Bruxelles
Phone: (32) 2 7630 738
Fax: (32) 2 7630 753

Burundi

Ambassade de la République Rwandaise
24, Avenue du Zaire
B.P. 400 Bujumbura
Phone: (257) 228 755
Fax: (257) 223 254

Canada

Embassy of the Republic of Rwanda / Ambassade de la République Rwandaise
121 Cherwood Drive
Ottawa, Ontario
K1 J3 V1
Phone: (613) 722 8350
Fax: (613) 722 4052

China

Embassy of the Republic of Rwanda
30, Xiushui Beijie
100600 Beijing
Phone: (861) 65321820
Fax: (861) 22104

Ethiopia

Embassy of the Republic of Rwanda
Africa Avenue, H-17K-20
No. 001
B.P. 5618 Addis Ababa
Phone: (251) 1 610300 / 610357 / 610987
Fax: (251) 1 610411

France

Ambassade de la République Rwandaise
12, Rue Jadin
75017 Paris
Phone: (33) 1 47 66 54 20
Fax: (33) 1 42 27 74 69

Germany

Botschaft der Ruandischen Republik
Beethovenallee 72
53173 Bonn
Phone: (49) 228 355 228
Fax: (49) 228 351 922

Israel

Embassy of the Republic of Rwanda
30, Heh-B?l-Iyor Street
P.O. Box 21572
Tel Aviv
Phone: (972) 3691 2319
Fax: (972) 3696 3408

South Africa

Embassy of the Republic of Rwanda
Suite 113, Infotech Building
1090 Arcadia Street, Hatfield
Pretoria
Phone: (27) 12 342 1741 / 342 1742
Fax: (27) 12 342 1743

Switzerland

Botschaft der Ruandischen Republik / Ambassade de la République Rwandaise
60 Eigerstrasse
3007 Bern
Phone: (41) 31 301 0611/301 8610
Fax: (41) 31 371 4475

Tanzania

Embassy of the Republic of Rwanda
32, Upanga Road
P.O. Box 2918
Dar es Salaam
Phone: (255) 30119
Fax: (255) 46917

Uganda

Embassy of the Republic of Rwanda
Nakaima Road, Plot No. 2 (near National Museum)
P.O. Box 2468
Kampala
Phone: (256) 41 343 662
Fax: (256) 41 258 547

United Kingdom

Embassy of the Republic of Rwanda
42 AV Lumer Road, No. 2
OBX London
Phone: (44) 171 9302 570
Fax: (44) 171 9302 572

United Nations

Permanent Mission of Rwanda to the United Nations
124 East 39th Street
New York, NY 10016
United States
Phone: (212) 679 9010 / 9023 / 9024
Fax: (212) 679 9133

United States

San Francisco
Scott Heldford
Consulate General of Rwanda
120 Montgomery St.
Suite 950
San Francisco, CA 94104
Phone: (415) 772 9181
Fax: (415) 772-9830

Washington, DC
Embassy of the Republic of Rwanda
1714 New Hampshire Avenue, NW
Washington, DC 20009
Phone: (202) 232-2882
Fax: (202) 232-4544

IMPORTANT ADDRESSES

IMPORTANT ADDRESSES

Office of Tourism and National Parks
Office Rwandais du Tourisme et des Parcs Nationaux (ORTPN)
B.P. 905
Kigali RWANDA

Phone: (250) 76515/7 or (250) 76514
Fax: (205) 76512

Chamber of Commerce and Industry
B.P. 319
Kigali RWANDA

Phone: (250) 83538 or (250) 83541
Fax: 250 83532

HOTELS

Kigali

Baobab Hotel
B.P. 1406
Kigali RWANDA
Phone: (250) 75633, 73281

Guest House Ituze
Kacyiru
B.P. 2797
Kigali RWANDA
Phone: (250) 84289
Fax: (250) 84289

Hotel Chez Lando
Remera
B.P. 1519
Kigali RWANDA
Phone: (250) 82050, 84328
Fax: (250) 84380

Hotel des Diplomates
B.P. 269
Kigali RWANDA
Phone: (250) 75111, 7511
Fax: (250) 75365

Hotel des Mille Collines
B.P. 1322
Kigali RWANDA
Phone: (250) 76530
Fax: (250) 76541

Hotel Isimbi
B.P. 1163
Kigali RWANDA
Phone: (250) 72578, 72581, 75109, 72795
Fax: (250) 75109

Hotel Umubano
B.P. 874
Kigali RWANDA
Phone: (250) 82176, 82177
Fax: (250) 82178

Butare

Hotel Faucon
Butare
B.P. 366 Butare
Butare RWANDA
Phone: (25) 30138 Butare

Hotel Ibis
Butare
B.P. 103 Butare

Butare RWANDA
Phone: (250) 30335 Butare
Fax: (250) 30335 Butare

Ruhengeri

Hotel Muhabura
Kigombe, Ruhengeri
B.P. 118 Ruhengeri
Phone: (250) 46296 Ruhengeri

Hotel Urumuli
Kigombe, Ruhengeri
B.P. 89 Ruhengeri
Phone: (250) 46702 Ruhengeri

TRAVEL AGENTS AND TOUR OPERATORS

Air Master Travel Rwanda
B.P. 10
Kigali RWANDA
Phone: (250) 74931, 73852
Fax: (250) 73853

B.P. 5649
Kampala UGANDA
Phone: (041) 250267

Changa Travel Agency
Avenue de la Justice
B.P. 3246
Kigali RWANDA
Phone: (250) 77564, 77103
Fax: (250) 77669
Represents Air Burundi

Flight Services
B.P. 865
Kigali RWANDA

GTS Gatera Travel Service
B.P. 2520
Kigali RWANDA
Phone: (250) 83866, 82177
Fax: (250) 83867

ITT
(International Tours and Travel Ltd.)
Immeuble SORAS
B.P. 924
Kigali RWANDA
Phone: (250) 74057
Fax: (250) 75582

Nord Sud International Travel and Tours Agency
Avenue de la Paix
B.P. 183
Kigali RWANDA
Phone: (250) 75310
Fax: (250) 75349

Rwanda Tours
B.P. 449
Kigali RWANDA
Phone: (250) 75037
Fax: (250) 85693

Rwanda Travel Bureau
B.P. 1395
Kigali RWANDA
Phone: (250) 77777, 78560
Fax: (250) 78565

Satguru Travel and Tours Service
B.P. 2111
Kigali RWANDA
Phone: (250) 73079
Fax: (250) 72231

SOMACO
B.P. 1108
Kigali RWANDA
Phone: (250) 82847, 77690

Transworld Tours and Travel
10 Avenue de la Paix
B.P. 1003
Kigali RWANDA
Phone: (250) 77472, 77070
Fax: (250) 77473

TRASER
(Travel Agency Services)
Bat. BRD
B.P. 3859
Kigali RWANDA
Phone: (250) 74990
Fax: (250) 73126

Travel Agency Services
B.P. 977
Kigali RWANDA
Phone: (250) 73124

CAR HIRE

Air Master Travel Rwanda
See Travel Agents and Tour Operators

Auto World Company
B.P. 1305
Kigali RWANDA
Phone: (250) 73138, 74390 Kigali
(250) 62652 Gitarama
Fax: (250) 74147

B.P. 12001
Kampala UGANDA
Phone: (041) 533450

EUROPCAR
B.P. 394
Kigali RWANDA
Phone: (250) 72983

GTS Gatera Travel Service
See Travel Agents and Tour Operators

ITT (International Tours and Travel Ltd.)
See Travel Agents and Tour Operators

Nord Sud International Travel and Tours Agency
See Travel Agents and Tour Operators

Orange Line
B.P. 1315
Kigali RWANDA

SOCOR s.a.r.l.
Boulevard de la Revolution
B.P. 10
Kigali RWANDA
Phone: (250) 78646
Fax: (250) 73853

Taxi Service du Rond Point
Hotel des Mille Collines
Phone: (250) 76586

Taxi Service Mille Collines
Hotel des Mille Collines
Phone: (250) 76530
Fax: (250) 76541

TRANSAFRICA
B.P. 2248
Kigali RWANDA
Phone: (250) 74543, 82347
Fax: (250) 72385, 82347

TRASER (Travel Agency Services)
See Travel Agents and Tour Operators

SELECTED OFFICIAL MATERIALS

IRIN INTERVIEW WITH ACTING PRESIDENT PAUL KAGAME

KIGALI, 7 April (IRIN) - The following is an interview conducted with Acting Rwandan President Paul Kagame. The wide-ranging interview, which deals with both foreign policy issues and domestic politics, took place on the eve of the sixth anniversary of the 1994 genocide.

Q. The survivors of the genocide are becoming critical of the government saying they have had a raw deal in the political and economic life of the country. Do you think their demands are taking on political overtones?

A. This is in the minds of very few people who want to build a constituency on the plight of some groups in our society. They overplay some of the problems for their own political benefit. This has happened in the past history of our country, but I think it is nothing extraordinary and unmanageable. In the last financial year, we spent 7.5 billion Rwanda francs [approximately US$ 24 million] on top of what they get like every Rwandese. We have really tried to help these people.

PRESIDENTIAL AMBITIONS AND POLITICAL FUTURE

Q. People say you like operating from the background. What has encouraged you to have a shot at the presidency?

A. When I became vice-president it was not according to a well-worked plan. I had been a leader in our liberation struggle and it [the vice-presidency] simply came up as a result of the 1994 situation. Today, I am acting president just because the other president resigned.

It was not planned. Again, I find myself in a situation where I am acting president. There is an on-going process to select a new president. It might be that I turn out to be the chosen president. I am always willing to serve my country in whatever capacity, be it out of circumstances or otherwise.

Q. As chairman of the Rwandan Patriotic Front (RPF), do you think the resignation of president Pasteur Bizimungu was inevitable? Did internal contradictions within the RPF lead to his resignation?

A. Yes, there were some problems. The RPF is built on an ideology where people must be modest in doing things. As Africans with all sorts of problems to overcome we have to behave and think in a certain way. For example, we believe that corruption must be fought. Along the path to achieve our goals, some people fall away. However, we always believe that with time people can rethink their positions and become part of the struggle again.

Q. If you become president, what will be your goals?

A. We shall continue with the current programme. Essentially, the goals would remain the same. These are: reconstruction, the reconciliation of our people who have been affected by all kinds of divisive politics, and the provision of security so that our people can live in peace internally and become part of the peace in our region.

Q. What other options are available for those who have genuine political grievances against your government?

A. It is a simple matter, we are saying those who have responsibilities in the genocide should be handled by the justice system and those who have no case to answer should go to their villages and live a normal life.

Q. Have you integrated any members of the former Rwandan government army into your forces?

A. We have so far integrated nearly 15,000 members of the ex-Rwandan government army and [they] are holding different areas of responsibility in the force. In fact, some of them are the ones in different units fighting in the Congo.

The integration has been extremely successful, I think most people do not know this, including some of our neighbours who have shown a lot of ignorance about what goes on here. Some of the ex-FAR [Forces Armees Rwandaises] had expertise in different areas and we used this as a yardstick for integrating them in the army. The door is open for those who had nothing to do with the 1994 events.

Q. Do you think the political parties sharing the transition administration with the RPF are up to the job of preparing the political future of the country? Do they share the agenda of the RPF?

A. I think the political parties in Rwanda have been doing well, given their background. They are inputting to our programmes. There is common ground on major issues like security, justice, reconciliation and economic development. We might disagree on small details, but that is not a problem. Indeed, that is politics.

Q. Is the RPF preparing for a future as a political force?

A. I think the future of the RPF is good, we have made our contribution to the liberation of our country. We might make mistakes, but we have a mechanism for sitting down and correcting them. I think this capacity to reexamine ourselves is good political culture and will help us consolidate as we go along. But our consolidation politically is not at the expense of other people. It is about reaching common ground with other people.

Q. Do you think Rwanda needs a new constitution?

A. Yes, absolutely. We have to work on putting in place a new constitution. In the past, individuals used to sit down and write constitutions based on their personal dreams. We intend to put in place a legal and constitutional commission, which is provided for in the Arusha agreement. This commission will go around the country collecting views. The commission will also travel to other countries both in the region and outside to get ideas about constitution making. Certainly it is a question of views and ideas and then writing a draft constitution. If there is a need, there will be a referendum to endorse the outcome.

JUSTICE - THE LEGACY OF THE GENOCIDE

Q. Justice is another major challenge to your government. Do you have any creative ideas how justice will be administered in a transparent manner?

A. Justice is another problem area we have been dealing with it for the last six years and we have managed to stabilize the situation. But we still have a big problem on our hands, with over 100,000 in our prisons on genocide allegations. We have been improvising by looking at different ways to deal with the situation. We created categories of responsibilities for the genocide. This has helped us to be able to focus on the main authors of the genocide and handle the lower categories in different ways. Then we have also come up with another improvisation known as

Gacaca, which means that people will be taken to their home communes to be tried in public assisted by the justice system here. This will probably see many cases tried at the same time and being tried in a manner there that is likely to result in many of them being forgiven or given small sentences to serve the community.

A legal basis has been created for the Gacaca process and the donors are supportive given other available alternatives. If we had to go by the normal standards of applying justice, we might take centuries dealing with the problem. Donors are on board and have promised to put in resources so that we can proceed with this process.

DOWNING OF HABYARIMANA'S PLANE AND UN RELATIONS

Q. Your name has been cited in a memo, implicating you as having masterminded the shooting-down of [former Hutu President Juvenal] Habyarimana's plane. Is this true? Do you have any clues about what happened to the plane?

A. We are told reliably that some people at the United Nations are very worried about the [former Swedish premier Ingvar] Carlsson report, which puts a lot of responsibility, in terms of the failures in Rwanda before, during and after the genocide on the UN.

I understand some of them have now devised ways of trying to intimidate some of us to keep quiet about these failures. The UN should know what happened. They are the ones who were in charge of the situation before the genocide and should not try to push responsibility elsewhere. We are getting more details about this network of people at the UN involved in this smear campaign, we are going to expose them when the time comes.

The situation has not been clear when it comes to the downing of Habyarimana's plane. It is stupid for some people to say that the genocide was as a result of the downing of Habyarimana's aircraft. Such people do not know the history of Rwanda. Genocide started in 1959. It was continued in the following years - 1963, 1967, 1973. Of course, we had killings in the 1990's when our struggle was on. If you remember, in 1993 we had to halt the negotiation process in Arusha because there were killings in the north and demand that the government should stop them. Towards the conclusion of the Arusha peace process, one colonel close to Habyarimana openly told people that he was going to Rwanda to plan an apocalypse. What is happening today is an attempt by some people to revise history by distorting facts.

About Habyarimana's death, I think the issue should be handled separately from the genocide because at that time there were all sorts of forces in charge of the city and neighbouring areas, which included the United Nations force, the Belgium contingent under the UN, the then-government forces. At the time, we [the RPF] had a force at a site near town which had no relationship with the place where the aircraft was brought down.

RELATIONS WITH UGANDA AND DRC

Q. Why has the relationship with Uganda, a close ally of Rwanda, remained tense since the fighting in Kisangani last year despite meetings between the top leadership of both countries?

A. I really do not fully understand the whole problem because as you said there have been problems before, during and after Kisangani. We have tried to lay them out on the table with our Ugandan brothers. We have had serious discussions on how to overcome this kind of situation. But serious shortcomings keep coming in the way of that process.

We are very concerned and we think our partners in this process have to put in a lot in terms of effort to put this history behind us and focus more on the importance of the relationship between the two countries.

Q. Do you think a complete fallout with Uganda would strengthen the position of [DRC President Laurent-Desire] Kabila and his allies and offset the military balance in the region?

A. Continued problems between the two allies, Uganda and Rwanda, would result in all sorts of negative things, including the strengthening of our enemies.

My advice to everyone involved in this war is to work for the implementation of the Lusaka agreement. I do not think there is likely to be any serious changes on the ground. What people did not achieve when there was serious fighting, they should not think that they will achieve now.

It would be a very wasteful exercise for anybody to think they can take advantage of the ceasefire to change the situation on the ground. So it will be costly for people who try to operate outside Lusaka. Let's implement the agreement and stop wasting time.

Q. Do you subscribe to the view that a deal between you and Kabila will end the war in Congo?

A. The problems in Congo are not between me and Kabila. If that were the case, it would be the simplest thing to deal with. The problem is much wider than that and it involves different sections of the Congolese population, it affects different neighbouring countries and countries far from the Congo border.

Q. There are credible reports indicating that ethnic hatred aimed at the Tutsi in Congo is on the rise. Do think this will result in mass killings?

A. I do not think this hatred has just been created. It has been in that part of Congo for some years. It has been sustained by people who exploit it for political ends. We should fight this hatred politically. Where there is use of arms, we have to face it with use of arms.

Q. Do you think people like the Banyamulenge are threatened with extermination?

A. Yes, they are in danger. They are in danger because of the unresolved problems in DRC and because there is fighting going on.

Q. Do you think the UN plan to deploy 5,500 troops and observers in the DRC is enough?

A. It is nowhere near enough, but one should say it is a good gesture. But even this gesture has yet to materialise. It is far early to talk of serious involvement by the international community, which we thought would come in the form of prompt UN involvement.

RWANDA REUNIFICATION 2000

Remarks by H.E. DR. Richard Sezibera Ambassador of Rwanda on the Occasion of Rwanda Reunificatinon 2000 Los Angeles, July 01, 2000

Fellow Rwandans,
Friends of Rwanda,
Ladies and Gentlemen:

It gives me great pleasure to say a few words on this occasion celebrating what Africa in general and Rwanda in particular so desperately needs - Unity.

In 1884, at Berlin in Germany, by the stroke of a foreign pen, our continent was divided into politico-economic structures with neither our input nor knowledge.
We have therefore in our hands the unenviable task of making sure that those structures and norms which we inherited are not turned into permanent barriers and sources of division, but rather serve as membranes, allowing for a free exchange of ideas and engendering co-operation in all fields.

Fellow Rwandans,
Friends of Rwanda,
Ladies and Gentlemen:

We in Rwanda, given our history, have come to the inevitable conclusion that Unity is not a luxury reserved for the few, but a sine qua none for national development.

As you may well remember, 6 years ago, Rwanda hit the nadir in its history, with the genocide that claimed over one million of its people.

A nation, in existence for over five hundred years, had been battered by colonialism and successfully resisted the slave trade, yet in mid 1994, within 100 days, was almost destroyed by its own citizens and came close to ceasing to exist as a state.

It was saved in extremis by some patriots, hung in the balance for some time as its sons and daughters fled it, but has now reestablished national equilibrium as it embarks on economic recovery and growth.

Rwanda is on a genuine search for workable political systems that will provide political space for all its citizens, and an opportunity for each of them to participate in developing the country's resources for their own economic well-being and the well-being of their families.

Fellow Africans,
Ladies and Gentlemen:

The near collapse of Rwanda as a state and its miraculous recovery has taught us a number of lessons, which I believe, are worth repeating because they bear universal significance.

With independence, all our countries inherited states that are in the long run, inimical to Africa's long term interests.
The colonial state was a parasitic organ, at the service of the metropole, indifferent and even detrimental to the self-actualization of the indigenous peoples. At independence, only the actors at the helm changed, but in many cases the concepts remained the same. The challenge is for us all to break through the mold and develop a Pan-African agenda. This cannot be done through official channels alone, thus the importance of this, and other gatherings.

Post genocide Rwanda believes that the fundamental challenges which Africa faces are to return sovereignty to the people, to redefine the development and national agendas, and to build inclusive politico-economic structures that break out of the enforced isolation of Africa's modern states forcing them to reach out to others.

In service of this strategic vision therefore, Rwanda has taken the following important policy decisions.

1. The state no longer defines who is Rwandese and who is not. The individual determines citizenship. If a person chooses to declare himself Rwandese, then to all intents and purposes they are. This is reflected in our laws and it is my hope that it will be enshrined in our new constitution which is in the process of being elaborated, and will be adopted by referendum. We believe that even though we are a small country, our richest resources are our people and we prefer to include instead of excluding those who would want to join us.

2. Governance is being returned to the local communities. Popular participation in decision making at all levels, and leadership accountability are the hallmark of the new policies. There always is a tendency for elites, be they political, intellectual, economic, or otherwise, to assume that they alone know what is best for the people. We have rejected this and are putting in place mechanisms to ensure that people make their own economic destinies and have sole control over the decision-making in all aspects of their lives. This includes, to the limits of the possible, even those arenas that have been traditionally the exclusive preserve of intellectual elites. This is the philosophy that underlies the recourse to our traditional forms of justice to handle the overwhelming demand for justice after genocide through the Gacaca courts.

3. Rwanda believes in, and is practicing collective and inclusive power sharing, instead of relying exclusively on competing interests of different political groups. Instead of open competition, all political parties take part in governance through their presence in Cabinet and Parliament. We believe that in a post conflict situation, it is important that all the actors on the national scene have a stake in governance. The alternative is that competing interests might lead to the total collapse of the state, and as Somalia has shown us, such a collapse has very few redeeming features.

4. We are promoting an anti-sectarian agenda. Rwanda was almost destroyed by state inspired sectarian policies. Exclusion based on perceived ethnic, religious, or regional loyalties superceded the national greater good. We believe that ethnic groups, especially in the Great Lakes region, are cultural categories transformed into self-conscious communities by leaders, elite groups, or states seeking to provide socio-economic and political advantages to the groups in question. Thus there is an ongoing creation of groups and subgroups in Africa. Some peoples and groups are even denied citizenship and turned into aliens at the whim of some rulers. In Rwanda one sometimes hears people claim they represent Hutus, others Tutsis or Twa, and some have even gone to the extent of planning for the extermination of others. Let us however ask ourselves the fundamental question. What links rich educated Tutsi or Hutu in the capital to a jigger infested poor, malnourished Tutsi or Hutu in the villages? Why would a poor Hutu peasant, who relies on his Tutsi and Twa neighbor to help him carry his sick wife to a far-off clinic, be encouraged to turn on him and kill him at the instigation of a chauffeur driven elite. I would contend that the fundamental problem for us all is to provide wealth and equal opportunities for all, and everything else is pure manipulation. Some of us have said an emphatic “no” to these manipulations and have dedicated our lives to the promotion of a nationalistic and ultimately Pan-Africanist agenda. The Government of National Unity cannot and will not be a tribal chieftainship - we have made that very clear.

5. Finally ladies and gentlemen, the fundamental challenge of post colonial Africa is search for appropriate and visionary leadership. The leadership that Rwanda had after independence was a recipe for disaster: Rwanda’s first President, Gregoire Kayibanda on 27/11/1959 made a strong appeal for the segregation of the Hutu and Tutsi into two separate zones. He compared the two communities to “Two nations in a single State… Two nations between whom there is no intercourse and no sympathy, who are as ignorant of each other’s habits, thoughts and feelings as if they were dwellers of different zones, or inhabitants of different planets.” With a head of state like this, Rwanda was an eruption waiting to happen. Compare this to the inaugural speech of H.E. President Paul Kagame, April 22 when he said: “I appeal to every Rwandese to rise up and fight against anything that divides our people. We must fight injustice against our people. Current and future legislation will ensure that the state has its full weight behind the fight against division and injustice. I would like to call every Rwandan to be his brother's keeper. Only when we commit ourselves to helping guarantee the security of others can we enjoy maximum security as a nation". From the backward leadership of 1959 to the visionary one of 1994 and beyond, as tectonic shifts go, this is a fundamental one in the vision of who we are as a people and where we should be headed as a nation and as a continent. I appeal to you to help us define the appropriate agenda and accompany us on that march.

Happy reunification day and I thank you.

GENOCIDE IN RWANDA

The 1994 genocide was a carefully planned and executed exercise to annihalate Rwanda's Tutsi population and Hutus who did not agree with the prevailing extremist politics of the Habyarimana regime. One million lives were lost in only one hundred days. It is the fastest and most vicious genocide yet recorded in human history.

The 1994 genocide was by no means the first time that the then government of Rwanda attempted to annihalate sections of the population they believed were opposed to their politics. throughout the 1960s the government of Rwanda launched vicious attacks on Rwanda's Tutsi population, resulting in a mass exodus into neighbouring Burundi, Tanzania, Uganda, Kenya and Congo. For the first time in Rwanda's six century long history, a large portion of the people of Rwanda became stateless, and were denied the right to live in their motherland. For the first time in Rwanda's long history, the Rwandan leadership preached a message of division, hate, and violence to the population, resulting in repeated cycles of genocide.

Other cycles of genocide occured in 1973 and 1979. In 1990, after the commencement of the struggle by the RPF to liberate Rwanda, the government launched yet another cycle of genocide. Between 1990-1994, the bagogwe people of Northern Rwanda were targeted by the Habyarimana regime, resulting in tens of thousands of deaths. There were similar attacks orchestrated against people of kibuye, Butare and elsewhere in Rwanda. On assuming power in July 1994, the Government of National Unity made it among the highest priorities to apprehend and bring to justice the perpetrators of these crimes. Thousands have been arrested and await trial, while some have already faced justice. The Government of National Unity believes that the people of Rwanda should reconcile after many decades of division and hatred. However, it is pertinent to the reconciliation process that Rwandese feel that justice is being done. There can be no reconciliation without justice.

The sheer bulk of genocide suspects and cases due for trial has placed severe strain on Rwanda's criminal justice system which is already crippled by poor infrastructure and the death of professional during the genocide. Rwanda's prison's are heavily congested, and the cost of feeding and clothing prisoners is a drain on the economy.

The lack of an adequate number of prosecutors, judges, and lawyers to try cases exacerbates the already bad situation. At the present rate, it would take over 200 years if Rwanda was to rely on the conventional court system to deliver justice.

The Government of National Government decided to ease pressure on the criminal justice system by categorizing genocide suspects according to the crimes of which they are accused. Category 1 - the 'planners,organizers, instigators, supervisors and leaders' of the genocide numbering 2,133, will be tried in the conventional courts. Categories 2-4, where involvement was slightly less serious, will be tried in traditional community courts or *GACACA* courts. This new process will significantly speed up trials and sentencing.

The *GACACA* courts also have the advantage of involving the community in the trial and sentencing process. The Government of National Unity believes that involving the population in the trials can also contribute significantly to reconciliation.

The government has also made it a priority to develop the criminal justice system. Special training has been provided to Magistrates and Judges, while courts around the country have been renovated. A national police force has been created and charged with civil security matters and criminal investigations.

CATEGORIZATION OF OFFENCES RELATING TO GENOCIDE

The Genocide Law of the Republic of Rwanda categorizes the crimes of Genocide and crimes against Humanity as follows:

Persons accused of offences set out in Article 1 of this organic law and committed during the period betwenn 1st October 1990 and 31st December 1994 shall, on the basis of their acts of participation, be classified into one of the following categories:

Category 1:

- Persons whose criminal acts or whose acts of criminal participation place them among the planners, organisers, instigators, supervisors and leaders of the crime of Genocide or of a crime against humanity;
- Persons who acted in positions of authority at the National, Prefectorial, Communal, Sector or Cell level, or in a political party, the army, religious organizations or in a militia and who perpetrated or fostered such crimes;
- Notorious murderers who by virtue of the zeal or excessive malice with which they committed atrocities, distinguished themselves in their areas of residence or where they passed;
- Persons who committed acts of sexual torture or violence

Category 2:

Persons whose criminal acts or whose acts of criminal participation place them among the perpetrators, conspirators or accomplices of intentional homicide or of seriuos assault against the person - causing death.

Category 3:

Persons whose criminal acts or whose acts of criminal participation make them guilty of other serious assualts against the person.

Category 4:

Persons who committed offenses against property

GACACA COURTS

GACACA COURTS initiative is very timely because it will make the following possible:

- It will enable the truth to be revealed about Genocide and crimes against Humanity in Rwanda.
- It will speed up the trials of those accused of Genocide, Crimes against Humanity and other crimes.
- It will put an end to the culture of impunity in Rwanda.
- It will reconcile the people of Rwanda and strengthen ties between them.
- It revives traditional forms of dispensing justice based on Rwandese culture.
- It demonstrates the ability of local communities to solve their own problems.
- Helps solve some of the many problems caused by Genocide.

ORGANISATION AND POWERS OF GACACA COURTS

Judges

The judges of the GACACA Courts will be respectable people of at least 21 years of age, and elected by people of voting age. They will take responsibility for ensuring orderly and fair proceedings.

The **Functional Hierarchies** of the Gacaca Courts are as follows:

- The General Assembly
- The Court Council
- The Coordination Committee

THE GENERAL ASSEMBLY

A.) **At Cellule Level**

The General Assembly at Cellule level consists of all the inhabitants of the Cellule over 18 years of age.

The main responsibilities of the General Assembly at the Cellule level are as follows:

- To compile a list of those who died in the Cellule as a result of the 1994 Genocide, as well as those who were raped and those who participated in those crimes.
- To compile a list of those who moved away from their usual residential areas during the genocide.
- To give evidence which incriminates or exonerates those who have been accused of having taken part in the genocide.

B.) **At the Secteur, Commune and Prefecture levels**

The General Assembly of the Gacaca Court at these levels consists of representatives from lower levels in the hierarchy.

The responsibility of the General Assembly of the Gacaca Court at these levels is to follow-up the work of the Gacaca Court Council at the same level.

The Gacaca Court Council

- The Gacaca Court has a court-council at eqach level. The gacaca Court-Council at the Cellule, Secteur, Commune, and Prefecture level consists of people elected by the General Assembly.
- The main responsibility of the Gacaca Court is to try cases.

The Coordination Committee

At each level, the gacaca Courts will have coordination committees composed of the Chairman and two Secretaries of the Gacaca Court.

Powers of the Gacaca Court

- **At Cellule level:** Has the power to try cases of persons who allegedly committed or conspired to commit crimes which fall under Category Four of genocide crimes.
- **At Secteur Level:** Has the power to try cases of persons who allegedly committed or conspired to commit crimes which fall under Category Three of genocide crimes.
- **At Commune Level:** Has the power to try cases of persons who allegedly committed or conspired to commit crimes which fall under Category Two of genocide crimes.
- **At Prefecture Level:** Has the responsibility of hearing and passing judgement on appeals from lower Gacaca Courts.

Working relationships

The office of Public Prosecutions will maintain their responsibility of investigations. However, case files will be sent to Secteurs for distribution.

The Department of Public Prosecutions will continue to supply the Gacaca Courts with evidence on cases where there has been investigation.

Monitoring and supervising the operations of the Gacaca Courts all over the country will be carried out by the coordination department due to be set up shortly within the High Court.

The Ministry for Justice and other local and central government departments will play a role in sensitizing the population to take part in the Gacaca Courts.

How you can help in the process

- Seek as much information as you need about the gacaca process from your local Cellule, Secteur, Commune or Prefecture.
- Encourage your friends and neighbours to also take interest in the process.
- You should volunteer any evidence or information you have about genocide.
- Select Gacaca Judges wisely

- Cooperate with local authorities to prepare whatever is needed to get the courts operational.
- Work openly and without fear to expose the truth.

Genocide Trials

Genocide trials are being conducted in Rwanda as well as at Arusha by the UN International Criminal Tribunal for Rwanda (ICTR). A few other cases have been heard in European courts. Over 2, 500 suspects have been tried and sentenced in Rwanda while ICTR has tried and sentenced eight suspects.

PRESIDENT CLINTON VISITS AFRICA BUILDING A NEW PARTNERSHIP

RWANDA: A FUTURE WITHOUT FEAR

Excerpts from President Clinton's remarks at Kigali Airport
-- Rwanda, March 25, 1998

I have come today to pay the respects of my nation to all who suffered and all who perished in the Rwandan genocide. It is my hope that through this trip, in every corner of the world today and tomorrow, their story will be told: that four years ago in this beautiful, green, lovely land, a clear and conscious decision was made by those then in power that the peoples of this country would not live side by side in peace. During the 90 days that began on April 6 in 1994, Rwanda experienced the most intensive slaughter in this blood-filled century we are about to leave.

The international community, together with nations in Africa, must bear its share of responsibility for this tragedy, as well. We did not act quickly enough after the killing began. We should not have allowed the refugee camps to become safe haven for the killers. We did not immediately call these crimes by their rightful name: genocide. We cannot change the past. But we can and must do everything in our power to help you build a future without fear and full of hope.

To that end, I am directing my administration to improve, with the international community, our system for identifying and spotlighting nations in danger of genocidal violence, so that we can assure worldwide awareness of impending threats.

We must as an international community have the ability to act when genocide threatens. We are working to create that capacity here in the Great Lakes region, where the memory is still fresh.

We must work now to remedy the consequences of genocide. The United States has provided assistance to Rwanda to settle the uprooted and restart its economy, but we must do more. I am pleased that America will become the first nation to contribute to the new Genocide Survivors Fund. We will contribute this year $2 million, continue our support in the years to come, and urge other nations to do the same, so that survivors and their communities can find the care they need and the help they must have.

Mr. President, to you, and to you, Mr. Vice President, you have shown great vision in your efforts to create a single nation in which all citizens can live freely and securely.

To help ensure that those who survived in the generations to come never again suffer genocidal violence, nothing is more vital than establishing the rule of law. There can be no peace in Rwanda that lasts without a justice system that is recognized as such.

We applaud the efforts of the Rwandan government to strengthen civilian and military justice systems. I am pleased that our Great Lakes Justice Initiative will invest $30 million to help create throughout the region judicial systems that are impartial, credible, and effective. In Rwanda these funds will help to support courts, prosecutors, and police, military justice and cooperation at the local level.

We will also continue to pursue justice through our strong backing for the International Criminal Tribunal for Rwanda.

We must make it clear to all those who would commit such acts in the future that they too must answer for their acts, and they will. In Rwanda, we must hold accountable all those who may abuse human rights, whether insurgents or soldiers. Internationally, as we meet here, talks are under way at the United Nations to establish a permanent international criminal court. Rwanda and the difficulties we have had with this special tribunal underscore the need for such a court. And the United States will work to see that it is created.

I know that in the face of all you have endured, optimism cannot come easily to any of you. Yet I have just spoken, as I said, with several Rwandans who survived the atrocities, and just listening to them gave me reason for hope. You see countless stories of courage around you every day as you go about your business here -- men and women who survived and go on, children who recover the light in their eyes remind us that at the dawn of a new millennium there is only one crucial division among the peoples of the earth. And believe me, after over five years of dealing with these problems, I know it is not the division between Hutu and Tutsi, or Serb and Croatian and Muslim in Bosnia, or Arab and Jew, or Catholic and Protestant in Ireland, or black and white. It is really the line between those who embrace the common humanity we all share and those who reject it.

It is the line between those who find meaning in life through respect and cooperation and who, therefore, embrace peace, and those who can only find meaning in life if they have someone to look down on, someone to trample, someone to punish and, therefore, embrace war. It is the line between those who look to the future and those who cling to the past. It is the line between those who give up their resentment and those who believe they will absolutely die if they have to release one bit of grievance. It is the line between those who confront every day with a clenched fist and those who confront every day with an open hand. That is the only line that really counts when all is said and done.

To those who believe that God made each of us in his own image, how could we choose the darker road? When you look at those children who greeted us as we got off that plane today, how could anyone say they did not want those children to have a chance to have their own children? To experience the joy of another morning sunrise? To learn the normal lessons of life? To give something back to their people?

When you strip it all away, whether we're talking about Rwanda or some other distant troubled spot, the world is divided according to how people believe they draw meaning from life.

And so I say to you, though the road is hard and uncertain, and there are many difficulties ahead, and like every other person who wishes to help, I doubtless will not be able to do everything I would like to do, there are things we can do. And if we set about the business of doing them together, you can overcome the awful burden that you have endured. You can put a smile on the face of every child in this country, and you can make people once again believe that they should live as people were living who were singing to us and dancing for us today.

That is what we have to believe. That is what I came here to say. That is what I wish for you.

TRANSCRIPT: CLINTON MEETS WITH RWANDAN GENOCIDE SURVIVORS

(Announces $2 million survivors' fund)
25 March 1998

KIGALI AIRPORT, Rwanda -- President Clinton March 25 began the third day of his six-nation visit to sub-Saharan Africa with a brief visit to Rwanda, where he spoke to survivors of the 1994 genocide in which up to one million Rwandans perished.

Included in the president's audience were relief workers as well as U.S. and Rwandan government officials, including Rwandan President Pasteur Bizimungu and Vice President Paul Kagame. Clinton announced that America will become the first nation to contribute to the new Genocide Survivors Fund. "We will contribute this year $2 million, continue our support in the years to come, and urge other nations to do the same, so that survivors and their communities can find the care they need and the help they must have," he said.

Clinton said, "I have come today to pay the respects of my nation to all who suffered and all who perished in the Rwandan genocide" of the summer of 1994. "It is my hope that through this trip, in every corner of the world today and tomorrow, their story will be told."

The president emphasized that "it is important that the world know that these killings were not spontaneous or accidental. These events grew from a policy aimed at the systematic destruction of a people. The ground for violence was carefully prepared, the airwaves poisoned with hate, casting the Tutsis as scapegoats for the problems of Rwanda, denying their humanity."

Acknowledging that the international community "must bear its share of responsibility for this tragedy," Clinton explained that "we did not act quickly enough after the killing began. We should not have allowed the refugee camps to become safe haven for the killers. We did not immediately call these crimes by their rightful name: genocide. We cannot change the past. But we can and must do everything in our power to help you build a future without fear, and full of hope."

Following is the transcript of President Clinton's Kigali Airport remarks:

(BEGIN TRANSCRIPT)

THE PRESIDENT: Thank you, Mr. President. First, let me thank you, Mr. President, and Vice President Kagame, and your wives for making Hillary and me and our delegation feel so welcome. I'd also like to thank the young students who met us and the musicians, the dancers who were outside. I thank especially the survivors of the genocide and those who are working to rebuild your country for spending a little time with us before we came in here.

I have a great delegation of Americans with me, leaders of our government, leaders of our Congress, distinguished American citizens. We're all very grateful to be here. We thank the Diplomatic Corps for being here, and the members of the Rwandan government, and especially the citizens.

I have come today to pay the respects of my nation to all who suffered and all who perished in the Rwandan genocide. It is my hope that through this trip, in every corner of the world today and tomorrow, their story will be told; that four years ago in this beautiful, green, lovely land, a clear and conscious decision was made by those then in power that the peoples of this country would not live side by side in peace. During the 90 days that began on April 6 in 1994, Rwanda experienced the most intensive slaughter in this blood-filled century we are about to leave. Families murdered in their home, people hunted down as they fled by soldiers and militia, through farmland and woods as if they were animals.

From Kibuye in the west to Kibungo in the east, people gathered seeking refuge in churches by the thousands, in hospitals, in schools. And when they were found, the old and the sick, women and children alike, they were killed -- killed because their identity card said they were Tutsi or because they had a Tutsi parent, or because someone thought they looked like a Tutsi, or slain like thousands of Hutus because they protected Tutsis or would not countenance a policy that sought to wipe out people who just the day before, and for years before, had been their friends and neighbors.

The government-led effort to exterminate Rwanda's Tutsi and moderate Hutus, as you know better than me, took at least a million lives. Scholars of these sorts of events say that the killers, armed mostly with machetes and clubs, nonetheless did their work five times as fast as the mechanized gas chambers used by the Nazis.

It is important that the world know that these killings were not spontaneous or accidental. It is important that the world hear what your president just said -- they were most certainly not the result of ancient tribal struggles. Indeed, these people had lived together for centuries before the events the president described began to unfold.

These events grew from a policy aimed at the systematic destruction of a people. The ground for violence was carefully prepared, the airwaves poisoned with hate, casting the Tutsis as scapegoats for the problems of Rwanda, denying their humanity. All of this was done, clearly, to make it easy for otherwise reluctant people to participate in wholesale slaughter. Lists of victims, name by name, were actually drawn up in advance. Today the images of all that haunt us all: the dead choking the Kigara River, floating to Lake Victoria. In their fate we are reminded of the capacity in people everywhere -- not just in Rwanda, and certainly not just in Africa -- but the capacity for people everywhere to slip into pure evil. We cannot abolish that capacity, but we must never accept it. And we know it can be overcome.

The international community, together with nations in Africa, must bear its share of responsibility for this tragedy, as well. We did not act quickly enough after the killing began. We should not have allowed the refugee camps to become safe haven for the killers. We did not immediately call these crimes by their rightful name: genocide. We cannot change the past. But we can and must do everything in our power to help you build a future without fear, and full of hope.

We owe to those who died and to those who survived who loved them, our every effort to increase our vigilance and strengthen our stand against those who would commit such atrocities in the future -- here or elsewhere. Indeed, we owe to all the peoples of the world who are at risk -- because each bloodletting hastens the next as the value of human life is degraded and violence becomes tolerated, the unimaginable becomes more conceivable -- we owe to all the people in the world our best efforts to organize ourselves so that we can maximize the chances of preventing these events. And where they cannot be prevented, we can move more quickly to minimize the horror.

So let us challenge ourselves to build a world in which no branch of humanity, because of national, racial, ethnic or religious origin, is again threatened with destruction because of those characteristics, of which people should rightly be proud. Let us work together as a community of civilized nations to strengthen our ability to prevent and, if necessary, to stop genocide.

To that end, I am directing my administration to improve, with the international community, our system for identifying and spotlighting nations in danger of genocidal violence, so that we can assure worldwide awareness of impending threats. It may seem strange to you here, especially the many of you who lost members of your family, but all over the world there were people like me sitting in offices, day after day after day, who did not fully appreciate the depth and the speed with which you were being engulfed by this unimaginable terror.

We have seen, too -- and I want to say again -- that genocide can occur anywhere. It is not an African phenomenon and must never be viewed as such. We have seen it in industrialized Europe; we have seen it in Asia. We must have global vigilance. And never again must we be shy in the face of the evidence.

Secondly, we must as an international community have the ability to act when genocide threatens. We are working to create that capacity here in the Great Lakes region, where the memory is still fresh. This afternoon in Entebbe leaders from central and eastern Africa will meet with me to launch an effort to build a coalition to prevent genocide in this region, where the memory is still fresh.

I thank the leaders who have stepped forward to make this commitment. We hope the effort can be a model for all the world, because our sacred task is to work to banish this greatest crime against humanity.

Events here show how urgent the work is. In the northwest part of your country, attacks by those responsible for the slaughter in 1994 continue today. We must work as partners with Rwanda to end this violence and allow your people to go on rebuilding your lives and your nation.

Third, we must work now to remedy the consequences of genocide. The United States has provided assistance to Rwanda to settle the uprooted and restart its economy, but we must do more. I am pleased that America will become the first nation to contribute to the new Genocide Survivors Fund. We will contribute this year $2 million, continue our support in the years to come, and urge other nations to do the same, so that survivors and their communities can find the care they need and the help they must have.

Mr. President, to you, and to you, Mr. Vice President, you have shown great vision in your efforts to create a single nation in which all citizens can live freely and securely. As you pointed out, Rwanda was a single nation before the European powers met in Berlin to carve up Africa. America stands with you, and we will continue helping the people of Rwanda to rebuild their lives and society.

You spoke passionately this morning in our private meeting about the need for grassroots effort in this direction. We will deepen our support for those grassroots efforts, for the development projects which are bridging divisions and clearing a path to a better future. We will join with you to strengthen democratic institutions, to broaden participation, to give all Rwandans a greater voice in their own governance. The challenges you face are great, but your commitment to lasting reconciliation and inclusion is firm.

Fourth, to help ensure that those who survived in the generations to come never again suffer genocidal violence, nothing is more vital than establishing the rule of law. There can be no peace in Rwanda that lasts without a justice system that is recognized as such.

We applaud the efforts of the Rwandan government to strengthen civilian and military justice systems. I am pleased that our Great Lakes Justice Initiative will invest $30 million to help create throughout the region judicial systems that are impartial, credible, and effective. In Rwanda these funds will help to support courts, prosecutors, and police, military justice and cooperation at the local level.

We will also continue to pursue justice through our strong backing for the International Criminal Tribunal for Rwanda. The United States is the largest contributor to this tribunal. We are frustrated, as you are, by the delays in the tribunal's work. As we know, we must do better. Now that administrative improvements have begun, however, the tribunal should expedite cases through group trials, and fulfill its historic mission.

We are prepared to help, among other things, with witness relocation, so that those who still fear can speak the truth in safety. And we will support the War Crimes Tribunal for as long as it is needed to do its work, until the truth is clear and justice is rendered.

Fifth, we must make it clear to all those who would commit such acts in the future that they too must answer for their acts, and they will. In Rwanda, we must hold accountable all those who may abuse human rights, whether insurgents or soldiers. Internationally, as we meet here, talks are under way at the United Nations to establish a permanent international criminal court. Rwanda and the difficulties we have had with this special tribunal underscores the need for such a court. And the United States will work to see that it is created.

I know that in the face of all you have endured, optimism cannot come easily to any of you. Yet I have just spoken, as I said, with several Rwandans who survived the atrocities, and just listening to them gave me reason for hope. You see countless stories of courage around you every day as you go about your business here -- men and women who survived and go on, children who recover the light in their eyes remind us that at the dawn of a new millennium there is only one crucial division among the peoples of the Earth. And believe me, after over five years of dealing with these problems I know it is not the division between Hutu and Tutsi, or Serb and Croatian and Muslim in Bosnia, or Arab and Jew, or Catholic and Protestant in Ireland, or black and white. It is really the line between those who embrace the common humanity we all share and those who reject it.

It is the line between those who find meaning in life through respect and cooperation and who, therefore, embrace peace, and those who can only find meaning in life if they have someone to look down on, someone to trample, someone to punish and, therefore, embrace war. It is the line between those who look to the future and those who cling to the past. It is the line between those who give up their resentment and those who believe they will absolutely die if they have to release one bit of grievance. It is the line between those who confront every day with a clenched fist and those who confront every day with an open hand. That is the only line that really counts when all is said and done.

To those who believe that God made each of us in His own image, how could we choose the darker road? When you look at those children who greeted us as we got off that plane today, how could anyone say they did not want those children to have a chance to have their own children? To experience the joy of another morning sunrise? To learn the normal lessons of life? To give something back to their people?

When you strip it all away, whether we're talking about Rwanda or some other distant troubled spot, the world is divided according to how people believe they draw meaning from life.

And so I say to you, though the road is hard and uncertain, and there are many difficulties ahead, and like every other person who wishes to help, I doubtless will not be able to do everything I would like to do, there are things we can do. And if we set about the business of doing them together, you can overcome the awful burden that you have endured. You can put a smile on the face of every child in this country, and you can make people once again believe that they should live as people were living who were singing to us and dancing for us today.

That's what we have to believe. That is what I came here to say. That is what I wish for you.

Thank you and God bless you.

WORLD BANK RWANDA-HUMAN RESOURCES AND DEVELOPMENT PROJECT

Region	Africa
Sector	Education Adjustment
Project ID	RWPE45091
Borrower(s)	Government of the Republic of Rwanda
Implementing Agency	Ministry of Education
Environment Category	C
Date PID Prepared	November 1, 1999
Projected Appraisal Date	January 15, 2000
Projected Board Date	May 15, 2000

1. COUNTRY AND SECTOR BACKGROUND

Country Background

The Country Assistance Strategy (CAS) Progress Report Update for Rwanda identifies the acute lack of human capacity and poor health standards as major constraints to fighting poverty. The Government has put very high priority on human development – education, training, knowledge development and all aspects of health including sanitation, nutrition and population. In education and related fields, the immediate priorities are to: (i) strengthen primary and secondary education, with relevant curricula, instructional materials, trained teachers and better resource management; and (ii) address the shortage of skilled manpower by improving quality and relevance at tertiary levels, and strengthening education in science, technology, management and vocational training. The project supports the two CAS goals in education.

SECTOR BACKGROUND

The average gross enrollment ratio at the primary education level dropped from about 80% before the crisis to 70% in 1997 due to the burden on the system of the return of large groups of people from neighboring Tanzania and Congo (DRC). The quality of education provided by the public school system is a further cause for concern. Between 1991 and 1996 the percentage of qualified primary school teachers dropped from about 59% to 33%. Furthermore, only 28% of the need in school books for teachers is covered. Textbooks for students are also in short supply. Further problems within the education sector include: (i) the inadequate numbers, qualifications and motivation of teachers; (ii) the low and uneven distribution of intake capacity; (iii) the inadequate information and planning systems; (iv) the shortage of students in priority disciplines; (v) the high wastage rates (high repetition and dropout rates) and the poor adaptation of curricula; and (vi) the highly centralized system of management. Success and quality remain limited at all levels and all sub-sectors.

2. PROJECT OBJECTIVES

The main objective of this project is to build capacity in Rwanda thereby making a significant contribution to achieving the development objective of poverty reduction. This will be done through: (a) support in developing a critical mass of human resources, and (b) assistance to elaborate and implement a sustained program of education and skills to fill the void caused by previous deficiencies and aggravated by the destruction of human capital during the genocide of 1994 and the refugee movement that followed.

Specific actions under the project will be geared to: (i) consolidating and improving the quality of primary education initiated under the First Education Sector Project (Cr. 2227-RW), including improving readiness for primary education through the development of early childhood care and development (ECCD) programs; (ii) expanding and improving the quality of secondary education and teacher training; (iii) selectively expanding and improving the quality of tertiary education; and (iv) HIV/AIDS education and prevention. The focus will be on improving access and the quality of secondary education and making it sustainable financially and in terms of human resources. However, given the links between secondary education and the other levels (providing teachers for the primary level, and the need for replacing lost skills and having secondary teachers trained at the higher level), as well as the need for a holistic and balanced approach, both primary and tertiary education will also figure prominently in this project.

3. PROJECT DESCRIPTION

ù Expansion and improvement of the quality of primary education: (i) improving access; (ii) improving equity in prefectures; (iii) promoting professional development and in-service training of teachers and supervisors; (iv) strengthening system of monitoring and evaluation and assessment of student learning; (v) strengthening applied pedagogical research; and (vi) improving readiness for primary education through adequate early childhood care & development (ECCD) programs.

ù Expansion and improvement of the quality of secondary education: (i) rehabilitating and building school infrastructure; (ii) reviewing and developing curricula; (iii) providing textbooks and other pedagogical materials; (iv) strengthening the examinations system and improving the assessment of students' learning achievement; and (v) developing a critical mass of qualified teachers.

ù Capacity building and the selective expansion and improvement of the quality of tertiary education

ù Strengthening of education sector management capacity: (i) strengthening planning, budgeting, financial control, human resources; and (ii) improving management information system for primary, secondary, and tertiary education.

ù improving HIV/AIDS education and prevention. On all of these, there will be a special focus on the gender dimension.

4. PROJECT FINANCING

IDA will finance US$35.0 million. Counterpart funds of about US$2 million will be expected from Rwanda. Parallel financing or co-financing from other donor (notably DFID), is also expected.

5. PROJECT IMPLEMENTATION

The project would be coordinated by a committee under the chairmanship of the Ministry of Education. The Secretary General of the Ministry will be in charge of the actual coordination of project activities. The management of each component will be the responsibility of the relevant Department. Management of the IDA Credit (including credit accounting coordination of procurement, and management of disbursement procedures) and logistical support will be provided by the current Project Office that has been implemented the First Education Sector

Project. The Project Office would be strengthened through the quantitative and qualitative improvement (through training) of its local professional and support staff, and the provision of equipment as necessary to help them adequately carry out the work involved.

6. PROJECT SUSTAINABILITY

The success of this project will depend on its financial and pedagogical sustainability The combination of chronic poverty, social tension and conflict and poor health standards make for bleak human condition. Development of human resources is urgent to sustain economic growth and reduce poverty. As regards pedagogical sustainability, every school in the country should be involved in a bottom-up school improvement initiative which could have a wide impact and ensure local ownership and sustainability of attempts to improve quality and reduce repetition rates. The capacity for evaluating student learning outcomes should be developed because it is an important tool for monitoring pedagogical sustainability.

Regarding financial sustainability, donor support in the education sector is critical until a sustainable growth path has been established. In the long-run, sustainability of the sector needs to be enhanced. Government commitment and the involvement of communities and the private sector in financing and implementation of the project, will enhance the project's sustainability in the long-run.

7. LESSONS LEARNED FROM PAST OPERATIONS IN THE COUNTRY/SECTOR

Completed projects under previous education Credits have focused on the development of primary and secondary education Following early delays attributable to the first education project complexity, poor accounting and the unfamiliarity of the authorities with Bank procedures, in the end the project was well-executed, and a commendable community effort was made in the construction of school workshops. Lessons learned under the first education project were incorporated in the design of the second and cumulatively in the design of the third and the subsequent First Education Sector Project. However, the participation of the communes in the construction of primary schools was discontinued under the First Education Sector Project because of the war. The proposed project should remobilize the active participation of the all the communes.

Lessons learned from the implementation experience point to the need for decision-makers and other stakeholders at the prefecture and commune levels to feel ownership of the project and to develop mechanisms for effective collaboration. In addition, there is a acute lack of coordination among all donors. The design of the proposed has incorporated these lessons, as well as those identified by supervision missions for the ongoing project.

8. POVERTY CATEGORY

This operation falls under the category of programs of targeted intervention (PTI) to reduce poverty and enhance human resource development.

9. ENVIRONMENTAL ASPECTS

The project is not expected to have any negative impact on the environment. There will be a very limited amount of civil works and these will be mainly rehabilitation of existing structures. New schools to be constructed under the project will be small and dispersed in rural areas. Construction methods would avoid putting pressure on scarce natural resources. The project would explore the use of hydraform block technology (based on pressure on a mixture of lots of soil and very little cement) and not baked bricks in order to reduce the need for firewood, avoiding any detrimental impact on the environment. Meanwhile, the construction of new schools and the rehabilitation of existing structures should result in improvements in sanitary conditions (portable water in schools and building of latrines). The planting of sapling shade trees and landscaping to prevent erosion as well as the building of latrines and water points, will all have positive effects on the environment. The project has been placed in category 'C'.

10. PROGRAM OBJECTIVE CATEGORIES

Poverty reduction and human resource development: These are at the core of the Bank's Country Assistance Strategy for Rwanda as indicated in the CAS discussed at the full Board on April 7, 1998 and recently updated. The thrust of the proposed project is poverty reduction and human resource development.

11. CONTACT POINTS:

The InfoShop
The World Bank
1818 H Street, NW
Washington, D.C. 20433
Telephone: (202) 458-5454
Fax: (202) 522-1500

Task Manager
Peter Ngomba
Human Resources 4
Africa Region
Telephone: (202) 473-4905
Fax: (202) 473-8107

Ministry of Education
B.P. 622
Kigali, Rwanda
Tel: (250) 83051
Fax: (250) 82162

Note: This is information on an evolving project. Certain components may not necessarily be included in the final project.

BASIC TITLES ON RWANDA

IMPORTANT!

All publications are updated annually!

Please contact IBP, Inc. at ibpusa3@gmail.com for the latest ISBNs and additional information

TITLE
Rwanda A "Spy" Guide - Strategic Information and Developments
Rwanda A Spy" Guide"
Rwanda Banking & Financial Market Handbook
Rwanda Business and Investment Opportunities Yearbook
Rwanda Business and Investment Opportunities Yearbook
Rwanda Business and Investment Opportunities Yearbook Volume 1 Strategic Information and Opportunities
Rwanda Business in Rwanda for Everyone: Practical Information and Contacts for Success
Rwanda Business Intelligence Report - Practical Information, Opportunities, Contacts
Rwanda Business Intelligence Report - Practical Information, Opportunities, Contacts
Rwanda Business Law Handbook - Strategic Information and Basic Laws
Rwanda Business Law Handbook - Strategic Information and Basic Laws
Rwanda Business Law Handbook - Strategic Information and Basic Laws
Rwanda Business Law Handbook - Strategic Information and Basic Laws
Rwanda Constitution and Citizenship Laws Handbook - Strategic Information and Basic Laws
Rwanda Country Study Guide - Strategic Information and Developments Volume 1 Strategic Information and Developments
Rwanda Diplomatic Handbook - Strategic Information and Developments
Rwanda Ecology & Nature Protection Handbook
Rwanda Economic & Development Strategy Handbook
Rwanda Energy Policy, Laws and Regulation Handbook
Rwanda Foreign Policy and Government Guide
Rwanda Foreign Policy and Government Guide
Rwanda Immigration Laws and Regulations Handbook - Strategic Information and Basic Laws
Rwanda Investment and Business Guide - Strategic and Practical Information
Rwanda Investment and Business Guide - Strategic and Practical Information
Rwanda Labor Laws and Regulations Handbook - Strategic Information and Basic Laws
Rwanda Land Ownership and Agriculture Laws Handbook
Rwanda Mineral & Mining Sector Investment and Business Guide - Strategic and Practical Information
Rwanda Mining Laws and Regulations Handbook
Rwanda Privatization Programs and Regulations Handbook
Rwanda Privatization Programs and Regulations Handbook
Rwanda Recent Economic and Political Developments Yearbook
Rwanda Recent Economic and Political Developments Yearbook
Rwanda Recent Economic and Political Developments Yearbook
Rwanda Taxation Laws and Regulations Handbook
Rwanda: Doing Business and Investing in Rwanda Guide
Rwanda: Doing Business and Investing in Rwanda Guide
Rwanda: How to Invest, Start and Run Profitable Business in Rwanda Guide - Practical Information, Opportunities, Contacts

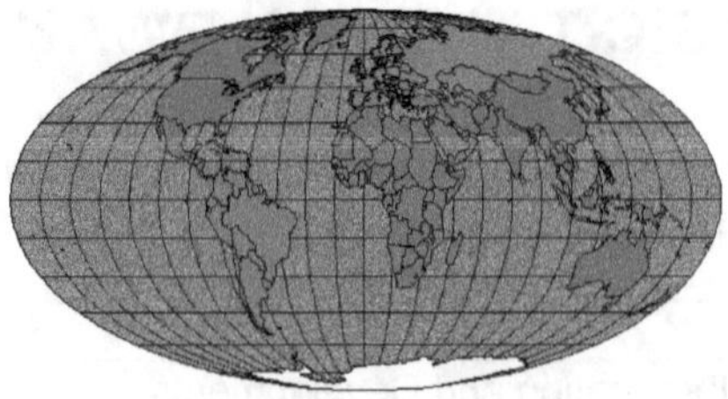

WORLD MINING LAWS AND REGULATIONS HANDBOOK LIBRARY

Price: $149.95 Each

Title
1. Afghanistan Mining Laws and Regulations Handbook
2. Albania Mining Laws and Regulations Handbook
3. Algeria Mining Laws and Regulations Handbook
4. Angola Mining Laws and Regulations Handbook
5. Argentina Mining Laws and Regulations Handbook
6. Armenia Mining Laws and Regulations Handbook
7. Australia Mining Laws and Regulations Handbook
8. Austria Mining Laws and Regulations Handbook
9. Azerbaijan Mining Laws and Regulations Handbook
10. Bahrain Mining Laws and Regulations Handbook
11. Bangladesh Mining Laws and Regulations Handbook
12. Belarus Mining Laws and Regulations Handbook
13. Belgium Mining Laws and Regulations Handbook
14. Benin Mining Laws and Regulations Handbook
15. Bolivia Mining Laws and Regulations Handbook
16. Bosnia and Herzegovina Mining Laws and Regulations Handbook
17. Botswana Mining Laws and Regulations Handbook
18. Brazil Mining Laws and Regulations Handbook
19. Brunei Mining Laws and Regulations Handbook
20. Bulgaria Mining Laws and Regulations Handbook
21. Burkina Faso Mining Laws and Regulations Handbook
22. Burundi Mining Laws and Regulations Handbook
23. Cambodia Mining Laws and Regulations Handbook
24. Cameroon Mining Laws and Regulations Handbook

Title
25. Canada Mining Laws and Regulations Handbook
26. Cape Verde Mining Laws and Regulations Handbook
27. Cayman Islands Mining Laws and Regulations Handbook
28. Central African Republic Mining Laws and Regulations Handbook
29. Chad Mining Laws and Regulations Handbook
30. Chile Mining Laws and Regulations Handbook
31. China Mining Laws and Regulations Handbook
32. Colombia Mining Laws and Regulations Handbook
33. Comoros Mining Laws and Regulations Handbook
34. Congo Mining Laws and Regulations Handbook
35. Congo, Dem. Republic Mining Laws and Regulations Handbook
36. Cook Islands Mining Laws and Regulations Handbook
37. Costa Rica Mining Laws and Regulations Handbook
38. Cote d'Ivoire Mining Laws and Regulations Handbook
39. Croatia Mining Laws and Regulations Handbook
40. Cuba Mining Laws and Regulations Handbook
41. Czech Republic Mining Laws and Regulations Handbook
42. Denmark Mining Laws and Regulations Handbook
43. Djibouti Mining Laws and Regulations Handbook
44. Dominican Republic Mining Laws and Regulations Handbook
45. Dubai Mining Laws and Regulations Handbook
46. Ecuador Mining Laws and Regulations Handbook
47. Egypt Mining Laws and Regulations Handbook

For additional analytical, business and investment opportunities information, please contact Global Investment & Business Center, USA at (202) 546-2103. Fax: (202) 546-3275. E-mail: rusric@erols.com

Title
48. El Salvador Mining Laws and Regulations Handbook
49. Equatorial Guinea Mining Laws and Regulations Handbook
50. Eritrea Mining Laws and Regulations Handbook
51. Estonia Mining Laws and Regulations Handbook
52. Ethiopia Mining Laws and Regulations Handbook
53. Fiji Mining Laws and Regulations Handbook
54. Finland Mining Laws and Regulations Handbook
55. France Mining Laws and Regulations Handbook
56. Gabon Mining Laws and Regulations Handbook
57. Gambia Mining Laws and Regulations Handbook
58. Georgia Mining Laws and Regulations Handbook
59. Germany Mining Laws and Regulations Handbook
60. Ghana Mining Laws and Regulations Handbook
61. Greece Mining Laws and Regulations Handbook
62. Guatemala Mining Laws and Regulations Handbook
63. Guinea Mining Laws and Regulations Handbook
64. Guinea-Bissau Mining Laws and Regulations Handbook
65. Guyana Mining Laws and Regulations Handbook
66. Haiti Mining Laws and Regulations Handbook
67. Honduras Mining Laws and Regulations Handbook
68. Hungary Mining Laws and Regulations Handbook
69. Iceland Mining Laws and Regulations Handbook
70. India Mining Laws and Regulations Handbook
71. Indonesia Mining Laws and Regulations Handbook
72. Iran Mining Laws and Regulations Handbook
73. Iraq Mining Laws and Regulations Handbook
74. Ireland Mining Laws and Regulations Handbook
75. Israel Mining Laws and Regulations Handbook
76. Italy Mining Laws and Regulations Handbook
77. Jamaica Mining Laws and Regulations Handbook
78. Japan Mining Laws and Regulations Handbook
79. Jordan Mining Laws and Regulations Handbook
80. Kazakhstan Mining Laws and Regulations Handbook
81. Kenya Mining Laws and Regulations Handbook
82. Korea, North Mining Laws and Regulations Handbook
83. Korea, South Mining Laws and Regulations

Title
Handbook
84. Kuwait Mining Laws and Regulations Handbook
85. Kyrgyzstan Mining Laws and Regulations Handbook
86. Laos Mining Laws and Regulations Handbook
87. Latvia Mining Laws and Regulations Handbook
88. Lesotho Mining Laws and Regulations Handbook
89. Liberia Mining Laws and Regulations Handbook
90. Libya Mining Laws and Regulations Handbook
91. Lithuania Mining Laws and Regulations Handbook
92. Macedonia Republic Mining Laws and Regulations Handbook
93. Madagascar Mining Laws and Regulations Handbook
94. Malawi Mining Laws and Regulations Handbook
95. Malaysia Mining Laws and Regulations Handbook
96. Mali Mining Laws and Regulations Handbook
97. Mauritania Mining Laws and Regulations Handbook
98. Mauritius Mining Laws and Regulations Handbook
99. Mayotte Mining Laws and Regulations Handbook
100. Mexico Mining Laws and Regulations Handbook
101. Micronesia Mining Laws and Regulations Handbook
102. Moldova Mining Laws and Regulations Handbook
103. Mongolia Mining Laws and Regulations Handbook
104. Morocco Mining Laws and Regulations Handbook
105. Mozambique Mining Laws and Regulations Handbook
106. Myanmar Mining Laws and Regulations Handbook
107. Namibia Mining Laws and Regulations Handbook
108. Nepal Mining Laws and Regulations Handbook
109. Netherlands Mining Laws and Regulations Handbook
110. New Zealand Mining Laws and Regulations Handbook
111. Nicaragua Mining Laws and Regulations Handbook
112. Niger Mining Laws and Regulations Handbook
113. Nigeria Mining Laws and Regulations Handbook
114. Norway Mining Laws and Regulations Handbook
115. Oman Mining Laws and Regulations Handbook

Title
116. Pakistan Mining Laws and Regulations Handbook
117. Papua New Guinea Mining Laws and Regulations Handbook
118. Paraguay Mining Laws and Regulations Handbook
119. Peru Mining Laws and Regulations Handbook
120. Philippines Mining Laws and Regulations Handbook
121. Poland Mining Laws and Regulations Handbook
122. Portugal Mining Laws and Regulations Handbook
123. Qatar Mining Laws and Regulations Handbook
124. Romania Mining Laws and Regulations Handbook
125. Russia Mining Laws and Regulations Handbook
126. Rwanda Mining Laws and Regulations Handbook
127. Sao Tome and Principe Mining Laws and Regulations Handbook
128. Saudi Arabia Mining Laws and Regulations Handbook
129. Scotland Mining Laws and Regulations Handbook
130. Senegal Mining Laws and Regulations Handbook
131. Serbia Mining Laws and Regulations Handbook
132. Sierra Leone Mining Laws and Regulations Handbook
133. Slovakia Mining Laws and Regulations Handbook
134. Slovenia Mining Laws and Regulations Handbook
135. Somalia Mining Laws and Regulations Handbook
136. South Africa Mining Laws and Regulations Handbook
137. Spain Mining Laws and Regulations Handbook
138. Sri Lanka Mining Laws and Regulations Handbook
139. Sudan Mining Laws and Regulations Handbook
140. Suriname Mining Laws and Regulations Handbook
141. Swaziland Mining Laws and Regulations Handbook
142. Sweden Mining Laws and Regulations Handbook
143. Syria Mining Laws and Regulations Handbook
144. Taiwan Mining Laws and Regulations Handbook
145. Tajikistan Mining Laws and Regulations Handbook
146. Tanzania Mining Laws and Regulations Handbook
147. Thailand Mining Laws and Regulations Handbook
148. Togo Mining Laws and Regulations Handbook
149. Trinidad and Tobago Mining Laws and Regulations Handbook
150. Tunisia Mining Laws and Regulations Handbook
151. Turkey Mining Laws and Regulations Handbook
152. Turkmenistan Mining Laws and Regulations Handbook
153. Uganda Mining Laws and Regulations Handbook
154. Ukraine Mining Laws and Regulations Handbook
155. United Arab Emirates Mining Laws and Regulations Handbook
156. United Kingdom Mining Laws and Regulations Handbook
157. United States Mining Laws and Regulations Handbook
158. Uruguay Mining Laws and Regulations Handbook
159. Uzbekistan Mining Laws and Regulations Handbook
160. Venezuela Mining Laws and Regulations Handbook
161. Vietnam Mining Laws and Regulations Handbook
162. Yemen Mining Laws and Regulations Handbook
163. Zambia Mining Laws and Regulations Handbook
164. Zimbabwe Mining Laws and Regulations Handbook

www.ingramcontent.com/pod-product-compliance
Lightning Source LLC
LaVergne TN
LVHW080034210926
848481LV00011B/3191